BY REASON OR FORCE

BY REASON OR FORCE

Chile and the Balancing of Power
in South America, 1830-1905

BY

ROBERT N. BURR

UNIVERSITY OF CALIFORNIA PRESS
BERKELEY, LOS ANGELES, LONDON

University of California Publications in History
Volume 77

University of California Press
Berkeley and Los Angeles
California

University of California Press, Ltd.
London, England

091640

FOR LIZ

ACKNOWLEDGMENTS

FOR THEIR CONTRIBUTIONS to this book I wish to thank the Doherty Foundation of New York and the University of California for financial assistance which made possible ten months of research in Chile and Colombia; the International Relations Program of the Rockefeller Foundation for a grant which, combined with a sabbatical leave from the University of California, provided an opportunity for writing; Don Eugenio Pereira Salas, Don Ricardo Donoso, Don Rául Silva Castro, Don Héctor Fuenzalida, Dr. Ned Fahs, Don Alberto Miramón, and Dr. Howard Cline for their friendly help in the pursuit of sources in Santiago, Chile, Bogotá, Colombia, and Washington, D.C.; Arthur P. Whitaker for reading the entire manuscript and making valuable suggestions; David Neukamm and Jack Bloc for drafting the line map; John Dougherty for preparing the index; and Miriam Morton and Grace Stimson for editorial help in preparing the manuscript for publication. Above all I am grateful to Elizabeth E. Burr for invaluable counsel and editorial assistance.

R. N. B.

CONTENTS

DISPUTED AREAS IN SOUTH AMERICA

Lima
Cuzco
La Paz
Sucré
Arica
Iquique
Antofagasta
Valparaiso
Santiago
Puerto Aisen
Strait of Magellan

LEGEND

DISPUTED AREAS

(A) Venezuela and England
(B) Venezuela and Colombia
(C) Ecuador, Colombia, and Peru
(D) The Gran Chaco

BRAZILIAN DISPUTES

(1) With Venezuela
(2) With Colombia
(3) With Ecuador
(4a)(4b) With Bolivia
(5) With Paraguay
(6) With Argentina
(7) With Uruguay
(E) PUNA DE ATACAMA

CHILEAN
EXPANSION NORTH

ANTOFAGASTA
Yielded by Bolivia to Chile

TARAPACÁ
Yielded by Peru to Chile

TACNA ARICA
Disputed by Peru and Chile

Border claims – Chile and Argentina

Bolivia and Argentina

Argentina and Chile

CHAPTER I

INTRODUCTION

IN INVESTIGATING the history of South American international life between the achievement of independence and the early part of the twentieth century, Latin-American and non–Latin-American historians have shared but a single major interest—international coöperation. Historians in the latter group, primarily concerned with relations between the Great Powers and South America, have neglected the history of the relations of South American nations among themselves. South American historians, in contrast, have put great stress upon the history of intra–South American relations.

Such divergence of interests is owing in part to the relative availability of source materials and the extent of historians' language training. But it is owing far more to the differing values of the respective historians. Non–Latin Americans have been largely the nationals of Great Powers. They have tended to evaluate South American international relations by the standards of Great Power politics and to see those relations as but one of many factors—and a distinctly secondary one at that—in the rivalries among the Great Powers. Also, because intra–South American relations in the century preceding World War I had little impact upon the structure of the Great Power world, they have been assigned minimal historical value.

South American historians, on the other hand, have lived in a world whose historical development, thought and action patterns, and nationalisms have all been profoundly affected by the rivalries and conflicts that characterized intra–South American relations in the nineteenth and early twentieth centuries, and whose historical importance is reflected in the human and material resources expended in six declared major wars and several undeclared armed conflicts. From 1825 to 1828 Brazil fought against the United Provinces of the Río de la Plata; Colombia and Peru waged war in 1828–29; Chile and Argentina battled the Peru-Bolivian Confederation between 1836 and 1839; "La Guerra Grande," which dragged on from 1836 to 1852, involved the Argentine Confederation, Uruguay, antigovernment factions in each of those nations, and Brazil, and brought intervention by France and Great Britain; Paraguay engaged a coalition of Argentina, Brazil, and Uruguay between 1865 and 1870, in the Paraguayan war; Chile fought Peru and Bolivia for a second time in the War of the Pacific, 1879–1884. In undeclared engagements, Peruvian forces battled those of Bolivia at Ingavi, in

1841; Peru landed troops in Ecuador in 1859; and Ecuador and Colombia invaded each other's territory in 1862 and again in 1863. Concerning these and other conflicts journalists, intellectuals, politicians, and diplomats of South America penned uncounted numbers of emotion-charged manifestos, articles, editorials, pamphlets, and books. And several South American states, in response simply to these rivalries, created military and naval establishments whose excessive costs bore no reasonable relationship to national income.

The rivalries that flourished during South America's first century of independence have, moreover, nourished a historicomythology that has influenced contemporary attitudes and actions and provided stimuli for nationalistic sentiment. Homage is still paid the heroes of nineteenth-century wars; litanies on national holidays celebrate those conflicts; international attitudes reflect the influence of these earlier events. Thus both Chile and Peru, haunted by the War of the Pacific, still regard with great fear any increase in the naval power of the other. Argentina and Brazil, acting out a century-old pattern of Platine rivalry, vie for the favor of Paraguay. Colombians and Ecuadorans still regard each other with the ambivalence born of the rapid shifts between conflict and coöperation which characterized their relations during the nineteenth century.

From the above it is clear that the intense preoccupation of South American historians with the intrarelations of South America has resulted not only from the subject's intrinsic importance but also from the emotional and intellectual climate in which those historians have worked. It is also clear that the non–South American cannot fully comprehend the realities of contemporary South America without an understanding of South American intrarelations of the nineteenth century.

To our knowledge of those relations South American historians have made a prolific contribution. Their best work has described the diplomacy of military and boundary conflicts and the lives and times of political and military figures. Several excellent general histories of individual nations have discussed foreign relations as manifestations of national development. Yet a study of this material, notwithstanding its individual scholarly and literary merit, leaves one with the feeling that South American international history was a series of discrete episodes. History so written, regardless of its intrinsic interest, does not provide the insights that we believe possible from the study of history. Our philosophical assumptions tell us that the phenomena of relations between and among nations are not discrete but continuous, and that if we know how and where to look for connections, we will find them. We are convinced, in particular, that the nations of South America have interrelated not in response merely to depraved or enlightened personal leaders, or to conditions that have been created out of a vacuum and subsequently swallowed up by it, but rather in response to broad trends in both their internal development and the totality of their international relations.

The telling of the entire story of nineteenth-century South American intrarelations must await completion of a tremendous amount of monographic study. But we should not, on that account, delay the attempt to find meaningful connections within the body of data already developed. On the contrary, it would seem desirable, both as a means of encouraging new and valuable research and as a method of extracting greater significance from that already done, to propose a general framework within which the events of South American intrarelations will have a meaningful place and a historical relevance to one another. In previous studies I have suggested that such a framework, to be sufficiently capacious, must be continental, and that the main developments in the international life of South America may fruitfully be regarded as phases in the evolution of a continental South American system of power politics.[1] In the present volume I attempt to follow my own prescription with regard to a segment of South American history.

But first, in order to devise more clearly the place of individual happenings within the evolution of a system of power politics, I have had to arrive at a definition—however personal and arbitrary—of that system. I view a system of power politics as a complex of several sovereign states, each intent upon maintaining its independence and upon competing with the others in order to advance national interests. An unsystematized group becomes a systematized one when the following conditions have come to prevail: (1) the group members share a conviction that any significant change in their relative power positions may threaten the interests of individual members, so that each nation simultaneously insists upon the need for maintenance of power equilibrium and strives for a power structure favorable to itself at the expense of others; (2) group members compete with other group members in the effort to increase their power and advance their national interests; (3) the leadership of group members accepts the basic axioms of power politics and is willing to use its techniques, including the various forms of uni- and multilateral coercion and the *divide et impera* principle; (4) the international political interests of member states are primarily, but not necessarily exclusively, centered upon intrasystem relations; (5) the members of the group possess the capability of shaping the system's power structure without significant or decisive out-group influence. With this definition to serve as a frame of reference, apparently scattered events assume a pattern, and the history of the first century of intra–South American relations, regarded as the history of the development of a South American system of power politics, becomes the comprehensible continuum that we believe it to be.

The history of South American intrarelations during the first century after independence falls into two periods of approximately equal length. The first period, the age of *regional* power politics, stretches from independence to the late 1860's. The second period, the age of *continental* power politics, makes its debut in the late 1860's and persists into the first quarter of the twentieth century. The boundaries between the regional and the continental periods are blurred, for the former did not give way to the latter without a struggle. Even in the age of regional power politics there existed some conditions necessary to a continental system. South American nations tended early to focus their political interests on one another, if only because of their confinement to a continent separated from the rest of the world by wide expanses of ocean. Moreover, rivalries and conflicts over elements of national power, and fluctuations in the power structure of the continent, produced interactions among South American nations during the regional period.

The earliest South American rivalries were the direct result of the colonial experience and the struggles for independence. Among the more deeply rooted conflicts was that between Brazil and Argentina, which perpetuated the Spanish-Portuguese struggle for control of the interior rivers emptying into the Río de la Plata estuary. Also colonially derived were contests between the commercial interests of Montevideo and Buenos Aires on the Atlantic, and between those of Callao and Valparaíso on the Pacific.

The major source of potential conflict which emerged after, and as a result of, independence concerned the structural and territorial delineation of the new states. Strong interests in the former viceregal capitals of Bogotá, Lima, and Buenos Aires wished to establish those cities as the capitals of nations encompassing entire former viceregal domains. But interests in the centers of lesser colonial administrative units, such as Chuquisaca, Quito, Montevideo, Caracas, and Santiago, wished to be free of the long-resented control of the viceregal capitals. By the end of 1830 the latter had prevailed, and Bolivia, Ecuador, Uruguay, Venezuela, and Chile were independent states. In the former viceregal capitals, however, there still existed attitudes of preëminence and aspirations for hegemony which inspired the fear and distrust of lesser nations, and provided elements of future discord.

Establishment of the territorial identity of the new states proved extremely difficult. An early understanding that national boundaries would in general correspond to Spanish colonial administrative limits failed to solve the problem, for Spain had seldom demarcated with precision its administrative units, particularly in such sparsely populated regions as the Atacama Desert, Patagonia, Tierra del Fuego, and the Amazon and Orinoco river basins. Moreover, there existed certain overlapping ecclesiastical and judicial administrative authorities for each of which might be claimed equal political jurisdiction. As Spanish colonial precedent was entirely inadequate as a legal basis for determining their boundaries, the new nations commenced to dispute their limits from the moment they agreed about their existence as separate states.

Spain, however, had not ruled alone on the continent. Consequently, the serious Spanish American boundary problem was further complicated by the fact that, except for Chile, all the new Spanish American nations fronted upon Brazil. Spain and Portugal had disputed their colonial boundaries strenuously and had reached several successive agreements which were never fully implemented. The expanding population of Brazil had pressed against its uncertain boundary and had spilled over into areas generally conceded to be under Spanish jurisdiction. With independence, a dispute promptly arose concerning the principle that should be applied to the determination of boundaries between Brazil and the Spanish-speaking nations; Brazil upheld the principle of effective occupation, while its adversaries claimed the boundaries indicated in previous Spanish-Portuguese treaties. The areas in dispute were always large, sometimes immense, but their small population and hostile environment dimmed their value, and, until the middle of the nineteenth century, they remained a latent rather than an active source of conflict.

Against a background of potential strife the new states sought to consolidate themselves, thus creating new areas of friction arising from fluctuations in the continent's power structure. Those changes varied widely in size and significance; some of them are discussed in detail in the following chapters. In general, they derived from revolutionary disturbances within states, from personal and national ambitions to rearrange political geography, or from the loss or acquistion, peaceful or otherwise, of wealth and commercial advantage on the part of certain nations.

A further early component of a system of power politics in South America was acceptance by its leaders of the axioms and techniques of power politics. The culture and education of the ruling elite were of

European derivation; European values and forms in literature, fashions, and politics tended to be accepted and imitated, along with the European state system. To be sure, some voices in the wilderness cried out against the transplantation to the New World of European-style power politics, damning them as decadent, corrupt, and un-American. But those who gained power did not seriously question the concept of a community of competing sovereign states, each with the duty to defend itself and to expand its interests, preferably by peaceful means but by force if "necessary," even at the expense of other states. The Great Powers of Europe, those leading practitioners of the art of power politics, were the specific models for the international behavior of the South American nations. And because South American culture was largely derivative, and because South Americans suffered from a sense of inferiority bequeathed by their former colonial status and by the relative weakness of their respective nations, high prestige was attached to the imitation of European models.

South American statesmen early showed their acceptance of the axioms and techniques of European power politics. They used its jargon, and did not hesitate to employ its forms of coercion in dealing with problems of intra–South American relations. For several decades after independence, the problems in those relations were bifurcated in two regional groupings—one on the Pacific and the other in the Plata. Not until later in the nineteenth century did these regional systems become fused into a single continental system.

The slowness with which that fusion occurred was due partly to the slowness with which South American leaders became aware of the importance of changes in the power positions of apparently distant nations. The continent's area was more than twice the size of the forty-eight contiguous states of the United States, and its urban centers were isolated from one another by formidable geographical obstacles. Because means of communication were at first painfully slow, contact between and among different peoples was infrequent. But even had the newly independent states been in closer early contact, they would have had neither the power nor the serious desire immediately to play continental roles. Most of them were grappling with financial and political crises; most of them lacked tradition and experience in self-government. The first demands upon the leadership of the new nations were domestic and regional rather than continental.

Difficulties in regularization of relations with the Great Powers further impeded development of a continental system by diverting the attention of the new states from intra–South American matters. Upon independence, recognition and expanded commerce had been sought from the Great Powers. South Americans wished, moreover, to borrow funds for both public and private purposes and to import the more highly developed technology and the skilled nationals of Europe and the United States. South America's attraction of money, people, and technology from Europe and the United States was indispensable to its fulfillment of urgent material and cultural aspirations. The more highly developed nations responded with alacrity to such an opportunity to exploit markets and resources, which Spain had so long denied them. But difficulties soon arose concerning the protection of the interests of Great Power nationals. Poverty often prevented South American governments from fulfilling their financial commitments; instability imperiled the persons and the interests of foreign nationals; the attitudes of the parties to resultant disputes made solution difficult. Xenophobia was prevalent among the Spanish-speaking peoples of South America to whom both the Spanish economic system and the Inquisition had for centuries denied contact with and knowledge of the outside world. In turn, immigrants from the Great Powers regarded the "backward" peoples of South America with contempt. They tended to enlist the superior coercive strength of their home governments to resolve conflicts of interest rather than to negotiate upon a basis of theoretical equality.

In the 1820's all but one of the embryonic nations borrowed funds from British sources at exorbitant interest rates and premature dates of call. In that decade each debtor nation defaulted. Moreover, throughout the military phase of the independence effort and in the immediately succeeding chaos, many European and United States nationals suffered personal and financial damages. In accordance with accepted nineteenth-century practice, the Great Powers responded with diplomatic pressure, threats, ultimata, and/or forceful intervention. Occasionally a Great Power would support exaggerated or baseless claims; sometimes a Great Power made real or supposed grievances the excuse for proving its "strong" foreign policy to the home front; sometimes such injuries were the pretext for contemplated imperialist expansion.

South American leaders, fearful that intervention by a Great Power might abort independence, fought back. They played off one power against another. They sought to establish legal doctrines favorable to small countries. They attempted to create a multinational defense. Sometimes they resisted with force. Such resistance helped to prevent Great Power political domination, as did efforts to ameliorate the conditions that provoked intervention. But it was, above all, the oper-

ation of the European system of power politics which protected the
new nations. Europe had little interest in dominating chaotic states
remote from the mainstream of its political life. One Great Power or
another might occasionally cast a covetous eye southwest across the
Atlantic, but serious consideration of the cost and the risks of such
a venture, and of its possible effects upon the world of Great Power
rivalries, dispelled dreams of domination. Particularly important was
the posture of Great Britain. Having lost enthusiasm for colonial venture after its experience of the American Revolution, Britain was not
interested in territorial expansion in South America, despite its possession of naval power sufficient, if it so desired, to discourage imperialist activities by other European nations. The policy of the European
Great Powers toward South America was thus the essentially negative
one of preventing the extension of rival influence. Nevertheless, because
the Great Powers did continue to intervene to protect the interests of
their nationals, South American attention tended to be diverted from
intra–South American rivalries.

Another factor inhibiting early development of a continental system
of power politics was a lingering spirit of solidarity among Spain's
former colonies. Sharing language and culture, as well as the emotions
of allies in a bitter struggle against a common enemy, these states
possessed a consciousness of dual nationality, tending to consider themselves both "Spanish American" and citizens of a particular nation.
After independence various leaders sought to organize for common
defense and maintenance of peace, and their tenacious utopianism
tended doubly to impede development of a South American system of
power politics. In the first place, independent Spanish America included not only the states of South America but also those of the
Caribbean and of Central and North America. *Spanish* American coöperation therefore tended to distract attention from any distinctly *South*
American system. In the second place, because the binding forces in a
system of power politics are competition and conflict, the trend toward
coöperation tended to inhibit the development of these forces. For four
decades the idea of Spanish American coöperation was kept alive by
periodic injections of threatened or actual intervention by the Great
Powers. From the 1820's through the 1860's proposals were devised for
leagues or confederations. In 1826, 1847–48, and 1864–65, varying numbers of Latin-American nations met in formal diplomatic congresses
and adopted modifications of these proposals. But their agreements
were seldom acceptable to their home governments, and, because basic
competitive and conflictive forces promptly reasserted themselves upon
withdrawal of the outside threat, they were never put into effect.

Before the 1860's forces antagonistic to a continental system were in the ascendancy. Nevertheless, events were continually taking place which would lead to the triumph of such a system. Important among them were the internal stability achieved by certain nations, subsequent material progress, and a stronger power position. Such nations secured an informal *modus operandi* with the Great Powers which permitted expanding economic and cultural relations without endangering independence. Under the unwritten *modus operandi*, a given nation would put its house in order, meet its financial and security obligations to Great Power citizens, and provide opportunities for foreign investment. In return Great Power investment, enterprise, and immigration, but not Great Power intervention, would be received.

The ability of certain South American nations to fulfill the *modus operandi* was heightened by the continent's accelerated integration into the world's economy. The initial impacts of that integration were felt even before 1850, were intensified between the 1850's and 1870's, and in the 1870's assumed greatly increased momentum. Economic integration manifested itself in the growth of commerce between the Great Powers and South American countries, in mounting Great Power demand for raw materials and foodstuffs, in greater European investment in public and private South American enterprise, in the introduction into South America of elements of advanced United States and European technology, and in the accelerated migration of Europeans to South America.

South America's integration into the world's economic pattern contributed to the formation of its continental system of power politics by combining with existing factors to differentiate the South American nations into major and minor powers. Nations that could offer good port and distribution facilities, or whose natural resources were coveted, or which offered attractions to capital and immigration, raced ahead to become the predominant powers. A predominant power tended to expand its influence into its own previously neglected lands and beyond into weaker nations where, upon confrontation with a similarly advancing predominant nation, an area of conflict would develop. Predominant powers were at first concerned mainly with regional affairs, but the forces that had created them and others pushed them steadily toward involvement in the affairs of the entire continent.

Participation in the world economy had the further effect of exacerbating rivalries among the South American nations over disputed territories suddenly found to be valuable on account of European demand for their raw materials. Finally, improved communications based upon imported technological innovations brought the peoples of South

America into wider contact with one another and made them come to feel that their own national interests could be affected by occurrences in areas of the continent once regarded as remote.

As South America was beginning to participate with mounting intensity in the mainstream of the world economy, and as certain South American nations were achieving a position of predominance upon the continent, the great powers of Europe were gradually relaxing their pressures upon South America. European relaxation resulted first from the greater reliability with which South American nations fulfilled their part of the *modus operandi* and from their increased ability to resist the demands of the Great Powers. Also, as a result of Germany's unification, France's defeat in 1870, and the dawn of the new imperialism in Africa and in the Orient, Europe was becoming more deeply involved in its own power politics. As European rivalries mounted, there was a corresponding decline in the possibility that any single European nation might succeed in exerting significant political influence in South America. But, although their primary non-European interests had been deflected to Africa and Asia, European nations would not have regarded lightly an attempt by one of their number to seize an opportunity for a South American imperialist adventure. Moreover, European developments had been arousing the mistrust of the rapidly maturing United States and were creating in the "Republic of the North" a growing resolve to oppose European "meddling" in the affairs of the Western Hemisphere.

The relaxation, voluntary or otherwise, of European pressures upon South America had the important effect of permitting its nations to concentrate more strongly upon intra–South American affairs, and to play power politics in an expanding continental arena with more vigor. In the 1860's the factors that had impeded the maturation of a continental South American system of power politics were forced to recede before the forces that were encouraging its growth. The history of South American intrarelations now entered upon its second period—the age of continental power politics—which reached its apogee in the early twentieth century.

In the pages that follow I fill in the details of the above broad outline by observing the way in which one South American nation affected and was affected by the development of a continental system of power politics in South America. That nation, the Republic of Chile, adopted in 1834 as its official national emblem a shield upon which is engraved a maxim befitting a nation that was to rise from obscurity and become a major force in South American power politics: *Por la razón o la fuerza* ("By reason or force"). I begin this study with the year 1830, when Chile forged the internal stability that was a prerequisite for its rise to a position of power. I break off in the year 1905, when Chile, having previously reached agreements with Argentina providing for a continental equilibrium giving Chile hegemony on the Pacific Coast, exchanged with Bolivia ratifications of a treaty symbolizing that hegemony.

Chapter II

THE FOUNDATIONS OF NATIONAL POWER

Chile in 1830

In 1830 the young Republic of Chile gave little indication of its future status on the South American continent. It encompassed less territory than all but two of the continent's eight states; it was smaller in population than all but three.[1] The seven anarchic years through which it had passed seemed to foretell disintegration rather than consolidation of national power. To be sure, between 1818 and 1823 Chile had shown considerable promise. The government of Bernardo O'Higgins had supported positive social and economic reforms. An expensive campaign had been mounted to liberate Peru from the grip of Spain. Chile had assembled a formidable navy, had secured a large British loan, and had obtained the recognition of the United States.

But the Peruvian campaign faltered. Its high cost stirred popular discontent. O'Higgins' liberal reforms and authoritarianism aroused the ire of the aristocracy. In 1823 the father of his country fled into Peruvian exile, leaving behind a land that promptly fell into disorder. Chile's long colonially-rooted tradition of military subordination to civilian control was replaced by military domination of the political arena. Government followed government in dizzy succession. Barracks revolts became commonplace. Presidents and cabinet members, in their fleeting tenure, proclaimed and forgot grandiose plans for the advancement of Chile. Public works lay abandoned. Government employees went without pay. Highwaymen infested the countryside. Murder and assault and robbery plagued the capital on the Mapocho River. At night only the very poor, the foolish, the criminal, or the well-guarded ventured forth. Economic life lay stagnant in the mire of social and political collapse. The Chilean navy had been reduced to a single ship. Payments were no longer being made on the British loan.[2] The infant republic had fallen upon evil days.

Most of the outside world knew little of Chile. But England—whose business it was to know as much as possible about other nations—placed Chile very low in the hierarchy of South American states. In the mid-1820's London recognized the governments in Bogotá, Rio de Janeiro, and Buenos Aires,[3] but ignored Santiago's wish for recognition on the grounds that Chile was "not completely organized."[4] That adverse attitude was confirmed early in 1830 by the British commercial agent in Valparaíso, who reported that "at present the State is so generally convulsed that it may be said there is no government in the country."[5] Nevertheless, the small, chaotic, politically unstable, crime-ridden, poverty-stricken Chile of the 1820's encompassed significant elements of potential power, foremost among which were the nature of its society, the character of its people, and its geographic configuration and location.

Chilean society was schematically similar to that of other Spanish American peoples, for after the founding of Santiago in 1541 a hierarchical society became firmly entrenched. In time, with the expansion of the colonists' activities beyond the capital's fortifications, Chile became dominated by a small aristocracy whose wealth, power, and prestige were based primarily upon landownership and, to a lesser extent, upon mining and commerce. A deep social, economic, and cultural chasm separated Chile's aristocracy from the landless, illiterate, ill-clothed, and powerless *pueblo*.[6] But only the form of Chilean society was similar to that of other Spanish American republics; its substance was very different, especially when compared with the two neighboring countries with which independent Chile was to have close relations. Those countries, Peru and Bolivia, has been opulent colonies where the peninsular social climber of moderate competence could luxuriate on returns from seemingly inexhaustible supplies of precious metals and cheap native labor. In contrast, Chile was a wretched frontier outpost, poor in valuable metals and cursed with a small, primitive, warlike aboriginal population. Chile held no attractions for the adventurer who wished to make a quick killing. The colonist who ventured there with foreknowledge, or remained there after his rude awakening, was a different man from the one who wanted "to get rich quick" in the more northern areas of the continent.

The desperate day-to-day fight for survival imparted a distinctive stamp to the progenitors of the Chilean nation. The emergent aristocrat was harder-working and tougher-minded than his northern counterpart. The "arrived" Chilean aristocrat of the later colonial period stayed near his hacienda, although he might send his family to Santiago for the "season." He was in intimate contact with his *inquilinos,* and treated them fairly well if only because they were so few. A relatively harmonious relationship came into being and, along with the increasing ethnic homogeneity that was so radically to distinguish Chile from its neighbors to the north, was gradually strengthened. By the time of the republic's establishment, Chile's population was the product of a miscegenation so complete that almost no Chilean, however "blue" his blood, could deny the presence of an Araucanian Indian somewhere in his family tree. Nor would he necessarily wish to do so. President O'Higgins, the bastard son of an Irish-born Spanish colonial administrator and a native Chilean woman, honored his mother's memory with a public monument. Chile's ethnic uniformity and lack of class conflict were the silver spoons with which it was born into republican life. Its wealthy neighbors on the northern "side of the tracks" were born in the wake of a brutal native revolt whose ruthless repression caused constant fear of reprisal. Chile's aristocracy was able to direct itself to the problem of founding a nation-state without the handicap of serious racial conflict within the country's settled areas.

Even as colonial Chile's unfavorable economic circumstances were ultimately to operate in its favor, so were its perennial Araucanian wars. Constant danger of surprise attack demanded fraternal cohesion and military readiness, and the birth of the republic found the Araucanians still unsubdued, thus providing a unifying common concern for many decades. The epic nature of the contest between their Spanish and Indian forefathers provided a heroic theme for the bards of Chile's nationalism to be.[7]

In the eighteenth century, expansion of mining and partial relaxation of Spanish trade restrictions eased Chile's economic hardships and attracted new colonists. But neither a higher standard of living, nor the new arrivals from Spain, nor the dislocations of the wars for independence altered the fundamental nature of Chilean society. The aristocracy did not rush to surround itself with luxuries. The new immigrants, many of them frugal and industrious Basques, fused with the old aristocracy and added vigor to its established values. From the wars for independence, which provided a second important heroic theme for nascent Chilean nationalism, the aristocracy emerged intact. That it fell immediately into fratricidal strife and violent political conflict was less in harmony with its essential character than that in 1830, at the end of seven anarchic years, it embarked, filled with disgust and dismay, upon a determined program of restoring order and building a nation.

In 1830, as Chile's governing elite commenced to reorganize the country, it found geographical as well as social factors on its side. The population of Chile was concentrated within the confined area of a fertile, amply watered, extremely pleasant valley whose communications were unobstructed. A central government was therefore able to function with an efficiency impossible to such capitals as Bogotá, Buenos Aires, and Lima. Chile's geography further endowed it with the formidable protection of the Atacama Desert to the north, the Andes mountains to the east, and the Pacific Ocean to the west and south. Those accidents of geography minimized the possibility of surprise invasion and, in addition, gave Chile the character of an island, forcing its sights toward the sea as a means of relating to the outside world. Chile's long seacoast, dotted with many small harbors, was favored with one excellent port within easy reach of the capital. That port, Valparaíso, was the first major stopping place for sailing ships that had rounded Cape Horn and was of great economic importance in Chile's effort to turn over a new leaf.

THE PORTALIAN ERA

The specific event about which the various forces that sought to end Chile's anarchy coalesced was a military revolt similar to those that had plagued the country. Its leader, Joaquín Prieto, managed to attract the support of certain aristocrats who opposed the "liberals" momentarily in power and who, in their search for a route to power, had been reorganizing the Conservative party. Prieto and the Conservatives triumphed in April, 1830, at the decisive battle of Lircay. There had been other "victories" during the anarchic period, but this one proved worthy of the name. The enduring effect of Lircay was owing to the encounter of a national climate and a man. The man was Diego Portales, a somewhat less than aristocratic Valparaíso businessman in his late thirties who had been instrumental in reorganizing the Conservative party. Brilliant, enigmatic, persuasive, withdrawn, Portales chose the role of the power behind the throne and exercised that power as a virtual dictator. The years between Lircay and Don Diego's death were so indelibly stamped with the effect of his policies that they became known as the Portalian era. The Portalian era succeeded in imposing in Chile a concept of government that set the tone of the nation's legislative, executive, and judicial administration for generations to come.

Reacting against the "liberal" turmoil through which Chile had passed, Portales demanded an end to exotic utopian political concepts, asserting that Chile must give itself a political structure in harmony with its socioeconomic reality. Moreover, Portales insisted, Chileans must subordinate class and individual interests to the nation's overriding need for orderly government.[8] Coming from another man, such ideas might have constituted simplistic reactionary verbiage. But Portales pushed and bullied and mercilessly drove President Prieto and the new Conservative government to the implementation of his precepts. From time to time, consumed with impatience, Portales would remove himself from Valparaíso to Santiago and there assume one or another cabinet post in order to expedite the realization of a policy. But he detested the limelight, and would return as soon as possible to the port city, wielding from there the long and powerful whip of his political authority.

The first steps of the new government were directed toward the reestablishment of law and order. Frank repression was instituted: political opponents of the new regime were ousted from positions of influence, and some of them were exiled; the military was restored to civilian control; the press was censored; political meetings were controlled and restricted. The second steps of the new government, commenced while the first were being carried out, were designed to reëstablish respect for government as such. Administrative abuses, inefficiency, graft, corruption, and disorganization were ruthlessly tracked down and stamped out. The government's financial structure was systematized, and government services were reinstituted and broadened. The number of government employees was reduced, and jobholders were required to perform their duties.

The juridical structure of the state was made to conform with the ideas of Portales and the Conservatives in a constitution completed in 1833, which created a strong central government with judicial, legislative, and executive branches. Within that framework only the president could act with complete independence, his extensive powers overshadowing those of a bicameral legislature composed of a senate and a chamber of deputies. The president might in times of crisis assume "extraordinary powers" and, with congressional consent, suppress opposition without judicial process. Chile's constitution of 1833 did not attempt to implant democratic institutions but, on the contrary, was designed to create and perpetuate government by oligarchy. High property and literacy qualifications were demanded for suffrage, and far higher ones were necessary for the holding of elective office. Such provisions restricted participation in government to approximately five hundred families. For three decades Chile's "five hundred"—linked by blood, marriage, friendship, or financial interest—supported and advised, or chastised and censured, those of its number whom it placed in public office.

COMMERCE AND INDUSTRY

As a businessman and resident of Valparaíso, Diego Portales took a special interest in industry, commerce, and shipping. Frenchman Claude Gay was commissioned to make and publish a detailed inventory of "the riches of the territory of the Republic in order to stimulate the industry of its inhabitants and attract that of foreigners."[19] Resolved to make Valparaíso the entrepôt for the trade of the entire Pacific Coast of America, the government lost no time in ordering repair, improvement, and enlargement of its docks and other facilities. Warehouses in which goods in transit might be cheaply stored without payment of duty were approved by a legislature impressed by the argument that "security and tax advantages to the world's merchants [would make] our principal port the marketplace of the Pacific and attract European and Asiatic manufactures for exchange with the valuable products of Mexico and Peru. In the geographical position of our coasts, nature has granted us a privilege that we must use."[10] Chile's port was to be improved not only for foreign use. Both a national merchant marine and coastal steam navigation were planned, and in 1835 Chile granted an exclusive ten-year concession to United States citizen William Wheelwright for the latter purpose.[11] Preferential tariffs for merchandise carried in Chilean-owned or Chilean-built ships were also enacted.[12]

By the time of the victory at Lircay, the national and the fiscal incomes of Chile had fallen to low points. But the new government's radical reforms had a marked beneficial effect even during the first two years, and, beginning in 1832, the entire economy was suddenly and sharply improved with the discovery of a rich new silver-mining area in the northern province of Copiapó. Exploitation of this new resource provided Chile with a firm financial basis upon which to proceed toward its ambitious goals.[13]

FOREIGN AFFAIRS

The post-Lircay government was building a nation-state that would become at one point the continent's strongest. But in the early 1830's considerations of relative power position were distinctly secondary to the special interests of the Chilean ruling elite, and that group did not yet comprehend clearly the relationship between Chile's growing wealth, stability, and internal strength and its relations with other nations. In the years immediately following 1830 few Chileans were interested in foreign policy or in balance-of-power politics. There was an urgent need for undivided concentration on internal problems. An international power structure favorable to Chile happened momentarily to exist, and isolationism was dominant in foreign policy. In fact, the run-of-the-mill Chilean aristocrat of that era was untraveled, poorly educated, and completely wrapped up in the interests of his own limited environment. His isolationism was closely related to Chile's physical isolation, for news from the outside world was hard to come by. The official government organ, *El Araucano,* complained in 1830: "It would appear that Chile had broken relations with the rest of the globe's peoples and had confined herself exclusively to the affairs of her own small corner."[14]

Chile's self-centeredness was expressed in the slender budget of the Foreign Department which, because it was believed not to merit its own ministry, was under the jurisdiction of the Ministry of Interior and Foreign Affairs. As late as 1836 it was granted, exclusive of the minister's prorated share, a mere 4,709 pesos.[15] Of that pittance almost half constituted the salary of the chief clerk, and the rest had to be stretched to pay the salaries of lesser officials, porters, and messengers and to purchase office supplies. An additional 18,600 pesos was allotted for a four-man foreign-service staff comprising chargés d'affaires in Paris, Washington, and Lima and a consul general in Central America.

ANDRÉS BELLO

There were in Chile, however, a few widely traveled and highly educated men with interest and experience in foreign affairs, chief among whom was Andrés Bello. Born in Venezuela, he had represented first its revolutionary group and then its independent government in London. He had remained in England, filling diplomatic posts for his own and other governments, and there came to know the Chilean statesman Mariano Egaña, through whose influence he entered the service of the Chilean government.

From the time of his arrival in Santiago in 1829, Andrés Bello exerted an influence upon foreign policy.[16] In 1832, with the publication of *Principios de derecho de gentes,*[17] his reputation as an internationalist was firmly established. The specific purpose of his work was to provide the new Spanish American nations with the legal knowledge to defend themselves against older and stronger powers. Speaking as he did for younger and weaker nations, Bello supported an international system wherein the rights of nations would derive from law and not from power. But Bello's work, which owed a great deal to such Europeans as Vattel and de Martins, frequently reflected the basic assumptions of the European system of competing sovereign states. *Principios de derecho de gentes* was published in Santiago (1832), Caracas (1837), Bogotá (1839), and Madrid (1843). Its revised edition, *Principios de derecho internacional,* appeared in Santiago (1844), Lima (1844), Caracas (1847), and Paris (1873). The scholarly excellence of Bello's work, together with the desperate need that it met, gave it an extraordinary influence upon subsequent South American concepts of international relations.[18]

It was in Chile that Bello's influence was first and most strongly felt, and it remained potent there for the many decades during which Bello actively participated in the formulation of policy, and even afterward. Bello assumed such varied responsibilities as editing the Foreign Department's reports to Congress and assisting in the drafting of the president's messages to the legislature. He edited and wrote countless other official government documents and papers.[19] He was editor of the official government organ, *El Araucano*. And within a decade of his arrival in Chile he was elected to the Senate. For many years the towering figure of Andrés Bello, thanks to his wide experience, wisdom, and tireless labor, provided logical continuity in the conduct of Chile's foreign relations.

THE SOUTH AMERICAN INTERNATIONAL SITUATION, 1830–1836

But not even Andrés Bello wanted to modify Chile's isolationism. The need to affirm domestic order was still overwhelming. Opponents were still plotting to overthrow the new government. Plans for economic development had barely been started. Chilean leadership felt it necessary to concentrate upon domestic matters, but its ability to do so was due less to intent than to a currently favorable international power structure.

Between 1830 and 1836 neither the great European powers nor the United States seriously endangered Chilean independence. Anti-imperialism was gaining ground in European circles. The two great maritime powers were busy at home with such serious matters as the British reform acts and the attempts of the "illegitimate" July monarchy in France to consolidate its power. Spain was still technically at war with Chile but, in spite of Chile's exaggerated fears, did not constitute a genuine threat. The United States was too busy fulfilling its "manifest destiny" to play a major role in southern South America. When the Great Powers did concern themselves with Latin America, they looked primarily to Mexico, the Caribbean, and the Río de la Plata. In distant Chile, too small and unimportant to tempt imperialist appetites, the Great Powers sought merely to protect their nationals and to promote their trade. As Andrés Bello asserted, "We have little to fear from Europe. The war in which it would become involved were an attempt made to succeed Spain [as possessor of South American colonies], the immense wall of the Atlantic, the love of independence of which we have given such signal proof, the self-confidence inspired by our triumphs, may not make danger vanish but will at least keep it at a distance."[20]

Fortunately, other South American states were not endangering Chile at that time, though they had by no means rejected the basic assumptions of power politics. Even before 1830 several states were involved in alliance-making attempts against several others; Colombia, Peru, Brazil, and the United Provinces of the Río de la Plata had resorted to war. But most of the South American nations were still too poor and too internally divided to mount an offensive, especially when lagging technology could not cope with the continent's vast extent and formidable physical barriers. Thus it was that power politics between 1830 and 1836 were confined to bilateral or regional relations, with rivalries among other South American nations tending to divert attention from a rapidly maturing Chile.

To Chile's east and northeast, beyond the Andes, lay two states whose size gave them potential power, but which, between 1830 and 1836, lacked the strength for foreign ventures. Bordering directly upon Chile was the United Provinces of the Río de la Plata, a wishful name encompassing fourteen feuding semiautonomous provinces theoretically governed from the former viceregal capital of Buenos Aires. Having no common boundary with Chile was the Empire of Brazil, an immense country possessing the largest population on the continent. It threatened Chile even less than did the Platine provinces, and came into no territorial conflict with it. Moreover, Brazil was preoccupied with the internal struggles that felled Pedro I and elevated the child Pedro II to the throne. Finally, Brazil and Buenos Aires were themselves rivals in the Río de la Plata region.

The conflict between Rio de Janeiro and Buenos Aires was a continuation of the colonial rivalry between their mother countries.[21] In 1825 war had broken out, but was resolved in 1828 by the creation of an independent new buffer state, Uruguay, which became the cornerstone of an embryonic Platine balance-of-power system. In the early 1830's, as Chile got on its feet, the Platine rivals were too involved in domestic problems to threaten the independence of Uruguay, much less that of any other South American nation.

Nor could Chile be threatened from the continent's far north, where once-great Colombia was falling into pieces. Bolívar, dreaming of a continental role, had marched his armies southward to destroy Spanish power in both Peru and Alto Peru. His influence in those areas had been strong, and he had even considered an anti-Brazilian alliance with Buenos Aires. Bolívar and other Colombians, imbued with the broad vision that accompanied their growing strength, had convoked a diplomatic meeting at Panama to consider the formation of a vast confederation of American states. By that time, however, Bolívar's power commenced to arouse mistrust throughout the continent. Chileans rejected his offer of help in ousting the Spaniards from their last foothold, the island of Chiloé; and they saw in the Panama congress a potential instrument for the extension of Bolivarian-Colombian power in South America. But the South American continent had not long to quake before Bolívar's widening sway. Great Colombia, base of his operations, failed to support his continental vision. While in Bogotá attempting to resolve domestic dissent, Bolívar saw his influence in Peru and Bolivia washed away in a wave of anti-Colombianism. By 1828 Peru and Colombia found themselves waging a war; Colombia emerged victorious, but in financial and political distress. Bolívar's prestige was declining; his health was ruined. In 1830, shortly before his death, he resigned as head of Great Colombia. Deprived of the binding force of Bolívar's personality, the one state that had seemed capable of playing a continental role in South America collapsed. Its three weak successors, New Granada, Venezuela, and Ecuador, posed no threat to Chile.

Peru alone of the South American countries constituted a potential threat to Chile in the early 1830's. The peoples of these two nations harbored a deep mutual loathing. Economic conflict of significant proportions already existed, and was growing. Sea communications between the two countries were relatively easy. But in the years between 1830 and 1836 Peruvian energies were absorbed by internal political warfare and conflicts with former Alto Peru, now Bolivia. The Altiplano was enjoying an unusual period of internal peace. An unsettled Atacama Desert boundary with Chile was no source of danger, for Bolivia considered the Atacama valueless and was primarily interested in the vital interests at stake in its relations with Peru.

The favorable international power structure of South America permitted the new Chilean government to delay the formulation of a broad foreign policy, and to concentrate on domestic development. It gave to foreign policy only the attention required to prevent foreign interference in Chilean affairs, to avoid involvement in the disorders and conflicts of neighbors, and, above all, to promote commercial relations with the outside world. Such was the gradually articulated three-pronged foreign policy of the first six years following Lircay. Chilean foreign policy faced two different sets of problems: those presented by the Great Powers and those posed by South American nations. The former refused to accept Chile as an equal. Paris sought extraterritorial rights in Chile; London refused recognition. Both supported the claims of their nationals against the Chilean government as a matter of course.[22]

Keenly aware of its weakness, Chile determined to avoid intervention-provoking controversies while striving to develop economic and commercial bonds with Europe. Chile's Great Power policy was thus a holding action pending the achievement of domestic goals which would earn it the respect and recognition of the world's more important states.

With respect to the South American nations, Chile could operate on a basis of relative equality and promote its interests with greater vigor. But between 1830 and 1836 Chile had significant relations with only three of the continent's nations: Peru, Bolivia, and the United Provinces of the Río de la Plata. With the latter it was necessary primarily to seek protection for Chilean commerce and nationals at a level of activity far lower than the level of relations with Peru.

RELATIONS WITH PERU

The odium that had long poisoned relations between Peru and Chile was accentuated in the early 1830's by the maturation of several basic conflicts. The mutual dislike was rooted in both the imperial-colonial past and the trials of the wars for independence. The sharp contrast between colonial Peru's luxurious viceregal spendor and colonial Chile's want of the simplest of life's amenities, which had made *Limeños* feel vastly superior to *Santiaguinos,* had aroused the envy of the latter. Peruvians were said to have mocked Chileans by telling them that in Lima "even mulattoes wear silk stockings, but in Chile gentlemen wear leggings."[23] True or not, the contemptuous expression well stated Peruvian attitudes. In addition, the frustrations of some two centuries of economic discrimination in favor of Peru added a sense of real material injury to the spiritual injury of which Chile felt itself the victim.[24]

Their common interest in ending Spanish rule served only further to embitter relations. Chile, having secured its independence earlier, mounted with Herculean effort and enormous expense an expedition for Peru's liberation. The expedition's leader, Argentine-born José San Martín, becoming the first chief executive of independent Peru, promptly assumed a Peruvian outlook which, however commendable in theory, aroused deep Chilean resentment. San Martín deprived Chilean expeditionary soldiers of their national insignia and drafted them into the newly established regular army of Peru. The Chilean navy retained its nationality, but San Martín's refusal to release its payroll so enraged its commander, Lord Cochrane, that he broke openly with the Peruvian chief executive. The unpleasant word "ingrate" increasingly became, in Chile, a synonym for "Peruvian."

But Chileans were nothing if not optimistic, for when San Martín was forced from Peru and Spanish forces returned to the attack, Chile went again to the rescue. A treaty was arranged to cover the terms of repayment of a loan of 1 million pesos and to provide for compensation of Chile's cost in sending arms, ships, supplies, and soldiers to prevent the retaking of Peru by Spain.[25] Amid subsequent political upheaval in Lima, the treaty was pigeonholed, and none of the various governments that held power in Peru during the 1820's attempted to fulfill the nation's obligations to Chile. As Chile was then experiencing dire financial difficulties, its bad opinion of Peru was confirmed. Now that Chile had put anarchy behind it, it was determined to seek repayment of the Peruvian loan through diplomatic channels, for any funds thus obtained would assist the new government to assert itself.

Peru was also economically important to Chile as its largest foreign customer. Both the national treasury and the bank accounts of landed aristocrats depended heavily upon the Peruvian wheat and flour trade, which in the late 1820's constituted 50 per cent of Chile's considerable total exports to Peru.[26] Every Chilean government had sought to regularize trade with Peru and to eliminate such obstacles as high duties, arbitrary official Peruvian actions and exactions, and United States competition in the Peruvian market.[27] But in 1830 that trade still suffered the hazards that had plagued it in the past, so that, along with the loan repayment, the new Chilean government sought a treaty that would rationalize commerce with Peru. No less a source of potential conflict than the loan and trade questions, however, was Chile's determination to make Valparaíso, at the expense of Callao, the major Pacific port of South America. In the resultant struggle Peru had a trump card; it could force the bypassing of Valparaíso by enacting a discriminatory tariff favoring ships that proceeded directly to Callao after rounding Cape Horn. An important object of Chile's Peruvian diplomacy was therefore to prevent such a move. A further matter of great concern to Chile in the early years of the Conservative government was the activity of Chilean political exiles in Lima, who were openly plotting revolution. It was therefore Chile's object to secure Peru's coöperation in preventing the organization and departure of a revolutionary expedition.

Chile's relations with Peru during the years 1830–1836 were difficult, not only because of the many questions at issue, but because it was often impossible to obtain policy definitions from Peru, and sometimes impossible to find a responsible authority with whom to negotiate. The frustrating situation resulted from two closely related factors:

Peru's political instability and its tangled relations with Bolivia. At issue in the latter problem was the ultimate political connection, or lack of it, between Peru and Bolivia, an issue closely tied to the aspirations of individual *caudillos* in each country and to the outcome of conflicts among them.

THE BOLIVIAN PROBLEM

Alto Peru, as Bolivia had been known in the colonial period, constituted part of the viceroyalty of Peru until 1776, when it was incorporated into the newly organized viceroyalty of the Río de la Plata. In 1810 newly independent Buenos Aires lost its jurisdiction to still-loyal Peru, and Alto Peru remained under the control of Lima until freed by military forces under Bolívar. At that crossroads in its sad history, Alto Peru rejected both Buenos Aires and Lima in favor of independent organization. Bolívar acceded, and was rewarded by the new state's choice of its name. Bolivia was born misshapen and doomed to weakness. Cobija, the seaport provided by Bolívar, was distant from the Altiplano and removed from traditional paths of commerce with the outside world, which ran overland through Peru to the latter's port of Arica. Bolivia's economic survival and development required a more adequate port, and many Bolivians sought either the forceful annexation of Arica or political union with Peru.

PROCONFEDERATIONISM

Peruvian opinion, which dreamed of building a single powerful nation upon the heritage of the viceroyalty of Peru, favored the second Bolivian solution as much as it opposed the first. From the first days of Peru's independence, its leaders had been working to frustrate Bolivian independence and to incorporate the Altiplano into Peru by fair means or foul. Bolivian proconfederationism, though somewhat weaker than Peru's because it was primarily economic rather than emotional, was nevertheless significant. In 1830, the first year of the new Chilean Conservative government, Peru and Bolivia each had a proconfederationist general as president. But agreement in principle could not possibly bring about union at that point, for the two generals were bitter personal enemies and each was resolved to destroy the other and to become the sole ruler of a unified Peru-Bolivia.

General Agustín Gamarra of Peru and General Andrés Santa Cruz of Bolivia had been comrades in arms under Bolívar in the war against Spain. Upon liberation they had together successfully plotted to oust the Liberator from Peru, and when their own designs to succeed Bolívar failed, they coöperated in the triumphant overthrow of his successor. When the time came for the two comrades to form their government, however, Gamarra drove Santa Cruz from Peruvian soil at gun's point. But Santa Cruz did not sink into political oblivion, as Gamarra had hoped. With great shrewdness he gained the presidency of Bolivia, where his superb administrative ability gave the Altiplano better government than it was to have in the rest of the century. As both general-presidents were fanatically dedicated to the establishment of a personally led Peru-Bolivian confederation, they were continually intriguing against each other and toward seizure of power in both countries. At the same time, in Peru several powerful caudillos were planning seizure of the presidency from Gamarra, each on his own account. Peru was thus in a state of constant inner turmoil at a time when war with Bolivia loomed on the horizon.

THE ZAÑARTU MISSION TO LIMA

Although the complex tensions to Chile's north seemed to offer security from aggression, they also hindered diplomacy, restricted commerce, and encouraged efforts by various Bolivians and Peruvians to attach Santiago to their respective causes. Chile, nevertheless remaining determined to press its Peruvian interests, dispatched Miguel Zañartu to Peru with orders to seek, among other things, a commercial treaty under which each nation's agricultural and manufactured products might be reciprocally imported free of duty. Chile argued that its reciprocal-trade proposal offered mutual advantages. Its wheat and flour would gain a favored position in its largest market, and other branches of Chilean enterprise would be stimulated, while Peru would secure a privileged position for its tropical produce, especially for the sugar of which Chile was the largest purchaser.[28]

But the Chilean proposal posed a major threat for the poverty-stricken government of Peru, a large part of whose financial support was derived from customs duties upon Chilean goods. Zañartu, anticipating resistance on that account, advised his government to ask merely for a wheat and flour monopoly[29] which would simultaneously free Chile from competition and maintain Peruvian government revenues. The Chilean Foreign Department rejected this suggestion on the grounds that United States interests would oppose a Chilean monopoly, that Peru would then blame Chile for its conflict with Washington, and that the Peruvian people would blame Chile for the high price of bread. Under such conditions no treaty could survive, and Chile was interested only in a permanent commercial agreement with Peru.

Santiago finally resolved to ask for a reciprocal removal of duties upon only its wheat and Peru's sugar, leaving all other articles subject to revenue-producing taxation. Chile was so eager to secure removal of the wheat tariff that it was even willing to offer as a last resort a substantial reduction in the amount Peru would have to repay on the independence loan. If Zañartu was unable to gain complete reciprocal removal of the sugar and wheat tariffs, he was to seek their reduction to the point where the products concerned would at least have an advantage over the same products of other nations. If Lima rejected this arrangement, Zañartu was to hint at possible Chilean reprisals in the form of an increase in Chile's tariff on Peruvian sugar, which would give Peru's competitors a preferential position in the Chilean market.[30]

Not one of Chile's proposals met with Lima's favor. Peru insisted upon reciprocal monopolies, together with a guaranteed market for its tobacco and a Chilean political commitment to the effect that if "the territory of either of the two nations is invaded, . . . the other is obliged to come to its assistance."[31] Lima's wish to couple commerce with a defensive alliance met a cold reception in Santiago, where war between Peru and Bolivia was regarded as inevitable. Moreover, Bolivia also wanted to entangle Chile in the struggle.

THE CHILEAN MEDIATION OF 1831

In March, 1831, President Santa Cruz of Bolivia requested that Chile mediate his country's difficulties with Peru.[32] The Chilean foreign minister suspected that the Bolivian general desired, not peace, but time in which to prepare for war,[33] and it was with the greatest reluctance that he instructed the Chilean minister in Lima to offer mediation, warning strongly against involving Chile in any responsibility for failure of a mediation effort and emphasizing the importance of Chile's absolute neutrality in Peru-Bolivian affairs.[34] The Chilean minister arranged a preliminary peace pact which was signed on August 31, 1831. It provided that each country would remove its army from the other's frontier and reduce the size of its forces in a manner to be specified in a subsequent definitive treaty of peace. The latter, also negotiated with Chilean help, was signed in November. In it Peru and Bolivia solemnly swore to maintain their armies at purely defensive levels, to remain eternally at peace, and never to intervene in each other's internal affairs.[35]

Chile did not rejoice in its successful mediation diplomacy, for the young Conservative government wished only to concentrate upon business at home. Now, having waded into the muddy waters of its neighbors' problems, it was faced with the choice of swimming or climbing back on shore, for both Peru and Bolivia requested that Chile act as guarantor of the November treaty. Chile got back on shore. In a major foreign-policy decision intended to avoid involvement in the conflict that would probably follow violation of the November treaty provisions, Chile declared a policy of "vigorous neutrality" in the dissensions among American states. Chile could not guarantee the peace between Peru and Bolivia, for it believed that any form of intervention in the disputes of other countries, except for friendly mediation, would merely create new problems and provide the basis for further disputes.[36]

Chile became even more committed to neutrality when threatened with deeper involvement in a Bolivian-Peruvian-Chilean triangle as the result of a Bolivian proposal for the negotiation of two treaties, one commercial and the other military. Santa Cruz sought a tripartite defensive alliance directed against any or all of three possible objectives: non–Spanish American nations; Spanish American nations; any one of the signatory nations of Chile, Peru, and Bolivia. Its answer to Bolivia sharply revealed Chile's contemporary attitudes toward Spanish American coöperation and South American power politics. Chile accepted the widely espoused theory that common language, common institutions, common religion, and common cause made of the Spanish American nations a "family," but saw no reason for its members to ally themselves against outsiders. Such alliances, in Chile's view, would be both ineffective and unnecessary. The weak and unstable members of the family would evade their obligations; the strong and orderly would fulfill them, whether bound by treaty or not. Chile thus indirectly indicated that it felt an obligation to defend any Spanish American nations endangered by an outsider. As for the Spanish American countries themselves, "Chile ... has based its relations with [them] ... upon complete impartiality, abstaining from any interference whatsoever in their internal or foreign affairs."[37]

According to Chile, its noninterventionist policy was due, not to lack of concern, but rather to the conviction that there existed a balance of power system in which

... the designs of an ambitious [Spanish American] government against the independence of other states will encounter ... insuperable obstacles in the very spirit that so powerfully influences the American peoples. ... Not long ago we witnessed the crumbling of grandiose projects based upon considerable military force and the prestige of America's most glorious name [Bolívar]. ... The spirit of mutual emulation and rivalry ... is the firmest bulwark of the independence of states. ... We do not believe ... pacts to be necessary.[38]

But Chile did think that certain positive but nonmilitary steps might discourage possible non–Spanish American aggression, and its foreign minister reminded the President of Bolivia that "the respect which the new nations inspire abroad depends mainly upon the consolidation of their domestic institutions and the development of their resources. . . . The public interest and . . . justice counsel the making of treaties of navigation and commerce granting moderate reciprocal preferences which, without damaging . . . foreign interests, might advantageously encourage agriculture."[39]

Chile clearly regarded the Spanish American nations as a separate international community whose intrarelationships were radically different from the relationships of its nations with the non–Spanish American world. In respect to the latter, the Spanish American states were joined by common defensive interests; but the outside world was too remote to constitute a genuine threat of the first order. What dangers it did hold could be warded off by affirmation of domestic political stability and by economic development. In contrast, Chile regarded Spanish American intrarelations as intimate affairs governed by the basic laws of power politics. The Spanish American nations were mutually competitive; any one of them might attempt to dominate any other, but natural forces would contain undue ambitions. This dichotomous view of international life provided Chile the intellectual basis upon which to reject commitments that it believed would hamper the pursuit of domestic goals. But it was in reality the favorable surrounding international power structure that permitted Chile enjoyment of its noninterventionist neutrality, leavened by occasional beneficent mediations which it hoped might encourage its trade and commerce. The ideal of Spanish American coöperation seemed to Chile highly impractical, but Chile was willing to exploit that ideal in the interest of securing advantageous commercial agreements.

THE PERUVIAN DECREE OF FEBRUARY 17, 1832

While Chile's negotiations with Bolivia were still under way, the Zañartu mission to Peru began to falter. For more than a year the Chilean minister had been attempting to secure a commercial treaty, when he learned to his dismay that Peru had declared Callao a port of deposit; this long-feared move was designed to improve that port's position with respect to Valparaíso. Because the step was neither unexpected nor illegal, it could not be officially protested. A subsequent decree did, however, elicit a strong official objection. Prior to sale, Chilean importers had been storing wheat and flour at the point of disembarkation in Callao. On February 17, 1832, it was ordered that wheat and flour be weighed and promptly removed whether or not they had been sold, subject to penalty. Viewing the decree as concrete evidence of Peruvian malice, Zañartu countered by demanding payment of the Peruvian independence debt to Chile. It was now Peru's turn to be resentful, and Zañartu informed Santiago that a commercial treaty could not be obtained without direct pressure. He advised that the duty on Peruvian sugar be raised, and that arrangements be made for the purchase of Brazilian sugar.[40] As the Chilean government's irritation grew, it ordered its minister in Lima to discontinue commercial negotiations but to maintain friendly diplomatic contact.[41] Then, surprisingly, Santiago placed a prohibitive duty upon imports of sugar from Peru.

Portales, then residing in Valparaíso, seriously doubted the wisdom of such action. It might, he felt, lead to reprisals that would hurt the port's economy. Portales advised the government to avoid fighting a tariff war and to prepare to fight a military one.[42] Don Diego was correct in his prediction of Peruvian reprisals, for Lima not only doubled the duty on Chilean wheat but also diverted some trade from Valparaíso by imposing an additional duty upon goods that had not come directly to Callao. Chile called home its minister, but left the door open by informing Peru that if the latter sincerely desired a commercial treaty its envoy would be well received in Santiago. A consul general was designated to protect Chilean interests pending reëstablishment of formal relations.

The consul general's instructions reveal that his functions were not merely commercial, as advertised, for he was ordered to investigate closely the activities of Chilean exiles in Lima and to "ascertain if any of them are approaching the Peruvian government and assisting its intentions with the purpose of discrediting the government of Chile, ... and what means they might try to use to disturb our republic."[43] Moreover, heeding Portales' advice in a now-grave situation, Chile sought to purchase a Colombian frigate, seeking a loan from Bolivia for that purpose. After a long delay Bolivia denied the loan, claiming that because Chile had announced it would not sign alliances, Bolivia could not compromise itself in the "ominous" Peruvian-Chilean conflict.[44]

Tension-reducing factors were, however, already coming into being. In December, 1833, President Gamarra of Peru finished his legal term in office and was forcibly ejected from the presidential palace by General Luís Orbegoso. Gamarra promptly organized a revolt whose suppression lasted several months; then, in mid-1834, the government of

General Orbegoso bowed to the demands of Peruvian sugar interests and accepted their offer to pay for a commercial mission to Chile. The mission reached Santiago in September, and in January, 1835, a commercial treaty was signed.[45]

THE COMMERCIAL TREATY OF 1835 WITH PERU

The 1835 Commercial Treaty with Peru fulfilled many of Chile's objectives. Article XIV provided that "the natural products or manufactures of ... the contracting republics, transported by Peruvian or Chilean ships, shall ... pay only one-half the import duties which are now or may in the future be charged on the same or equivalent merchandise of the most favored nation transported by ships not having, because of their flag, this privilege." Such a provision assured Chile rationalization and stabilization of the wheat trade, a preferred position for its wheat in the Peruvian market, an end to Peruvian retaliatory measures, and growth and prosperity for the Chilean merchant marine under a protective umbrella.

Article XXVI was also favorable to Chile, providing that "foreign merchandise taken from the bonded warehouses of either of the two states and transported in Peruvian or Chilean ships to the ports of the other will be charged no more than the customary import duties." Thus not only would Chile's merchant fleet benefit, but Valparaíso was virtually assured Pacific commercial supremacy, as its location to the south of Callao made it certain to be the first port of call for ships rounding the southern tip of the continent. As further indication of its goodwill, Peru promised to negotiate, as soon as possible, a special treaty providing for the payment of its debt to Chile.

The Chilean government, highly pleased with the results of its commercial negotiations, rushed to complete the treaty. It convoked a special session of Congress which approved the agreement without opposition and then rapidly dispatched the warship *Aquiles* to Callao, bearing on board the signed treaty and a commission empowering the consul in Lima to effect an exchange of ratifications.

By the time the *Aquiles* reached its destination, however, revolution had again engulfed Peru. President Santa Cruz of Bolivia had renewed his intrigues to detach southern Peru from Lima and incorporate it into Bolivia. President Orbegoso of Peru had reacted by leading an army to the southern city of Arequipa. While Orbegoso was away from the capital, General Felipe Salaverry proclaimed himself president of Peru. And then former President Agustín Gamarra, who had been in Bolivian exile, reëntered Peru with an army and attempted to reinstate himself at the head of the government. In the midst of this tremendous upheaval the Chilean consul was confronted with the perplexing problem of with whom, or with what Peruvian clique or government, he should effect the exchange of ratifications of the commercial treaty. In June, 1835, after a period of hesitation, Salaverry seemed to be in control of most of Peru, and the Chilean agent exchanged ratifications with him as apparent victor in the Peruvian struggle for power.

News of the exchange of ratifications was joyously greeted in Chile. In July the President issued a proclamation providing that

... inasmuch as ... ratifications have been exchanged of the treaty of friendship, commerce, and navigation between the republics of Peru and Chile, and as it is proper to celebrate this happy event ... with all possible signs of joy, I therefore order and decree:

1. On the 23d, 24th, and 25th days of the month, doors and balconies shall be festooned with decorations. . . .
2. During the nights of those three days there shall be lights and the general ringing of bells.[46]

The President's proclamation accurately reflected the importance to Chile of the Peruvian commercial treaty. The agreement was a triumph of Chilean conservatism, whose proponents believed that Chile's national interests lay in the maintenance of stable orderly government and in the development of the nation's economy. The Chilean conservatives believed that what was good for business was good for the country, and that their goals for their country could best be achieved by retaining Chilean freedom of action in the international sphere and by expanding Chilean commerce with the outside world. To be free in its dealings with the Great Powers, Chile had sought to raise its international status so that it might merit equal treatment; and it had sought to avoid controversy. In dealing with the nations of its own continent, Chile had sought also to retain freedom of action through nonintervention and avoidance of entangling alliances. At the same time Chile had tried to promote its commerce with important South American nations by maintaining the peace among them through friendly mediation and by negotiating advantageous commercial treaties.

In the period 1830–1835 Chile's major objective in relation to other nations was avoidance of involvement. It can scarcely be maintained, therefore, that the Chilean government engaged in power politics during that period. Nevertheless, in propounding the notion that an American aggressor would be contained automatically by competitive forces operating among the American nations, Chile was clearly basing its policy upon a fundamental assumption of power politics. Moreover, Chile, as well as Peru and Bolivia, had used, or had tried to use, techniques of power politics to forward their national interests. Alliances had been proposed; economic warfare had been waged; armies had been threateningly deployed. Chile, in attempting to increase its naval power, had sought Bolivian aid. A regional system of power politics, based upon a Chilean-Peruvian-Bolivian triangle, was in gestation.

But the system was not yet in active existence. Chile had so far been successful in remaining physically aloof from the international conflicts of the anarchic nations that surrounded it. It had gathered domestic strength and had improved its international power position. Its port of Valparaíso had grown immensely, tripling its customs receipts between 1831 and 1835. By the latter year the government's fiscal reforms enabled it to recognize and regularize the internal debt. Within less than six years Chile had made political and economic strides that even the most dedicated supporter of the conservative regime might have hesitated to predict upon its assumption of power. The wresting of a commercial treaty from Peru was thus public proof of the success of the policies of the government and of Portales. Well might Chilean leaders wish to light lights and ring bells.

CHAPTER III

CHAMPION OF THE AMERICAN EQUILIBRIUM

THE COMMERCIAL TREATY of 1835 with Peru, so joyously proclaimed at midyear, did not survive to fulfill its promise. During the eighteen months following its promulgation, the South American power structure, previously so favorable to Chile, underwent radical alteration. Chile's commercial aspirations and internal political stability were endangered. To meet that challenge the Chilean oligarchy began to think of practical power politics in concrete terms, and reached the decision to wage war in order to restore the balance of power. In the course of that war Chile came to see itself as a member of a system of power politics. And, finally, its leadership began to regard Chile as "Champion of the American Equilibrium."

FORMATION OF THE PERU-BOLIVIAN CONFEDERATION

The central figure in the events that carried Chile into war was General Andrés Santa Cruz, president of Bolivia. He had improved the Bolivian economy, implanted a certain degree of law and order in the Altiplano, and organized a well-trained and obedient army.[1] Santa Cruz had never ceased to intrigue toward the confederation of Peru and Bolivia, and mid-1835 found him ready to stop plotting and go into action.

General Felipe Salaverry, whom Santa Cruz regarded as an able and dangerous adversary, was in control of much of Peru, and any delay might allow him to unify Peru and turn upon Bolivia.[2] Setting aside their old and bitter enmity, Peruvian ex-President Agustín Gamarra and Santa Cruz agreed to join forces and seize power in Peru, establishing two independent Peruvian states, one in the north and the other in the south, which would later be united with Bolivia in a tripartite Peru-Bolivian Confederation.

Gamarra, without awaiting written formalization of his understanding with Santa Cruz, entered Peru with some hastily mustered men and proclaimed against Salaverry. But Gamarra had reckoned without the desperate circumstances of Orbegoso in Arequipa, and the opportunism of Santa Cruz. The former, who had for some time been seeking Santa Cruz's assistance against Salaverry, was so frightened when he learned of Gamarra's invasion that he immediately met the terms for aid previously advanced by the Bolivian general. It was a golden opportunity for Santa Cruz, as Orbegoso still claimed the legal presidency of Peru, and his invitation to enter the country would tend to free Santa Cruz of charges of aggression. Gamarra was therefore eliminated from the Bolivian general's plans.

On June 15, 1835, less than ten days after the exchange of ratifications of the Chilean-Peruvian commercial treaty, Santa Cruz and Orbegoso arranged a pact stressing the point that only after repeated requests was the former entering Peru, and then for the sole purpose of restoring the order disturbed by Salaverry's proclamation and uprising. Upon restoration of order, the pact stipulated, the peoples of "north" Peru and those of "south" Peru would freely choose the form of government they desired.[3] Needless to say, the pact did not disclose the private understanding of the two generals concerning confederation.

Promptly upon the signing of the agreement with Orbegoso, Santa Cruz publicly announced his intentions, directing explanations not only to the army and the people of Bolivia, but to the outside world as well. For the enlightenment of the latter he published a long argument entitled *Exposición de los motivos, que justifican la cooperación del Govierno de Bolivia en los negocios políticos del Perú.*[4] In that manifesto Santa Cruz insisted that stable and peaceful Bolivia had repeatedly denied Peruvian requests to bring order to that country and that he was now going to the aid of Peru only because Salaverry had created "a tyrannical and monstrous authority whose legal code is torture, whose basis is terror, whose rights are . . . bayonets and which . . . enriches itself upon the ruins of the unfortunate peoples who tremble under its yokes, . . . terrified by the sight of blood running in its fields and plazas."[5] After painting so horrifying a picture, Santa Cruz affirmed that Peru's social structure was in a state of such utter collapse and anarchy that "the security, the repose, and the legal regime of neighboring peoples are immediately threatened." The Bolivian general claimed that he could not, as one of Peru's menaced neighbors, reject the pleas of the Peruvian people and of the country's legal government.

Santa Cruz insisted that Bolivia's intervention in Peru was in accordance with "the principles of the most respected nations of the Old World," and cited a British declaration of November, 1793, which justified war against France on the grounds that the reforms of the French Revolution " 'have given rise to a system destructive of all public order' " and that " 'this state of things cannot continue without involving all bordering powers in a common danger.' " On the same day that this justification was issued to the world, June 15, 1835, Santa Cruz entered Peru. Gamarra defected to Salaverry and held out until

August 13, when he fled into Lima, leaving Salaverry and Santa Cruz to prepare for a direct confrontation.

The events to its north now forced reluctant Chile to formulate a more comprehensive Peru-Bolivian policy. In October, 1835, Orbegoso angrily charged that Chile's exchange of ratifications of the commercial treaty had constituted recognition of Salaverry at a time when Orbegoso was the only, and the legal, president of Peru.[6] At the same time representatives of both Salaverry and Orbegoso arrived at the Foreign Department as agents of Peru and requested accreditation. Alleging that it could not depart from its traditional policy of neutrality, and wishing to avoid alienation of either faction before knowing who would win, Chile made the blunder of officially receiving both agents.[7] Peru was thus simultaneously represented in Santiago by two mutually hostile envoys[8] whose home factions were angered by the dual accreditation maneuver. Salaverry asked for recall of the Chilean representative in Peru, but the chancellery in Santiago ignored his request in the hope that there would occur a change either of tempers or of governments. Salaverry had not attempted to enforce his recall demand prior to his departure from Lima to take the field against Santa Cruz.[9]

ENTRANCE OF ORBEGOSO INTO LIMA AND DEFEAT OF SALAVERRY

In his anxiety to confront Santa Cruz with a maximum array of power, Salaverry, failing to demonstrate his usual tactical ability, left the capital insufficiently garrisoned. Pro–Santa Cruz forces took advantage of the error to enter Lima. With them rode Orbegoso who, assuming the title of "Supreme Chief of Peru," annulled the "acts" of the Salaverry regime, among which was the one providing for the exchange of ratifications of the Chilean trade treaty. Santiago, seeking to compel the treaty's acceptance, placed upon Peruvian goods an additional import duty which was to be returned upon Orbegoso's adherence to the agreement.[10] But the Supreme Chief had already acted, decreeing on January 4, 1836, that the treaty would expire at the end of a four-month grace period to allow for the readjustment of Peruvian commercial interests.[11]

Chile feigned indifference, *El Araucano* claiming that invalidation of the treaty had been expected, and that in any event it had not really served Chile's interests.[12] But the private mood of Chilean leaders was very different. The Foreign Minister denounced the invalidation as "unjustifiable ... before the tribunal of national honor and public faith." The chargé d'affaires in Lima was informed that "for Chile's part there would be no obstacle" to the agreement's reconsideration.[13]

Meanwhile, although the grace period was still in effect and permitted some hope for a change in Peru's position, Chile was increasingly disturbed by the growing power of General Santa Cruz.

In February, 1836, Santa Cruz definitively eliminaied significant Peruvian opposition by crushing Salaverry's army and shooting its leader to death. The Bolivian general then proceeded to advance the confederation of his country with Peru by arranging for his designation as "chief" of the separate state of "South Peru," whose independence was especially declared for the purpose. Orbegoso, now "supreme chief" of a similarly independent "North Peru," was fully prepared to coöperate in the confederation. In sum, the information at Chile's disposal gave it every reason to believe that Peru and Bolivia were about to be united under the undivided power of Santa Cruz.[14]

With relations with Peru strained to the utmost, the Chilean government asked a number of wealthy citizens for a secret loan for the purchase and equipment of warships. At the same time *El Araucano* conveniently began to advocate a large navy for the protection of Chile's expanding foreign commerce, a navy that incidentally might prove useful for defensive purposes should the need ever arise.[15] The official Chilean journal attempted to make it appear that any enlargement of the navy would have nothing to do with current international conditions, but Peruvians were not deceived. The Chilean agent in Lima reported that a rumored Chilean naval loan "had caused some alarm in government ... [circles]."[16]

Commercial Treaty Abrogated

As Chile moved, quietly but with determination, to strengthen its military position, Santa Cruz elements gained the ascendancy in the government of Orbegoso. Juan García del Río, an intimate of the Bolivian general, was named finance minister and asked to review the commercial treaty with Chile. His report, dated May 16, 1836, sounded the agreement's death knell. García, pointing out that the treaty would prevent Peruvian commercial hegemony on the Pacific, recommended that Peru's basic commercial goal be *direct* trade with the United States and Europe. He warned, however, that such a goal would not be reached if Chile was assured enjoyment of the advantages inherent in its geographical location, and advised definitive nullification of the treaty.[17] On the day the García report was published, the agreement was officially decreed void in an order purporting to restore Peruvian-Chilean trade to its pretreaty status, but which was in fact designed to obtain for Peruvian sugar a preferred situation in the Chilean market under threat of doubling the duty on Chilean wheat.[18]

Upon learning of the May 16 decree, *El Araucano* removed its mask of indifference and reprinted all the relevant Peruvian documents in full. In a lengthy and indignant editorial comment it betrayed the government's deep concern, asking if there could "... be seen in this behavior the slighest indication of a desire to reach a commercial agreement, much less to cultivate peaceful relations."[19] The journal assured its readers that the government was giving undivided attention to the serious situation created by Peru's unfriendliness. But to calm any undue fears *El Araucano* also promised that in the "examination of these questions there will be no place for the emotions of irritation to which the disdainful coolness and dictatorial tone of the Peruvian government toward this Republic would naturally give rise."

THE FREIRE EXPEDITION

Whatever their intentions, Chilean statesmen were unable to suppress their irritation when commercial defeat was followed by a direct threat to internal Chilean order and the power of the Conservatives. That threat took concrete form at the beginning of July, 1836, when Peru leased two allegedly deactivated naval ships to a group of Chilean exiles who had been plotting seizure of power in Chile under the leadership of former President Freire. The Peruvian government, moreover, made no effort to prevent departure from Callao of the ships and men of the well-armed expedition, which set sail for the Chilean island of Chiloé which Freire planned to seize for his headquarters. On July 28, when the Chilean government learned of the expedition, the President declared martial law, informing the people of Chile that "the news so far received confirms the publicly notorious fact that the expedition has been organized with the full knowledge of the Peruvian government. ... Until I come into possession of irrefutable documented proof, I shall not regard the peace between the two nations as broken."[20]

The Chilean government's moves to suppress Freire's expedition were seconded from an unexpected source when the crew of Freire's *Monteagudo* mutinied, sailed into Valparaíso Harbor, and handed both the ship and valuable documentary information over to Chilean authorities. Promptly incorporated into the Chilean navy for action against Chiloé, the *Monteagudo* freed other Chilean vessels, including the *Aquiles,* for use elsewhere. The *Aquiles* effected, in late August, a reprisal for Peruvian help to the Freire expedition, which at a single blow weakened the sea power of Chile's potential enemy and strengthened Chile's own badly lagging naval strength. Penetrating the harbor of Callao, the *Aquiles* made off with three ships of the Peruvian navy.[21]

General Santa Cruz, enraged, cast the Chilean chargé d'affaires into
prison, though only for a few minutes,[22] and war seemed about to
break out.

It was the British who prevented open conflict at this point by bringing together Victorino Garrido, commander of the *Aquiles*, and a representative of the Bolivian general. Garrido agreed to seize no more
Peruvian ships and to retain those taken only until final settlement of
questions pending between Santiago and Lima. The agent of Santa
Cruz agreed that Chile might permanently retain the ships of the Freire
expedition, promised to keep Chilean exiles under surveillance, and
agreed to undertake no economic retaliation for the seizure of the
ships.[23] Santa Cruz approved the agreement because he needed peace to
concretize his cherished Peru-Bolivian Confederation. And for that
very reason Chile rejected it, having decided even before Garrido's
return that the confederation must perish.

PORTALES PLANS DESTRUCTION OF THE PERU-BOLIVIAN CONFEDERATION

On September 10, 1836, Portales confidentially informed Manuel Blanco
Encalada, naval hero of the wars for independence, that he would
shortly be asked to lead a campaign "to achieve . . . the second independence of Chile." In explaining what he meant by "second independence," Portales demonstrated clear comprehension of the danger to
Chilean interests implied in the change of the international power
structure to the north. He asserted that

Chile's position in relation to the Peru-Bolivian Confederation is untenable. It
can be tolerated neither by the people nor by the government, for it would be
equivalent to suicide. . . .
. . . the confederation must forever disappear from the American scene. By its
geographical extent; by its larger white population; by the combined wealth of
Peru and Bolivia, until now scarcely touched; by the rule that the new organization,
taking it away from us, would . . . exercise in the Pacific; by Lima's larger number
of cultured white people closely connected with influential Spanish families; by
the greater intelligence, if indeed inferior character, of its public men, the confederation would soon smother Chile. . . .
The navy should act before the army, dealing decisive blows. We must rule forever
in the Pacific. . . . The armed forces of Chile will triumph by reason of their national
spirit; . . . if not, . . . they will leave the impression that it is difficult to dominate
people of character.[24]

Chile's dominant political figure thus proved himself to be the possessor of a thoroughly sophisticated concept of power. In evaluating the
relative strength of opposing forces, he went beyond the mere summa-
tion of obvious quantitative elements to such components as the nature

of the citizenry, its leadership, character, and intelligence, and the strength of the national spirit. And in his sense of Chile's inferiority to the former viceregal capital, Portales reflected the attitudes of Chilean leaders as they confronted the growing power of Santa Cruz, and decided that that power must be definitively destroyed.

A few days after Portales had written to Blanco concerning Chile's "second independence," Garrido returned from Lima bearing a copy of his agreement and a personal letter from Santa Cruz to President Prieto. Santa Cruz wrote that notwithstanding Chile's hostile actions he strongly wished to reach an amicable settlement of misunderstandings, toward which end he was sending Dr. Casimiro Olañeta to Santiago for discussions.[25] In replying to Santa Cruz over Prieto's signature, the Chilean government openly stated for the first time its view of the Peru-Bolivian Confederation, informing its leader that Chile's policy was a reaction to a "new order of things which, disturbing the equilibrium of the republics of the South, has imposed upon each of them the obligation to provide not only for the conservation of secondary material ... rights but also of their very existence."[26]

Prieto went on to deny Santa Cruz's charge that Chile's relations with Salaverry had implied hostility to Orbegoso, claiming that Chile had simply attempted to cope neutrally with an existing situation and that it was in fact Orbegoso who had expressed hostility by "clothing [rejection of the commercial treaty] in the most odious and repulsive garb." As for the seizure of the Peruvian ships, that had taken place only after the launching from Peru of the Freire expedition, and for the very good reason that "if the plan hatched under the nose of the Peruvian government to set fire to this Republic [had not failed], ... it is extremely probable that we would have had to fight the whole Peruvian navy." To conclude, Prieto informed Santa Cruz that Chile wished only for assurances of peace and just reparations, and was sending a plenipotentiary to Lima for negotiations.

THE EGAÑA MISSION TO PERU; DECLARATION OF WAR

Moving relentlessly to bring matters to a head, the Chilean government received congressional authorization to declare war "if it does not obtain from the government of Peru reparations adequate to the injuries inflicted upon Chile under conditions that ensure the independence of the Republic."[27] The power to declare war was delegated to Mariano Egaña, who was sent to Lima with instructions to insist upon five points: satisfaction for the jailing of the chargé d'affaires, Lavalle; Peru's recognition of its independence debt to Chile; limitation of the

Peruvian navy; a reciprocal trade treaty; and exemption of Chilean nationals from forced loans and from service in the Peruvian army. In addition, and more importantly, the major objective of Egaña's negotiations was "the independence of Bolivia. The incorporation of the two republics into one ... clearly endangers neighboring states. ... We do not care whether General Santa Cruz rules in Bolivia or in Peru; what we do care about is the separation of the two nations. ... If Austria or France seized Spain or Italy ... to form a single political body, ... would the other nations be indifferent?"[28]

Egaña, aboard one of a squadron of five warships under the command of Admiral Blanco Encalada, reached Callao on October 30, 1836, but was refused permission to anchor pending explicit guarantees concerning the fleet's intentions. With the matter still unresolved, four of the squadron's units proceeded to Guayaquil to prevent departure of three Peruvian ships known to be in the Ecuadoran port.[29] On November 11 Egaña, concluding that further efforts to negotiate with Santa Cruz would be fruitless, declared war.

Egaña's return to Santiago found Casimiro Olañeta feverishly attempting, on behalf of General Santa Cruz, to keep the Peru-Bolivian Confederation out of war.[30] But his every offer was rejected as the Chilean government now broadened its demands by insisting that "the independence of Bolivia and Ecuador is regarded by Chile as absolutely necessary for the security of the other South American states."[31] Olañeta countered that Ecuador's independence could not be discussed because Ecuador, as an independent nation, could speak for itself without the intercession of Chile; and as for Bolivia, Olañeta affirmed that it was at liberty to associate itself with Peru if it wished to do so.[32]

Although the end of the road had in fact been reached, before putting an official close to discussions Portales wrote Olañeta a letter asking if

... an event such as the fusion of two nations into one, planned without the participation of neighboring states and obviously and notoriously consummated by means of force, would have been regarded in Europe with the cold indifference that you recommend to the government of this Republic; and if it would not have spread war from one end of that continent to the other. ... Long and bloody wars have been ... brought about by the occupation of a small district which slightly altered power relationships among the various states.

In conclusion Portales explained that

In asking for Bolivia's independence as a condition for peace, we refer to independence in its most absolute sense; for any system in which the population, wealth, and resources of Peru and Bolivia might be at the disposition of a single government, and of a government that has given us incontestable proof of its ill will, is incompatible with the security of this Republic.[33]

On December 21, 1836, President Prieto reported to Congress at great length upon the state of Chile's relations with Peru and Bolivia. Justifying Chile's peace demands—demands that had been rejected—Prieto recapitulated the five points of Egaña's instructions, but he especially emphasized other requirements, including the "maintenance of political equilibrium among the republics of the South."[34] He also reminded Congress that the "history of civilized peoples is a continual lesson . . . in the justice of resisting the earliest acts of ambition. It shows us the results of that guilty indolence that causes people after people to fall into the abyss. . . . The national pact of the new Peru-Bolivian people has been concocted partly of treason and partly of force and cleverness. Chile is not stepping into this situation to defend foreign interests; it is defending its own welfare."

On December 24, 1836, in compliance with the government's request, the Congress of Chile resolved that

1. General Don Andrés Santa Cruz, president of the Republic of Bolivia, unjust withholder of Peruvian sovereignty, menaces the independence of the other South American republics.

2. The Peruvian government, under the influence of General Santa Cruz, has in peacetime permitted the invasion of Chilean territory by warships of the Peruvian Republic for the purpose of introducing discord and civil war among the Chilean people.

3. General Santa Cruz has, against the precepts of international law, injured the person of a public minister of the Chilean nation.

4. The National Congress, in the name of the Republic of Chile, whose honor has been insulted and whose internal and external security has been menaced, solemnly ratifies the declaration of war.[35]

The pivotal point in Chile's justification for war was that it had to restore the balance of power for the sake of its own security. Whether this was a true motive or merely a hastily devised rationalization is a question whose answer is central to any evaluation of Chilean policy. General Santa Cruz claimed that Chile waged war to retain its commercial and political hegemony, and that before the confederation was established Chile had attempted to subordinate Peruvian commerce to its own, using for the purpose the commercial agreement of 1835. Reflecting the influence of the García report, Santa Cruz affirmed that "Chile . . . intervened in our internal affairs only for the purpose of preventing direct trade with all the peoples of the earth by the states of the confederation, and in fear that Valparaíso would lose the mercantile supremacy that it had possessed for years as a consequence of Peru's disorders and . . . economic errors. . . . The cabinet of Santiago planned perfidiously and conspiratorially a ruinous war with the pur-

pose of acquiring naval supremacy in the Pacific."[36] Although Santa
Cruz may have been partly correct, his argument did not exclude the
possibility that Chile felt it necessary to restore the South American
balance of power.

Chile's leaders, nurtured in European traditions, clearly related their
nation's naval and commercial position to its total power status. Even
before Santa Cruz loomed menacingly upon the horizon with the confederation, Chilean statesmen were familiar with the basic principles of
power politics. As early as 1825 Mariano Egaña wrote: "...now that
the independence of Alto Peru has been established, Chile has nothing
to fear from its neighbors."[37] And Chile's policy of nonintervention in
the early 1830's was based upon the belief that among competitive
nations the balance-of-power principle would operate so as to prevent
the consummation of aggressive plans. Nor can the part that Andrés
Bello played in the formulation of Chilean policy be overlooked. As a
Venezuelan agent in London he had closely watched the efforts of Great
Britain to form a coalition against Napoleon, and the subsequent reestablishment, at Vienna, of the European equilibrium. In his powerful
treatise on international law, Bello maintained that

Power and the intention of wrongdoing are not necessarily united. Only, therefore,
when a power has given repeated proof of pride or boundless ambition is there
reason to regard it as a dangerous neighbor. But even then arms are not the only
means of preventing the aggression of a powerful state. Confederation with other
nations, which, combining their forces, make themselves capable of equilibrating
those of the mistrusted power is the most effective means of imposing respect. One
may also demand guarantees, and, if they are refused, the refusal itself would be
basically suspect and would justify war. Ultimately, when a power makes known its
ambitious plans, attacking the independence of another..., the rest may legally,
...after having tried peaceful means,...favor the oppressed nation.[38]

In the opinion of Chilean statesmen, General Santa Cruz and his confederation had fulfilled Bello's indicated *casus belli.*

It is possible, but unlikely, that Chile first decided to go to war and
then sought a justification in Bello, for the government's procedures
did follow rather closely the prescriptions of the treatise. It is, however,
more reasonable to suppose that the government, whose influential members already accepted, either consciously or unconsciously, the basic
principles of balance-of-power politics, was shocked into full realization
of their meaning for Chile only after feeling the direct impact upon
Chilean national aspirations of the attempt to unite Peru and Bolivia.
It was then that the idea of power balancing came to represent, not
merely a respectable, if somewhat remote, European dogma, but a concrete workable solution to an immediate problem.

Chile's post-1830 leadership had acted with decision in coping with domestic problems, and now did likewise in handling an international one. If less than the entire leadership at first clearly realized the stakes involved in the war against the Peru-Bolivian Confederation, by the end of the conflict there was no doubt that unanimity prevailed. During the progress of the war the Chilean government became increasingly ruled, both in relations with neutrals and in the formulation of peace terms, by the idea that it was of paramount necessity to restore the South American balance of power to its preconfederation position. During the more than two years of Chile's effort to destroy the Peru-Bolivian Confederation, its statesmen encountered problems that deepened their understanding of the interests involved in intra–South American relations and clarified and enlarged their concept of the system of power politics of which Chile was a member. If, as implied by Santa Cruz, the principle of maintaining a balance of power had been a rationalization in mid-1835, by the middle of 1838 it was an immovable cornerstone of Chilean foreign policy.

WARTIME DIPLOMACY

Preparations for a successful campaign, guided at every point by the tireless and ubiquitous Don Diego Portales, included the organization not only of the requisite armed forces but also of a diplomatic offensive calculated to win friends to Chile's position against Santa Cruz and to prevent unwanted interference. In its broad strategic planning, moreover, Chile differentiated between the nations it considered to be within its own system and those it viewed as "outsiders." It sought to deny the latter any role in the settlement of the war, while it assiduously courted the former. Chile consistently strove to prevent subordination of South American interests to those of the Great Powers, and thus to make it possible for South American countries to interact as sovereign independent states, in imitation of their European models. Chile early rejected a Santa Cruz proposal that would have involved arbitration by agents of Great Britain, France, and the United States because, as Portales explained,

... their ardent zeal in promoting their commercial interests ... predisposes them to regard as of secondary value other considerations of vital importance, ... [such as] independence, honor, domestic tranquility, and the stability of institutions and governments. To inspire the necessary confidence, an arbiter's decision must be completely impartial, not only with respect to the contending parties, but also with respect to the various interests concerned.... The great nations that trade with us ... have until now refrained from taking sides ... among our American states. They have advised their agents to be most delicately circumspect upon this point.

Let us adopt this enlightened policy ourselves and avoid any move that might
motivate ... foreign intervention.[39]

In seeking the help of South American nations believed by Chile to
have a stake in the maintenance of the equilibrium, Santiago was disheartened by the relative indifference of its should-be allies to broader
continental concerns. One such state was Ecuador. In international
affairs Ecuador could at best play a secondary role, for it was poverty-
ridden, sparsely populated, and torn by extreme geographical and
political strife. The political, economic, and international orientation
of its hot coastal region, dominated by the commercial port city of
Guayaquil, was almost diametrically opposed to that of the mountain
plateaus, dominated by the political capital of Quito. Of the caudillos
who during the war personified Ecuador's traditional coast-mountain
schism the two most influential were Juan José Flores and Vicente
Rocafuerte. The former had been president from 1830 until 1835 and
had become commander of the armed forces upon Rocafuerte's assumption of the presidency.

THE LAVALLE MISSION TO ECUADOR

Had Santiago been more informed about conditions in Ecuador, it
might have refrained from seeking Quito's assistance. Nevertheless, an
Ecuadoran alliance was not to be totally despised. Quito's adherence
would have reinforced Chile's argument that Santa Cruz was threatening other nations besides Chile itself. And Ecuador might have helped
the war effort by preventing Peru-Bolivian use of Guayaquil's shipyards, or even by contributing a fighting force to the planned invasion
of Peru.

Designated to seek an Ecuadoran alliance was the former briefly
jailed envoy to Peru, Ventura Lavalle. Upon his arrival in Guayaquil,
Lavalle was greatly encouraged by General Flores' declared eagerness
to take up arms against Santa Cruz.[40] But upon completing the ascent
to Quito the Chilean chargé d'affaires found that President Rocafuerte
had no intention of becoming involved. In fact, he had recently signed
a treaty with the three states of the confederation, and now offered to
sign a similar one with Chile.[41] Lavalle, convinced that the President's
sentiments lay with Santa Cruz, believed that Chilean hopes lay with
Flores;[42] and indeed, early in 1837, the Ecuadoran Congress, swayed by
the latter's influence, rejected the triple treaty with Santa Cruz. It did
not, however, express itself in favor of an alliance with Chile. In reporting his failure to Santiago, Lavalle deplored the fact that

The Congress [of Ecuador] resists war because it does not see the dangers that threaten Ecuador, and thinks that ... the interests of the country demand rigorous neutrality. Neither do these gentlemen wish to believe that if Santa Cruz defeated Chile there would be serious reason for fear ... [imagining]that the two or three thousand men Ecuador could arm would be able to destroy as many battalions as Santa Cruz might command. You cannot imagine the pride and haughty presumption of these people.[43]

The Ecuadoran Congress, having rejected both a treaty with Santa Cruz and an alliance with Chile, commenced to see the nation's role as a mediating one, and in May, 1837, the government made a formal offer of mediation, apparently removing itself from the list of possible Chilean allies.

It was so obvious that New Granada would not want to become involved in the Peru-Bolivian conflict that Chile had not even taken the trouble to send a propaganda agent to Bogotá. But Lavalle, grasping at straws in the face of his Ecuadoran failure, took it upon himself to write a long personal letter to President Santander explaining that Chile's major purpose in the war was "to contain ... the tremendous power being established in Peru which threatens to involve its neighbors in frightful disasters."[44] In reply, New Granada's president expressed no direct opinion concerning the justice of Chile's cause, but he did clearly indicate disapproval of Santa Cruz. Santander admitted that both New Granadans and Venezuelans were aware of the fact that a "great power is being raised at the expense of the liberties of the Peruvian people, which, if consolidated, would endanger the peace of neighboring peoples."[45] But the president of New Granada did not believe it was his nation's duty to restore the equilibrium, and predicted that a combination of the arbitrary methods of Santa Cruz and the divisive forces within Peru and Bolivia would prevent ultimate consolidation of the confederation. Santander believed that New Granada itself had nothing whatever to fear, and that in any event it was perfectly capable of defending itself. He advised Lavalle to accept Ecuador's mediation offer and through it to end the war.

RELATIONS BETWEEN BOLIVIA AND BUENOS AIRES

Buenos Aires was more disturbed by the Peru-Bolivian Confederation than either Bogotá or Quito, for the northwesternmost of the feuding provinces which it attempted to govern had long been closely associated with Bolivia in both commerce and sentiment. Factions on either side of the frontier had become intimately involved in each other's strife and caudillo warfare. In the early 1830's President Santa Cruz of

Bolivia had given moral and material support to Argentine Unitarios
of the interior in their conflict with the Federalistas led by Governor
Juan Manuel Rosas of Buenos Aires. When Rosas decisively defeated
them, many Unitario leaders fled across the border into Bolivia, where
Santa Cruz gave them financial help and closed his eyes to their con-
spiratorial activities. After Rosas' assumption of dictatorial power in
1834, relations between Bolivia and Buenos Aires became increasingly
hostile. By 1836 the failure of Rosas' ruthless effort to exterminate the
opposition and consolidate his political position throughout the provinces led the Buenos Aires governor to fear that Santa Cruz, following
the pattern he had used with respect to Peru, might use the Unitarios to
secure the incorporation of the northwest provinces into Bolivia.[46]

THE PÉREZ MISSION TO BUENOS AIRES

Santiago, aware of the concern of Buenos Aires, sent José Joaquín
Pérez there to seek an alliance. Pérez, arriving at his destination in
February, 1837, assured representatives of the Rosas government that
Chile had gone to war only "after ... making use of other means
adopted in similar instances by the most cultured peoples of Europe,
and advised by the most renowned writers on international law."[47]
Pérez then presented a four-point proposal: (1) Buenos Aires would
declare that it was "opposed to the system of incorporation announced
by General Santa Cruz because it was incompatible with the security of
the other South American states"; (2) Buenos Aires and Chile would
form a coalition which would seek guarantees of security and independence by use of arms; (3) Buenos Aires and Chile would sign a treaty of
offensive and defensive alliance against Santa Cruz; and (4) a representative of Buenos Aires would participate in peace negotiations,
which would be held in Chile.

Buenos Aires countered with a nine-point proposal, two of whose
points were especially unacceptable to Chile: postwar incorporation
into Argentina of the Bolivian province of Tarija, claimed by Buenos
Aires as part of its province of Salta,[48] and postwar reduction in the
size of the Bolivian army. The Chilean negotiator rejected the demand
for Tarija on the ground that Santiago's information was insufficient to
permit it to judge the claim's validity. He rejected the second as being
properly the subject of actual peace negotiations. But Pérez, who had
already represented his country in Paris and would one day be its
president, surely realized that the postwar structure envisioned by
Rosas would be less favorable to Chile than the preconfederation structure which Chile was attempting to restore. It was important to Chile

that Bolivia emerge from the war not only completely independent of Peru, but sufficiently strong to maintain that independence and to constitute a counterpoise to Peru.[49]

ROSAS DECLARES WAR ON SANTA CRUZ

Pérez' negotiations foundered upon differences over Bolivia's postwar status, but dictator Rosas was not thereby deterred from leading his country to war against the Peru-Bolivian Confederation. He was not only opposed in principle to the confederation and to the person of its leader, but he was also a practical politician who well knew how much Argentine unification might benefit from a foreign threat.[50] Rosas made his first moves toward war while still negotiating with Chile. On February 13, 1837, he suspended all commercial and mail communications with Bolivia in retaliation for alleged aggression by Santa Cruz. Three months later, on May 19, Rosas declared war on "the government of General Andrés Santa Cruz," accusing the General of interference in Argentine internal affairs, of duplicity in relations with Chile, and of unbridled ambitions. Rosas, also charging Santa Cruz with upsetting the balance of power, declared: "No one would dare to deny to the Argentine Confederation the right to prevent by use of arms the excesses of a power that since its birth has been occupied in creating anarchy in the Republic, has enlarged itself by means of conquest, and has culminated in upsetting the political equilibrium of South America."[51]

Chile meanwhile prepared to invade enemy territory. The navy was being equipped both to do battle at sea and to transport men to Peru. Soldiers were being conscripted, put into uniform, issued shoes and guns, and trained. But, in spite of the government's great efficiency, all was not proceeding as planned. The army was being penetrated by antigovernment elements. Isolationist and pacifist propaganda was being circulated secretly among conscripts, and a rash of barracks revolts, attributed to Santa Cruz agents, plagued the high command and delayed formation of the Chilean expedition to Peru. The government responded by establishing a number of "Provincial Permanent Councils of War," a species of un-Chilean activities committees empowered to use any means they saw fit to identify and stamp out sedition, disloyalty, and criticism of government policies.

ASSASSINATION OF PORTALES

Finally, in June, 1837, the expeditionary force had been assembled, equipped, and trained, and was ready to board ships of the Chilean

navy for the trip north. Portales, guiding genius of the new Chilean
nation-state's war of destruction against the Peru-Bolivian Confederation, was to accompany the expedition in person, determined to see
through to the end the achievement of Chile's "second independence."
En route from Santiago to Valparaíso to board ship, Portales was am-
bushed, kidnapped, and then shot to death. The un-Chilean activities
committees had signally failed to accomplish their purpose.

The murder of Diego Portales stunned the Chilean nation and government. In the days immediately following the tragedy, it seemed to
many that Chile could not hope soon to recover from the loss of Portales;
General Santa Cruz himself was confident that Chile would promptly
ask for peace. But both the Bolivian general and Chile's anguished
leadership proved altogether wrong. The efficient administrative organization and the respect for government, which had been implanted
in the Portalian era, now stood firm. *Caudillaje,* personalism, and anarchy had been replaced, as Portales had strived to replace them, by a
government able to stand above private and class interests. The Chilean
public, revolted by the crime which was attributed to agents of Santa
Cruz, threw its support solidly behind the war effort.[52]

After Portales' death, as before it, Chile's ruling oligarchy continued
to envision a system of nations, of which Chile was a member, bound
together by a common interest in maintaining among themselves a balance of power. During the war's second phase, which now commenced,
Chile evaded British mediation by claiming, among other things, that
Buenos Aires and Ecuador, as interested parties, would have to be con-
sulted.[53] In fact, however, Chile distrusted British impartiality, for
London had officially recognized the Peru-Bolivian Confederation; this
circumstance acted powerfully to reinforce Chile's opposition in principle to Great Power intervention in South American affairs.

Chile flatly rejected Ecuador's offer to mediate the Peru-Bolivian
conflict, informing Quito tartly that "the principal motive of Chile and
the Argentine Provinces has been the danger to the security of these
peoples and even to all South America. . . . It is entirely clear that
Ecuador is as immediately concerned as are Chile and the Argentine
Provinces; for this reason Ecuador is not a disinterested third party."[54]
Moreover, in commenting upon the matter to his Ecuadoran envoy, the
Chilean foreign minister insisted that the "security of the states of the
South, founded upon the equilibrium of their forces, is a base that we
cannot abandon; any mediation on other principles would be useless if
not positively pernicious."[55]

A CHILEAN PHILOSOPHY OF HISTORY

While the Foreign Department was educating other South American chancelleries in balance-of-power politics, the official publication of Chile was doing the same for its own people. In an interesting attempt to make such concepts meaningful, *El Araucano* compared the nations of Spanish America, established upon the ruins of the Spanish Empire, with those of Europe, founded upon the remains of the Roman Empire. The newspaper preached that the former could avoid the terrible past experiences of the latter if they would but learn from history what the European nations had learned from sad experience. Two basic truths were to be extracted from that history:

1. That the zeal of European nations in containing powers that menaced their security has raised almost insuperable barriers to conquest . . . ,
2. That the same zeal was somehow born of the equality and multiplicity of the powers that simultaneously established themselves, and the importance that they, from the first, attached to their foreign relations.[56]

It appeared that Chile was enunciating principles applicable to the future as well as to the present. No longer did it seem concerned solely with restoration of the preconfederation structure. It was now designing a model system for all the Spanish American nations, a system embracing an "equality and multiplicity" of powers, each aware of the importance of international relations. The war against Santa Cruz was being waged to establish and defend principles of supreme importance to the future of all Spanish America. And indeed, Chile seemed to have ended by being convinced of its own argument.

THE FIRST EXPEDITION OF RESTORATION

On September 15, 1837, a reorganized Chilean "Expedition of Restoration," comprising more than 3,000 men, together with some 400 Peruvian exile volunteers, embarked at Valparaíso under the command of Admiral Blanco Encalada. When victory had been achieved Admiral Blanco, with Antonio José de Irisarri, was to negotiate "an honorable peace . . . granting full reparations for injuries . . . and reëstablishing the equilibrium of the states of the South."[57] At this date Chile's minimum peace terms were the familiar ones of satisfaction for Lavalle's imprisonment, independence for Bolivia and Ecuador, settlement of Peru's debt to Chile, Peruvian naval limitation, and a commercial treaty granting Chile most-favored-nation status. Chile, convinced that nothing less than total deprivation of power and authority would remove the threat of Santa Cruz, also instructed Blanco and Irisarri to obtain his ouster as president of Bolivia.

The expedition's departure found Chile willing to modify somewhat the territorial *status quo,* but only if Argentina took an active part in the war, "making efforts proportionate to those of Chile." In that event Chile might support Buenos Aires' claim to Tarija, compensating Bolivia with part of Peru's department of Arequipa so that the Altiplano might be provided with an adequate seaport. Here for the first time was sounded a note henceforth recurrent in the diplomatic annals of Chile—the solution of Bolivian problems through the appropriation of Peruvian territory. At the time of the launching of the Expedition of Restoration, Chile may have revised its Tarija position merely to force Buenos Aires' more strenuous participation in the war, or to remove a future source of intra–South American conflict, or merely to prepare Chilean opinion for a *fait accompli* in the event that Buenos Aires occupied Tarija. In any event, such a territorial rearrangement would have created an international power structure highly favorable to Chile. Bolivia, freed of commercial dependence upon Peru, would be stronger; Peru would be weaker. Simultaneously there would be created a source of controversy which would keep those two nations at each other's throats. And the addition of Tarija to anarchic Argentina could hardly affect its power position with respect to Chile.

The Expedition of Restoration disembarked in southern Peru without difficulty, but could not win a decisive victory. An expected Argentine offensive did not materialize; an anticipated revolt in Bolivia failed to occur; the inhabitants of Peru were decidedly apathetic in support of their "restorers"; and quarreling broke out between the Chilean command and the Peruvian volunteers. When General Santa Cruz arrived to confront the restoration army, he took up a tactical position so strategically superior that Chilean victory in battle became most unlikely. Santa Cruz promptly offered to negotiate, and the Chileans accepted. On November 17, 1837, Chile and the Peru-Bolivian Confederation signed a treaty of peace at Paucarpata.

THE TREATY OF PAUCARPATA

Although the Treaty of Paucarpata did permit the safe return to Chile of the expeditionary army, thereby saving hundreds if not thousands of lives, it fell far short of the government's minimal expectations.[58] Santa Cruz did make concessions: trade relations would be on a most-favored-nation basis, pending conclusion of special relevant agreements; Chile would mediate the peace between Santa Cruz and Buenos Aires; both parties accepted the principle of nonintervention; each government promised to prevent use of its territory as a base for revolutionary activities against the other; and Santa Cruz assumed Peru's debt to Chile, with interest.

Chile's concessions were, however, far more impressive. Its negotiators agreed first to return the three ships kidnapped by the *Aquiles*, a move that granted naval superiority to the Peru-Bolivians. Second, in signing the treaty with "the government of the Peru-Bolivian Confederation," Blanco and Irisarri gave recognition to a political body whose destruction was the main purpose of Chile's war effort.

In late December, 1837, the Chilean government learned of the treaty and promptly dissociated itself from the acts of its two negotiators, notifying General Santa Cruz that a state of war still existed.[59] The government not only obtained legislative approval of its disavowal, but secured a congressional resolution urging renewed and vigorous prosecution of the war.[60]

THE BRITISH VIEW

During the third and final phase of the Peru-Bolivian war, which now commenced, the Chilean government was forced into major exertions in three directions: achievement of an absolutely decisive military victory so that its peace terms would be unconditionally accepted; justification of its treaty repudiation; and the prevention, or at least the control, of possible British intervention. It was no secret that British agents on the west coast of South America liked Santa Cruz. The General's government of Peru would be efficient, and he would impose order. With efficiency and order would come great commercial and economic benefits both for the confederation and for Great Britain. British agents also wished the war to end, as both Peru and Chile had defaulted on British loans, and the sooner peace was reëstablished the sooner payment would be resumed. Even before the departure of the first Expedition of Restoration, the decidedly impatient British consul in Santiago had unsuccessfully tried to mediate the conflict.

When news of the Paucarpata treaty reached Santiago, the British agent was greatly relieved, only to become consumed with anger upon learning of its repudiation. Trembling with wrath he demanded an interview with the President, and in the course of a heated three-hour conference made scarcely veiled threats of dire consequences should Chile continue its war against Santa Cruz.[61] While making every effort to soothe the British consul, the Chilean government stood firm on its peace terms and refused to reverse its decision. To prevent immediate drastic action by the British, Santiago agreed to accept British mediation, but only under conditions that would not thwart Chile's major objectives. And when Buenos Aires failed to respond promptly to the British mediation offer, the Chilean chargé in that city was ordered to "agitate" the matter so that "Chile ... may not be accused of having received with indifference the mediation of a respectable power from which we have much to gain."[62]

CHILE'S SECOND EFFORT TO SECURE AN ARGENTINE ALLIANCE

To strengthen its military position, Chile again sought support in Quito and Buenos Aires. The latter, despite its official state of war, had been militarily phlegmatic. Chile's new suggested alliance terms therefore included an Argentine commitment to invade Bolivia with a 5,000-man army within a specified period of time, together with a Chilean commitment to do the same in respect to Peru. The Chilean negotiator was instructed to encourage the acceptance of those terms by hinting that Chile might otherwise be forced to review its currently favorable stand on Buenos Aires' claim to Tarija.[63]

The Argentine counterproposal reflected the divergent vital interests of the east and west slopes of the southern Andes, for Buenos Aires wanted both parties to concentrate upon invasion of Bolivia, setting aside the problem of Peru. In fact, Buenos Aires offered to undertake alone the responsibility of invading Bolivia if Chile would grant it a substantial subsidy. Argentina would, upon completion of the invasion, demand, on behalf of itself and of Chile, the mutual independence of Peru and Bolivia, together with recognition of Argentine sovereignty over Tarija.[64] Chile's rejection of those terms led to suspension of negotiations for alliance, but Buenos Aires continued to be officially at war against the Peru-Bolivian Confederation and to prepare to invade the Altiplano.

CHILE'S SECOND EFFORT TO SECURE AN ECUADORAN ALLIANCE

Santiago's second attempt to secure assistance in Quito was undertaken by Ventura Lavalle, who had remained as chargé d'affaires after the failure of his original mission. From Quito, Lavalle had waged a tenacious propaganda war in New Granada, Venezuela, and Ecuador, and, with the passage of time, had been able to inform Santiago that both the press and the government in Bogotá were becoming decidedly alarmed by the implications of a concretized Peru-Bolivian confederation. A New Granadine agent had even come to Quito to discuss possible common measures against Santa Cruz with the Ecuadoran government.

Above all, Lavalle, having become familiar with the people and the politics of the entire region, was able to suggest that the place to seek an Ecuadoran alliance was in the capital of New Granada.[65] Lavalle's reports to his government forced it to expand its spatial concept of the system of power politics to which it belonged, pushing back the horizon of Chile's concerns. Chile now had to take into consideration a far-northern capital which had seemed very remote only months before.

RELATIONS WITH NEW GRANADA

In April, 1838, Chile made its first official wartime contact with New Granada. The Foreign Minister traced the development of the Peru-Bolivian conflict in a communication informing Bogotá that Chile's insistence upon total destruction of the confederation was based upon its conviction that such destruction was "necessary to the independence and repose of the rest of the South American nations."[66] The Chilean foreign minister, claiming that Ecuador was immediately threatened, suggested that New Granada press Quito to take an active part in efforts to end confederation between Peru and Bolivia. Chile followed this letter with an attempt to give its relations with Bogotá greater continuity and regularity. Lavalle was authorized to communicate with the government of New Granada; there was instituted a program designed to cultivate cordial relations not only with New Granada but with the other American republics, especially those of South America which, according to the Foreign Minister, "form a special system whose members are bound together in such a manner that it is impossible to commit against one of them an illegal act without its having ramifications upon the others."[67]

THE SECOND EXPEDITION AND THE "PERUVIAN ARMY"

It was not upon alliances, however, but upon its own army and anti-Santa Cruz sentiment within Peru itself that Chile was most strongly depending to extinguish the Peru-Bolivian Confederation. Peruvian and Bolivian exiles in Chile were assuring and reassuring the government that anti-Santa Cruz sentiment abounded. To exploit that sentiment and at the same time to prevent repetition of the misunderstandings between Peruvian volunteers and the Chilean command which had marred the first expedition, in the second expedition Peruvians constituted a separate "Peruvian Army" led by Santa Cruz's notorious enemy, Agustín Gamarra, a former president of Peru. Although the "Peruvian Army" was in reality under the military command of General Manuel Bulnes of the Chilean expeditionary forces, Chile did agree, in exchange for expected important assistance from Peruvian elements, to limit its action to destruction of the confederation and to refrain from subsequent intervention in Peru's domestic politics.[68]

The government did not attempt to hide its reliance upon the Peruvian citizenry. *El Araucano,* emphasizing that the enemy was not Peru but Santa Cruz, noted that Chile could not defeat united Peruvian opposition and attempted to mitigate the public's anti-Peruvianism by insisting that Peruvian exiles in Chile were just as interested in restoring Peru's independence as were the people of Chile. At the same time the official journal tried in every way to assure Peruvians of Chile's benevolence and good intentions.[69]

Chile's felt need for support from within Peru wrought a subtle change in the government's manner of expressing its war aims. Before Paucarpata, Chile had stressed restoration of Bolivian autonomy and asked for guarantees of Ecuadoran independence. Such an orientation was in some ways more a reflection of Chilean antipathy toward Peru than of the reality of the situation. It was, after all, a Bolivian general at the head of a Bolivian army who had entered Peru for the purpose of bringing its independence to an end. After Paucarpata, the Chilean government recognized this fact by making increasingly frequent references to the liberation of Peru. And in January, 1838, *El Araucano* asserted that restoration of Peruvian sovereignty "is the cornerstone of Chile's security."[70]

THE IRISARRI AFFAIR

Crucial to the Chilean war effort were issues raised by its repudiation of the Treaty of Paucarpata. More than British ire was involved, for the opinion of the Chilean public and of potential South American allies was at stake. It was in the exceptional importance of the negotiators whose work had been nullified that the main challenge to Chilean policy lay. Both negotiators were lauded heroes of the wars for independence, and Guatemalan-born José Antonio de Irisarri had made distinguished contributions to Chilean public and intellectual life, had been its first officially accredited diplomat in Europe, and had for a short time held the office of president.

After Paucarpata, Irisarri had remained in Peru as his government's diplomatic agent, and, upon learning of the treaty's rejection, refused to return to Santiago, threw his support to Santa Cruz, and burst into print with vitriolic charges against the government of Chile. Irisarri flatly denied that he had exceeded his authority, insisting that the agreement fully met Chile's legitimate needs. Chile's rejection of the treaty, affirmed Irisarri, was proof that it was waging an unjust war.[71]

The eminent *prócer's* allegations aroused a furor in Chile and throughout the continent. The Chilean government threw the strenuous efforts of all its appropriate branches into their refutation. *El Araucano,* under the editorship of Andrés Bello, published a series of seven long articles in May and June, 1838, which denied in minute detail all the allegations that Irisarri had published in Lima, seeking especially to erase the impression that Chile was waging an unjust war.[72] The government also issued an *Exposition of the Motives of the President of Chile in Disapproving the Treaty of Peace Concluded in Paucarpata . . . and Renewing the Hostilities Interrupted by It,* which reiterated the entire range of Chile's charges against Santa Cruz, and again insisted that Chile's internal peace and security were absolutely dependent upon the "American equilibrium." Referring indignantly to the Freire expedition, the pamphlet charged that "Chile's . . . era of tranquillity and good fortune ended at the very moment when the equilibrium of neighboring peoples was destroyed." Chile assured the continent that it did not seek to impose any government upon the peoples of Bolivia and Peru, but desired only to liberate them from a scheming usurper. When they had been freed, Chilean troops would withdraw, and the newly freed peoples would determine their own destinies. In conclusion, Chile affirmed that "the mission of Chileans is to intervene for the sole purpose of destroying intervention; and experience will demonstrate that they are worthy of the title of champions of the American equilibrium and of the rights of peoples."[73]

THE EGAÑA MISSION OF 1838

On July 10, 1838, the second Expedition of Restoration set sail under General Bulnes, a tough, wily, experienced veteran of the Araucanian frontier wars who was determined not to repeat the tactical blunder that had led to Paucarpata. While the expedition was en route, one of the three states of the confederation—North Peru—revolted against Santa Cruz and proclaimed Orbegoso. Upon reaching Peru, however, Bulnes found Orbegoso as opposed to Chile as was Santa Cruz. Brief negotiations ended in a pitched battle, which culminated in Chilean occupation of Lima and the proclamation of Agustín Gamarra as provisional president of Peru. The spilling of Peruvian blood by Chilean forces virtually eliminated the expedition's hope of arousing broad popular support among Peruvians. Bulnes therefore marched his army into the interior and prepared to make a stand against Santa Cruz who, fresh from a decisive defeat of Argentine forces, was moving on Lima to restore his control of North Peru. On November 10, 1838, General Santa Cruz recaptured Lima, ousted Gamarra, and entered the capital city in triumph.

At this turn of events the Chilean government became the prey of serious self-doubts. It seemed that anti–Santa Cruz sentiment in Peru was far weaker than promised by Gamarra, and although Santiago did not yet know that Argentina had been defeated, it did know that Buenos Aires was involved in so serious a dispute with France that little help would come from that source. At the same time the British were harshly pressing for mediation.[74] Before events could take an even worse turn, the Chilean government decided to ask for a peace whose terms would save face while preserving as favorable a position as circumstances permitted. Mariano Egaña was to speak for Chile, and was given one official and one secret set of instructions. The former closely followed Chile's demands in its two previous attempts to reach an understanding with Santa Cruz. The latter gave Egaña wide latitude in determining peace terms, even to the extent of granting official recognition to the confederation and of commencing the cultivation of friendly relations with the hated Bolivian general.[75]

Santa Cruz, displaying his usual willingness to seek negotiated peace, approached Egaña through an English intermediary and offered safe-conduct to the Expedition of Restoration in exchange for recognition and Chile's acceptance of naval and military parity with the confederation. Egaña countered with the proposal that both sides withdraw and permit the Peruvian people freely to vote upon the question of the confederation. When Santa Cruz rejected this suggestion, Egaña returned to Santiago without a treaty.[76]

YUNGAY

In the interior of Peru, General Bulnes, awaiting his inevitable encounter with Santa Cruz, had been assiduously training the Chilean army to do battle with an enemy far superior in numbers. On January 20, 1839, the general from Chile faced the general from Bolivia on a Peruvian field of battle at Yungay. The Chilean army inflicted upon the forces of the Peru-Bolivian Confederation a bloody, stunning, and decisive defeat. Santa Cruz took flight, first to Lima and thence back into Bolivia. Returning to the Altiplano, Santa Cruz found his remaining troops in revolt and was forced to flee to Ecuador, where he was granted political asylum.

Separate governments came into being in Peru and Bolivia and promptly demonstrated their mutual independence by preparing for war against each other. In April, 1839, General Bulnes commenced the withdrawal of Chilean troops from the soil of Peru. By October the last members of the Expedition of Restoration had returned to their native land. The Peru-Bolivian Confederation had collapsed as if it had been a house of cards. The South American equilibrium had been reëstablished. Chile had earned the title of champion of the American equilibrium on the field of battle at Yungay.

CHILE'S NEW VIEW OF ITS INTERNATIONAL ROLE

During the course of Chile's struggle to destroy the Peru-Bolivian Confederation, the concepts of its leaders concerning their nation's international role had evolved. Isolationism, nonintervention, and "no entangling alliances"—policies that less than a decade earlier had formed the basis of Chile's foreign policy—no longer guided its international thought. In the eyes of its leadership, Chile had become part of a system of international relations in which Peru, Bolivia, the provinces of Argentina, and Ecuador figured actively, in which New Granada figured peripherally, and in which all the South American republics figured theoretically. Those nations formed, it was believed, a sealed system of power politics because of their common interest in maintaining an equilibrium of power among themselves. The great nations of the non–South American world lay outside that system, in the Chilean view, because their concentration upon purely commercial matters blinded them to the vital political interests at issue in intra–South American relations.

In fighting for the destruction of the Peru-Bolivian Confederation and for the restoration of the balance of power, Chile was fighting for no abstract principle. Chileans firmly believed that fulfillment of transcendental domestic goals was threatened. Chileans saw their future economic and social progress hanging in the balance. Every Chilean leader vividly recalled the dislocations, poverty, crime, and political chaos which had preceded Lircay. Chile was convinced that restoration of the preconfederation power structure was a necessary prerequisite for its continued advance as a nation-state. The doctrine of equilibrium became transformed, therefore, into a Chilean national doctrine. And the dramatic victory at Yungay consecrated in the minds of Chilean leaders the idea that their nation's security was dependent upon maintenance of a balance of power.

Chapter IV

ASPIRATION VERSUS REALITY
IN THE POSTWAR WORLD

CHILE EMERGED from the Peru-Bolivian war with national goals similar to those whose threatened obstruction had paved the way into conflict. In forwarding those purposes Chile was buttressed not only by its victory on the field of battle, but also by wartime's blunting of internal divisive elements and an awakened spirit of nationalism. A popular postwar ballad rejoiced, "Let us sing the glory of the martial triumph which the Chilean people obtained in Yungay,"[1] and the hero of Yungay, General Manuel Bulnes, was in 1841 rewarded by elevation to the presidency. The government was now so certain of broad national backing that it proceeded to rehabilitate opposition leaders who had been in Coventry after Lircay.

In the management of foreign affairs the Chilean government displayed mounting self-confidence and acted with increased effectiveness. Its wartime alliance seeking had made it wiser in the ways of practical diplomacy. Policies that evolved in the course of the conflict were at hand to serve as a guide for the future. Above all, Chile emerged from the Peru-Bolivian war with a power position superior to that of any South American state then capable of affecting its policy.

RELATIONS WITH THE GREAT POWERS

Chile's highly advantageous postwar position was the sum of its own assets and the liabilities of its neighbors; among the former was the skill with which Chile conducted its relations with the Great Powers. After the war, as before it, Chilean leaders recognized their inability to influence Great Power policy. As a Chilean foreign minister lamented in 1841, "The Great Powers . . . hold in their hands the fate of the universe . . .—a state of affairs we can neither prevent nor ignore."[2] An avoidance-of-controversy policy therefore continued to govern Chile's actions with respect to France, the United States, and Great Britain, but was implemented more effectively than before as a result of Chile's postwar progress. The Foreign Department was assiduous in its protection of the interests of Great Power nationals, and gave prompt and courteous attention to damage claims. Above all, by resuming payment on the British debt, Chile concretely demonstrated its solidity and good intentions, paving the way for better relations with all the Great Powers.[3] In 1841 Great Britain officially recognized Chile's upward advance in the hierarchy of South American states by raising the rank of its Santiago representative from consul general to chargé d'affaires.⁴ The absence of serious Great Power problems enabled Chile to attend closely to the affairs of its own continent.

CHILEAN STABILITY

Naval power was a further source of Chile's strong postwar position, for, though the navy had been cut back after the war for reasons of economy, Chile's skilled seamen, plus the lack of naval power in neighboring states, served to establish Chilean power in the continent's Pacific waters.⁵ But on the balance sheet of postwar power, the asset that was most decisively in Chile's favor lay in the realm of national spirit, social order, and political stability.

Upon the solid basis of Portalian reforms, the events of the war had forged a highly unified nation-state which proceeded to move consistently toward the achievement of its goals, while Peru, Bolivia, Ecuador, and the Argentine Confederation were being plagued by paralyzing domestic and international strife. Among the governments of its system, Chile alone enjoyed freedom from the constant fear of being overthrown. Alone it could rely on broad popular support for its foreign policies.

The extent of Chile's postwar power and prestige was vividly illustrated by the fact that in the half-dozen years after the war all the nations of the west coast of South America appealed to it for some form of assistance or support. Even distant New Granada sent its first official minister to Santiago, observing that "Chile . . . is distinguished by an active commerce and by the influence that its position and progress gives it on the Pacific."⁶

EQUILIBRIUM

Expanding foreign trade, the prevention of external interference in its domestic affairs, and peaceful relations with its neighbors were, after the war as before it, primary objectives of Chilean foreign policy. But the framework within which Chile envisioned the achievement of these goals was different. Having come to see herself as part of a power-politics system, Chile now equated the attainment of her ends with "equilibrium." In the immediate postwar years equilibrium was somewhat naïvely defined as the maintenance of the *status quo ante bellum.*⁷ And because Chile possessed a superior power position before the war, her concept of equilibrium was actually that of an international situation favorable to her own interests. At the same time, however, that Chilean policy stood firm upon the status quo ante bellum, it encouraged

the domestic stability and international peace of its neighbors. Overlooking the potential challenge to its own relative position, Chile believed that peace among these nations would favor her commerce, and
that their stronger domestic order would discourage international ad-
ventures that might threaten the equilibrium.

A BILATERAL ALLIANCES POLICY

The success of its forceful approach in dealing with the Peru-Bolivian
Confederation convinced Chilean leadership that the former passive
isolationist approach to foreign affairs was unworkable. Chile therefore
adopted a twofold policy, and prepared actively to implement it. On
the one hand, Chile sought to create a stable international order in
South America by giving a more formal organization to the system of
power politics of which it was a member. On the other, it acted as an
individual nation to secure its own goals.

Chile's changed policy was exemplified by its position on alliances.
Before the war Santiago had rejected a tripartite alliance of Bolivia,
Peru, and Chile as undesirable and unnecessary. But in August, 1839,
while its troops were still evacuating Peru, Chile initiated a program to
secure a series of bilateral alliances designed primarily to prevent reestablishment of a Peru-Bolivian state, but intended also to provide "a
reciprocal guarantee of the independence and the sovereignty of each
state against any aggression from one or more of its neighbors."[8] Chile
proposed first to arrange treaties with Bolivia, the Argentine Confederation, and Peru, states forming the heart of the system. It saw in those
pacts, if completed, "a general system of reciprocal guarantees among
all contracting nations." Chile believed that such a system would, by
enforcing the territorial status quo ante bellum, maintain equilibrium
among the participating states. On August 6, 1839, a treaty was signed
with Bolivia, and on the same day negotiations commenced for a similar
pact with Peru.[9] Chile, envisioning the desired series of bilateral treaties
as the first step toward "the organization of a definitive system embracing all the Spanish American Republics,"[10] shortly took steps to negotiate a similar agreement with Ecuador.[11]

But Chile's aspiration for a broad Hispanic-American system of
guarantees based upon multiple bilateral agreements foundered on the
realities of contemporary international relations. The Bolivian treaty
expired amid disagreement over responsibility for the cost of the Expedition of Restoration. Relations with the Argentine Confederation
cooled sharply because of the refuge granted by Chile to victims of the
Rosas tyranny. Ecuador incurred Chile's displeasure by continuing to

grant asylum to General Santa Cruz. Peru and Bolivia seemed chronically on the verge of war.

AN AMERICAN CONGRESS: THEORY AND PRACTICE

Although these harsh realities dispelled Chile's hopes for a tightly knit treaty organization, they did not end its desire for a more stable international order. Santiago began to consider the convocation of an assembly, or congress, of American plenipotentiaries. The congress idea was not original with Chile. Its most widely known exponent had been Simón Bolívar who, in planning a meeting in Panama in 1826, had advocated an exclusively Spanish American gathering. It was against his wish that Brazil and the United States, although they did not attend, had been invited. At Panama, four countries—Peru, Central America, Colombia, and Mexico—had negotiated a treaty of "Union, League, and Confederation" which committed them to work for the peace among themselves and "mutually to uphold, defensively and offensively, . . . the sovereignty and independence of each and all of the confederated American powers against all foreign domination."[12] Ratified by Colombia alone, the Panama treaty did not take effect, but the idea of an American congress in the Bolivarian tradition was a persistent one, and within a few years Mexico began to plan for another meeting.

Highly suspicious of United States intentions regarding its territory of Texas, Mexico sought to establish a counterpoise to Washington by bringing together a Spanish American assembly, thereby excluding Brazil as well as the United States. Chile became involved, almost by chance, when in 1831 its homeward-bound United States minister detoured through Mexico City to establish formal diplomatic relations. The Chilean minister signed a treaty of friendship and commerce which included, at Mexico's suggestion, a mutual commitment to promote a general American congress.[13] Chile ratified the treaty but made no move to fulfill this commitment. In 1834, pressed by Mexico, Santiago even expressed doubts concerning the practicability of such a meeting. It felt that anarchic conditions would prevent attendance of many nations and that the actions of those that did attend would be ineffective. Chile further doubted that the Spanish American nations could contribute equally to one another's defense; many were weak, and some were separated from others by vast distances. Chile, though suggesting that bilateral pacts might gain the objectives sought, nevertheless indicated that it would send representatives to a general congress.[14]

No meeting had materialized by the time the Peru-Bolivian war began, and at its end Mexico renewed her invitation. Chile accepted, assuring Mexico that "Chile is inclined with the greatest zeal toward the establishment of a situation which, by strengthening the union of the new republics, may provide effective guarantees of their dignity, integrity, and independence."[15] Nevertheless, the Foreign Minister's report of the invitation to the congress betrayed the fact that Chile's reservations had not diminished, for previously advanced objections to such meetings, alleged to have been proved well founded in intervening years, were explicitly reiterated.[16] In late 1840, however, after her efforts to arrange a series of bilateral security pacts had been frustrated, Chile began to view a congress with more favor. When Mexico's internal problems halted its action on the meeting, the Chilean government took up the initiative. For the next five years its leaders continued to display interest in the project, exchanging correspondence with several South American nations and annually reporting to the Chilean Congress on the problems being encountered and the progress being made.

Upon assuming the organizational leadership of the general congress, Chile modified the Bolivarian and Mexican concepts of such a meeting in ways that reflected both her national concerns and her assumptions concerning the power-politics system of which she now saw herself to be part. In the first place, Chile wanted to include Brazil. During the war against Santa Cruz a Brazilian agent had been received in Santiago, and in 1838 a Brazilian-Chilean treaty of friendship and commerce had been signed and was awaiting ratification.[17] In 1840, without consulting Mexico, Chile invited the Empire of Brazil to the congress, later explaining to the governments of Mexico, Ecuador, New Granada, and Venezuela the connection between Brazil and the Spanish states of South America. The foreign minister of Chile emphasized the fact that Brazil shared boundaries with all save Chile, and was the "exclusive owner of the Amazon, holding the key to the maritime communications of an immense part of the continent."[18] The Foreign Minister added that he would "omit other points of view which hold it extremely important for all Spanish America that Brazil should participate in a system called upon to consolidate the integrity and the independence of all those associated in it."

Second, both Mexico and Bolívar had envisioned important roles in the congress for Mexico and Central America, as well as for South America. Chile did not explicitly reject that idea, but its interest was plainly, if not publicly, in a South American meeting. When Mexico's domestic problems lessened its interest in the meeting, Chile suggested that "it would perhaps be well for the South American plenipotentiaries to meet together ... without awaiting the arrival ... of their Mexican and Central American colleagues. ... The republics of South America and the Brazilian Empire form a compact system whose ties with Mexico and Central America are comparatively weak."[19] Chile believed the proposed congress might serve three major purposes: furtherance of peace, development of commerce, and consolidation of integrity and independence.[20] With respect to the last, the Chilean government still opposed, as impractical and dangerous, alliances directed against the Great Powers. It still believed that Spanish American nations could best consolidate their independence by eliminating domestic disorder and concentrating upon economic progress. If such a policy had worked for Chile, it would probably work for the others.

Chile's primary purpose in promoting an American congress, however, was to achieve preservation of the status quo. The Chilean government was vague about the precise means of doing so. It suggested that peace might be preserved through conciliation or mediation by the congress; that integrity and independence might be consolidated through bilateral treaties or through the adoption of rules of international law which would buttress a government threatened with internal disorder. As the congress would be composed of governments constantly involved in international conflict and threatened by domestic instability, Chile was far from confident that such objectives would be gained, but it felt, nevertheless, that the "meeting presents us with a hope, however remote, of someday terminating the disgraceful continuous agitations of these unfortunate countries."[21]

In the years immediately following the Peru-Bolivian war, Chile's efforts to convoke a congress proved fruitless. Her aspirations to bring order out of the chaos of South American international life were frustrated, as had been her hopes for the bilateral treaty program, by the reality of continuing bitter domestic and foreign strife in which the other South American countries were enmeshed. But even had those countries been able to come up for air and take the long view, it is unlikely that a congress, having been convoked, would have reached significant decisions affecting the continent as a whole. In the 1840's the primary foreign interests of the South American nations were still bifurcated along the lines of the relatively easy communications within the Plata region and along the Pacific Coast. The Argentine Confederation of the Plata region, and the states of the Pacific, having related briefly during the Peru-Bolivian war, immediately afterward refocused their attention upon their own affairs.[22] Even those Chileans who had glimpsed a continental system recognized that their primary interests lay on the Pacific. There lay Chile's commercial destiny, and there lay the potential threats to interests that Chile must defend unaided so long as its aspiration for a stable international environment remained unrealized.

Without abandoning efforts to secure international coöperation, Chile proceeded to take unilateral action to maintain the territorial status quo on the Pacific, and to preserve the peace and promote commerce. Because Chile and Peru had abandoned their mutually discriminatory tariff policies, and Chilean commerce was therefore operating on the advantageous basis of equality, Chile's international problems were, in the immediate postwar years, primarily political ones. The most serious of these problems was the threat to peace and the political status quo.

PERU AND BOLIVIA, 1839–1841

Chile was greatly concerned lest General Santa Cruz, in Ecuadoran exile, succeed in his constant intriguing to regain power in Bolivia or to reconstruct the confederation. As the best defense against Santa Cruz was strong, stable government in Peru and Bolivia, and peace between those two countries, a significant part of Chile's international action was directed to that end.

Crisis was the normal state of affairs in Peru and Bolivia after the collapse of the confederation. General Agustín Gamarra, president of Peru, remained as dedicated as ever to confederation, notwithstanding his personal participation in the Expedition of Restoration. From 1839 to mid-1841 Gamarra worked unceasingly for that objective. Tragic Bolivia, torn by internal disorder after the downfall of Santa Cruz, was ripe for Peruvian intervention.

THE SCHEMES OF JUAN JOSÉ FLORES

The tensions between Peru and Bolivia were further aggravated by the tireless ambitions of Ecuadoran General Juan José Flores, who became president of his country for the second time in 1839. The single most important item on Flores' agenda was enlargement of his nation's territory at the expense of either Peru or New Granada, or both. Seeking to exploit Chile's known interest in equilibrium, Flores approached the Chilean chargé d'affaires in Quito with the suggestion that Chile coöperate with Ecuador, using force if necessary, to partition Peru. Flores recommended that part of Peru be annexed to Ecuador, and that the remainder be divided into two independent states. He claimed that much of Peru legally belonged to Ecuador because the provinces of Jaén and Maynas had once been recognized by Peru as belonging to Great Colombia, of which Ecuador was a successor state.[23] Other Peruvian territory upon which Flores had designs was to represent payment of a debt. To encourage Chile's participation, Flores pointed out that implementation of his proposal, by creating a more equitable territorial distribution on the west coast, would "offer hope of stable order and peace."[24] Flores predicted that failure to carry out his plan would have dire consequences, as "Ecuador is today a state so miserable and so lacking in resources that it cannot possibly maintain its independence; its revenues cover barely a third of its needs, exclusive of the service of an enormous debt; they decrease daily and imagination offers not the remotest hope of a change for the better."[25] Flores predicted that Lima would annex the Ecuadoran provinces of Cuenca and Guayaquil, pointing out that "if Peru with its present boundaries presents so dreadful an example, always threatening the tranquility of neighbors, with how much greater reason must [we] fear [its] acquisition of a rich territory and a shipyard like Guayaquil."[26]

The Chilean envoy in Quito transmitted Flores' Peruvian dismemberment proposal to Santiago with the observation that there was some weight in the argument for Peruvian partition. But Flores did not wait to learn the reaction of Chile before moving to bring the matter to a head. Early in March, 1840, he ordered his chargé d'affaires in Lima to seek a boundary settlement recognizing Ecuador's rights to Jaén and Maynas. Touching on a matter of deep concern to Chile, Flores told the chargé that if current tension between Peru and Bolivia resulted in war, he should "take advantage of that propitious circumstance ... to wrest from the government of Peru the act of justice demanded."[27]

Flores next turned his acquisitive attentions to New Granada, much of whose southern part he had attempted to annex during his previous administration; he had been compelled, however, to withdraw his occupying troops and to recognize the sovereignty of Bogotá. Since 1839 New Granada's southernmost province of Pasto had been torn by a revolution raising the specter of secession. Flores, after setting the stage by intrigue, entered Pasto and in May, 1841, declared it "reincorporated" into Ecuador.[28] Driven out of Pasto the next year, Flores turned again toward Peru, threatening to seize Jaén and Maynas by force if Peru did not voluntarily hand them over to Ecuador.[29]

The involved schemes of General Flores were characteristic of the maze of intrigue through which Chilean diplomacy had to thread its way in seeking to maintain the equilibrium of the Pacific Coast. The deceit-laden atmosphere in which Chile's northern neighbors conducted their relations with one another inspired in Chilean diplomats a certain degree of contempt and demanded of them great skill. Chile's actions

in that arena reflected its positive postwar foreign policy and indicated
its adherence to enunciated principles. But its actions also revealed
willingness to use force only to protect immediate vital interests, and
then only when there was every expectation of success. In rejecting the
Ecuadoran plan to carve up Peru, Chile stated that partition would be
contrary to

... the fundamental principle of [Chile's] American foreign policy, the 1835 status
quo.... The general adoption of the status quo would be good for the peace of
America. Once the dismemberment of one state by foreign intervention has been
accepted, the door is open wide for ambitious plans. Our republics are too weak,
too ready to regard others as rivals and enemies, to think of subdivisions that would
increase their weakness and would more and more bottle up our political system,
in which the elements of dissolution are excessively preponderant.[30]

Chile was not, however, ready to spill blood to maintain the "1835
status quo" in northern South America. In 1841, when General Flores
moved into Pasto, Santiago seems not to have lifted a hand; and in 1842,
when Peru and Ecuador stood on the brink of war over Jaén and
Maynas, Chile responded with merely polite interest to a New Granadine request for help in preventing war. Praising Bogotá's peace moves,
Chile agreed to join Colombia in a mediation only if current measures
proved inadequate to halt hostilities.[31] Chile, confident that New
Granada's influence over Ecuador could prevent war,[32] also rejected a
Peruvian appeal for its mediation in the same dispute. Instructing his
agent in Lima to keep Chile out of unstable Peru's affairs, the Chilean
foreign minister expressed doubt that Ecuador would accept its mediation. Only if both Lima and Quito sought its good offices would Chile
consider making an offer.[33]

Peru-Bolivian Tensions

In sharp contrast with its reluctance to employ force in the far north
was Chile's strong stand on Peru-Bolivian affairs. Early in 1840, when
Lima refused Chilean mediation and prepared to fight Bolivia, the
Chilean foreign minister sent Peru a virtual ultimatum declaring that
war between Peru and Bolivia would ease Santa Cruz's return to power.
He added:

... in view of such grave dangers ... menacing the security of Chile and the public
order of all the nations of the South, [Chile] feels called upon to support these
great objectives with all possible means.... The question pending between its two
allies is a rigorously Chilean question. Whichever of them sets aside conciliatory
methods of securing justice ... will be ... a disturber of the peace, an enemy of
the common interests of the new states and of Chile's special interests. These principles will influence the line of conduct which Chile will deem just and convenient.[34]

Santiago then named a new chargé d'affaires to Bolivia with orders to assist in reëstablishing cordial relations between Peru and Bolivia, or if hostilities had already commenced upon his arrival, to bring them to an end. In either event the new appointee was to oppose any form of Peru-Bolivian unification and to prevent Bolivia's dismemberment. If Bolivia was invaded, the chargé was to inform the Peruvian commander that "the Republic of Chile regards this step as a hostile act against itself."[35] Less than a decade earlier Chile had, though reluctantly and conditionally, allowed its minister to Peru to mediate between Peru and Bolivia. Now Chile, viewing a Peru-Bolivian conflict as "a rigorously Chilean question," appeared ready to use force in its resolution. After the Chilean note arrived, Peruvian and Bolivian negotiators signed a preliminary peace convention, and the threat of war momentarily subsided.

In October, 1841, however, President Gamarra of Peru invaded Bolivia suddenly and without formal declaration of war. Gamarra's purpose was to annex Bolivia, but he publicly claimed to have acted to prevent the return of Santa Cruz. Santiago was caught completely off guard. Lacking detailed recent intelligence, it could not disregard the possibility that Santa Cruz had indeed been on the point of reëntering Bolivia. Chile's minister in Lima was ordered to Bolivia. If the principles of the Expedition of Restoration were being compromised, he was to offer mediation upon conditions that would assure Bolivian independence, guarantee freedom of commerce for the Bolivian port of Cobija, and continue the exile of Santa Cruz. So that Chile might retain freedom of action until it had obtained all the facts, its minister was to make no commitment, but was to keep the contending parties in doubt concerning possible Chilean action.[36]

By the time Chile's minister to Peru had received the above instructions, Gamarra had been killed in battle, the Peruvian army had been routed, Bolivian forces had invaded Peru, and Bolivia seemed about to demand the port of Arica as the price for peace. As Peru was now so ravaged by domestic strife that it might be unable to resist the Bolivian demand, Chile ordered its chargé d'affaires in Lima to seek Bolivian evacuation and a peace pact guaranteeing the territorial status quo ante bellum. Chile was so anxious to secure the status quo that it was willing to guarantee the territorial integrity and independence of both Peru and Bolivia.[37] Equally determined to protect its nationals residing in the warring republics, it sent the frigate *Chile* into Peruvian waters "to impose the respect due to the justice of the claims that . . . it might be necessary and convenient to place before the Bolivian or Peruvian authorities."[38]

After prolonged negotiations Peru and Bolivia accepted the media-

tion of Chile and in June, 1842, reached a preliminary treaty of peace
which affirmed the belligerents' unalterable friendship and provided
for Bolivian withdrawal from Peru.[39] Although the Chilean mediator
was a signatory to the preliminary treaty and was named as the agent
through whom ratifications would be exchanged, it was not necessary
for Chile to act as guarantor of the pact in order to obtain its signing.

THE CAPTURE OF SANTA CRUZ

Soon afterward Chile moved with equal vigor to crush another threat
to west coast stability. Notwithstanding strong pressure from Santiago,
Ecuador failed to inhibit the activities of General Santa Cruz. As
early as 1841 rumors reached Chile of an imminent Santa Cruz expedition against either Peru or Bolivia. Convinced that such an expedition was only a matter of time and that the only way to ensure the
Bolivian general's abstinence from Peru-Bolivian politics was to obtain
possession of his person, the Chilean government devised various alternative plans whereby that end might be accomplished. One set of plans
provided that the warship *Chile* would intercept a presumed seaborne
expedition near its point of disembarkation and take the General prisoner. The details of this scheme indicated that Chile still wanted to
avoid controversy with the Great Powers, for the ship was to set aside
its plans if Santa Cruz was under escort by one or more European or
United States vessels.[40]

It was, however, an alternative plan that effected the Bolivian general's seizure. In October, 1843, Santa Cruz, seeking to exploit an especially severe Peruvian civil war and Bolivian unrest, managed to land
clandestinely in Peru, only to fall into the hands of a South Peruvian
revolutionary junta. Chile acted quickly, requesting the prisoner's custody allegedly both for his own protection and to prevent further agitation of an already disturbed Peruvian political scene. The *Chile*
was at the same time ordered to Arica, and the Chilean foreign minister, to conceal its true mission, informed his consul in Arica that the
ship's visit was owing to "the uninterrupted series of grave events in
Peru ... which have made the government fear enormous damages to
Chilean commerce and citizens."[41] After the *Chile*'s arrival in Arica, the
deceived Chilean consul traveled up to Cuzco to negotiate with the
junta for Santa Cruz's protective custody. The junta, reluctant to
relinquish so splendid a prize, prolonged the Cuzco talks while on the
coast the commander of the *Chile* successfully concluded his secret
mission by persuading the prefect of Arica, in whose safekeeping the
Bolivian general had been placed, to put Santa Cruz aboard the Chilean
ship for his greater safety. As the *Chile* prepared to bear its prisoner

southward, the unaware consul was reaching an agreement with the Cuzco junta under which Chile would be given temporary protective custody of Santa Cruz in exchange for a promise to leave the General's ultimate fate to the decision of Peru. Santa Cruz was interned comfortably in Chile, whose leaders, unwilling to leave to the decision of Lima the fate of the ubiquitous general whose defeat had cost their country so great an effort, refused steadfastly to ratify the Cuzco agreement. Finally, in November, 1845, Peru, Bolivia, and Chile reached a tripartite agreement under which Santa Cruz was provided financial support and sent into European exile for a period of no less than six years, during which time he was not to set foot in South America without the unanimous consent of the signatories.[42]

ECONOMIC AND INSTITUTIONAL ADVANCES

The varying degrees of forcefulness with which Chile implemented its policies in the near and far north, respectively, indicated that while Chile in principle related its interests to the entire continent, it was guided in its actions by the realities of its palpable concerns and restricted power. Having so far failed to bring about collective establishment of international security, Chile had unilaterally assumed the role of regulator of the equilibrium in the southern region of the Pacific Coast. "Stability," "maintenance of the status quo," "equilibrium"— these were the concepts of a successful conservative government seeking to pursue its domestic goals without molestation from an international community composed of disorganized states which Chile regraded with a blend of impatience, compassion, and contempt. The rigidly ordered international community sought by Chile was unattainable, but in the six years following the Peru-Bolivian war Chile did succeed in imposing sufficient stability upon its immediate northern neighbors to permit a clear advance along its chosen domestic course.

The extent of Chilean progress was visible on many sides. In the six-year period following the war government revenues averaged 55 per cent more than in the equivalent prewar period.[43] In the same span of time the government was able to give vastly increased attention and financial support to education, crowning a group of major reforms with the opening of the University of Chile in 1844. In 1842 Chile refunded the British debt and resumed payments. Foreign credit rose during that period more than that of any other South American government, so that by 1844 Chile's 100-peso bonds were selling for 3 to 6 pesos more than their face value on the London market.[44] In addition to such immediately visible strides, two other developments were to have far-reaching impact upon the future economic development

and foreign relations of Chile. Both developments were early manifestations of South America's integration into the economy of Europe;
both served to revise sharply upward the aspirations of Chile. Together
they were to lay the foundations for war.

GUANO

The hitherto despised substance deposited by waterfowl upon the rain-
free shores and adjacent islands of the Pacific coast was called *huanu*,
or dung, by the Quechua Indians and *guano* by the Spanish; but it
was a Frenchman who, in about 1840, discovered its great value as a
fertilizer. Europe's fast-multiplying population and its need for food
were rapidly exhausting the possibilities of its prescientific agriculture,
thus creating a continually rising market for guano. The government
of Chile, cognizant of the technology of guano production and aware
of its commercial implications, suspected that large deposits existed
in the bleak and uncharted Atacama Desert. In 1842, having completed
a preliminary exploration of the area, Chile declared that the northern
limits of its territory lay in the Atacama near the 23d parallel and
that the region's guano deposits were national property, exploitable
only under government concession. Bolivia angrily protested, demanding that Chile rescind its new law of limits and recognize Bolivian
sovereignty south to the 26th parallel. Chile's rejection of Bolivia's
demands set in motion a conflict that would in time pass from the conference table to the field of battle.

THE PACIFIC STEAMSHIP NAVIGATION COMPANY

The second far-reaching development of the immediate postwar period
concerned the introduction into South America of European capital
and technology, and the growing competition among Europe's com-
mercial-imperialist powers to attract less developed areas of the world
into their orbits. One such area was the west coast of South America
where, in 1835, William Wheelwright had been given a Chilean government concession to ply Chile's waters with steamships. Wheelwright had been delayed in the realization of his plans by the venture's
highly speculative nature and by the Peru-Bolivian war. But with the
latter's end he obtained the backing of British capital and formed the
Pacific Steamship Navigation Company whose first two ships, the
Chile and the *Peru,* left England in August, 1840. Passing through
the Strait of Magellan without difficulty, the two steamships dropped
anchor in Valparaíso in October.

British support of Wheelwright was based not so much on interest
in Chile as on British concern for transport and communications fa-

cilities that would link Great Britain with the entire west coast of South America and with its colonies in Oceania and the Far East. Under this global plan travel time between England and Panama via Valparaíso would be substantially reduced, and the entire west coast of South America would become more closely involved in the main-stream of world commerce, of which Great Britain was the nerve center.[45]

The Steamship Company intended to serve, and eventually did serve, all the countries of the west coast, but it was of highest significance to the economic and commercial advance of Chile. Establishing head-quarters at Valparaíso, the company became closely identified with Chile's development. Its operation facilitated and proliferated contacts between Chile and other west coast nations and among those nations themselves. The increase in contacts was reflected in more closely linked international relations. In the immediate postwar period the benefits of more frequent and more rapid steamship communications were felt chiefly in the relations between Chile and Peru, for not until 1845 was the company able to secure a concession to operate in the waters of Colombia's province of Panama.

THE FOUNDING OF FORT BULNES

The most immediate and most dramatic impact of the steamship company was in its focusing attention on the Strait of Magellan. The strait's unfavorable winds had for centuries forced sailing vessels to make the stormy and longer trip around Cape Horn. No action had been taken on various suggestions that steam-powered tugboats be used to pull sailing vessels through the strait, but after the *Chile* and the *Peru* had traversed the strait, its economic and strategic attributes became suddenly clear. Chile now deemed control of the strait neces-sary to its maintenance of Pacific Coast commercial hegemony, and began to fear that European powers with Far Eastern interests might seek such control.

In 1843, after months of careful preparation, a Chilean expedition established Fort Bulnes on the Strait of Magellan, strengthening by occupation Chile's claim to that waterway.[46] In addition the Chilean government made plans to establish regular steamship service through the strait in order to "broaden and strengthen the advantages that Chile has by virtue of its geographical position, making it the em-porium of European commerce on the Pacific."[47] When Buenos Aires somewhat belatedly protested Chile's occupation of the Strait of Ma-gellan as a violation of Argentine sovereignty, another serious intra–South American conflict came into being.

A Larger Navy

To control and protect the more extensive territory that it had claimed under the impetus of guano and steam, Chile would need to improve its naval position. In 1844 the Minister of War and Navy advised Congress that the country's long coastline made it particularly vulnerable to sea attack and, although admitting that war was not just over the horizon, reminded his listeners that "no American republic . . . has not had, in the brief days of its existence, to resort to arms in defense of its territory." Warning that Chile could not afford to wait for actual conflict to provide for adequate naval defenses, the minister insisted that "for Chile, the navy is its future." Strongly pleading for a larger naval appropriation, he quoted a statement by the commandant-general of the Chilean navy which reflected both Chile's aspiration to a dominant Pacific role and its tendency to accept the Great Powers as models. The commandant made light of the expense involved in a large navy: ". . . if you cast a glance over the rest of the world and observe that the two most free and industrious nations are precisely those that possess the greatest naval forces, you will be tempted perhaps to study the intimate relationship between war and merchant fleets, and between merchant fleets and the greatness of a people."[48]

In 1845 Congress authorized the addition to the navy of a 900-ton steamship and the replacement of two existing small schooners with sailing vessels of 240 tons each. In the debate prior to the naval bill's passage, one senator affirmed his conviction that "Chile's interest lies in having its naval force at a level that may give it domination of the Pacific."[49]

The decision to enlarge the navy was not, however, to be interpreted as an indication that Chile was embarking upon a foreign policy stronger than those of the preceding five years. The decision merely constituted recognition of the fact that the South American international order would be unstable within the foreseeable future, and that Chile could rely only upon itself to uphold its interests and to preserve a power structure favorable to its progress. A more powerful navy had become necessary as a result of Chile's extension of its active jurisdiction south to the Strait of Magellan and north to the 23d parallel. And a more powerful navy had become possible as a result of the government's financial strength, which had steadily grown with better internal order and greater material advance of the Chilean nation.

Chapter V

REGULATING THE PACIFIC COAST
BALANCE OF POWER

In the decade preceding 1845, Chile, in the process of seeking support against the Peru-Bolivian Confederation, had recognized the existence of a South American system of politics based upon a chain of interlocking interests. It had tried to give that system a formal organization but had failed, largely because of widespread domestic and international chaos; yet the same chaos had enabled Chile to preserve with a minimum of effort a power structure favorable to its interests. As Chile had considered forceful action necessary only in Peru and Bolivia, however, it is clear that in spite of its theoretical vision of a continental system, Chile was still part of a system whose dimensions were limited.

In the period 1840–1845 the Chilean government did not abandon the idea of continental equilibrium, but did keep it in abeyance at a time when neither South American nor Chilean interests seemed to require its implementation. In this period, the continental equilibrium was to a large degree maintained automatically by the relative weakness and the rivalries of the other South American states. Between 1845 and the later 1860's, similar conditions prevailed east of the Andes, and there was no need for a positive Chilean position with respect to that region's power structure. But on the Pacific Coast the situation that confronted Chile in the two decades following 1845 heightened its awareness of a system of power politics and extended the sphere of its forceful action to maintain equilibrium. Concurrently, in response to its encounter with new conditions, Chile's concept of "equilibrium" became more sophisticated.

Chile's sharpened awareness of a Pacific Coast system was stimulated by the expanding operations of the Pacific Steamship Navigation Company[1] and by successive short-lived threats to the common security of the west coast. Both factors propelled the area's states into closer contact. Chile's concept of its system was also affected by its own rapid economic development, by an upward surge in Peruvian power, by the highly unstable far-northern situation centered in Ecuador, and by the growth of radicalism in New Granada. These four elements fused to produce a volatile west coast power structure, creating apparent threats to the status quo which induced the Chilean government to assume the role of regulator of the balance of power along the entire coast.

Economic Advances

Chile's especially rapid economic growth in the two decades beginning in the mid-1840's was based upon its continued stability, marred only briefly by abortive revolts in 1851 and 1859; upon vastly expanded silver and copper mining; and upon important short-term gold-rush markets for wheat and flour in California and Australia.[2] During the two decades the government's revenues rose some 75 per cent; foreign trade increased approximately 225 per cent.[3] By 1851 President Bulnes was able to inform Chileans that "Our commercial and diplomatic relations . . . now embrace all the countries of the civilized world, with few exceptions."[4] By 1865 Chile had exchanged ratifications of commercial treaties not only with France and Great Britain, but also with Belgium, Prussia, Sardinia, and Spain.

But the nature of Chile's foreign trade at this time tended to direct its attention to the Pacific Coast. Beginning in the 1850's, Valparaíso suffered somewhat from the competition of the United States port of San Francisco, from a revival of Callao's direct trade with Europe, and from competition of the completed Panama railroad. But at the same time the growth of these commercial centers created new opportunities for Chilean commerce.[5] The Chilean merchant fleet doubled in number of ships and tripled in total tonnage between 1849 and 1864, and in the mid-1850's almost 20 per cent of its fleet was plying the Pacific along the coast as far north as San Francisco.[6] The Chilean government did not leave its expanding commerce unprotected. In 1851 the Minister of War and Navy announced plans for a regular tour of duty by a Chilean warship all the way from Valparaíso to San Francisco, so that "our merchant fleet will be encouraged and our consuls will have nearby a force with which to make their decisions respected, aside from the not inconsiderable importance that it will give Chile in the eyes of those peoples." Advocating enlargement of the navy, the minister added: ". . . without wishing to inspire fear, . . . Chile understands that [naval] expansion must be based upon the needs born of its growing commerce and shipping, the position that Chile occupies among the republics of the Pacific, and the demands of its . . . defense."[7] By supplying Chile the resources necessary to a more forceful role, and by bringing it into more intimate contact with the peoples and the problems of the entire Pacific Coast of South America, Chile's economic growth tended to push the interests of the nation northward.

THE REHABILITATION OF PERU

The post-1845 rehabilitation of Peru was the result of both economic development and internal order. In the early 1840's Peru had established a national guano monopoly which soon began to give increasing support to the government budget and to stimulate the Peruvian economy in general. Revenues of approximately 4.2 million pesos in 1846 and 1847 had by 1854 reached almost 10 million, and ten years later some 23 million.[8] Order was imposed upon Peru's warring cliques by caudillo-statesman Ramón Castilla, who seized power in 1844. President from 1845 to 1851 and from 1855 to 1862, and a dominant force in the interval, Castilla brought independent Peru the greatest internal stability it had thus far enjoyed. During his first term Peru's finances were reorganized and steps were taken toward liquidation of the British, Chilean, and New Granadine debts. Educational and military reforms were initiated; merchant shipping was encouraged; a navy was established.

Peru's mounting wealth and more stable order constituted a challenge to Chile's leadership. In the ensuing rivalry Peru's population and wealth were pitted against Chile's governmental efficiency, civil and political stability, and more unified citizenry. But international factors were also to affect the ultimate outcome of the contention. Peru was enmeshed in many disputes. Its conflict with Bolivia was endemic. Ecuador posed serious, if sporadic, problems. Relations with New Granada were anything but cordial. Peru's growing Amazon interests were bringing it into conflict with several countries, including Brazil, whereas Chile was spared serious problems over its unsettled Bolivian and Argentine borders, at least until late in the period under consideration.

Other factors, however, tended to mitigate the Chilean-Peruvian rivalry. Peru's international problems prevented it from giving undivided attention to the Chilean question. The possibility of Peru-Bolivian unification had declined, and thus the tension in Chile's relations with both those states had somewhat relaxed. The formerly bitter economic conflict between Chile and Peru had lost its edge after Chilean adoption of a free-trade policy, development of new foreign markets, and steady improvement in Peruvian demand for Chilean products.

THE FLORES THREAT OF 1846-47

The potential sharpness of the rivalry between Chile and Peru was further lessened by a threatened invasion of the west coast of South

America, which gave Peru the opportunity to assume a leading position in Pacific Coast affairs. General Juan José Flores, a former president of Ecuador, was in European exile, after the failure of one of
his revolutionary attempts. Late in 1846 it was strongly rumored that
Flores, with the support of the Queen of Spain and the connivance
of the Madrid government, was preparing an expedition to retake power
in Ecuador. It was said, moreover, that he intended to establish an
Ecuadoran monarchy under a Spanish prince;[9] that Bolivian General
Andrés Santa Cruz, also in European exile, was involved in the conspiracy; and that a government other than the Spanish—presumably
that of Great Britain—was supporting the contemplated invasion.

To the Chilean government it appeared that, if these rumors proved
correct, the South American continent would be confronted with two
unpleasant possibilities, each disturbing to the equilibrium: a monarchy under European sponsorship—intolerable under any circumstances—which would probably expand beyond the confines of Ecuador;
a Flores–Santa Cruz duarchy that might attempt to reconstitute the
Peru-Bolivian Confederation and to set up a similar alliance on another
front. Upon confirmation of preparations for an expedition which would
depart from Great Britain, Chile, believing that South American security was jeopardized, decided to resist the Flores invasion with all
the means at its disposal.

Among the measures that Chile took in defense of South American
security was exploitation of the mutual suspicions of the Great Powers.
France and the United States were asked to exert their influence
against a project that had the support of England and Spain.[10] British
banking and commercial houses doing business in South America were
asked to use their influence to force British intervention against
Flores.[11] A Chilean agent was sent to Madrid to protest Spanish connivance in the expedition. Plans were laid to sever Chilean trade
relations with Spain.[12] Feverish attempts were made to reinforce the
Chilean navy; the army was alerted for action.[13]

Moves similar to those of Chile were made by Ecuador, New Granada,
and Peru. Peru went even further, convoking an American congress
to deal with General Flores[14] and to devise measures to protect the
general security of the American countries in the future. Although the
British government did step in to thwart the Flores expedition, Peru
proceeded with arrangements for the congress, which convened in Lima
in late 1847. When the delegates had assembled, however, they constituted not the all–Western Hemisphere conference for which invitations had been issued, but rather a "concert" of Pacific Coast powers:
Bolivia, Chile, Ecuador, New Granada, and the host country.

THE CONGRESS OF LIMA, 1847–48

Chile's position was not elaborated before the congress opened, but it was already clear that Santiago would oppose creation of a complex collective security organization and would seek to confine the agenda to purely intra–South American questions. The Chilean government's expectations were moderate. It hoped for limited steps toward international stabilization, among them agreement on legal principles applicable to such matters as political asylum, extradition, and arbitration. Chile was unwilling to grant arbitrative power to the congress, but merely sought acceptance of the principle that participating nations would submit their differences to one or more arbitrators of their own choosing.[15] But the delegates, Chile's included, had more grandiose ideas. On February 8, 1848, they signed a treaty of confederation which provided for a permanent congress of plenipotentiaries and endowed it with major peace and security functions.[16] All disputes among and between the confederated states would have to be submitted to arbitration by the Congress of Plenipotentiaries, which was empowered to enforce its decisions by imposition of sanctions. The congress, moreover, would unite under a single command the separate military forces of the confederated nations in order to defend their territorial integrity and independence against foreign aggression. And it could commit member states to the use of force by plurality vote.

This visionary treaty expressed the deep longing of the delegates for international peace and order. Only one of its clauses, however, coincided with fundamental Chilean policy, and it provided that "if an attempt is made to unite two or more of the confederated republics, or to detach from one in order to add to another of the same republics, or to a foreign power, one or more ports, cities, or provinces, it will be necessary that the governments of the other confederated republics declare expressly that such a change is not prejudicial to the interests and security of the confederation." Had such an agreement existed before 1835, the Peru-Bolivian war might have been prevented. But Chile's objections to other aspects of the treaty, which was not even submitted to its own Congress for approval, were overwhelming.[17]

Chile maintained that the powers granted to the Congress of Plenipotentiaries would limit national sovereignty and governmental freedom of action. Chile also opposed certain treaty provisions directed against the Great Powers; it objected to the preamble which indirectly charged them with "usurpations" and "affronts" to the "interests, dignity, and independence" of the signatories.[18] Chile was too realistic to consider an alliance against all the nations of the globe, above all one that would command use of its military power and impose economic sanctions, not only in defense of the signatories' territory and independence, but also in the event of Great Power intervention or "offense." The treaty did provide for prior arbitration, but Chile thought it inconceivable that any Great Power would accept the arbitration of its enemy's allies as stipulated in the treaty. In short, the Foreign Minister of Chile was convinced "it would be impossible to adopt a line of conduct more calculated to involve us in external conflicts and to justify ... the ill will of powerful states."[19]

But even if these serious objections could be overcome, Chile did not believe that the joint actions envisioned in the treaty would be effective. The combined military strength of all the signatories would hardly dent the power of a nation such as Great Britain, or so it seemed to Chile's foreign minister, who also felt that economic sanctions, or the breaking of commercial relations with such countries as England, France, or the United States "could be more damaging to any of the American republics than to the offending power."[20] The government of Chile was not alone in its objections to the Treaty of Confederation produced by delegates to the Lima Congress. The opposition of a number of nations, together with general apathy and the collapse of the current Flores threat, consigned the draft to oblivion. The coöperative impulse subsided. Rivalry and competition again became the determinative elements in the international behavior of the states of the Pacific Coast of South America.

THE PERUVIAN NAVY

At this point the Chilean government awoke to the implications of Peru's improving power position, especially to the fact that Peru, powerless on the sea at the end of the Peru-Bolivian war, once again had a navy. In the first year of his administration, Castilla had assembled a sqadron of one frigate, two brigantines, two schooners, and a transport. In 1847 Peru's navy moved toward modernization with the incorporation of the steamship *Rimac.*[21]

Meanwhile Chile's sea power had remained static, in spite of the government's intentions, partly because Congress had failed to appropriate sufficient funds to implement its 1845 authorization to increase the navy. The Flores menace and the Argentine protest of 1847 against Chilean occupation of the Strait of Magellan had evoked flurries of interest and demands for a larger navy, but only the growing strength of Peru succeeded in turning words into action. In March, 1848, the commandant of the navy insisted that "the steady enlargement of the

Peruvian navy requires similar efforts on Chile's part ... to maintain between the two states the peace that is so greatly desired."[22] That same year a Frenchman residing in Valparaíso was awarded a contract for the construction of the first warship to be built upon Chilean soil.

Chile's sense of naval inadequacy became particularly acute when its leaders suspected that Chilean nationals were being treated unfairly in Peru. The Foreign Minister charged that Peruvian "antipathy against Chile has become a national sentiment."[23] Not many years earlier, in the face of similar difficulties, a warship had been dispatched to Callao to instill proper respect for Chilean rights, but in 1848, lamented the Foreign Minister, "forceful but prudent representations ... are our only recourse, for threats unsupported by visible force ... would merely inflame the ... malevolent spirit of which Peruvian authorities have given us repeated examples."[24] But, apparently hopeful of Chile's planned naval expansion, he added that "the day may not be distant when we can acknowledge such insulting conduct and treat it as it deserves to be treated."

It was the seemingly eternal Ecuadoran crisis, however, rather than the mounting but long-to-be-delayed crisis in Chile's relations with Peru, which served to push Chilean activity farther to the north. After Juan José Flores had been exiled in 1845, Ecuador, whose trials had always been severe, began to suffer even more appalling problems. By 1850 it had entered a dark age which would keep it immersed in bloodshed for ten years, creating a vacuum irresistible to neighboring states. At the same time that Ecuador was sinking deeper into its chaos, Peru was gaining strength, and New Granada was experiencing an exciting ideological transformation which had profound implications for its neighbors. Chile's primary concern in the Ecuadoran situation was the possible expansion of Peruvian influence into the Ecuadoran vacuum. Chile became involved secondarily in the affairs of New Granada because of the latter's influence upon Quito.

RADICALISM IN NEW GRANADA

The increased interest and influence of New Granada in the affairs of South America derived from the lessening of its nagging fears over the possible loss of its province of Panama. Prior to 1848 such a blow had seemed possible. It was forestalled, however, in 1846, when mounting Anglo–United States rivalry in the Caribbean made Washington willing to sign the Mallarino-Bidlack Treaty with New Granada guaranteeing the latter's sovereignty over the isthmus in return for certain commercial concessions. In the Clayton-Bulwer Treaty of 1850 Great

Britain and the United States agreed not to extend their territorial possessions in Central America, and jointly to control any interoceanic canal that might be built. This treaty, by establishing a balance of power in the Caribbean between the United States and Great Britain, indirectly gave Bogotá an additional guarantee of its Panamanian sovereignty and permitted it to turn its attention from the north to the south.

New Granada's ideological ferment sprang from the European revolutions of 1848. In 1849 New Granadine radicals peacefully gained control of the executive and legislative branches of government, and immediately implemented their anticlerical and egalitarian ideas. Looking backward rather than forward, they favored closer ties among the successor states of Great Colombia. The government publicly announced that it considered relations with Venezuela and Ecuador to be of paramount importance.[25]

REVOLUTION IN GUAYAQUIL, 1850

Radicals were already in power in Bogotá when a revolution broke out in Guayaquil, Ecuador, whose ultimate purpose Quito believed to be annexation of that port to Peru. Aware of Bogotá's Bolivarian bent, Quito asked its help, warning that the addition of Guayaquil to Peru would imperil "the maintenance of the political equilibrium among the other Hispano-American states."[26] New Granada, agreeing that such an event would have "lamentable consequences for the welfare and security of the states neighboring on Ecuador,"[27] promised aid if the annexation took place. The President of New Granada made public his country's commitment, notifying Chile by sending a copy of the letter that promised aid to Quito.

Santiago, knowing even before Bogotá[28] of the trouble in Guayaquil, was making every attempt to ascertain the exact relationship between the port revolt and the government of Peru.[29] As Chile's information indicated "a basis for the fear that the revolutionaries of Guayaquil adhere to the ambitious designs that Peru has long cherished of adding to Peruvian territory that interesting province,"[30] Santiago was tensely watching the situation.[31]

JESUIT EXPULSIONS

As the three capitals—Santiago, Quito, and Bogotá—anxiously awaited the outcome of the Guayaquil revolt, a new source of international unrest was created when New Granada ousted the Company of Jesus. The Jesuits, who had only recently returned after their preindependence expulsion by the Spanish Crown, were given but forty-eight hours in which to leave the country. Many of them fled to Guayaquil.³² Bogotá immediately charged that their presence there constituted a threat to the internal stability of New Granada, whose Congress authorized a declaration of war; troops were massed at the Ecuadoran frontier.³³ War seemed inevitable and Chile promptly offered its mediation. But by the time Santiago's offer was received in Bogotá, harmony had been restored.³⁴ The conservative faction in Guayaquil had been overthrown, and a new liberal regime in Quito was attempting to govern the strife-torn land. To smooth its thorny path, it placated New Granada by promptly agreeing to expel the Company of Jesus.

ANOTHER FLORES THREAT

In keeping with Ecuadoran political tradition, the enemies of the new liberal regime began at once to plot its overthrow. Juan José Flores, a former president who had quit European exile and was now residing in Lima,³⁵ was busily laying the groundwork for seizure of the government, and because the Peruvian leadership of the moment shared Flores' conservatism and dreaded the liberalism of the New Granadine and Ecuadoran governments, it was assisting Flores with the same ill-disguised secrecy that had characterized its aid to Chilean ex-President Freire some fifteen years earlier.³⁶ Quito, charging Peru with intervention, prepared for war and called upon Chile and other American governments to seize the ships of the Flores expedition. Bogotá, whose relations with Peru had been deteriorating, promised Quito help and commenced to prepare for war.

FRANCISCO BILBAO, FIREBRAND

Even had Francisco Bilbao not chosen that moment to swoop down upon Chile, the government's decision on the complex events to the north would have been most difficult. But the presence of Bilbao made the decision agonizing. On February 2, 1850, the twenty-seven-year-old firebrand, filled with the fanatical fervor that had been inspired in him by anticlerical radicalism, returned from Europe to his native country. Starting at once to agitate for reforms similar to those that were being effected in New Granada, Bilbao founded the Egalitarian Society. Through its meetings and publications, the society became an extremely effective propaganda instrument, and was branded as subversive by a rattled aristocratic government. It influenced an abortive revolt, and then a more serious revolutionary effort late in 1851. Largely because social unrest was a phenomenon virtually unknown to post-

Lircay Chile, the discontent aroused by the inspired preaching of Bilbao seriously frightened the Conservative government and caused it to regard with deep distrust and fear the radical government of New Granada.

The Chilean government did not know which of the two evils it stood between—the growing power of Peru or the radicals in New Granada and Ecuador—was worse. Its ambivalent and contradictory steps toward resolution of the problems of the north reflected its dilemma. But at the same time Chile's actions revealed its willingness and ability to manipulate the nations of the Pacific Coast in order to maintain a power structure favorable to its own interests.

CHILE'S RESPONSE TO THE NORTHERN PROBLEM

Reacting to the Peruvian-based Flores expedition against Ecuador, Chile notified Lima that it "would vigorously oppose any threat to the independence of any sister republic."[37] But only a few weeks later Chile decided to offer its mediation if the Flores expedition failed and if New Granada and Ecuador, in reprisal, invaded Peru. And if its mediation failed to halt such a war, Chile was prepared to take more active steps "against the immoderate pretensions of the enemies of Peru."[38] In view of the total unpredictabilty of the Ecuadoran situation, the Chilean chargé d'affaires in Lima was provided with a general policy guide: Chile wanted "the peace of the continent; continuance of the present order of things, with neither dismemberments nor annexations; and the protection of Chilean persons and property."[39]

In order to learn the exact extent of Bogotá's influence in Quito, and how prepared both radical governments were to go to war against conservative Peru, the Chilean government sent a special agent to Ecuador. But travel was slow in the 1850's, and by the time Chile's man arrived matters had already come to a head. The Flores expedition had been dispersed, and Peru, which was at the moment being threatened by Bolivia, was preparing to defend itself against the combined assault of Ecuador and New Granada. The latter two had invited Bolivia to join them in laying waste to Peru, which now turned to Chile for help.[40]

Peru's overture was regarded with some sympathy in Santiago. The Chilean government, which at the onset of the latest Ecuadoran problem had been disposed to think the worst of Peru's intentions, had become even more fearful of the potential Bolivian–Ecuadoran–New Granadine combination, viewing with particular alarm "the influence of the present government of New Granada upon the affairs of the continent, [which] would be dangerous for the social and political institutions of all these peoples. As the Flores expedition has been dissolved, it is much to be feared that the latest moves of New Granada are primarily for the purpose of propagating its exaggerated principles."[41]

Hitherto "malevolent" and "insulting" Peru was now a conservative bulwark against radical subversion, and Santiago's Quito agent was ordered to warn Ecuador that any move against Peru might lead Chile to intervene "as a party interested in the maintenance of the political order of the new states, which New Granada seeks to disturb."[42] The Chilean representative was to offer his government's mediation and attempt to counteract the political and ideological influence of New Granada upon Ecuadoran affairs. The recently completed *Constitución* was ordered to the ports of Ecuador and Peru,[43] and a chargé d'affaires was accredited to La Paz with instructions to frustrate the intentions of New Granada.[44]

It proved unnecessary, however, for Chile to support Peru openly. Lima, preparing at full speed for war with Bolivia and therefore determined to settle its northern question, sent an agent to Bogotá to negotiate. Meanwhile, Quito, overwhelmed by domestic chaos, impoverished as usual, and fearing complete isolation in event of an understanding between Lima and Bogotá, dispatched an envoy to Lima to seek settlement of their dispute. In March, 1853, Peru and Ecuador reached an agreement under which Peru promised to keep Flores out of its territory. The agreement resolved all questions arising from the most recent expedition, except for the disposition of Flores' ships, which was to be entrusted to Chilean arbitration.[45]

As Peru disentangled itself from disputes with Ecuador and New Granada, its war with Bolivia drew nearer. While Chile was fruitlessly attempting to mediate,[46] Peru seized the Bolivian port of Cobija and relations between the disputing nations were broken off. Then, when Bolivia found itself engulfed in domestic disorders even more serious than those to which it was accustomed, and when Peruvian attention was distracted by revolution, the war withered on the vine.

EVOLVING CHILEAN POLICY

The diplomatic activity centered on Ecuador in the early 1850's showed that the horizon of Chile's political interests had moved far to the north. In safeguarding its northern interests Chile sought to maintain the balance of power through preservation of the status quo, demonstrating a decidedly more than theoretical wish for the "continuance of the present order of things." Chile had not used force. That had been unnecessary. But Santiago had made clear its stubborn opposition to territorial dismemberment, and its reputation for tough-mindedness and seriousness left no doubt among its Pacific Coast colleagues that Chile would take action against any nation that threatened "the present order of things." Chile had served notice, in effect, that it was assuming the role of regulator of the balance of power along the entire western rim of the continent. Several incidents of the 1850's and early 1860's, each stemming fundamentally from the perpetual Ecuadoran crisis, illustrate the manner in which Chile performed its self-appointed task of regulating west coast equilibrium.

THE ECUADORAN–UNITED STATES CONVENTION OF 1854

In the first incident, Chile pitted its diplomacy against one of the Great Powers, though usually it sought to avoid controversy with them. The United States had been inspiring a great deal of mistrust as a result of its territorial acquisitions in the Mexican War, its interest in Cuba and in the Lobos Islands off northwestern Peru, and filibustering forays by its citizens in Baja California. Chile became seriously alarmed about Washington's policy when, in 1854, Ecuador and the United States signed, in Quito, a convention that Santiago believed to threaten the independence of Ecuador. The agreement provided that, in return for a Galapagos Islands guano concession, the United States would pay Ecuador 3 million dollars and would protect both the Ecuadoran coastline and the islands. In Chile's view the arrangements threatened the peace of South America, for the equilibrium would be upset by Ecuador's greater power as a recipient of United States aid and its increased ability to commit aggression. Sooner or later, believed Santiago, Ecuador would lose its independence altogether, and become just one more United States possession. When that had happened other South American nations would be endangered by the voracious appetite of the northern colossus.

A threat of that magnitude required action. A special mission was dispatched to Quito to prevent ratification of the convention, or, if it had already been ratified, to proffer financial aid to Ecuador so that it might extricate itself from its commitment to the United States. Further, Santiago circularized the entire continent asking full coöperation in frustrating the establishment of a United States protectorate over Ecuador." Then, overlooking no potential source of assistance, the Chilean government sent copies of its South American circular to several European nations so that they would become aware of the expansive posture being assumed by the United States in South America.

Chile's new minister to Ecuador found circumstances promising for the success of his mission. It was rumored freely in Quito that the United States Senate would reject the convention, in which event Ecuador would be deprived of its 3-million-dollar windfall precisely when it was nervously fearing an unfavorable turn in its relations with Peru. Lima had just announced its intention to annul its 1853 agreement to keep Flores out of Peru; the Ecuadoran chargé d'affaires had already asked for his passports and returned to Quito. Now the Ecuadoran government was eager to curry the favor of Chile and gain its help in preventing another, and possibly successful, Flores expedition.[48]

Ecuador's President Urbina informed the Chilean minister that the agreement with the United States had been signed only in order to purchase ships to be used either against Flores or against the United States itself. Therefore Urbina would be glad to heed Chile's advice in respect to the convention, but he insisted that "the powers of the Pacific need to combine their forces ... to assure the integrity of their territorial sovereignty and to guarantee the freedom of these seas. [Ecuador] ... would agree to a serious commitment in this respect if Chile offered it naval assistance against a piratical expedition by the *cabezilla* Flores, or against any similar threat."[49] In requesting instructions on the mutual-assistance treaty proposed by Ecuador, the Chilean minister warned his government that Ecuador's fear of another Peruvian-based Flores expedition was so strong that it might accept United States protection in spite of its apparent readiness to set aside the 1854 convention. With this turn of events Peru once again became the major Pacific Coast concern of the Chilean government.

CHILIAN AND PERUVIAN COUNTERPROPOSALS

Chile, which had for some time sought Peruvian guarantees against another Flores invasion attempt, now demanded a prompt and unequivocal statement. Peru was reluctant to commit itself, but neither did it wish to alienate Santiago whose coöperation it needed in preventing the organization of a revolutionary coup on Chilean soil by Peruvian exiles. Peru was also disturbed by the activities of United States filibusterers in Central America, where the government of Nicaragua had been seized by William Walker. Peru had even sent financial aid and dispatched a naval vessel to stand by in Costa Rica and help in the fight against Walker. As it wanted Chile's help in that effort, it countered Chile's demand for guarantees against Flores with a dual proposal. First, Chile and Peru would send armed forces to Central America if the Peruvian minister there thought it necessary. Second,

the two governments would sign a treaty of defensive and offensive
alliance which would provide for the creation of a union of American
nations for their common defense.[50]

In its initial form the Peruvian proposal was unacceptable to Chile,
for, although Chile deplored the depradations of *yanqui* filibusterers,
it was not prepared to dispatch an army to end them. Further, the
proposed alliance was objectionable for reasons similar to those that
had caused Chile's rejection of the 1848 Lima congress treaty. Also,
Santiago was convinced that prior efforts to unify Spanish America
had failed because solid economic and cultural bonds were still lacking. But one aspect of the Peruvian proposal—that concerning a guarantee of the peace—was acceptable to Chilean policy and might help
to solve the urgent Ecuadoran problem. Chile therefore advanced a
counterproposal which emphasized the promotion of commercial and
cultural relations, provided a mutual guarantee of independence, and
declared filibustering expeditions illegal, but placed no emphasis upon
measures of common defense against the outside world.

THE "CONTINENTAL" TREATY OF 1856

A treaty embodying Chile's ideas was discussed in Santiago, at first
bilaterally with Peru and later, at Chile's suggestion, with Ecuador.
The result was the tripartite "continental" treaty of 1856, which was
signed with the understanding that other Latin-American states would
be asked to subscribe to it.[51] The agreement fulfilled two major Chilean
objectives: broader bases for trade and commerce, and a Peruvian
commitment to nonintervention in Ecuadoran affairs. It also met one
of Santiago's objections to continent-wide formal organization in its
provision that future implementational meetings of plenipotentiaries
be rotated among the capitals of the signatories, thus helping to ensure
against Peruvian domination.

PERU INVADES ECUADOR

Any hopes aroused by the signing of the continental treaty faded fast.
The Peruvian government objected to its terms and fell promptly to
quarreling with Ecuador, this time over Ecuador's latest efforts to
solve its perpetual financial crisis. Hard pressed by Great Power creditors, Ecuador had decided to raise money by selling "unused" Amazon
Basin territory to European colonists. Peru claimed sovereignty over
the lands being sold and demanded that Ecuador rescind the sales
contract it had signed. As Peru prepared to go to war to enforce its
demand, both Chile and New Granada offered mediation, the latter

sending an envoy to Santiago to discuss the matter in person with the Chilean government. But to no avail. In 1859 President Castilla of Peru invaded Ecuador at the head of a large expeditionary force.

THE GUAYAQUIL TREATY OF 1860

Castilla soon encountered a plethora of mutually hostile factions claiming or exercising control over various regions of Ecuador, none of which could possibly represent the government as a whole. But, wishing to have in his possession some kind of document to prove his "victory," Castilla signed a "treaty" with the Caudillo of Guayaquil. The agreement provided that Ecuador would nullify the Amazon lands contract and would accept Peru's territorial pretensions as the basis for any future boundary settlement. Castilla then withdrew, apparently leaving to Ecuador's various rival caudillos the settlement of their power struggle, but actually continuing to support the Guayaquil faction which had signed a treaty so favorable to Peru. This faction, seeing its fortunes declining in the Ecuadoran power contest, began to entertain ideas of annexation to Peru.

Rumors of such an annexation had already raised an outcry. As the Peruvian expeditionary force was landing in Guayaquil, New Granada asked for and obtained assurances. But for Santiago that was not enough, even after Castilla's withdrawal. Chile had long deeply mistrusted the relationship between Lima and Guayaquil. Six months after Castilla's evacuation the Foreign Minister informed his chargé d'affaires in Peru that "Chile can regard with indifference . . . neither the direct intervention of Peru in the internal affairs of Ecuador, nor territorial acquisitions which are the result of pacts with the government of a fraction of Ecuadoran territory . . . in a time of civil war."[52]

A few weeks later Chile, believing the Guayaquil affair serious enough to warrant joint action by the diplomatic corps in Lima, ordered its chargé to seek the issuance of a joint protest. The Chilean government considered Peru's Guayaquil policy illegal and insisted that "dismemberment of any American republic in order to enlarge the territory of another is a very serious matter and one that cannot be accepted without very compelling reasons. Unless justified by considerations of an exceptional character, such dismemberments and annexations, which alter the respective situations of the various states of the continent, cannot be accepted by Chile."[53]

But the strong action that Chile was clearly prepared to take was not necessary. Lima's support of Guayaquil led to the momentary cooperation of several warring Ecuadoran cliques against the "foreign enemy" in Guayaquil. The coalition defeated its prey and set up a "unified" national government which promptly repudiated the Guayaquil treaty of 1860. Satisfied that the Peruvian threat to Ecuador had substantially declined, Santiago ordered its envoy to drop his efforts to secure a joint protest, but asked him to continue a careful watch for evidence of further Peruvian designs upon the independence and territorial integrity of its neighbors.[54]

ECUADOR SEEKS HELP

The distressing international problems of Ecuador were, of course, far from ended. Although now governed by authoritarian ultraconservative President García Moreno and returned General Juan José Flores as commander in chief of the army, the country had achieved no real unity. Relations with Peru were antagonistic, for its President Castilla was believed to be supporting the intrigues of Ecuadoran exiles. Quito, trembling with insecurity, was ready to take help where it could find it. It negotiated with France for the establishment of a protectorate[55] and at the same time sought help from Chile, to which it sent an envoy in search of an anti-Peruvian alliance. But in this instance the Chilean government was willing only to use its good offices to encourage Lima to settle its Ecuadoran question.[56] Two years later, when Ecuador appealed to Chile for assistance in a conflict with Colombia, Santiago asked Bogotá to explain its open preparations for war. But by the time the explanations reached Santiago war had broken out, had been fought, and had come to an end with the signing of a peace treaty which halted, for at least a time, hostilities between Colombia and Ecuador.

THE BOUNDARY CONFLICT WITH ARGENTINA

While Chile was exerting its influence in the far north, it was strongly affirming its interests in southern South America. The preoccupation of Buenos Aires with an Anglo-French intervention in the Plata had inhibited its forceful support of an 1847 protest against Chilean occupation of the Strait of Magellan. But Buenos Aires had commissioned a study in support of its position, and in 1852 Pedro de Angelis' *Memoria histórica sobre los derechos de soberanía y dominio de la Confederación Argentina a la parte austral del continente americano . . .*, the result of the study, was published. De Angelis' argument was so persuasive that Chile asked Miguel Luís Amunátegui to undertake its refutation. Amunátegui's response, published the following year, contended that not only the strait, but Patagonia as well, was Chilean.[57]

The inclusion of Patagonia in Chilean claims was a radical departure from Santiago's traditional position, for the constitution of 1833 specified the cordillera of the Andes as the Republic's eastern boundary, thus excluding Patagonia.

In attempting to explain so important an "omission" to European opinion, Chilean publicist Vicente Pérez Rosales unconsciously reflected the degree to which Chile's improved power position affected its role in South American affairs. Pérez "explained" that the cordillera had been designated as the eastern boundary at the time of independence because "the Republic took the only limits that it could defend against . . . the Spanish forces; but it never alienated its rights to the rest of its legal . . . [territory]. Thus, when general peace, population, power, and wealth permitted it to carry its civilizing action to the population of Patagonia, it founded the colony of Magellan upon the waters of the strait of the same name, as the principal base of its later operations."[58]

Neither Chile nor Argentina, however, was ready to make conflicting territorial claims a major issue to be supported by force. A treaty signed in 1856 recognized their boundary as the one that had divided them in 1810, and agreed to submit to arbitration any differences concerning the exact location of that boundary.[59] With Chile remaining in physical possession of the Strait of Magellan, resolution of the conflict was postponed.

THE ATACAMA DISPUTE WITH BOLIVIA

Chile's Atacama dispute with Bolivia was not so easily postponed. For almost fifteen years the Chilean government had allowed its claim to territory north to the 23d parallel to stand unsupported by force. But in 1857, by which time Peru's mounting wealth had given ample proof of the riches to be extracted from guano deposits, Chile moved to demonstrate its jurisdiction *de facto*. A warship was sent to the port of Mejillones, Bolivian authorities were expelled and replaced by Chilean officials, and the permission of the Chilean government for the exploitation of guano deposits was made mandatory. When Bolivia protested, a few years of desultory negotiations ensued.

It was the discovery of vast new guano deposits in the Mejillones region which suddenly brought the dispute to a head, as Bolivians were shocked into the realization of how much they were in danger of losing by failing to affirm sovereignty south to the 26th parallel in the Atacama Desert. On May 27, 1863, the Bolivian National Assembly, called into session to consider the "illegitimate possession that

Chile has taken of Bolivian territory," empowered President Acha to declare war if he failed to obtain an "honorable" solution to the problem.[60] Chile and Bolivia stood on the threshhold of bloodshed. A flurry of new negotiations and Peruvian mediation efforts were obviously proving useless to halt the onrushing war, when the attention of the disputants was suddenly attracted and held by the maneuvers of Spanish ships that had earlier rounded the southern tip of the continent and were now making their way northward along the Pacific coast.

INTENSIFIED EUROPEAN INTERVENTION IN THE WESTERN HEMISPHERE

The subsequent actions of Spain would have seemed less suspicious to the states of the west coast had they not appeared to be part of a pattern of intensified European intervention in the Western Hemisphere. As the flames of the United States Civil War were rising, Spain had "reannexed" Santo Domingo; France, Great Britain, and Spain had intervened in Mexico to support demands that the Juárez government make payments on the Mexican foreign debt; and France had launched its tragically prolonged attempt to implant a monarchy upon the soil of Mexico. Those events deeply shocked the entire hemisphere, especially the Spanish American nations, which saw in them a threat to their own independence.

Peru issued a stinging denouncement of Spain's action in Santo Domingo and called for joint action. Lima also dispatched to Mexico a minister who so effectively supported the cause of Juárez that the monarchy to which he was accredited handed him his passports.[61] Chile was more cautious. While unequivocally condemning Spanish occupation of Santo Domingo, it declined to join Peru in further action on the ground that it did not possess sufficient information.[62] With respect to Mexico, Chilean agents were instructed to work diligently but quietly to force France's respect of Mexican sovereignty and independence.[63]

But the movements of the Spanish fleet in Pacific waters brought close to home the question of European activities in the Americas. That fleet, commanded by Admiral José Manuel Pareja, was alleged by its government to be carrying out scientific investigations. Not one of the uneasy governments of the west coast believed that pretext, although none could have known that in fact Pareja bore instructions to support Spanish damage claims against various countries of the region.[64] The fleet passed from port to port without incident, reaching Callao in July, 1863, a few weeks after the Bolivian National Assembly had authorized a declaration of war against Chile.

Bolivia's readiness to go to war, together with the appearance of the Spanish fleet, spurred Chile to enlarge its navy. Naval circles, and indeed the government as well, wanted to acquire one of the newfangled ironclads "which are vastly superior to all the ships we have in our America, and one possessed by Chile would be the only one in all the neighboring republics."[65] But the funds authorized by the Chilean Congress in December, 1863, were sufficient only for the acquisition of less powerful wooden vessels suitable for service in peacetime as well as in time of war.

THE "TALAMBO" MATTER

After the departure of the Spanish fleet from Callao, violence broke out in Peru. Hitherto contained emotions burst their bounds on the hacienda of "Talambo," where immigrant Spanish workers were in conflict with the *hacendado* to whom they were contracted. When the "Talambo" matter ultimately reached the courts, the judicial findings favored the Peruvian landowner. While a strong protest from the Spanish consul was still pending, the Peruvian government issued invitations to a second Lima congress which it hoped would devise measures for common defense against Europe's newly aggressive posture. But the Lima congress had not yet convened when the Spanish fleet returned to Callao to give forceful support to a Spanish commissioner who had been sent from Madrid to demand justice in the "Talambo" affair. Peru refused to enter into discussions with Madrid's emissary until Spain officially recognized Peru's independence.

SEIZURE OF THE CHINCHA ISLANDS

The rebuffed Spanish agent responded by ordering seizure and occupation of Peru's extremely valuable guano-producing Chincha Islands. The Spaniard alleged that, as a merely *de facto* truce existed between Spain and its former colony, Spain was justified in "revindicating" the islands. The Peruvian government reacted by obtaining from Congress extraordinary powers and permission to seek in Europe and the United States arms and naval vessels, and the money with which to pay for them. It also decided to seek a direct settlement with Madrid.

The seizure of the Chinchas greatly alarmed the government of Chile, and on May 4, 1864, it circularized the American nations denouncing the principle of revindication as a euphemism for reconquest. It strongly protested occupation of the islands, declaring that Chile would never recognize any but Peruvian sovereignty over them and demanding immediate Spanish disavowal of its agent's actions. The entire tone of the Chilean circular made it clear that force would be used if necessary,[66] and Santiago rushed an agent abroad to purchase four additional ships.[67]

At the same time Santiago sought to bolster the forthcoming Lima congress, and through it the Spanish American postion vis-à-vis Spain.[68] Former President Manuel Montt, a figure of great prestige, was named Chilean delegate to the meeting in the hope that his presence would assist in securing a satisfactory solution in the Peruvian-Spanish dispute. In the face of Ecuador's resistance to participation in any meeting sponsored by Peru, Santiago dispatched an agent to Quito who was successful in persuading the Ecuadoran government of the overriding threat of Spain.

By the time the Lima congress convened, Spain had somewhat lessened the fear and anger of Spanish American leaders by recognizing Peru's independence and disavowing revindication. But Madrid stood firm on its refusal to relinquish the Chincha Islands until its citizens' claims for damages had been satisfied. Peru met that situation with total indecision. The country, pressed from one side by the advocates of appeasement and from the other by those who demanded war, was entirely unprepared for war. Too politically and militarily weak to confront the issue clearly, the Peruvian government seemed paralyzed.

THE LIMA CONGRESS OF 1864–65

Against this hazardous backdrop the delegates to the second Lima congress met and set aside the official agenda in order to deal immediately with the Peruvian crisis. Led by Manuel Montt of Chile, the congress protested against the Chincha occupation, and in October and again in December negotiated with the chief of the Spanish forces for their return to Peru and for restoration of friendly relations between Lima and Madrid. In the course of considering the Peruvian-Spanish dispute, Montt became convinced, as did his colleagues, that Peru's military unpreparedness and political dissension made its resistance to Spanish demands hopeless.[69] When their negotiations with the Spanish commander failed, the delegates of Chile, Peru, Bolivia, and Argentina advised Peru to seek direct talks with Madrid and simultaneously to attempt to organize an army for war. Neither of those recommendations had been carried out when Admiral Pareja issued an ultimatum to the effect that Peru would never regain the Chinchas unless it paid Spain an indemnification of 3 million pesos.

As the Peruvian government attempted to reach a decision whether to prepare for submission or for resistance to Spain's demands, the American congress returned to its planned agenda. Much of its discussion centered upon an international organization of American states. The need for such a body was generally accepted but opinions differed as to its form. Two schools of thought were apparent in the Lima deliberations in early 1865. Colombia, Venezuela, and Ecuador favored a compulsory confederation which would deëmphasize sovereignty and whose members would delegate defensive and peacemaking measures to a powerful congress of plenipotentiaries, similar to the one that would have been created under the treaty drawn up at the first Lima congress, seventeen years before. Montt of Chile convincingly argued for a voluntary arrangement, emphasizing the merits of unrestricted national sovereignty. This point of view envisioned a governing body that would function largely as a kind of clearinghouse for the drafting of multilateral mutual assistance and arbitration treaties, whose signatories would remain free to interpret their applicability in any given instance.

The Treaty of Union and Defensive Alliance and the Treaty on the Conservation of Peace, signed at the second Lima congress, represented the triumph of the voluntary tendency and of Manuel Montt of Chile. Those two treaties encountered a no more cordial reception with the home governments than had their predecessor. But the debates that preceded their signing made unequivocally clear the fact that however much the participating nations might be willing to coöperate against a common external threat, they saw themselves primarily as entities in an "every-man-for-himself" system of power politics, where the maintenance of stable power relationships was of the utmost importance. A Colombian proposal and the reactions it aroused illustrate the degree to which such a concept was accepted.

Colombia's proposal reflected the internal political collapse which, beginning in the 1850's, had caused the centralized national government of New Granada to be transformed into a loosely allied group of "sovereign states" under the name "United States of Colombia." In 1864 Venezuela, having suffered similar decentralization, adopted a loose federal constitution as the "United States of Venezuela." As the internal parts of the Colombian states became increasingly unstuck, their leadership developed a new interest in gluing back together, as a "federal union" of Colombia, Venezuela, and Ecuador, the once-powerful Great Colombia of the Bolivarian era. As early as 1853 Chile learned that the Lima representatives of those three countries had devised a plan "to reëstablish the former Republic of Colombia"; Chile's minister in Peru had warned that the implementation of such a plan "would alter the political equilibrium that exists among the

South American states."⁷⁰ Colombian federal union of the three states
had not been achieved, but the idea had remained alive and the Colombian constitutions of 1861 and 1863 made specific provision for such
union.⁷¹

It was against this background that the Colombian delegate to the
second Lima congress proposed approval of the principle that two or
more nations might voluntarily join together in a union. The Chilean
delegate countered with the suggestion that such a privilege, if granted,
be limited to successor states to those that had at independence formed
a single state, thus excluding all but the successor states of the Central
American Federation and Great Colombia. Manuel Montt, commenting upon the departure from Chile's traditional adherence to the principle of maintaining the 1835 territorial status quo, pointed out that
"while there is nothing . . . inconvenient in the reunification of the three
republics of former Colombia, nor the five of Central America, and
it might even be well for [the latter] to do so, the same may not be
said for the incorporation into Peru of Bolivia or Ecuador, for example.
The existence . . . of each of these republics is necessary not only to
maintain the necessary equilibrium among the states of the continent
but also . . . for their own security, thwarting the machinations of ambitious caudillos."⁷²

The Lima congress, finding itself unable to agree on the unification
question, resolved merely that individual cases should be decided "in
accordance with the general principles of international law."⁷³ But,
as with other unresolved questions, the spotlighting of these issues at
an international meeting, and their discussion, served to elicit important insights into the reality of contemporary international life and
into the national interests of the participants. In the discussion of the
unification issue at the second Lima congress, the mere fact that Bogotá
sought the meeting's approval showed that it was aware of membership in a system all of whose other participants would be concerned
about any major change in the territorial status quo. That no agreement was reached indicated that, in spite of their professed desire to
achieve solidarity in the face of foreign aggression, the delegates in
Lima considered the power relationships among their own countries
to be of fundamental importance.

Chile's position was particularly significant, for it made evident the
fact that, although Chile still adhered to a policy of maintaining the
equilibrium, she had modified her idea of what constituted a threat
to the equilibrium. In the immediate postwar years Chile had believed
that continuance of the 1835 territorial status quo would ensure South

American equilibrium. In the first Ecuadoran crisis Chile had sought "the peace of the continent, the continuance of the present order of things with neither dismemberments nor annexations." And although Chile had viewed Peruvian influence in Ecuador with displeasure, she had been equally disquieted by the potential influence of New Granada. When New Granada and Ecuador had seemed ready to attack Peru, Santiago had considered intervention on the latter's side "as a party interested in the political order of the new states, which New Granada seeks to disturb." It was after that threat had subsided that Chile was informed of plans to reconstruct Great Colombia. The failure of such plans to materialize had relieved Chile of the need to define her policy in regard to a move that might "alter the political equilibrium of the South American states."

But by 1865 the Chilean delegate to the Lima congress did not consider Colombian unification a threat to the equilibrium, whereas the incorporation of either Ecuador or Bolivia into Peru was still regarded as dangerous. Montt's position seemed illogical. If the "existence ... of each of these republics is necessary," as he had stated in objecting to Peruvian incorporation of Ecuador, why should Ecuador's existence, when the question was its absorption into Colombia, be less necessary? Merely because the Chilean delegate had abandoned the doctrine of the territorial status quo with respect to the far north, while retaining it for Peru and Bolivia. Chile's doctrinal modification was a realistic response to alterations that had taken place in the South American power structure. The power position of Colombia had declined along with the disintegration of its internal administrative system and the increased domestic strife which had accompanied adoption of its extreme form of federalism. The course of Venezuela had been similar.

Former President Manuel Montt, Chile's delegate in Lima, was well aware of the weakness of the northern republics. He suspected that "they seek in a [confederative, compulsory] league of republics ... the force and the respectability which they are losing through the fragmentization of their internal unity.'"[4] It was obvious that the three Colombian republics, even if united, would be too weak to threaten a South American power structure favorable to Chilean interests. On the contrary, their unification might serve as a counterweight to Peru. On the other hand, as Peruvian power was mounting in spite of its domestic and international problems, it could not be permitted to gain control of either Ecuador or Bolivia.

Although Chile had modified its doctrine of status quo, it had by no means relinquished the policy of maintaining a power structure favorable to its interests. Chile still wanted equilibrium among the nations of its system; it had merely adopted a more flexible standard for identifying a threat to the equilibrium. Chilean diplomacy in the two decades preceding the second Lima congress was concerned primarily with the balancing of power among the nations of the Pacific Coast. For that very reason these countries constituted the system of power politics to which Chile then belonged, even though Chilean statesmen were wont to equate Chile's interests with the "continental" or "South American" equilibrium. In the two decades following the second Lima congress the simultaneous waging of two wars was to combine with fundamental changes in the continent's power structure to stimulate more far-reaching Chilean efforts to regulate the balance of power.

CHAPTER VI

THE BRIDGE THAT TWO WARS BUILT

ON JANUARY 27, 1865, the government of Peru bowed to Admiral Pareja's ultimatum and agreed to pay Spain an "indemnification" of 3 million pesos. The ransomed Chincha Islands were returned to Peruvian control, but the Pacific operations of the Spanish fleet continued, for Pareja now felt compelled to chastise Chile for alleged "hostile acts." In May, 1865, Spain's minister, pressed by the Admiral, reluctantly handed the Chilean Foreign Office a list of complaints including claimed public insults to the flag of Spain, Chile's circular protesting the Chincha seizure, and the closing of Chilean ports to the ships of Pareja's fleet during the period of Peruvian conflict.

Santiago was in a conciliatory mood, for Spain had renounced the doctrine of revindication and had returned the islands to Peru. And if it was true, as rumor had it, that Spain was contemplating severe reprisals against Chile, it might be all the wiser to rely on conciliation, for little help was likely to be forthcoming from either Peru or other west coast countries. Chile therefore replied to the protest in pacific terms which the minister accepted, subject to final approval by Madrid. The Spaniard fully expected approval and so did the Chilean foreign minister, who assured Congress that "we have no reason to doubt that [Madrid] will approve an understanding as honorable and reasonable for Spain as for Chile."[1]

WAR WITH SPAIN; THE QUADRUPLE ALLIANCE

Conciliatory elements in both Chile and Spain had reckoned without the influence of Admiral Pareja, a superpatriot who considered the Chilean affair a matter of Spanish national honor and therefore absolutely nonnegotiable. Madrid rejected the proffered explanations of Chile, rebuked its minister, and placed the entire matter in the Admiral's hands. On September 17, 1865, Pareja demanded that Chile not only apologize for its alleged offenses, but also pay homage to the flag of Spain with a twenty-one-gun salute. Chile, feeling in its turn that the matter was one of its own national honor, declined to make the required obeisance. Pareja announced a blockade. Chile declared war on Spain.

At the outbreak of hostilities Chile confronted an enemy whose naval power was unquestionably superior. Santiago's plans to augment the navy had not yet borne fruit. Two corvettes were under construction, but Chile's belligerent status would probably cause their detention under British neutrality regulations. Chile's fighting fleet in September, 1865, consisted of one 18-cannon corvette and one 4-cannon steamship. It was a pitiable fleet with which to confront Pareja's eight warships, carrying a total of 207 cannon. Chile rushed agents abroad to find ships, meanwhile making every effort to reinforce onshore defenses against a possible Spanish landing and to secure the closing of the continent's ports to the Spanish fleet.

Chile also sought alliances against Spain as a matter both of military necessity and of American principle. Now if ever was the moment for the American states to implement their determination, so often expressed, to coöperate in the preservation of one another's independence and integrity. Santiago warned that Madrid's action against Chile was part of a grand Spanish plan to resubjugate its former American colonies. Chile therefore was acting as defender of all the Spanish American nations. Her position was that these countries, in their own self-interest as well as in obedience to the principle of hemispheric coöperation, should join with her to drive Spain once and for all from the Western Hemisphere.

But the government of Peru was not moved, and it was the one that Chile most strongly desired to bring into the war because of the Peruvian navy. The government that had bowed to Pareja had been overthrown, but even the one that replaced it proved loath to fight Spain. Since, however, all that Chile really wanted was use of the navy, Santiago was willing to settle for less than open alliance. In the face of Peru's continued cool response, the Chilean government began to view the Peruvian government as both hostile to it and "a danger for America."[2] To put an end to that threat, Chile determined to act forcefully, but in an unspecified manner, coöperating if possible with Ecuador and Bolivia.[3] But drastic three-power action was obviated when the Chilean minister in Lima succeeded in making contact with certain elements who believed that Peru should be fighting openly on Chile's side against Spain. It may be assumed that the November, 1865, coup which placed pro-Chilean Mariano Ignacio Prado in the presidency received Chile's blessing, if not its more concrete financial backing. One of the new regime's first acts was to sign an anti-Spanish alliance with Chile.[4] Four Peruvian ships, with a total of 90 cannon, were assigned to Chile, and Peru's ports were closed to the ships of Pareja.

Ecuador's response to Chile's request for an alliance was hesitant. Undefended Guayaquil was vulnerable to Pareja's cannon, and Quito was too poverty-stricken to undertake its defense. But Chile insisted, wishing to present a united front to world opinion and to secure the closing of Ecuadoran ports. Finally, on January 30, 1866, after Chile and Peru promised financial and military assistance, Ecuador joined the alliance against Spain.[5]

The problem of Bolivian adherence to the anti-Spanish alliance was even more delicate. Formal diplomatic relations between the Altiplano and Santiago were severed; the Bolivian National Assembly had authorized a declaration of war. A confidential Chilean agent traveled to Bolivia with assurances of Santiago's good intentions in regard to the Atacama boundary dispute, which Chile suggested be set aside until the threat of Spain was overcome.[6] Bolivia responded favorably and, in February, 1866, after an agreement between Chile and Bolivia was signed, Spain found herself at war against a quadruple alliance of South American west coast states.

The quadruple alliance constituted a formidable obstacle to Pareja's plans to punish Spain's former colonies. Although Ecuador and Bolivia could not mount a naval offensive, the closing of their ports seriously handicapped the movements of the Spanish fleet, forcing it to Atlantic ports for purposes of refueling and reprovisioning. Madrid responded to the formation of the alliance by authorizing any action, however drastic, which might be needed to bring the war to a speedy and successful finish. On March 24, 1866, Pareja issued another ultimatum to Chile: if Chile failed immediately to accept Spanish demands, the port of Valparaíso would be destroyed. Upon Chile's rejection of his ultimatum Pareja turned cannon upon the port city, killing two people and inflicting great damage upon its facilities. Satisfied with the results of the attack, the Admiral sailed north to besiege the fortified Peruvian port of Callao. After four days the Spanish were forced to retire, but without serious loss.

THE LASTARRIA MISSION TO ARGENTINA;
GENESIS OF THE PARAGUAYAN WAR

The nations of the quadruple alliance did not consider that the Spanish withdrawal from Callao ended the dispute, but continued to prosecute the war and to strengthen their own solidarity. Chile and Bolivia presumably settled their long-standing boundary dispute by treaty in August, 1866.[7] The alliance accelerated efforts to gain assistance against Spain from the states of the east, Santiago having moved in that direction even before the outbreak of the war.

In January, 1865, José Victorino Lastarria reached Buenos Aires at the head of Chile's first diplomatic mission to Argentina since the end of the war against the Peru-Bolivian Confederation. Lastarria's major objective was an anti-Spanish alliance. In fact, only a few months earlier President Bartolomé Mitre of Argentina had himself suggested the desirability of such an understanding. Upon reaching the Platine port, however, Lastarria found that conditions in Argentina had changed so as virtually to preclude the chance of a treaty. Not only had Mitre come to feel that Spain, having officially disavowed the doctrine of revindication, no longer constituted a serious threat,[8] but Argentina had reluctantly become involved in a complex and dangerous pan-Platine power struggle.[9]

The 1828 establishment of Uruguay as a buffer state had not succeeded in preventing sharp and frequent fluctuations in the Platine system's power structure. In the late 1830's the equilibrium had been threatened by Juan Manuel Rosas, who, having brought some slight order to the Argentine provinces, set out to dominate Uruguay. The Platine structure was further shaken in the early 1840's when Paraguay emerged from the absolute isolation imposed during the long dictatorship of xenophobic Dr. Francia.[10] The interference of landlocked Paraguay in Platine affairs radically affected the region's power politics, with an early promise of dispute in Argentina's refusal to recognize Asunción on the ground that Paraguay was legally an Argentine province. The Empire of Brazil, fearing that Rosas would gain domination of both Uruguay and Paraguay, sought to prevent it by recognizing the independence of Paraguay and negotiating an alliance with it. Brazil also pressed Great Britain, France, and the United States to act against the dictator of Argentina, and when Anglo-French intervention failed to topple him, the Brazilian government allied itself with anti-Rosas groups in Uruguay and Argentina.[11] In 1852 Rosas was overthrown by the military force of this Brazilian-backed alliance. The disappearance of Rosas from the Argentine scene left the provinces free to return to their disputes, and for most of the following decade two independent and rival governments ruled upon Argentine soil. While Argentina seemed to have reverted to its traditional divisions, Brazil was enjoying increasing political stability and was expanding economically. The scales tipped, and the Empire assumed hegemony in the Plata.

While Brazil was dominant in Platine affairs it advanced its interests in several major respects. Treaties guaranteeing the independence of Uruguay and Paraguay were secured. Free navigation of the Paraná-Paraguay–Plata river system, of extreme importance to the economy of Brazil's interior provinces, was diplomatically sanctioned. Brazil intervened in Uruguay on several occasions in order to protect the interests of its nationals. In 1856 Brazilian naval vessels pointed their guns at the harbor of Asunción to force Paraguayan compliance with navigation and boundary demands.

But Brazil's maintenance of its hegemony became increasingly difficult after 1862, when an Argentine national government was formed and an important change in leadership occurred in Asunción, where Francisco Solano López succeeded his father in the Paraguayan dictatorship. The new dictator was the victim of intense fears and of unrealistic ambitions. Haunted by a paranoid fantasy, he was determined to force upon the outside world respect for Paraguay and to play a stellar role in the affairs of the Plata region. He immediately began to construct a formidable military machine, and in 1863 Paraguay's strong military position was recognized in the form of a Uruguayan request for an alliance against possible Argentine and/or Brazilian intervention. But López was not yet ready to make his move, and for the time being edged away from alliance with Montevideo.

But by August, 1864, López was ready to state his intentions. He chose a threatened Brazilian intervention in Uruguay as the opportunity, warning Rio's Asunción minister that Paraguay would regard any foreign occupation of Uruguayan territory "as an assault against the equilibrium of the states of the Plata which interests the Republic of Paraguay as a guarantee of security, peace, and prosperity."[12] The Empire of Brazil, not allowing itself to be swerved by the threat of the Paraguayan man-on-horseback, sent troops into Uruguay in October. By November, when López seized a Brazilian ship on the Paraguay River and sent troops into the Brazilian province of Mato Grosso, the war was on.

The recently formed national government of Argentina now confronted an extraordinarily difficult policy decision. President Mitre knew that both time and peace were required to assure his government's consolidation and to prevent the return of political chaos. He was convinced, moreover, that Brazil's intervention in Uruguay was motivated by its stated desire to protect the interests of its nationals, and not by the wish to achieve permanent political control of Uruguay. He therefore decided that vital Argentine interests were not threatened and that the nation would remain neutral in the war between Brazil and Paraguay. This position had already been taken when López demanded permission to move his army across the Argentine province of Corrientes. When Mitre denied his request, the Paraguayan dictator declared war upon Argentina, invaded Corrientes, and prepared to wage war against two countries, each of which was incomparably superior to his own in wealth, population, and territorial extent.

López did not seek out his third enemy as he had the first two. But neither did the third constitute any considerable addition to the formidable power of the foes against whom the Paraguayan was determined to charge. Uruguay, whose independence Asunción had presumed to protect, was being governed, as a result of revolution, by elements friendly to Brazil and Argentina. On May 1, 1865, Argentina, Brazil, and Uruguay formalized their common enmity against Paraguay in an agreement whose terms were surrounded with the utmost secrecy.

When it sent José Victorino Lastarria to Buenos Aires, the Chilean government had been but dimly aware of the trend in Platine affairs. Upon his arrival Lastarria, although correctly concluding that he would not obtain the desired anti-Spanish alliance, complied with his instructions to the extent of presenting a formal proposal, which he then withdrew in the face of certain Argentine objections.[13] Santiago was not dismayed, for it still believed that war with Spain might be avoided. Informed by Lastarria of the conflicts in the Plata, Chile offered its mediation; when this and other conciliation efforts failed to prevent war, Chile became a mere observer of the Platine bloodshed, justifying its passivity upon the grounds that "the independence and territorial integrity of no American nation appear menaced."[14]

In Buenos Aires Lastarria awaited a more propitious occasion to make a new offer of Chilean mediation, and to suggest once more an alliance against Spain. Meanwhile, with the best of intentions, he tried to turn his mission to some account by seeking settlement of the boundary question. His instructions had been to uphold Chile's claims to both the Strait of Magellan and Patagonia. But, as Lastarria was not personally convinced of the validity of all his country's claims, he suggested a direct settlement in which Chile would relinquish half of the strait and almost all Patagonia, a proposal that Argentina nevertheless rejected.[15] The Chilean foreign minister regretted that Lastarria had not adhered to his instructions, but no official disavowal was forthcoming,[16] and future Argentine governments were armed with a potent weapon in their Chilean boundary negotiations.

When war broke out between Spain and Chile, Lastarria once again sought an alliance and was again rebuffed. This time the Chilean government was first irritated, then bitter, then angry. It regarded as a pretext rather than a reason Argentina's explanation that it could not afford to become involved in two wars at the same time. Chile seemed unable to believe, from its Pacific distance, that puny Paraguay could constitute anything but a minor irritant to the great lands of Argentina and Brazil. Certainly the excesses of destruction and blood-letting to which Francisco Solano López' fanatic determination would lead were not yet evident west of the Andes. So deeply disconcerted was Chile by Argentina's failure to join it in the face of the Spanish threat that Santiago sent its minister in Buenos Aires a letter of retirement to be used in the event that it "be desirable to let . . . [Argentina] know that we consider its conduct hostile. . . . The terms in which your letter of retirement is couched are not at all friendly, but its presenta-tion should not have the character of an open break in diplomatic relations. . . . Limit yourself in your departing remarks to an astute indication of the bad impression made upon us by that government's conduct, replacing any manifestation of friendship with an expres-sion of concern for the cause of America."[17]

Lastarria did not choose to present the letter of retirement and was still at his post when the Spanish fleet, having bombed Valparaíso, moved on to the seige of Callao. The nations of the quadruple alliance had closed their ports to the enemy fleet, but now discovered that Pareja could not be stopped unless Atlantic ports were similarly closed. To accomplish this objective the friendly coöperation, if not the formal alliance, of Uruguay, Brazil, and Argentina would be needed. As such coöperation was not probable so long as they were at war against Paraguay, it was decided at a Santiago conference of April, 1866, to offer the joint mediation of the members of the quad-ruple alliance.[18] This offer was intended explicitly to bring the Para-guayan War to an end and to unify the continent against Spain. But the Foreign Minister of Chile also saw a chance to unmask Argentina, for "if [as is claimed] the only cause of Argentina's ambiguous policy in respect to us is the Paraguayan War, mediation provides Argentina with the means to remove that reason for abstaining from the Ameri-can alliance. If, on the contrary, it does not wish to enter this alliance it is well to strip away all honorable pretext . . . for its desertion of the interests of America."[19]

Although Chile had little hope for the success of the mediation offer, Lastarria was instructed to lay the groundwork in Buenos Aires and to prepare to coöperate with other agents of the quadruple alliance in the event that mediation was accepted. Lastarria, for his part, doubted that the offer would be well received, and even questioned the wisdom of making it at all.[20] But he did carry out his instructions, and on June 20, 1866, informed the Argentine foreign minister that a mediation offer from the quadruple alliance would be forthcoming at an appropriate time. Along with this trial balloon Lastarria presented to Argentina a proposal for its adherence to the Pacific Coast alliance against Spain, which "was received with sentiments little favorable to its good results."[21]

A BREACH OF CONFIDENCE

The month following the Santiago quadruple-alliance conference, ill will between east and west rose sharply as a result of Great Britain's violation of a confidence. The government of Uruguay had in utmost secrecy informed England of the details of the May 1, 1865, secret treaty of the triple alliance. When the British made public the terms of the treaty, the signatories' reason for wishing to conceal them became clear.[22] The triple allies had promised to bear arms until the Paraguayan dictator had been completely crushed. Moreover, they agreed to guarantee the independence, sovereignty, and territorial integrity of a presumably totally defeated Paraguay for only five years. Although the treaty stated that the allies were not warring against the people of Paraguay but rather against the government, it was the Paraguayan people who were to indemnify the three allies for the total cost of the war, at a time when López had presumably been killed and was no longer the government. Paraguay's boundaries were to be redrawn in accordance with the most exaggerated claims of Brazil and Argentina. Paraguay was to be deprived of the attributes of national sovereignty by being forced to accept river-navigation regulations favorable to the interests of its enemies and unfavorable to its own interests. Paraguay's fortifications would be permanently dismantled; the country would be completely disarmed. Only when Paraguay had agreed to accept these humiliating terms would it be granted peace.

West coast governments were shocked and surprised by the exorbitant price of peace. In July, 1866, Bolivia, protesting that the treaty's boundary provisions affected its own territory on the west bank of the Paraguay River, massed troops on the Argentine frontier to make clear its intention to defend that territory.[23] The members of the triple alliance hastened to reassure the Altiplano, for they had actually guaranteed Bolivian rights in their secret treaty and wished to avoid further involvement.[24] Peru's objections to the treaty were more general. Accusing the signatories of attempting to destroy Paraguayan sovereignty, it declared that "to make of Paraguay an American Poland would be a scandal which America could not witness without being covered with shame."[25] The Peruvian minister in Buenos Aires complemented his government's official protest by informing the Argentine foreign minister that "the treaty against Paraguay seems to demonstrate that the final aim of the war . . . is none other than the carrying out of overt attacks against the law of nations, which would at the same time be a threat to the continental equilibrium and an injury to the principles that constitute the public law of the American states."[26]

The Chilean government's initial reaction, in spite of inflamed public opinion, was cautious. Before Great Britain's violation of its confidence concerning the terms of the secret treaty, Chile had seen in the Paraguayan War no menace to the independence or territorial integrity of any American nation. Now Chile awoke to "the whole of the tragic extent to which that pact conspires against the sovereignty and independence of Paraguay"[27] and to the possibility that the "pact could injure the territorial rights of our ally, the Republic of Bolivia."[28] But practical Chile nevertheless felt that it must win the war against Spain before mounting a white charger to rescue Paraguay.

Spanish ships were taking on provisions in Platine ports. If Chile alienated Brazil, Argentina, and Uruguay by publicly and strongly supporting Paraguay, the war against Spain might be prolonged. And there did exist the slim possibility that the mediation offer of the quadruple alliance might be accepted by the members of the triple alliance. If so, the way would be paved for the Platine-Pacific entente sought by Santiago.[29] An official Chilean protest would of course strip Santiago of a mediator's requisite neutrality. But, with time, Chile's official taciturnity became both less necessary and more difficult to maintain. In August, 1866, and again in October, the Chilean minister in Buenos Aires emerged with little hope from conferences with the Argentine foreign minister on the proposed joint mediation; he was told on both occasions that no mediation would be accepted until the triple alliance had achieved the objectives of its no longer secret treaty.[30]

At the same time the issue of Spanish use of Platine ports became critical. In possession of specific and documented information, Santiago ordered an agent to Montevideo and Rio de Janeiro with instructions to protest Spanish refueling and reprovisioning operations. Chile's protests were entirely unheeded,[31] and by November, 1866, Chile found it impossible to hold its official tongue. The Foreign Minister informed Congress that "there are stipulations [in the treaty of the triple alliance] that deeply wound the sovereignty and the independence of an American republic. The government of Peru was quick to protest such stipulations, and if we did not from the first explicitly adhere to its just and well-founded protest, it was only in consideration of the pending offer of mediation."[32]

In the months that followed, the embittered relations between Chile and the members of the triple alliance continued. Protest after protest against Spanish use of Atlantic ports went unanswered, as did Santiago's request that Argentina officially dissociate itself from a "scandalous and hostile" anti-Chilean article published in a semiofficial newspaper.[33] In June, 1867, the President of Chile told Congress that attempted mediation in the Paraguayan War had failed because Argentina had refused, "after long delays," to accept Chile's offer. He further asserted that prolongation of the Paraguayan War "alarms vital interests common to the nationalities of our continent." He then denounced Brazil and Uruguay for having "converted ... the ports of Montevideo and Rio de Janeiro into military bases" for Spain.[34] A month later the Foreign Minister informed Congress that Brazil and Argentina had protested the President's remarks, but added that their protests "have not succeeded in modifying our opinion concerning that lamentable conflict."[35] He also charged that Montevideo and Rio de Janeiro had been converted into "military bases for our enemy."[36]

These denunciations of Argentina, Uruguay, and Brazil marked the high point of Chilean resentment over the Paraguayan War and the reluctance of the Platine nations to coöperate with the west coast against Spain. But the danger of renewed Spanish hostilities seemed to be receding. Within a few months the war's active military phase appeared to be at an end. As the need for Platine assistance diminished, Chilean leaders turned their attention to matters closer to home.

SIGNIFICANCE OF THE EAST-WEST ENCOUNTER

The two concurrent wars, involving eight of South America's ten states and marking the end of the first half century of independence, were of the utmost significance in the evolution of South American power politics. The attention of Chile and of the other west coast countries was at last sharply focused upon the power politics of the Platine system. The eastern states were told that western interests should be important to them. The number and kind of diplomatic contacts between Pacific and Plata rose sharply. Landlocked Paraguay, once hidden from view behind its isolationist ramparts, had been exposed as part of the continent, and moreover as a part that concerned the entire continent. Above all, as their reactions to the terms of the 1865 secret treaty demonstrated, west coast leaders were now aware of the interdependence that had developed between the power politics of the Pacific Coast system and those of the Plata system. During the decade that followed the encounter of east and west in two wars, the awareness of the interrelatedness between Plata and Pacific increased, and the arena in which Chile sought to regulate the power structure advanced eastward, beyond the Andes.

Chapter VII

CONTINENTAL POWER POLITICS: BEGINNING OF A NEW ERA

Even during the war against the Peru-Bolivian Confederation, Chilean leaders had expressed their belief in the existence of a South American system of international relations; they had later included Brazil in their schemes for Latin American coöperation; they had pointed to the existence of special South American, as contrasted with pan–Latin-American or pan–Spanish American, interests; and they had made much of the need to maintain "the South American equilibrium." But, notwithstanding such professions, the Chilean government had shown limited practical political interest in the vast area that lay to the east of the Andes. The slowly maturing Argentine boundary question had not yet reached the peak of its first crisis. Platine power struggles, regarded with more curiosity than concern, were not thought to affect vital Chilean interests. Chilean actions designed to maintain a favorable power structure had in actual practice been restricted to the nations of the west coast.

In the 1870's, however, the policies and actions of the Chilean government came to reflect the genuine conviction that a power structure favorable to Chile required the balancing of power on a continental scale. The Pacific Coast, although still Chile's major sphere of interest, ceased to be the sole area in which Chilean leaders engaged in political action. Regular diplomatic activity was extended across the Andes and was intensified throughout the continent. There developed in Chile a consistently mounting concern for the totality of intra–South American affairs. In short, the 1870's witnessed the beginning of a profound change in Chilean policy, a change from a regional to a genuinely continental outlook.

The closing of the gap between continental ideals and continental policies was the result of an extremely complex concatenation of events which was to culminate in the integration into a single system of the previously separate Platine and Pacific regional systems of power politics. Chilean attitudes and policies played no small part in bringing about that integration. Chile's image of its role on the continent, together with the way in which its Argentine and Bolivian policies evolved, had a direct bearing upon the ultimate linking of the two systems. But of more fundamental significance in the creation of a continental system was the acceleration of basic existing economic and political forces. These forces, by building a series of interlocking interests among the continent's nations and intensifying competitive elements in intra–South American relations, contributed heavily to the fusion of the regional systems of power politics.

INTEGRATION OF SOUTH AMERICA INTO THE WORLD ECONOMY

The economic forces of which we speak were a part of the complex process of the integration of South America into the economy of the world.[1] The concrete manifestations of this process were the growth of trade between South America and the more developed nations of the Atlantic world; the investment of surplus European capital in South America; the introduction of more advanced European technology; and migration to South America from the United States and Europe.

The process of economic integration was not a smooth and constantly advancing one. There was a spurt of activity in the 1820's when citizens of the great commercial powers sought to take advantage of the collapse of Spanish and Portuguese monopolies. In the 1830's and 1840's, however, a sharp decline had resulted from debt defaults, failure to perceive anticipated high returns on investments, and the falling into disorder of most South American states. But even during the period of foreign retrenchment, commercial activity had been maintained in some areas and had even slowly expanded in such a way as to have a direct bearing upon the continent's power politics. Thus the Platine system developed around rivalry for control of the several commercial routes provided by the Paraguay-Paraná–Plata river system; thus Chile's determination to make Valparaíso an entrepôt for Pacific commerce played a major part in the formation of a Pacific Coast system of power politics. Nevertheless, although commercial activity contributed to the development of regional systems, it did not forge lasting links between the separate regional systems so as to form a continental system.

In the 1850's, however, at first slowly and then with increasing momentum, both extra– and intra–South American factors began to work toward the continent's integration into the world economy. Several nations besides Chile succeeded in establishing domestic situations favorable to such participation. Peru moved toward somewhat greater internal order under the tutelage of Castilla. Brazil entered a period of political stability and progressive leadership. In Argentina, elements anxious to expand economic relations with the outside world participated in the overthrow of antiforeign Rosas.[2] These developments coincided with the extension and intensification of the industrial revolution in Europe and the United States, and with the concomitant phenomena of population growth, urbanization, surplus capital formation, and growing rivalry for markets and sources of raw materials. Demand mounted for such South American products as rubber, nitrates, guano, tropical woods, quinine, wool, minerals, and foodstuffs. Immigrants came in increasing numbers to employ their technical and business skills in the exploitation of South America's resources. Foreign investors, regaining confidence, began to purchase government bonds and to finance mining ventures and public utilities.[3] Certain elements of advanced technology were introduced into South America.[4] It was in response to such developments that in the 1850's, the 1860's, and the 1870's South America's economic relations with the outside world sharply increased.

Of the many political consequences that these economic developments held for the South American states, among the more dramatic was the way in which changing economic considerations attracted attention to regions of the continent hitherto neglected. Disputed boundaries that lay near or within regions whose value, either in fact or in speculative fancy, was enhanced overnight by the continent's integration into the world economy became more significant. In the Atacama Desert, for example, competition within the Pacific Coast system was intensified. Rivalry between Chile and Bolivia increased when valuable guano deposits were discovered in the Atacama in the late 1850's. Twenty years later, when nitrates and silver were also found, the Chilean-Bolivian competition became even more intense, and Peru, itself a major nitrate producer, also turned its attention to the Atacama.

Another example of the impact of South America's changing economic position vis-à-vis the world was the Amazon Basin, where interlocking interests were created among nations of the Pacific and Platine systems. For centuries the basin had been considered not only of little economic value, but also potentially dangerous to civilized man because of its hostile aborigines and a climate believed to be unhealthful. The adjudication of its boundaries had therefore not been pressed. Beginning in the early 1850's, however, attention was drawn to the rubber resources of the Amazon by discovery of the process of vulcanizing rubber, by a rising demand for rubber products in the world market, and by the introduction of steam navigation on the long, tortuous interior river system of the Amazon Basin.[5] In the 1860's and the 1870's,[6] as world demand for rubber and other tropical products multiplied, the Amazon's unsettled boundary and navigation questions assumed ever-mounting importance to the nations that claimed rights in the area.

The fact that the Empire of Brazil possessed the lion's share of the vast Amazon Basin did not make solution of the problem easier. Bolivia, Peru, Ecuador, Colombia, and Venezuela all claimed territorial and navigation rights. Thus five non-Platine nations found themselves in conflict with the Platine system's largest power. Their prolonged, involved, and sometimes bellicose efforts to affirm their claimed rights led to a proliferation of contacts and developed a series of rivalries which forged constantly stronger links between the Platine and Pacific regional systems of power politics. Chile did not itself have claims to press in the Amazon, but its involvement in Pacific Coast politics gave it an important interest in the rising tide of international developments related to the Amazon Basin.

Although the introduction into South America of improved means of communication was a phase of its integration into the world economy, and as such exercised the impact that has been discussed above, those improved communications in themselves exerted an important influence upon the evolution of the continent's power politics. On the domestic level the railroad, the telegraph, and steam navigation accelerated economic productivity and strengthened national unity and governmental efficiency. On the international level they hastened the integration of regional systems of power politics, a process that had already begun. Issues dividing Argentina and Chile were exacerbated when the Buenos Aires–Santiago telegraph service was inaugurated in 1872; the completion three years later of a cable between Peru and Chile similarly heightened conflicts pending between Lima and Santiago. Steam and rail and cable all served to bring the peoples of South America into more frequent and often more abrasive contact, and to force upon them the necessity of taking into account the actions and the opinions of nations in all parts of the continent.

DIFFERENTIATION AMONG SOUTH AMERICAN NATIONS

Finally, the integration of the South American nations into the world economy helped to bring about a fundamental change in the power structure of the continent by contributing to the further differentiation of its nations into great and small powers. Nations possessing resources in world demand, or controlling strategically located ports and distribution facilities, or offering attractive conditions to foreign capital or immigration became more rapidly integrated into the world economy than others. These nations profited most from technological innovation, and attracted the largest amounts of foreign capital. Their foreign commerce and their government revenues also increased most rapidly. When these nations also possessed sizable territory and population, they became the great powers of South America in comparison with less fortunate states.[7] And as they expanded economically, the political horizons of their leaders also tended to expand.

The emerging great powers of South America were at first primarily concerned with regional affairs, but as they became more involved in worldwide economic affairs they adopted a more continental view. To support their widening interests, they came into possession of financial resources which enabled them to buy modern war matériel, and this ability further differentiated them from states whose less advantageous position was forcing them into the classification of small South American powers. Chile had gained the peak of the Pacific power pyramid as a result of its victory over the Peru-Bolivian Confederation, its continued internal order, and its national unity, together with its advantageous commercial location and its possession of valued minerals and metals. A decade later Peru found itself a great power partly as a result of increased domestic stability, but largely because of the tremendous wealth that was pouring into its coffers from sales of guano. By the late 1840's Brazil had achieved a significant degree of internal stability, and commenced to move forward to become the third South American great power.

Brazil, Peru, and Chile had been concerned, well into the 1860's, primarily with the power politics of their respective regional systems. But all of them had given prelusive demonstrations of a more continental view. Chile and Peru had been stirred to continental considerations by the tragic events of the Paraguayan War. And in 1867 the Foreign Minister of Brazil suggested to parliament that the empire needed "a diplomatic agent in each of the republics of South America."[8] It was, however, the emergence of a fourth South American great power which served to impel integration of the Platine and Pacific Coast systems of power politics and which opened the "Age of Continental Power Politics" in South America. That fourth power, Argentina, began its climb to greatness in the 1860's and 1870's.

THE RISE OF ARGENTINA

In 1862, after half a century of political anarchy, the provinces of Argentina succeeded in establishing a single national government. But Buenos Aires and the interior provinces did not immediately begin to live together happily. Yet the fact that union had been achieved did satisfy a long-frustrated yearning, freeing Argentine energies for action in other areas. In its international relations Argentina proceeded to define its national interests with increasing exactitude, and to promote and defend those interests with greater efficiency.

As if the formation of a national government had been the starting signal for which they had been waiting, the population and the wealth of Argentina promptly raced forward. Between 1864 and 1880 foreign trade climbed 128 per cent.[9] Between 1860 and 1876, £12 million in government bonds were successfully floated in London.[10] By 1880 British interests alone had invested approximately £20 million in Argentina, about one-third of it in railroads.[11] The 39 kilometers of railroad track in 1860 had mushroomed two decades later into a formidable 2,516 kilometers. By 1874, 3,100 miles of telegraph line were serving the nation. And between 1864 and 1880 government revenues rose almost 180 per cent. Argentina's growth in population and immigration was even more dramatic. In the six years following 1868 approximately 280,000 Europeans, a number representing one-eighth of the nation's total population at the time, settled in Argentina. Between 1864 and 1880 the population climbed from approximately 1,500,000 to 2,500,000![12]

Because the energies of the new Argentina were at first directed toward the long Paraguayan War, it was not until the 1870's that the impact of South America's emerging fourth great power was felt in the broader continental sphere. Then, as Argentine wealth and population proliferated, Buenos Aires became increasingly interested in the exploration, exploitation, and settlement of more remote regions, including Patagonia and the Strait of Magellan, where hitherto minor boundary disputes with Chile were to assume increasingly acrimonious overtones and eventually lead to the threat of war.

Chile, taking a careful, if belated, look at the trans-Andine landscape, finally realized that the once weak and warring Argentine provinces were rapidly being transformed into a national power which Chile could ignore only at its own peril. The stage had been set for a bitter rivalry which would inextricably entangle Platine and Pacific interests, for the time had long since passed when either Argentina or Chile could regard their boundary dispute as merely a bilateral question. Both had become so deeply enmeshed in regional rivalries whose manipulation was proving more and more difficult that no change in the boundary dispute failed to have its effect upon regional political position. In turn, every alteration in the regional situation directly affected the status of the boundary dispute. For example, every time Argentina faced a crisis in its relations with Brazil it was forced to soften its stand on its Chilean boundary problem, and Chile, of course, exploited its advantage to the fullest extent possible. In short, in the South America of the 1870's, the narrowly regional viewpoint was becoming obsolete and lacking in viability. The emerging great powers, to promote and protect their vital interests, were forced to assume an increasingly continental approach. As they did so, a South American continental balance of power system came into being.

The alterations that occurred in South America's power structure after the Peru-Bolivian war had created formidable difficulties for Chilean statesmen. Chile was no longer the only strong and stable state in the system that encompassed its immediate and vital concerns. Moreover, its immediate system had been enlarged by the uninvited membership of a new and challenging Argentina. And Argentine membership in the system was forcing Chile to expand its vital interests into the Plata region at the obvious risk of diluting the force it could exert in the direction of Peru and Bolivia. A threat of this kind to the power position of any major state would, under the best of circumstances, have produced tension in South American international relations. But in the 1870's such tension was heightened by changes that had occurred in the governmental structure and the national self-image of Chile.

THE CHILEAN SELF-IMAGE, 1830–1879

Chile's national self-image underwent a significant transformation during the three decades that followed the Peru-Bolivian war. Historical hindsight enables us to discern the considerable strengths with which Chileans were endowed at the opening of their national period. But at the time Chileans themselves did not believe that they were particularly superior to other nationalities of the continent. Even the archnationalist Diego Portales was able to write of the "greater intelligence of [Peru's] public men" and of "Lima's larger number of cultured white people." As Portales was himself perhaps the continent's ablest public man of the times, as Chilean intellectual ferment was even then producing a cultural flowering of great merit, and as Portales wrote with complete sincerity, we may conclude that he did not believe Chileans to be superior to other South Americans.

Chile's victory over the Peru-Bolivian Confederation brought a flush of self-confidence to the nation, enhanced its nationalistic tendencies, and initiated a process of change in the Chilean self-image. It was in the three decades following Yungay, however, rather than in the fact of Yungay itself, that Chile's view of itself was to undergo the profound change that was to have so decided an influence upon its foreign policies of the 1870's. During that long period Chileans became aware of the extraordinary contrast between their own law and order and the chaotic turbulence of their neighbors. The more the Chileans learned about others, the more convinced they became that they were unique among Spanish American peoples in being able properly to govern themselves and to make orderly social and material progress.

Viewing with dismay the deplorable conditions in other states, and unable to understand the precise cause of those conditions, Chileans came to the conclusion that it was their own special personal virtues that had given rise to their greatness and stability. They came to see themselves as more intelligent, thrifty, modest, honest, capable, industrious, reliable, and virtuous than other Spanish American peoples, whom their spokesmen described with contempt as disorganized, prideful, lazy, disorderly, dishonest, and untrustworthy. In 1853 diplomat Victorino Garrido wrote from Peru: "When I compare our nation . . . with other American countries, I confess . . . frankly that I must make great efforts to repress the pride that is the natural result of contemplating the immense material benefits we enjoy, benefits that other peoples, including Peru, are unlikely to acquire."[13] Several years later Vicente Pérez Rosales informed the public of Europe that "in Spanish America Chile is the only refuge of peace, order, and progress."[14] Still later, future President Domingo Santa María wrote from Panama that "along the entire coast, as far as Cape Horn, Chile stands alone. In other lands you find but the remains of past vigor and the deep footprints of Spanish power fallen into ruins, which time respects in spite of men, I know not whether to shame or to glorify the name of Spaniard. . . . I am leaving Panama, for I do not wish to touch a corpse by its feet."[15]

Chile's growing sense of superiority over other Spanish American peoples, together with the reality of its power position, imparted a self-assured and markedly self-righteous tone to its relations with less fortunate states. By the 1870's, as positivism became the philosophical vogue in Chile, Chilean leaders had become firmly convinced that their country's long history of orderly progress entitled it to a position of leadership.

The Chilean self-image of the 1870's reflects the way in which such images tend to lag behind reality. For if in the 1830's Chile was more powerful than it believed itself to be, by 1870 it was less so. Chile's immutable belief in its mission of predominance heightened the tensions in a continental power structure that was straining itself to accommodate the rising pretensions of Peru and Argentina.

A Stronger Legislature

A notable evolution in Chile's governmental structure constituted the second additional source of tension in its international relations in the 1870's. In the previous decade Chile departed from its traditional pattern of a strong, virtually autocratic presidency and began to operate under a system that granted significantly increased powers to the legislature. Well-defined political parties began to press their divergent views upon the executive branch and to seek the support of a larger electorate. The Chilean leadership elite had to be more responsive to Congress, and had to defend its policies in a broader public arena. Foreign policy was more openly debated in and out of Congress. The debates produced heated and often intemperate expressions of opinion, expressions that the government found it difficult to ignore. It was inevitable that Chile's new political atmosphere would complicate the solution of the foreign problems that the nation was to face in the 1870's.

Relaxation of European Pressures

We have been reviewing here, in broad outline, the factors that lay behind the increasing tendency of regional South American systems to become fused into a continental system of power politics, together with elements contributing to the heightened tension in South American intrarelations during the 1870's. But before examining the concrete manifestations of these general tendencies, we must consider an additional factor, the element that permitted the South American states to act out their continental rivalries with a minimum of hindrance or influence from extracontinental sources.

It is an interesting circumstance that, as the nineteenth century passed its mid-point and as European capital, technology, and immigration found their way into certain parts of the South American continent, the political pressures of Europe within those regions declined. The more advanced nations were living up to their commitments in a generally satisfactory manner. They were protecting foreign nationals and business interests more effectively than before. A significant proportion of non–South American enterprise, and many influential non–South American individuals, had come to identify themselves closely with the national interests of their new residence, no longer looking to their countries of origin for protection.

Furthermore, several nations made it very clear that they were ready, willing, and able to resist European intervention. In the 1840's

Argentina stood off a combined British and French intervention. By the 1860's Brazil had shaken off the Britsh political influence that had been a codicil to its Portuguese inheritance.[16] In the 1860's Chile declared war against Spain in the face of Pareja's unreasonable demands, and secured the help of other west coast states in driving the powerful Spanish fleet from the Pacific. Far to the north the French had failed to extinguish Mexican nationalism and the United States, once more united after its Civil War had strengthened its resolve to oppose European meddling in the Western Hemisphere.

Finally, Europe itself was experiencing a sharp upsurge of activity in the field of power politics. Germany had been unified. France had been defeated. And the nations of Europe found themselves committed not only to the intensified rivalries on their own continent but to a sharp competition engendered by the new imperialism in Africa and the Orient. The European powers watched one another to guard against a rival's achievement of greater political influence in the New World, but they were too enmeshed in other spheres to be greatly concerned about the affairs of South America. The relaxation of European pressures removed what would have otherwise constituted a formidable barrier to South America's concentration upon its own intrarelationships. That easing was taking place as dynamic forces were bringing the South American nations closer together and intensifying the competitive elements in their relations with one another. The South American nations began to play politics on a continental scale.

Reflecting the operation of the forces discussed above, the diplomacy of the Pacific nations in general and of Chile in particular moved gradually from coöperation in the quadruple alliance against Spain to a conflict of major proportions. The war that overtook the Pacific in 1879 made clear the degree to which the continent of South America had come to constitute a single system of power politics.

CHAPTER VIII

FROM COÖPERATION TO CONFLICT: CONTINENTAL CROSSCURRENTS

IN 1864 the Pacific Coast system had swept its conflicts under the rug and attempted to put its best coöperative foot forward in meeting its uninvited visitors from Spain. But even at the height of the Spanish fleet's depradations the disputes among the west coast states had never been out of mind, and with the passing of the active phase of the war against Spain they began to reassert themselves with increased vigor. Chile and Peru resumed their contest for hegemony on the west coast. Bolivia and Chile renewed their Atacama Desert disagreements, for their treaty of 1866 had in fact raised more questions than it had solved. And now the resolution of these and lesser conflicts was to be complicated by the involvement of the Platine great powers in the diplomacy of the Pacific.

NAVAL POLICY

During the war against Spain, Peru was displeased by the selection of a Chilean naval officer as commander of the joint fleet while it was operating in Chilean waters, for Peru's vessels outnumbered those of Chile.[1] In turn, Chile resented what it considered Peru's insufficient appreciation of the Chilean war effort.[2] But it was the question of naval power which most clearly illustrated the persistence of the strong rivalry between Chile and Peru, even while the two countries were allies in a war against Spain.

The naval disparity between Chile and Peru increased during the course of the war. Chile, prevented by British neutrality laws from taking delivery of the two modern corvettes it had ordered, was able slightly to better its position through the capture of two small Spanish units and the purchase of certain miscellaneous ships. In contrast, Peru had secured delivery of two extremely powerful ironclads which departed Great Britain before news of Peru's declaration of war against Spain had reached London. Those ships, the *Huáscar* and the *Independencia,* were superior in every respect to any vessel in the Chilean navy.

The Spanish threat already seemed to be on the wane when a reputedly anti-Chilean revolutionary movement succeeded in overthrowing the Peruvian government. Betraying its inner conviction that Peru was more dangerous than Spain,[3] the Chilean government resolved to

improve its naval position as quickly and as substantially as possible.
For that purpose it initiated negotiations with Spain in London in
order to reach an agreement that might secure the British lifting of
neutrality regulations. These regulations were applied to ships of both
countries which had been completed in British shipyards and were
now standing idle pending the war's end. Spanish and Chilean agents
in London had reached an understanding approved by the British government when the Peruvian agent there issued an official protest and
secured a delay in the release of both the Chilean and the Spanish ships.[4]

The Chilean foreign minister responded by accusing Peru of "ill-
concealed hostility,"[5] while the Peruvians in their turn were indignant
at Chile's "disloyalty" to their country. They insisted that, because
the Spanish ships were stronger than the Chilean ships, the London
agreement would strengthen the Spanish position in future peace negotiations, and that Chile was more interested in strengthening its forces
vis-à-vis Peru than in preparing for a possible encounter with Spain.[6]
The Peruvians were correct. After Chile had forced Lima to withdraw
its objection to release of the corvettes, the Chilean minister of war
and navy, strongly attacked by the opposition for dealing with the
enemy, was forced to confess the government's true purpose. In doing
so he reminded the Chamber of Deputies that it "must not lose sight
of the fact that Chile's honor and its interests demand that it be represented upon the seas in a manner befitting its past history. It must not
continue to play the fool, supporting only four insignificant ships in
the Pacific. . . . Chile possesses the legitimate right to expect that its
flag—the most glorious flag of the republics of Spanish origin—will
figure nobly in the Pacific, maintaining forever the country's superiority."[7]

The delivery of the two corvettes did not give Chile its desired naval
predominance, for Peru, already possessing the *Huáscar* and the *Independencia,* soon matched Chile's new corvettes with two of its own.
The agreement between Santiago and Madrid did, however, make it
clear that the fleeting period of coöperation between Chile and Peru
had ended amid renewal of fundamental rivalries. During the next
few years those rivalries became increasingly bitter as Chile attempted
to challenge Peruvian naval supremacy and as Chile and Bolivia revived
an angry dispute over boundary differences supposedly laid to rest
in 1866.

RELATIONS WITH BOLIVIA

The treaty of 1866, signed by Bolivia and Chile in a moment of anti-
Spanish solidarity, designated their boundary in the Atacama Desert

as the 24th parallel. It gave to Chile, however, virtual condominium with Bolivia over the territory between the 23d and 24th parallels, the region possessing the Atacama's most valuable known resources. Under the condominium provisions Chilean business enterprise was assured equal rights with that of Bolivia, and the Chilean government was guaranteed half of any tax revenues realized from the production and sale of mineral resources. The efficient and aggressive business interests of Chile quickly began to exploit the region, pouring into it quantities of capital, technical and managerial skill, and hard-working labor. They created in the Atacama Desert a mining-industrial complex vastly superior to anything the Bolivians could achieve.

Differences soon arose over interpretation of the 1866 treaty. Because the document failed to specify by name the individual items from which Chile was to derive 50 per cent of the fiscal revenues, Bolivia sought to restrict the number of such items, with the predictable acrimonious consequences. Another difference concerned Bolivia's contention that Caracoles, an immensely valuable Chilean-discovered silver region, did not lie within the zone of condominium.[8] But during the five years immediately following the treaty's signing Santiago managed to uphold its claims. The Bolivian government, habitually on the brink of total impoverishment, watched the profitable activities of Chileans with envy and distrust, but while Mariano Melgarejo, with whom the treaty had been negotiated, ruled Bolivia, Chile's large and growing interests in the coastal desert between the 23d and 24th parallels were never seriously threatened.

In 1871, when Melgarejo was forcibly ejected from office, the Atacama question became critical. In March Chile sent a new chargé to the Altiplano to settle treaty differences that had arisen during the preceding regime.[9] The new chargé, though failing to reach an understanding on any major item in his instructions, was not discouraged, for it seemed to him that Bolivia's political chaos would prevent rapid progress in any event.[10]

THE BUSTILLO MISSION TO CHILE

Notwithstanding the hopefulness of the Chilean chargé, a substantial change in the Altiplano's policy was already in the making. In April the new government accredited to Chile Rafael Bustillo, who as foreign minister in the late 1850's had strongly opposed Chilean claims in the Atacama. Bustillo's instructions included revision of the 1866 treaty and abolition of its condominium aspects.[11] Although the new Bolivian envoy sought to conceal his full purpose, within a few months the Congress of Bolivia took action which left his intentions in no doubt. It declared null and void all the acts of the "usurping Melgarejo regime," making it clear that the treaty of 1866, and with it extremely powerful Chilean financial interests, were separated from dire peril only by the implementational action of the Bolivian chief executive.[12]

ERRÁZURIZ ADMINISTRATION

On September 18, 1871, while Bolivia was moving openly to challenge Chilean rights and interests in the Atacama, a new administration under Federico Errázuriz Zañartu was inaugurated in Santiago. The new president showed himself to be more forceful than his predecessor in the management of Chile's foreign relations. The new Council of State, at its first meeting early in October, reached decisions in two matters of exceptional importance in the realm of foreign affairs. Within a few months these decisions were enacted into law by the legislature. First, the administration of foreign affairs was radically reorganized. The Foreign Department was removed from the Ministry of Interior and transformed into the Ministerio de Relaciones Exteriores y Colonización, headed by a minister with full cabinet status. Second, the navy was substantially increased in size.[13] Congress authorized the President to borrow the funds necessary to purchase two of the new ironclads that seemed destined to revolutionize naval warfare,[14] and also a steamship to be used in patrolling the Strait of Magellan. Clearly Chile's new administration was embarking upon a positive program of international relations.

The fact that not only Peru[15] but Argentina as well promptly reacted to news of Chile's naval purchase plans shows the extent to which a new international order was emerging in South America. Within a few days of the congressional authorization, Argentina's minister in Santiago requested an explanation, asking particularly if Chile sought by naval expansion to influence the outcome of the boundary question. The Chilean foreign minister reassured the Argentine minister to the contrary,[16] but in writing to his minister in Paris, who was to arrange for purchase of the ironclads, he made it obvious that Chile saw a direct relationship between its naval power and its diplomatic success. "Our gain or loss of many millions," he warned, "and many leagues of territory may depend upon your greater or lesser diligence."[17]

But the new Chilean administration did not await naval improvement to press for settlement of urgent international problems. On February 7, 1872, provisional proposals were presented to Argentina which it was hoped would lead to settlement of the boundary question.[18] These proposals initiated a long and increasingly bitter exchange of views between Buenos Aires and Santiago. Of more immediate concern to the new administration, however, was the Bolivian question. It now appeared that Bolivia was determined to secure annulment of the treaty of 1866 and was looking for support among the other west coast republics in the event of open conflict with Chile.[19]

Chile prepared to deal with Bolivia through direct negotiations and to secure Brazilian support of its position. The latter move was based upon the common interest of Rio de Janeiro and Santiago in insisting upon Bolivian adherence to the commitments of the previous administration, for in 1867 Brazil had secured a highly favorable boundary treaty, now threatened by annulment. Chile's minister in Buenos Aires was sent to Rio de Janeiro to learn from the Brazilian government "how far it would go . . . to defend with us the clear principles of international law which legalize both treaties."[20] Chilean leadership, beginning to think in terms of the emerging new international order, was turning to a Platine state for support, this time not against Spain but against a potential enemy on its own coast.

THE LINDSAY MISSION TO BOLIVIA

On April 2, 1872, Chile ordered Santiago Lindsay to La Paz for direct negotiations. Lindsay was to seek complementary agreements guaranteeing Chile's rights under the treaty of 1866. He was further to obtain the inclusion of the Caracoles silver mines within the area of condominium and to secure acceptance of nitrates as one of the "mineral products" from which Chile received a share in tax revenues. Lindsay was also to insist upon conditions that would in effect grant Chile a degree of joint sovereignty over the littoral between the 23d and 24th parallels, for he was instructed to obtain Chilean participation in the determination of tax rates and appointment of customs inspectors. Moreover, it appears that Lindsay was empowered to settle the entire dispute, once and for all, by outright purchase of the area, if Bolivia agreed.[21]

Chile did not expect quick results, for it realized that its own interests and those of Bolivia were extremely far apart. And, in fact, from the very first Lindsay encountered difficulties so serious that Santiago concluded that Bolivia would reject any agreement specifying the condominium features of 1866. By mid-June, 1872, the Chilean government was convinced that the Bolivian question "has reached a genuinely critical situation which cannot be prolonged."[22] And yet the moment

was not propitious for direct action. Relations with Argentina were
strained, and Peru might go to Bolivia's assistance. Lindsay was therefore instructed, with fervent appeals to his patriotism and persistence,
to make every possible effort to reach a satisfactory understanding with
Bolivia.

THE PAQUETE DE LOS VILOS AFFAIR

While Lindsay was struggling to carry out his instructions, an incident
occurred on the coast which threatened to make his mission even more
difficult. Following a respected tradition, Bolivian exiles had been con-
spiring to return to the Altiplano and overthrow the government in
power. In July, 1872, a small expedition left Valparaíso aboard the
Paquete de los Vilos and seized the port of Antofagasta, only to be
promptly ousted by forces of the Bolivian government. Members of
the expedition took refuge aboard the Chilean warship *Esmeralda,* then
at anchor in the harbor. On August 27 the Bolivian chargé d'affaires,
Bustillo, protested, accusing Chile of complicity and of planning to
seize the Bolivian littoral for itself. Chile rejected Bustillo's charges
and demanded a retraction. When the chargé refused, Chile demanded
his recall.[23]

Foreign Minister Ibáñez, fearing an unfavorable Peruvian reaction
to the affair, instructed his minister in Peru to inform that government
of the "true" facts of the case.[24] And Peru was indeed very disturbed.
Already troubled by Chile's plan to acquire two ironclads and by the
deterioration in Chilean-Bolivian relations, Peru felt that what had
happened at Antofagasta might threaten its own interests. On August
29, 1872, the Peruvian foreign minister directed his Santiago envoy
to inform Chile that "Peru ... cannot be indifferent to the occupation
of Bolivian territory by foreign forces."[25] Peru also put on a show of
strength, maneuvering the *Huáscar* and the *Chalaco* off the Bay of
Mejillones, and at the same time ordered its agent in Bolivia to work
for an amicable settlement between Chile and the Altiplano.[26]

Nothing came of those efforts, nor of the attempts of Lindsay, the
Chilean minister, to obtain guarantees for his nation's interests from
the Bolivian government. The Altiplano steadfastly resisted Chile's
demands and, as reports to Lima from its agent indicated, relations
between La Paz and Santiago were going from bad to worse. The Bolivian minister to Peru agreed that matters were deteriorating, and
expressed fear that Chile might seize some portion of the Bolivian
littoral in order to force the Altiplano's settlement of the dispute. The
Peruvian and Bolivian governments, now regarding the Chilean question as one of utmost seriousness, acted quite separately to lay the

groundwork for coöperation against Chile. On November 8, 1872, the Bolivian legislature authorized negotiation of a defensive alliance with Peru.[27] Eleven days later the Peruvian cabinet, unaware of the Bolivian move, discussed the Chilean situation and agreed that "the Peruvian government will support that of Bolivia in rejecting Chilean demands which it considers unjust and threatening to the independence of Bolivia."[28] Were Chile to attempt seizure of the Bolivian littoral "Peru could not remain an indifferent spectator, and would feel itself obliged to support Bolivia in protecting interests that would be common to us, as we could not permit Chile, by breaking the American equilibrium, to gain ownership of a littoral that does not belong to it. Peru would at once offer its mediation, and, if Chile rejected it and the attempted occupation of that littoral thereby continued, alliance with Bolivia would be for us the necessary and inevitable consequence."[29] What the Peruvian government seems to have wanted by way of settlement was an agreement that would leave the littoral under Bolivian control. Moreover, Peru was eager to solve the question before arrival in Chile of the two new ironclads, for, as the Peruvian foreign minister put it, in "the definitive resolution of this question, the influence that today we exercise by virtue of our naval preponderance may be of weight."[30]

THE LINDSAY-CORRAL AGREEMENT OF 1872

As impossible as an agreement had seemed earlier, on December 5, 1872, after a new Bolivian administration more sympathetic to Chile than the preceding one had seized power, Bolivia and Chile signed in La Paz a treaty presumably ending the littoral dispute. The Lindsay-Corral agreement granted Chile the right to name customs officers who would coöperate with those of Bolivia in the zone of condominium, stipulated that no unilateral alterations could be made in tax rates, and affirmed Bolivian acceptance of nitrates and borax as products falling within the terms of the treaty of 1866. Chile claimed that it had gained no enlargement of its rights and that the agreement merely clarified the treaty of 1866. Bolivia disagreed, regarding the 1872 agreement as an extension of Chilean influence in its littoral; indeed, opposition to the document arose in the Bolivian National Assembly.[31] Peru also considered the Lindsay-Corral agreement an enlargement of Chilean influence and advised Bolivia to reject it. Peru further suggested that if rejection of the Lindsay-Corral agreement resulted in a break with Chile, La Paz should seek the mediation of Argentina or Peru. And, to provide Bolivia with full assurances, Peru acceded to its request for a formal alliance.[32]

THE SECRET TREATY BETWEEN PERU AND BOLIVIA

On February 6, 1873, Peru and Bolivia secretly agreed to guarantee each other's independence, sovereignty, and territorial integrity. Joint action would ensue when one of the allies was threatened with loss of any part of its territory, with the imposition of a protectorate, or with the imposition of any condition restrictive of sovereignty or independence. Each party to the secret treaty retained the right to decide for itself whether or not a specific act demanded action under the agreement's terms. If cause was seen to exist, peaceful measures would be tried first; if they failed, Peru and Bolivia would together declare war on the offending nation. Although Chile was not specifically named in the treaty, the negotiators clearly had Chile in mind as the potential aggressor. Article X of the treaty revealed the negotiators' awareness of the international order that was emerging on the South American continent. Providing for the adherence of other powers to the treaty, it opened the way for inclusion of a Platine state in an alliance of Pacific nations and took into account the rapidly worsening relations between Chile and Argentina.

THE ARGENTINE BOUNDARY QUESTION

By the 1870's the Chilean-Argentine boundary question concerned three distinct geographical areas: the fertile inter-Andine plateaus nesting between the eastern and western heights of the cordillera, Patagonia, and the Strait of Magellan and Tierra del Fuego. The combined extent of these virtually uninhabited and uncharted regions was about thrice that of the territory over which Chile then had undisputed jurisdiction, but it was less the size of the disputed areas than their strategic and productive capabilities that excited Chilean interest.

In 1872 the Foreign Minister wrote that "our present interests, as well as the future development of our industry, and even our position on the South American continent, are in large part dependent upon Chilean possessions and sovereignty over the Strait of Magellan, for it is now the route of most European commerce ... to the Pacific."[33] Control of the strait by an enemy power might endanger not only Chile's commercial position in time of peace, but its strategic military situation in time of war. Patagonia was potentially useful for agriculture and cattle raising and as living space for future population. But, as Chile's entrepreneurial energies and interest were centered in the Atacama Desert in the 1870's, Patagonia was viewed primarily as a prestige item and bargaining tool in connection with the rest of the disputed territory.³⁴ Argentina, also viewing Patagonia as an area where its expanding population might develop future great wealth, firmly insisted that Chile's boundary was the Andes and that Chile had no plausible claim to land east of the cordillera. Because of the nature of its trade and its geographical position, however, Argentina had less interest in controlling the Strait of Magellan than did Chile.

The boundary conflict between Argentina and Chile, though commencing before the South American wars of the 1860's, aroused little serious controversy until the 1870's. Then four developments operated to make it a matter of major concern to both governments. First, Argentina emerged from the Paraguayan War with a sharpened sense of national identity, and quickly moved toward greater political stability and economic progress. Optimistic and expansive, it renewed its interest in the southern regions of the continent, where it came into conflict with Chilean claims. Second, during precisely this period, Chile reached a policy decision forcefully to support the Patagonian claim. Third, the boundary dispute took on overtones of national pride and prestige among peoples who were in the process of becoming highly nationalistic. Fourth, the establishment of telegraphic communications between Buenos Aires and Santiago in 1872 fanned the flames of the argument by permitting the rapid exchange of charges and countercharges and informing the people in both countries, day by day and even hour by hour, of what was being said, written, and done about the boundary question on the other side of the mountains.

Late in 1870, having learned that Argentina was prepared to dispute Chilean control of the territory of Magellan, Santiago sent a minister to Buenos Aires to negotiate the boundary. The envoy's instructions forbade cession of actually occupied or legally possessed territory— what this territory comprised was not explained—but also stated that "it is the spirit and the character of your mission to obtain as much as possible, but the government of Chile does not in the least desire to make territorial acquisitions from which it would gain no positive advantage, any more than the Republic of Argentina would want to dispute the sovereignty of vast undeveloped territories over which it cannot establish effective jurisdiction."³⁵

Although these instructions did not indicate a disposition to make of Patagonia a major issue, by 1872 Adolfo Ibáñez, who attached great importance to Patagonia, had become Chile's foreign minister. He commenced negotiations in Santiago with the Argentine minister. The latter's initial proposal asked control of all Patagonia, the eastern mouth of the strait, and half of Tierra del Fuego. Ibáñez countered with an offer to relinquish half of Patagonia in return for the remainder of the disputed territory, suggesting the matter be turned over to arbitration in the event of Argentine rejection of the proposal. The Argentine minister, irritated, objected to arbitration on the ground that Chile had no right to Patagonia at all; he added that his country could not afford to provide Chile with the Atlantic outlet implicit in Chile's possession of the eastern mouth of the Strait of Magellan. Ensuing discussions became more bitter and in March, 1873, Ibáñez informed the Argentine minister that "My final word, sir, is that the government of Chile believes itself to have a right to all Patagonia and that, when the occasion arrives for proving it, will present the documents that support its right."[36]

PERU APPEALS TO BUENOS AIRES

Relations between Argentina and Chile were very tense when Lima confided to Manuel Yrigoyen the mission of securing Argentine adherence to the secret Peru-Bolivian alliance against Chile.[37] Conferring with the foreign minister of Argentina, Yrigoyen accused Chile of "showing a tendency to expand its territory to the north and south at the expense of its neighbors and of the South American equilibrium."[38] In spite of certain common Peruvian-Argentine fears and interests, upon which Yrigoyen astutely played, the foreign minister of Argentina had marked reservations about an anti-Chilean alliance. He dreaded above all the precipitation of a Chilean-Brazilian accord, and also objected to signing any treaty that included Bolivia until his country's dispute over boundaries with La Paz had been finally resolved. But the Peruvian agent was persistent, persuasive, and patient, and the Argentine government finally succumbed to his importunities and agreed to adhere to a secret anti-Chilean pact, pending settlement of its question with the Altiplano.

On September 25, 1873, a triple treaty of alliance against Chile was submitted to a special secret session of the Argentine Congress. Approval by the lower house was promptly secured, but, as a prolonged Senate debate seemed likely, it was decided to delay final action until May, 1874, when the senators would have reconvened after their vacations. No sooner had Congress gone into secret session than rumors concerning a secret treaty began to be heard. During the months of legislative recess those rumors reached many South American chancelleries, stirring up suspicions in an international atmosphere that was already very ill at ease.

ARGENTINE-BRAZILIAN RELATIONS

Brazil regarded any possible Argentine secret diplomacy very unfavorably. Buenos Aires and Rio de Janeiro may have been allies during the Paraguayan War, but that time was past. Even during the war mutual distrust had hampered military strategy. Afterward the suspicions had mounted to the point where disagreement over peace terms and division of the spoils was delaying completion of the joint peace treaty demanded by the original secret alliance of May 1, 1865.[39] In 1872 Brazil came to the brink of war with Argentina by signing a separate peace with Paraguay. Bloodshed was prevented only by the intervention of former President Mitre of Argentina, who rushed to Rio de Janeiro and succeeded in negotiating a preliminary agreement designed to lead to a final peace treaty between Paraguay and all the members of the triple alliance. Then Mitre set out for Asunción, site of the final peace conference, to represent Argentina in the negotiations.

In 1873, in the Asunción peace talks, a question again came to the fore which had been at issue prior to Brazil's signing of the separate peace with Paraguay—the extent of Argentine rights in the Chaco. Immediately after the crushing of López, Buenos Aires, notwithstanding a previous presidential proclamation that "victory gives no rights," ordered occupation of the Chaco up to the Pilcomayo River. There Argentina had halted, largely because of pressure from Brazil, but strong sectors of Argentine opinion demanded that Villa Occidental, beyond the Pilcomayo, be incorporated into Argentina. In the course of his hurried mission to Rio, ex-President Mitre accepted the Pilcomayo as the Paraguayan-Argentine boundary, and Buenos Aires had granted its approval. But in the midst of the final Asunción peace talks Buenos Aires changed its mind, ordering Mitre to insist upon Villa Occidental. Argentine armed forces invaded and occupied the area. Peace negotiations collapsed, and Argentina and Brazil were again on the point of an open break.

The maturing of a South American continental system was made plain by the fact that, in this crisis of its relations with Argentina, the Empire of Brazil turned to Chile for support. In response, the Chilean chancellery assured Rio that it could at least count upon its benevolent neutrality, and left the door open for more positive assistance by suggesting that the Brazilian and Chilean envoys in Buenos Aires "together study the situation that acts of the Argentine Republic appear to be creating for both countries."[40]

At the time of its approaches to Chile, however, the Brazilian government did not suspect the existence, much less the nature, of the secret
Peruvian-Argentine talks which led to the signing of an anti-Chilean
pact. When, for an unannounced reason, the Argentine Congress was
called into special secret session, Brazil assumed that it was on a matter
of Brazilian-Argentine relations. Perhaps, feared Rio, an anti-Brazilian
alliance on the part of the Spanish-speaking nations of South America
was being considered. So disturbed was the Empire that it asked Argentina formally to declare that the matter being secretly considered was
not potentially adverse to Brazilian interests. At the end of October,
1873, Brazil received those assurances. But by then rumors of the anti-
Chilean treaty had already reached the Brazilian chancellery which,
seeking to verify them, asked its minister in Peru to find out as much
as he could as quickly as possible, and to report back to his government
at once.[41]

BOLIVIA AND THE LINDSAY-CORRAL AGREEMENT

Meanwhile relations between Bolivia and Chile continued to deteriorate.
On May 19, 1873, the Bolivian National Assembly officially expressed
disapproval of the Lindsay-Corral agreement by delaying its consideration until the following year.[42] The Chilean agent in the Altiplano
reported that anti-Chilean sentiment had never been stronger, and that
Peru had supposedly offered Bolivia the use of its navy in the event
of war with Chile.[43] In the face of such diplomatic reverses and ani-
mosities, the Chilean agent in Bolivia believed that only a major shift
in Chilean policy could prevent further deterioration of relations. Santiago, grappling at the same time with the Argentine boundary dispute,
agreed. In August, 1873, new talks commenced in La Paz between
Bolivia and Chile.[44]

While the new Bolivian-Chilean talks were in progress, Santiago
first heard rumors of an Argentine alliance with Peru and Bolivia. Chile
did not at first take them seriously,[45] but as reports continued to pour
in from various capitals, and as the Bolivian negotiations dragged on
at a suspiciously slow pace, Santiago began to consider the possibility
that the rumors were true. In December, 1873, the foreign minister of
Chile wrote to the Chilean representative in France that "the lack of
punctiliousness on the part of the government of Bolivia, coinciding
with certain rumors of an alliance between it . . . and Peru, has made
us wonder whether or not it is one of the said alliance's aims to provoke
at all costs a conflict in order to prevent the departure of our ships from
the waters of the United Kingdom."[46] Once that possibility had pre-

sented itself, the government of Chile urged rapid completion of the ironclads and their prompt departure for Chile. At the same time Chile began to seek allies of its own.

On January 21, 1874, Foreign Minister Ibáñez proposed an alliance to the Brazilian minister in Santiago.[47] But the Brazilian government knew how inferior Chile's naval position would be to that of an Argentine-Peruvian alliance, and that Chile could be of little help to Brazil if it should go to war with Argentina. Moreover, Brazil, fearing that the very signing of such an alliance with Chile would bring war upon it, instructed its minister to advise Chile that he was not authorized to negotiate an alliance. Brazil was nevertheless anxious to keep and strengthen Chile's friendship, and to assist the country when possible, short of formal alliance. Within a short time Brazil was able to prove its good intentions in a most dramatic maner.

BRAZILIAN-PERUVIAN RELATIONS

Rio de Janeiro had ordered its Lima envoy to investigate a rumored Peruvian-Bolivian-Argentine alliance, with special reference to any implications such an agreement might have for Brazil in its deteriorating relations with Buenos Aires. The Brazilian envoy encountered virtually no difficulty in fulfilling his instructions. Peru had by now come to attach great importance to the Amazon Basin. It wanted to develop trade with Brazil via that region; it sought to avoid any possible conflict there with Brazil; it desired Brazilian support in its Amazon conflicts with Ecuador and Colombia. Employing the discreet diplomatic representations customary on such occasions, the government of Peru not only assured the government of Brazil that the rumored treaty did not affect its interests in the slightest, but, in order to remove every last trace of doubt, showed the Brazilian envoy a copy of the secret treaty. The envoy carefully noted the contents of the pact and informed his government, which promptly passed along the information to the Brazilian minister in Santiago, who in turn wasted no time in arranging for a full confidential briefing for the foreign minister of Chile.[48] This gesture on the part of Brazil toward an extremely grateful Chile augmented existing mutual goodwill, buttressed by lack of conflicting interests. Within a few years the fund of goodwill would pay interest in the form of an important Chilean-Brazilian entente.

But Brazilian diplomacy had not yet finished its work in connection with the secret anti-Chilean alliance. Even while confiding the treaty's terms to Chile, Brazil was asking of Peru a condition that was to contribute to the ultimate frustration of the attempt to secure Argentina's adherence. Behind Brazil's further move was its fear that, Peruvian assurances notwithstanding, Argentine adherence might somehow come to involve Peru and Bolivia in a future conflict between Argentina and Brazil. Peru, for its part, began to see that a Chilean-Brazilian alliance might be all the more likely if Rio was confronted by a triple alliance of Peru, Bolivia, and Argentina. At the same time that Lima wished to avoid the strengthening of Chile, it wanted also to protect and nurture the community of interests which it was developing with Brazil in the Amazon region. In February, 1874, Peru and Brazil formalized their palpable community of interests in a convention (which Colombia was shortly to protest as a violation of her sovereignty) providing for the demarcation of their frontier in the Putomayo region.[49] At Brazil's request, therefore, in order to remove all possible cause of friction in future relations, Peru asked Bolivia and Argentina to approve an additional treaty clause specifically excluding Brazil as an object of the secret alliance.[50]

Peru's request aroused misgivings in both La Paz and Buenos Aires, for the former had an unsettled Amazon boundary with Brazil and the latter did not wish to tie its hands in the matter of the Chaco question and the unachieved final peace that would end the Paraguayan War. But after extended discussions which served to delay Argentina's adherence to the anti-Chilean treaty, Buenos Aires accepted the exclusion of Brazil. There was, however, still another matter to be settled before Argentina was willing to join the alliance—the question of its boundary dispute with the Altiplano. Buenos Aires had a minister in La Paz, but at the end of 1874 he was still inconclusively attempting to negotiate.

THE BOLIVIAN TREATY OF 1874

In the meantime Chile had managed to find a temporary solution to its major west coast problem, protection of Chilean interests in the Atacama Desert between the 23d and 24th parallels. In August, 1874, after a year of difficult negotiations, Bolivia and Chile signed a treaty replacing that of 1866. The 24th parallel was recognized as the boundary; except for retention of its claim to 50 per cent of the region's guano deposits, Chile relinquished its former rights of condominium. Although these provisions were distinctly favorable to Bolivia, Chile did secure an important twenty-five-year guarantee against any increase of taxes on either Chilean commercial interests or their exported products.[51]

The 1874 treaty relieved west coast international tensions and strengthened Chile's position by removing what had been a serious challenge to its power and its diplomacy. Within a short time Chile's position was further improved by two other developments. First, with the arrival of the ironclad *Valparaíso* in January, 1875, following the arrival of the *Cochrane* the month before, the Chilean navy attained at least equivalence with that of Peru. Second, it was becoming increasingly evident that Peruvian finances were in a less healthy state than they had appeared to be.

Peru, intoxicated by the seemingly inexhaustible supplies of wealth derived from exploitation of guano deposits, had begun to spend money like a drunken sailor. The government had been spending so much in excess of its income that by 1869 it was forced to begin borrowing in order to finance not only its ambitious program of railroad building, but also its routine expenditures. In floating gigantic European loans Peru had counted on income from the sale of guano to help service them. But the richest guano deposits were already being depleted, and those of lesser yield were substantially less profitable. At the same time nitrates were beginning to provide considerable competition to guano. As a result, in the mid-1870's the government of Peru unexpectedly found itself on the brink of bankruptcy. It remained in that unhappy state until 1879.

The relaxation of Pacific Coast tensions by no means eliminated the problems in Chile's relations with Peru and Bolivia. With regard to the former, in fact, new problems arose which bore a striking resemblance to those that had troubled the relations between Chile and Bolivia. The well-financed, efficient, and aggressive mining and industrial interests of Chile, not content to restrict their exploitation to the Bolivian littoral, had extended their operations into the Peruvian province of Tarapacá. By 1875 more than 10,000 Chilean workers, engineers, and managerial personnel and approximately 20 million Chilean pesos were hard at work in the nitrate fields of Peru's Tarapacá.[52] Minor clashes, some of which elicited the protests of the Chilean government, were frequent. In 1876 the Chilean foreign minister informed Congress that the many instances in Peru of anti-Chilean sentiment "may be interpreted as an expression of systematic hostility toward the [Chilean] nationality."[53] Nor did Peru's 1875 move toward establishment of a nitrate monopoly, threatening as it did the expropriation of private nitrate interests, serve to calm the ruffled sensibilities of Chileans.

In the wake of an 1876 revolution which brought a new government to power, the Altiplano also experienced a new upsurge of anti-Chilean feeling. Chilean nationals residing in the littoral were allegedly being

subjected to constantly increasing harassment by minor Bolivian officials.[54] But at this time the friction in Chile's relations with Peru and
Bolivia was not sufficient to upset the relative calm that prevailed on
the west coast after the Chilean-Bolivian treaty of 1874 and the addition to the Chilean navy of two fast new ironclad warships. From the
standpoint of Santiago the west coast calm was fortunate, for its relations with Buenos Aires were rapidly deteriorating.

CHILE AND ARGENTINA

An August, 1874, exchange of notes gave only a slight promise of ending the bitter boundary dispute between Chile and Argentina,[55] for
action based upon it was delayed first by a change of Argentine administration and then by sharp differences concerning implementation
of the arbitral procedures referred to in the notes. It seemed clear
to Santiago that Argentina's new government was far from eager to
settle the dispute. Not only was Buenos Aires delaying implementation
of the August notes, but it also protested Chile's construction of a new
lighthouse in the Strait of Magellan.[56] Since Buenos Aires appeared
at the same time to be working feverishly to settle its problems with
Brazil, Chile believed it was seeking to delay solution of the boundary
question until it was in a stronger diplomatic position. In June, 1875,
acting on that assumption, Chile sent its Argentine minister to Rio
de Janiero, reminding him that "Chile . . . cannot remain indifferent to
the conduct that the Argentine government seems disposed to observe,
and it is indispensable that we follow closely and attentively the course
of negotiations being carried on in the empire, attempting to extract
from them, if circumstances permit, some advantages favorable to our
interests."[57]

If Argentina's delaying tactics and approaches to Brazil irritated
Chile, deliberations of the Argentine Chamber of Deputies in June,
1875, aroused outright indignation in the Chilean government. The
lower house of the Argentine legislature, with the approval of the
chancellery, was considering a bill to establish maritime communications "between Buenos Aires, the colony of Chubut, and, necessarily,
the Patagonian coast south of the Santa Cruz River."[58] As preservation
of the status quo in the Santa Cruz region had been agreed to in the
August, 1874, exchange of notes, Chile immediately protested. Nevertheless, the legislation was passed, and the bill was signed by the
President of Argentina. Again Chile protested, asking Buenos Aires
if arbitration would not be preferable to bloodshed.[59] But while asking
for arbitration, Chile prepared for the possibility of war. On August 2,

1875, the Foreign Minister requested his chargé in Buenos Aires to keep him informed on Argentine preparedness, warning that "possible future developments ... make indispensable ... exact knowledge concerning the military force that Argentina now commands or may in the future command."[60]

As Chilean-Argentine relations worsened, Peru became increasingly uneasy. Its 1873 proposal for Argentina's adherence to the secret anti-Chilean treaty was still pending. Lima, suddenly anxious to avoid involvement in any war between Argentina and Chile, instructed its envoy to Buenos Aires to stop pressing for Argentine adherence to the alliance and to help solve the Argentine-Chilean boundary dispute.[61] Peru's good offices, however, were not required. In September, 1875, Argentina took a milder stand, agreeing to negotiate the boundary matter and even to submit the dispute to arbitration should negotiations prove unfruitful.[62] During the next nine months Chilean-Argentine boundary negotiations proceeded without satisfactory results; and while they were taking place the broader diplomatic situation of both countries became altered so as to change the nature of the negotiations.

The diplomatic position of Argentina improved as of February, 1876, with the signing of agreements by Argentina, Brazil, and Paraguay which in effect ended the Paraguayan War. Both the Brazilian and Argentine armies were to be withdrawn from Paraguay, and the Chaco question was to be submitted to United States arbitration.[63] Relations between Rio de Janeiro and Buenos Aires were thus placed on a better footing, but their traditional rivalry continued and their boundary dispute remained unresolved.

THE BARROS ARANA MISSION TO ARGENTINA

In April, 1875, Adolfo Ibáñez was replaced by a new foreign minister who was responsive to influences which considered Patagonia of less vital importance than had Ibáñez. The Chilean government, now willing to relinquish some of its more extreme claims to Patagonia,[64] moved to implement its modified boundary policy by accrediting to Buenos Aires a mission whose purpose was to obtain a direct settlement. Diego Barros Arana, a scholar and close personal friend of many Argentine aristocrats, was entrusted with the mission. Barros Arana himself considered Patagonia of less than vital importance, and his instructions revealed the government's intention of acquiring the Strait of Magellan with sufficient surrounding territory to ensure its adequate defense.[65] For nearly two years Barros Arana worked hard to fulfill his mission. Two obstacles, however, frustrated his efforts.

The first was an incident that took place while Barros was en route to Buenos Aires. The *Jeanne Amélie,* a French merchant vessel bearing an Argentine permit to collect guano off the shore of Patagonia, was seized by Chile on the charge of operating in Chilean territory without authorization. The rising hosts of Argentine nationalism, together with other more moderate elements, were greatly angered, so that from the very first Barros found the success of his mission in doubt. The second obstacle was Argentina's inability to accept the idea that Chile should have an outlet to the Atlantic Ocean. This attitude was decisive in preventing direct settlement of the boundary dispute. As control of the entire strait would give Chile such an outlet, no agreement could be reached without Chilean compromise. And, indeed, Barros finally exceeded his instructions and signed a treaty granting Chile only partial control of the strait. But the Chilean government disapproved both that treaty and an agreement that was signed to resolve the affair of the *Jeanne Amélie.* Finally, on May 17, 1878, the Chilean government recalled Barros Arana with the statement that future boundary negotiations might better be carried on in Santiago.[66]

In October, when public emotion was still high on both sides of the cordillera, relations between the two governments still strained to the utmost, and boundary negotiations still suspended, another Patagonian incident fanned the flames of Chilean-Argentine discord. A United States merchant ship, the *Devonshire,* whose Argentine license Chile refused to recognize, was seized off the coast of Patagonia, in the Atlantic Ocean, just north of the mouth of the Santa Cruz River. The Argentine public reacted violently to this act by the Chilean navy, and the government announced that it was sending a naval squadron south to the Santa Cruz River. Chile replied by ordering its navy, including the two new ironclads, to stand at the ready, and war seemed about to engulf Chile and Argentina.[67]

The Fierro-Sarratea Treaty

Neither government really wanted military confrontation, in spite of strong public pressure. New negotiations between the Chilean foreign minister and the Argentine consul in Santiago therefore resulted in the signing of the Fierro-Sarratea treaty on December 6, 1878. The agreement provided for an elaborate series of steps, culminating in arbitration, by which the ownership of disputed territory was to be determined. Pending final settlement, Chile was to "exercise jurisdiction over the waters and shores, canals, and adjacent islands of the Strait of Magellan," and Argentina was to do likewise with respect to "the waters, shores, and adjacent islands of the Atlantic."[68]

The Fierro-Sarratea treaty, as its provisions actually settled nothing at all, was primarily a demonstration of the desire to avert war. Within forty-eight hours of its signing, the agreement was submitted to the Chilean Congress. The upper house assented within twenty-four hours, but the lower house, more responsive to the passions and the pressures of press and public, was reluctant to renounce a violent solution to the Chilean-Argentine boundary dispute. The Chamber of Deputies was still debating the question in the second week of January, 1879, when news of a crisis in Chile's relations with Bolivia reached Santiago.

CHILE AND BOLIVIA

The new Bolivian crisis concerned the affairs of the Antofagasta Nitrate Company, a powerful industrial complex created in the early 1870's by the merger of several smaller Chilean companies. In 1873 the company's concessions had been confirmed and extended by a Bolivian government decree. The Bolivian National Assembly delayed its formal approval, but the company continued to operate without interference under the terms of the 1873 understanding.

In 1876, after a new government had seized power in La Paz, the company began to experience mounting difficulties: its operations met with harassment, and its personnel were molested. In February, 1878, the Bolivian National Assembly approved the 1873 decree with the important and material condition that the company must pay a higher export tax on its products than stipulated in the Chilean-Bolivian treaty of 1874. The government of Chile, supporting the company's position that any increase, however slight, in the export tax would damage its competitive position in respect to Peruvian nitrates, and would furthermore establish a lamentable precedent, seconded the company's strong protest and persuaded the Bolivian government not to implement the stipulation raising export taxes. But the law remained on the books.

Chile was still seeking clarification of the rights of the Antofagasta Nitrate Company from the Bolivian government when, in December, 1878, it was notified by the Altiplano that the February, 1878, law would henceforth be implemented. Notwithstanding Chile's protest that such a step would violate the treaty of 1874, Bolivia ordered the company to make payment of the larger tax for the entire year 1878. News of the demand reached Santiago during the debate in the lower house on the Fierro-Sarratea treaty with Argentina, and seems to have brought certain dissident deputies over to the government. On January 14, 1879, the treaty with Argentina was approved.[60]

Chile dealt with the new Bolivian crisis by suggesting first that the treaty dispute be submitted to arbitration, as stipulated in the agree-

ment of 1874. Bolivia refused, declaring that, unless the company
obeyed the tax decree by February 14, its properties would revert to
the state. The threat of expropriation without compensation elicited
from Chile a demand that Bolivia withdraw the decree and submit the
matter to arbitration. When Bolivia rejected this virtual ultimatum,
Chile declared that the treaty of 1874 had been voided and that she
would proceed to revindicate her rights to the territory between the
23d and 24th parallels. On February 14, 1879, the day set by La Paz
for expropriation of the Antofagasta Nitrate Company, Chilean soldiers disembarked from vessels of the Chilean navy, occupied the port
of Antofagasta, and commenced to extend Chilean control northward
to the 23d parallel.

Peru, altogether unprepared for war, viewed the crisis in Chilean-
Bolivian relations with profound distress. Its recent financial reverses
had led it to neglect its military establishment; yet its supposedly secret
alliance with Bolivia was very much in effect. Turning a deaf ear to
Bolivian demands that it rush to its ally's defense, Peru sent a minister
to Chile in March, 1879, with orders to attempt mediation. The Peruvian
minister had been in Chile but a short time when Bolivia formally declared war upon Chile. At this point the Chilean government, having
full knowledge of Peru's secret alliance with Bolivia, asked the envoy
from Lima to make a formal declaration of his nation's neutrality.
When the Peruvian would-be mediator was finally forced to admit that
his nation could not make such a declaration because it was secretly
an ally of Bolivia, the Chilean government charged the government
of Peru with unpardonable duplicity. On April 5, 1879, Chile declared
war upon both Bolivia and Peru.

RÉSUMÉ

South America diplomacy in the decade preceding the declaration of
the War of the Pacific, viewed from the Chilean standpoint, clearly
demonstrated the ushering in of a new era in intra–South American
relations. A basic change had taken place in the continent's power structure. Four great powers, each with sufficient stability and wealth to
play continental rather than purely regional roles, had come to the
fore. Under the impact of their integration into the world economy,
they had become rivals for influence over lesser states. At the same
time they had become loosely bound together by a network of interlocking interests.

As a result of the changed South American international structure,
the manipulation of the Pacific Coast system was no longer sufficient

to preserve Chile's freedom of action and to advance its vital interests. The attempts of great Platine and Pacific powers to form alliances and ententes on a diagonal and intersecting, as contrasted with a vertical and parallel, basis, together with the interplay between the crises in Chile's relations with Bolivia and Argentina, had demonstrated beyond a doubt that Chile must now think in terms of continental rather than regional power balancing.

CHAPTER IX

RECASTING THE SOUTH AMERICAN POWER STRUCTURE

CHILE'S MOTIVATION in its war effort of 1879–1883 is still a matter of controversy.[1] Chile's foes have charged that Chile chose an aggressive path long before 1879. They point to its Patagonian claim, its activities in the Atacama, and its naval policy as proof of militant tendencies and maintain that, at the time of its signing, the Peru-Bolivian secret alliance was purely defensive. Chile's critics agreed with the foreign minister of Peru that "the true cause . . . of the war . . . is to be found in [Chile's] unbounded ambition, in the vehement desire to gain control of the Bolivian littoral which contains great riches in guano, nitrates, and minerals."[2]

The Chilean position has been that until the very last minute Chile assumed a conciliatory posture toward Bolivia; that in 1866 it gave up territory to which it had title; and that in 1874 it relinquished rights provided in 1866. In exchange for these significant concessions Chile received in 1874 a guarantee that taxes on Chilean interests would not be altered for a period of twenty-five years, and that because Bolivia abrogated the pact of 1874, first by imposing a tax increase and then by refusing arbitration, Chile was amply justified in seeking to revindicate its territorial rights. Chile claimed that it had become "indispensable to establish, once and for all, that it is not legal for a nation systematically to frustrate and avoid the rigorous fulfillment of the treaties to which it has subscribed."[3]

Chile justified war against Peru on the basis of an alleged conspiracy to destroy Chilean nitrate operations and establish Peruvian predominance. It was claimed that since established Chilean interests and rights in the Bolivian littoral stood in the way of that scheme, Peru became secretly allied with Bolivia which it then encouraged to resist Chile's just demands. The extent of Peruvian treachery became evident when it sent to Santiago a mediator even as it prepared for war. In the face of Peru's refusal to declare its neutrality, Chile had no alternative to a declaration of war.

A detailed evaluation of the merits of these and other versions of war guilt in the Pacific conflagration of 1879–1883 is beyond the scope of this work. Several conclusions do present themselves, however, in connection with the circumstances and forces that affected Chile's decision to wage war and its formulation of war objectives. The most immediately obvious *casus belli* was the conflict of interests arising from one country's economic predominance on the soil of another. That inherently dangerous situation was in this instance aggravated by the Bolivian littoral's distance and isolation from the seat of government and the center of population. Communications between the Altiplano and the coast were poor, and control of the capital over the coast was limited. Bolivians came to entertain fears concerning ultimate Chilean political domination of the littoral. But fearful, impotent, poorly governed Bolivia could neither strengthen its economic and political position in the littoral nor develop an effective policy toward Chile. For their part Chileans came to regard the coastal desert as their own in all but name. Not only were Chilean economic interests predominant, but development of the littoral was due almost exclusively to Chilean capital, labor, and technology. The spasmodic efforts of frequently corrupt local Bolivian officials to carry out the often arbitrary orders of the Altiplano were met by Chileans with angry resentment.

This conflict-laden situation was further complicated by the injection of Peruvian diplomacy. Chilean activities in the Bolivian littoral assumed increasing importance to Peru as its own nitrate industry in Tarapacá, near the Bolivian border, expanded. Whether or not Peru sought an ironclad nitrate monopoly, Chile's activities in the Atacama Desert would have appeared ominous to Lima. Moreover, although the War of the Pacific was precipitated by a dispute with Bolivia, Chile viewed Peru as its major enemy. Peru was not only far more powerful than Bolivia and the possessor of significant naval strength, but it was also Chile's traditional rival for Pacific hegemony.

TERRITORIAL STATUS QUO AND THE EQUILIBRIUM

So strong were Chile's fear of and hostility toward Peru that shortly after the outbreak of war the Chilean government revised a fundamental tenet of its past foreign policy. From the 1830's Chile had operated on the assumption that an equilibrium of power among the South American states was essential to its own preëminence on the Pacific and to the advancement of its interests. Prior to 1865 Chile regarded the 1835 territorial status quo as indispensable to maintenance of the equilibrium. At the Lima congress, however, its position was modified to include possible voluntary unification of the three Colombian nations, because, from Chile's point of view, such unification could not threaten the equilibrium. Chile, however, still applied the doctrine of the 1835 status quo to the continent's other nations. Unification of Peru with either Ecuador or Bolivia was classified by

Chile as dangerous, and Paraguayan dismemberment was viewed with distrust.

But within a few days of the declaration of war, Chile had begun to convince itself that maintenance of the South American equilibrium might demand a radical alteration in territorial arrangement. On April 19, 1879, Chile's immediate war goals included, "in respect to Bolivia, to assure Chile the definitive possession and permanent domination of the territory lying between the 23d and 24th parallels; and, in respect to Peru, to obtain the total abrogation of the secret treaty of February, 1873, and assurances sufficient to avoid future repetition of the state of affairs which it has been and is creating with its insidious actions and its disloyal policy toward ... [Chile]."⁴ At the same time the Chilean government expressed the opinion that "although the extension of the Republic's territory with foreign acquisition has not entered into [the government's] considerations, ... that object might be sensibly modified by the course of events. Thus, a serious blow to the Peruvian navy, the separation of Bolivia from the alliance with Peru in order to place itself at our side ... , would be a reason for modifying the present aims of the government, perhaps placing it in the position of seeking, as a result of the war, alterations of Peru's boundaries which, completely assuring the Republic's tranquillity, might make it impossible for that nation to constitute a threat against the South American equilibrium."⁵ These views, expressed at a meeting of a coalition cabinet sworn in two weeks after the declaration of war, suggest that Chile was ready to consider abandonment of its 1835 position on the territorial status quo, that it regarded Peru as the primary enemy, and that it already had in mind the detachment of Bolivia from its Peruvian alliance.

THE BOLIVIAN PORT QUESTION

Chile hoped to detach Bolivia from Peru by exploiting the Altiplano's desperate need for an adequate seaport. After colonial Alto Peru was transformed into independent Bolivia, the Altiplano's commerce with the outside world had been largely carried on via the Peruvian port of Arica—a dependent relationship that had contributed to dreams of Peru-Bolivian confederation and to consequent political and military conflict. Although confederation was no longer a matter for serious consideration, Bolivia chafed under its dependence upon Peruvian goodwill for access to the sea. It was this aspect of the relations between Peru and Bolivia which Chile hoped to exploit in order to detach La Paz from Lima.

Chile planned to seek an alliance with Bolivia; its goal would be the conquest and incorporation into Bolivia of the Peruvian provinces of Tacna and Arica. In return for so bounteous a gift, Bolivia would recognize Chilean sovereignty over the littoral between the 23d and 24th parallels, already "revindicated," and over the coastal region north to the river Loa as well. Chile had not previously claimed the latter area.[6] In addition to its territorial aspects, such an alliance would add Bolivian manpower to the anti-Peruvian army, would establish Peru and Bolivia as enemies too bitter ever to combine against Chile, and would, by solving its seaport question, make Bolivia both a stronger nation and one friendly to Chile in the event of future trouble with Peru or Argentina, or both.

A POLICY OF PERUVIAN DISMEMBERMENT

During the war's early weeks Chile made several unsuccessful attempts to form a Bolivian alliance. Nevertheless, the idea of dismembering Peru for the purpose of providing Bolivia with an adequate seaport became fixed in Chilean thought and was to play a significant role in the manipulation of South American power politics well into the twentieth century.

Dismemberment of Peru was considered by the Chilean cabinet to be dependent upon "a serious blow to the Peruvian navy" which might enable Chile to insist upon alteration of Peru's boundaries. But in April, 1879, Chile did not believe that it could inflict a "serious blow" upon Peru. Santiago was therefore greatly surprised by the series of stunning defeats inflicted by the Chilean navy on the Peruvian navy, which finally gave Chile control of the seas. Then Chile began to speak openly of territorial concessions; next, she insisted on them; and, finally, she enforced her demands by military might.

The War of the Pacific thus caused Chile completely to abandon its former policy of maintenance of the territorial status quo, and to replace it by a policy of territorial dismemberment which would "make it impossible for [Peru] ... to constitute a threat against the South American equilibrium." The redefinition of Chilean policy at this time was particularly significant because the new head of the cabinet, Antonio Varas, had expressed a sharply different view when he had served as foreign minister in past administrations. In 1852, during an Ecuadoran crisis, Varas had stated Chile's policy as maintenance of "the peace of the continent; the continuance of the present order of things, with neither dismemberments nor annexations." Eight years later, when Ecuador again seemed threatened, Varas had asserted that "the dis-

memberment of any American republic in order to enlarge the territory
of another is a very serious matter. . . . Unless justified by considerations
of an exceptional character, such dismemberments and annexations,
which alter the respective situations of the various states of the continent, cannot be accepted by Chile."

The possibility obviously presents itself that Chile's justification of
Peruvian dismemberment on the ground that it would preserve the
equilibrium was either a transparent pretext or, at best, a tortured
rationalization. Yet the meetings at which this matter was first raised
and justified were secret, and the nature of Chilean deliberations was
unknown to the public. A review of the records of the discussions makes
it appear that the Chilean cabinet believed that Peruvian dismemberment was necessary to the maintenance of the South American equilibrium. Moreover, an examination in perspective of Chilean foreign policy
from the time of Portales makes it reasonable to conclude that Chile was
merely continuing to implement its traditional policy of maintaining
the balance of power which its leaders believed essential to their country's Pacific Coast hegemony.

But why did maintenance of the 1835 territorial status quo no longer
seem to Chile a sufficient guarantee of the balance of power? In the
early decades of the post-1830 period, Chile's dominant position derived
from a combination of an internal stability vastly superior to that of
its neighbors with a strategic geographical location as entrepôt between
the Atlantic world and the west coast of South America. While chaos
and anarchy continued to prevail in Bolivia, Peru, and Argentina, it
was merely necessary for Chile to make sure that none of those nations
enlarged its gross mass to the point where it could by such means alone
gain an undeniable advantage over a country whose territory and population were as small as those of Chile. Under such circumstances an
insistence upon preservation of the territorial status quo had sufficed
to maintain a balance of power. And as those conditions continued
decade after decade, the two terms became almost interchangeable in
the minds of Chilean statesmen. But the emergence of Peru and Argentina as great South American powers altered the power structure upon
which Chile had based its policy. The implications of the new arrangement became evident to Chile after it became involved in the diplomatic
complexities associated with the Peruvian-Bolivian-Argentine negotiations for an anti-Chilean alliance. The effectuation of such a triple
alliance could have destroyed Chilean hegemony on the Pacific. And
to Chile the destruction of that hegemony was equivalent to destruction
of the South American balance of power. Now, with the power structure

of the late 1870's having a shape so different from that of earlier decades, Chile might create a new order of power favorable to its Pacific hegemony by dismembering Peru and making it impossible for her, either alone or in combination with other nations, to challenge Chile. In other words, it was a matter of changing some of the weights in the balance.

However the members of the new coalition cabinet may have reasoned or rationalized in the process of deciding to alter Peru's boundaries, Chile's war aims came to include not only the initially stated revindication of the Bolivian littoral, but also the perpetuation of Chilean hegemony on the Pacific Coast.

MILITARY FACTORS

To attain its war objectives, Chile would have to crush two nations whose combined population was more than twice that of Chile, and one of which possessed significant naval power. During the first six months of the war Chile was disheartened by successive destructive Peruvian naval forays along the coast, and by the generally unfavorable aspect that the military picture seemed to be assuming.

But in spite of its unpromising early position, Chile had in its favor some of the same factors that had enabled it in the past to hold its own against nations whose territories and populations were far larger; these factors did not fail Chile in the conflict of 1879–1883. As the training, organization, and equipment of its army and navy commenced to garner victories, Chile became convinced that one Chilean soldier was worth many Peruvian or Bolivian fighting men. And, in fact, Chile's small population was not a disadvantage in the War of the Pacific, for Chileans were accustomed to military and civil discipline and were endowed with a sense of national identity which was almost entirely lacking among the ill-equipped, badly trained soldiery of Peru and Bolivia. The Chilean army, moreover, knew what it was fighting for, whereas the forces of Peru and Bolivia were uncertain of their purpose. They had become so accustomed to fighting now for one caudillo and now for another that the furthering of a larger national goal in a total war effort was a concept alien to them.

In the higher direction of the war, Chile was further favored by a well-organized and efficient central administration and by its traditional stability, both of which were virtually unknown to Peru and Bolivia. Finally, in terms of military strength, the two ironclads of the Chilean navy turned out to be superior to any two ships possessed by its enemies.

But these advantages operated in Chile's favor in the long rather than in the short run. The War of the Pacific was hard-fought and long. Chile's achievement of victory was extremely difficult. During the first stage of the war, from April to October, 1879, Chile and its enemies were locked in a bitter struggle for naval supremacy.[7] During that period Chile tried desperately to get help from nonbelligerents in the form of war matériel, direct military aid, ships, benevolent neutrality, or at least moral support. At the same time Chile sought by every possible means to prevent its enemies from obtaining any of these aids from nonbelligerent states.

THE NONBELLIGERENTS

Among the nonbelligerents, the United States and the European nations did not in the early stage of the war present a major problem for Chilean policy. The Great Powers were interested in protecting the interests and the lives of their nationals, but were not sufficiently concerned with the war to seek to affect its outcome. Chile's major task with regard to those nations was therefore to keep a sharp eye upon enemy procurement activities and to attempt to frustrate them where possible.

South American nonbelligerents were another matter altogether. Not only did there exist among them bitter rivalries which might lead one or another of them to favor one or another of the belligerents, but in the decade before the outbreak of the War of the Pacific the major South American nations had shown a growing tendency to play power politics. At first Argentina presented the greatest danger to Chilean interests. Strong hostility to Chile existed in influential Argentine groups and was demonstrated in Argentina's flirtation with the secret Peru-Bolivian anti-Chilean alliance of 1873. Moreover, the Chilean-Argentine boundary dispute was still very much alive, for, although the Chilean Congress had approved the Fierro-Sarratea agreement in January, 1879, the legislature of Argentina had not yet taken action on it.

THE BALMACEDA MISSION TO ARGENTINA

In March, 1879, anticipating the possibility of war, Chile sent José Manuel Balmaceda to Argentina to expedite a boundary settlement and to frustrate Argentine adherence to the Peru-Bolivian alliance. Upon arrival in Buenos Aires, Balmaceda found that powerful anti-Chilean pressure groups were demanding both Argentine assistance to Peru and Bolivia in event of war and rejection of the Fierro-Sarratea treaty. He further discovered that the Argentine government had lost interest in the treaty and now wished a direct unarbitrated settlement on terms much less advantageous to Chile.

THE LASTARRIA MISSION TO BRAZIL

In response to Balmaceda's discouraging reports, the Chilean government on May 2, 1879, sent José Victorino Lastarria to Brazil with instructions to seek an alliance, or, at the very least, assurances of Brazilian sympathy "for the purpose of neutralizing or destroying the action of the Argentine Republic."[8] The foreign minister of Chile expected a favorable Brazilian response because of "the absolute lack of antagonistic interests between Chile and Brazil" and "the advantages these two countries could gain from an alliance or an intimate understanding which could assure their preponderance in the South American continent forever." Although Brazil remained a neutral, its government gave Chile such pleasing assurances that Lastarria felt it unnecessary to press for an alliance, and proceeded to Uruguay on a similar mission.

Lastarria had been in Montevideo but a short time when instructions arrived from Santiago urging him to rush back to Rio to counteract the activities of a new Peruvian minister named Lavalle. But Lastarria demurred, assuring Santiago that "twenty Lavalles will not change the concept that is held in Rio of the justice of Chile in the question of the Pacific, nor much less the political interests that the empire has in helping us in our differences with Argentina."[9]

Balmaceda's Buenos Aires negotiations were making no progress, but Santiago sought to keep them alive in the hope that a resounding Chilean military success might occur to alter Argentina's negative policy. The desired event occurred in May, 1879, when Chilean forces destroyed Peru's great ironclad, the *Independencia,* in the naval battle of Iquique. Encouragingly, two weeks after Iquique, the Chilean minister reached an agreement with the Argentine foreign office. But then, to Chile's distress, the Argentine legislature rejected both this agreement and the earlier Fierro-Sarratea treaty. A month later Balmaceda discontinued negotiations and returned to Santiago, leaving only a token staff to tend the Chilean Legation. Diplomatic relations between Chile and Argentina were now virtually severed.

ARGENTINE MILITARY NEUTRALITY

Despite their great strength, the pro–Peru-Bolivian elements in Argentina did not succeed in pushing their country into war against Chile.

Certain influential individuals felt that Argentina's interests required a negotiated and peaceful Chilean boundary settlement, rather than one reached through bloodshed. Others opposed war because it would interrupt the remarkable economic progress that Argentina was experiencing.[10] Still others were sure that by war's end Chile would be so drained of strength that Argentina could easily impose a favorable settlement of the boundary question.[11] Further influencing Argentina's decision to remain militarily aloof from the war was fear of possible Brazilian action.[12] Nor can there be any doubt that Chile's victories at sea, beginning with Iquique, made a strong impression upon military leaders in Argentina. By October, 1879, Chile had captured the *Huáscar,* thereby depriving Peru of its sole remaining ironclad and securing firm control of the sea lanes along the south Pacific coast.

Failure to ally itself with Peru and to declare war on Chile did not prevent Argentina from constituting a diplomatic and strategic problem of the first order. Buenos Aires took advantage of Chile's preoccupation with the war to make moves that it felt Chile could not counter, such as occupying Chilean-claimed territory in Patagonia. Moreover, Chile found it necessary to protest the alleged use of Argentine territory for transshipment of war matériel to Bolivia.

But it was hostile Argentine diplomacy that created for Chile its most serious challenge, one that persisted during the entire active phase of the War of the Pacific and for many years afterward. One effect of the unfriendly diplomacy was to keep alive the resistance of Peru and Bolivia well beyond the time when other military and political considerations would have normally caused its collapse. This objective Argentina accomplished by encouraging Peru and Bolivia to believe that it would eventually go to their support with something stronger than words.

THE GODOY MISSION TO ECUADOR

Although Chile was forced to give primary attention to the Argentine problem, it was simultaneously called upon to deal with two nations of the far north, Colombia and Ecuador. Quito nourished strong anti-Peruvian feeling as a result of Peru's past interventions in its affairs and Peru's refusal to return the "lost" provinces of Jaén and Maynas. Moreover, Ecuador had come to attach great importance to Amazonian claims which Peru was contesting. Complementing Ecuador's anti-Peruvianism was its friendship for Chile, based on that country's past efforts to preserve Ecuador's independence.

In March, 1879, Chile assigned to expert diplomatist Joaquín Godoy the task of bringing Ecuador into the War of the Pacific on Chile's side. Godoy was to suggest that the occasion was ripe for sending Ecuadoran troops into the various Ecuadoran-claimed but Peruvian-occupied territories. Godoy was to promise that if such action led to war with Peru, Chile would go to Quito's aid if the latter openly declared itself an ally of Chile. In spite of his skill, Godoy failed to drag Ecuador into the war; although it was true that in Quito, the political capital, sympathies against Peru and for Chile were intense, in Guayaquil there was still much of the pro-Peruvian feeling noted there in the past. The dictator of Ecuador, caught in the perpetual conflict between mountain and lowland, was probably unwilling to risk power by committing the country to the Chilean cause, notwithstanding the valuable territorial gains promised by Santiago. By the time Godoy gave up his mission as a lost cause he had been able to extract from the Ecuadoran dictator only the promise, for whatever its doubtful worth, that Ecuador would not assist Peru.[13]

COLOMBIA IN 1879

With respect to Colombia, Chilean diplomacy operated on an entirely different level. While Ecuadoran involvement would have had the advantage of immediately diverting Peruvian forces, Colombia was both militarily impotent and geographically removed from the area of conflict, so that no strategic benefit could be gained by its direct participation.

Colombia's adoption in the early 1860's of a policy of extreme federal decentralization had left Bogotá powerless to impose order among and within provinces wracked by violent conflict. The nation's power position had rapidly declined, and it was involved in disputes with each of its neighbors. With Brazil, Colombia was in conflict concerning territorial rights in the Amazon and free navigation of the Amazon River system. With Venezuela, diplomatic relations had been severed five years before the outbreak of the War of the Pacific as a result of boundary conflicts and Venezuela's refusal to permit Colombian use of the Zulia River, a major commercial outlet. With Ecuador, Colombia's relations, traditionally vacillating between angry conflict and anti-Peruvian coöperation, were in 1879 suffering a setback because of a riot and an attack against Colombian nationals residing in Ecuador. With Costa Rica, a boundary dispute momentarily quiescent might break into open warfare at any moment. Looming beyond Colombia's dismal relations with its immediate neighbors was a potential conflict with the United States, which was disturbed by Colombia's concession to a

French combine for the building of an interoceanic canal through the Colombian province of Panama.

At the outbreak of the War of the Pacific it thus seemed that the sum of Colombia's domestic and foreign problems would act to keep it well on the margin of the conflict. But appearances did not take into account the transisthmian railway, completed in 1855 by United States interests, which connected Colón on the Caribbean with Panama City on the Pacific. No sooner had active hostilities commenced than the railroad began to assume great importance in the transshipment of war matériel purchased by the belligerents from the industrial nations of the Atlantic world. The isthmian route was especially important to Peru, for its use shortened the traditional southern route by several thousand miles and by many weeks, making transportation of military supplies cheaper and less subject to Chilean attack. As Chile could secure its military supplies freely via the southern route—unless Argentina became an active belligerent on the side of Peru—it sought to prevent use of the Panama Railroad by its enemies. In the bitter conflict of interests that followed, Colombia was trapped between the claws of Chile and those of Peru.

The Panama issue came to the fore in May, 1879, when the Chilean consul in Panama City first officially protested that shipments of arms destined for Chile's enemies had been transported by rail in violation of an existing Colombian-Chilean treaty of commerce and of the principles of neutral conduct accepted under interational law. Bogotá responded to the protest by issuing a formal neutrality declaration whose terms only aggravated Chile's irritation, for it stated that Colombia, having designated Panama as a route of transit free to the commerce of the entire world, could not assume the obligation of determining the origin, classification, and destination of merchandise using that route.[14]

Not content with its ambiguous and unenforceable neutrality declaration, Colombia attempted to end the War of the Pacific through mediation, sending Pablo Arosemena as "minister to the Republics of the Pacific" with instructions to use his good offices. Colombia's desire to end the war was not, according to Ernest Dichman, United States minister to Colombia, entirely altruistic. Dichman noted widely circulating rumors that Chile was negotiating treaties with both Ecuador and Brazil which would enable them to extend their Amazonian territories at the expense of Peru and Bolivia.[15] As Bogotá was involved in disputes with both Ecuador and Brazil, it could not contemplate their strengthening without concern, and it was therefore to its interest to end the war quickly. By so doing Colombia would both diminish the danger of Chilean alliance with Ecuador and Brazil and extricate herself from the growing isthmian dispute.

By late June, 1879, the reports of its consul in Panama had convinced Chile that Colombia's strategic importance was not negligible. Chile therefore sent Francisco Valdés Vergara to Bogotá as chargé d'affaires, with the mission of informing the Colombian government that "Chile . . . cannot accept in any form the principles of neutrality . . . being practiced at Panama."[16] Valdés, reaching Bogotá early in August, found it necessary to make one protest after another against the shipment of arms to Peru via Panama. Colombia's minister to the "Republics of the Pacific" reached Santiago in September and encountered refusal to discuss any Colombian mediation until the isthmian neutrality question had been settled.[17] The matter was still in dispute when Chile captured Peru's ironclad *Huáscar* and the first phase of the War of the Pacific came to a close.

In the second phase of the war, from October, 1879, to June, 1880, the belligerents' military activities moved from sea to land. Chile, having won naval superiority, could safely transport it troops to Peru and disembark them at will. By the end of November Peru's rich nitrate province of Tarapacá was in Chilean hands, and the governments of Peru and Bolivia had been ousted and replaced by others that vowed to continue the war against obviously mounting difficulties. After the occupation of Tarapacá, Chilean forces invaded the Peruvian provinces of Tacna and Arica. By June, 1880, defending allied armies had been decisively routed and Chile was in firm control of those two provinces.[18]

Chile's relations with Argentina, Brazil, and Ecuador remained much the same during the war's second phase as during its first. The new challenges facing Chilean diplomacy in the second phase derived, first, from the deteriorating Colombian situation and, second, from the mounting concern of the United States and some European nations over the effects of the war on their interests.

Chile's achievement of naval superiority had forced Peru to depend almost entirely upon the Panama Railroad for delivery of war matériel. From Panama City, of course, supplies had to be carried to Callao aboard ship, but Chile was still unable both to transport and support its expeditionary forces and closely to patrol the sea-lanes between Panama and Peru. Prior to April, 1880, when Chile was able to release several ships for a blockade of Callao, Santiago sought to cut Peruvian supply lines by diplomatic means. Bogotá was increasingly pressed to adopt and enforce a strict neutrality policy, but although Valdés was able to frustrate isolated shipments to Peru, supplies continued to reach the enemy in large quantities, greatly to the annoyance of Santiago. The angry atmosphere in the Chilean capital moved the Colombian minister to "the Republics of the Pacific" to send repeated warnings to his government that it must deal with the neutrality question or risk possible conflict with Chile. He thought the situation grave enough to advise Bogotá to straighten out its troubles with Ecuador and Venezuela and build up its military defenses against a direct threat from Chile.[19] Its minister's ominous reports, together with Chile's continued sharp protests, seem finally to have taken effect, and by April, 1880, Valdés was able to report to Santiago that Colombia feared possible Chilean use of force if a change in its neutrality policy was not forthcoming.[20] From Chile's point of view this was a step in the right direction.

THREAT OF EUROPEAN INTERVENTION

French, German, Italian, and above all, British interests were being adversely affected by the War of the Pacific. Early in 1880 Prime Minister Gladstone seriously discussed with statesmen of other European nations the possibility of joint intervention designed to impose peace upon the belligerents. His plan did not materialize, largely because Bismarck regarded it as excessively costly,[21] but Washington watched the European discussions with great concern. United States policy could not tolerate European intervention on the scale implied by such high-level multinational negotiations. Washington therefore began to seek an end to the war through its own good offices, but had not succeeded in bringing the belligerents to the conference table by the time of Chile's triumphant victory in the Battle of Tacna, early in June, 1880, which brought the war's second phase to a close.

During the third phase of the war, from June to November, 1880, the battlefields were quiet but maneuvers on the diplomatic front were feverish. By now Bolivia, whose participation in the fighting had been notable largely for its ineptitude, had virtually deserted the lists. The dictates of "reason" should have convinced Peru of its defeat, but its leaders stubbornly opposed Chile's terms for peace. In Santiago there was a great debate as to whether or not Chile should be content with its current military positions in the hope that Peru would "come to its senses" and sue for peace. By the end of July, 1880, the argument had been won by those who wanted to carry the military campaign directly to the seat of government in order to give Peru no alternative to unconditional surrender. While preparations were under way for the capture of Callao-Lima, there occurred on the diplomatic front two major developments: settlement of the Colombian question and a United States mediation effort.

THE COLOMBIAN-CHILEAN ARBITRATION CONVENTION OF 1880

Victory at Tacna paved the way for settlement of the isthmian neutrality question by enabling Chile to blockade Peruvian ports so that Colombia's neutrality, while still important in principle, was less important in practice, and Chile could afford a more relaxed posture toward Bogotá. At the same time, Chile's conquests were arousing fear throughout South America, and Santiago hoped "to avoid any new conflict that might . . . weaken its prestige or alienate the sympathies . . . of other American republics."²³ Five days after Tacna, Santiago ordered its Colombian agents to soften their protests and instructed its chargé d'affaires to sound out Bogotá on the arbitration of Chilean-Colombian differences. Colombia responded favorably, for it was beset on all sides by grave international difficulties and had just received another warning from its minister in Santiago that Chile might at any moment break off relations because of irritation over the neutrality question.

On September 3, 1880, after a month of discussions, a convention on arbitration was signed in Bogotá, the Chilean chargé affixing his signature *ad referendum*. The agreement seemed to meet the needs of both nations. For Chile it relaxed tensions with Colombia and allowed greater freedom in attempting to conclude the war as soon as possible. Moreover, the convention served the public relations function of demonstrating to a concerned continent that Chile was willing to arbitrate a dispute that it could presumably settle by force if it so desired. For Colombia the agreement removed the threat of unpleasantness with Chile at a time when Bogotá was overburdened with troubles with its neighbors and the "Colossus of the North." Moreover, the arbitration convention might encourage some of Colombia's more powerful neighbors to eschew force and follow Chile's example in solving their disputes with Colombia.

The text of the arbitration convention seemed clear and simple. It provided for the settlement of all differences by compulsory arbitration and named as arbiter—lacking accord by the two parties—the President of the United States. At the suggestion of Colombia the agreement also included a clause stressing the desirability of similar treaties with other nations, and this apparently innocuous provision soon involved Chile in a diplomatic struggle of large proportions. Within six weeks of the convention's signing, and before its ratification by either government, Colombia, without consulting Chile, plunged toward its implementation, in its haste acting so as to embarrass and even endanger the interests of Chile.

In seeking to implement the provision that it had suggested, the government of Colombia did not merely initiate negotiations looking toward the strictly bilateral agreements that an exact interpretation of the relevant clause would have demanded. The foreign secretary of Colombia, under date of October 11, 1880, invited fourteen Spanish American nations to a conference to be held in Panama, asking them to grant their representatives full authority to sign with each of the nations present a convention on arbitration like the one that Chile and Colombia had signed, a copy of which was enclosed with the invitation. Colombia stressed the importance of the proposed conference as a means of avoiding war through the general adoption of arbitration for the settlement of international disputes.[23] The stage was thereby set for the proposed conference at Panama to become a pawn in the South American power struggle. But for the time being the signing of the arbitration convention quieted at least one of Chile's preoccupations, as it prepared during the lull in the fighting to carry its military might into the capital of Peru.

The Conference of Arica

While Bogotá and Santiago were settling their isthmian transit differences, the United States succeeded in bringing the belligerents in the War of the Pacific to the peace table. As the result of misunderstandings concerning Washington's bases for its proffered mediation, the allies and Chile met in October, 1880, aboard the United States cruiser *Lackawanna,* off Arica. Although the Conference of Arica [24] was a total failure, it had the important consequence of compelling Chile publicly to state its price for peace.

Accusing the allies of total war guilt, Chile demanded indemnification for the war's entire cost. The indemnity included the astronomical sum of 20 million United States dollars, together with the cession to Chile in perpetuity of the Pacific littoral from the Chilean border north to the valley of the Camarones River, within which lay the entire Bolivian seacoast and the Peruvian province of Tarapacá. Chile, moreover, demanded the right to occupy the Peruvian provinces of Tacna and Arica until the defeated allies had paid their indemnity in full, and finally demanded that Peru limit its sovereignty by agreeing to leave the port of Arica permanently unfortified. Both Peru and Bolivia flatly rejected consideration of territorial concessions, but were willing to consider arbitration of the monetary indemnification. Chile refused such arbitration, and the conference adjourned on October 27 after five days of fruitless discussion.

As Chile rushed preparations for the capture of Lima, its enemies embarked upon a propaganda campaign well-armed with the ammunition provided by the revelation of Chile's harsh terms for peace.[25]

ARGENTINA'S ANTI-CHILEAN DIPLOMACY

Foremost among the nations from which Peru and Bolivia hoped to receive help was Argentina. Its sympathies had long been obvious, although not expressed in active military participation. The failure of the Conference of Arica sparked Buenos Aires into action on the diplomatic front, for it was deeply concerned about the additional power that Chile might gain as the result of territorial acquisitions from the defeated allies. Argentinians who had drawn back from war in the hope that Chile would be so weakened by it as to be forced to accept Argentina's terms for a boundary settlement now faced the possibility that the reverse might occur.

On November 9, 1880, the Argentine chancellery launched a campaign to contain Chilean expansion. First, it sought joint Brazilian-Argentine mediation to end the war. Argentina proposed to Brazil that the two powers would "support ... all propositions that tend to achieve peace with the exception of those that might offend the national honor of the interested parties or deprive them of their rights of sovereignty and property."[26] Moreover, if the joint mediation failed, the two countries would withdraw their arbitrators and, "deploring the obstacles which they may have encountered ..., leave to the judgment of civilized peoples the evaluation of the facts that may have stood in the way." Since Chile's expectations were now known, Argentina's joint-mediation proposal constituted open support of the Peruvian and Bolivian positions, and Brazil's acceptance of it would have dealt a severe blow to the position and prestige of Chile.

While its proposed joint mediation with Brazil was still being discussed, Argentina received Colombia's invitation to the Panama congress on arbitration. Departing from his country's traditional aloofness toward such meetings, Argentina's foreign minister, Irigoyen, seized the occasion to extend the anti-Chilean campaign to wider circles. He replied to the invitation with comments and suggestions that seemingly made Argentine participation conditional upon the acceptance of premises that could prove extremely damaging to Chilean interests. Irigoyen expressed his country's acceptance of arbitration in principle, and its desire for peace among the nations of Spanish America, but insisted that peace could not be secured by the mere acceptance of the principle of arbitration. If the proposed Panama congress hoped to achieve peace, wrote Irigoyen, it must adopt principles regulating relations among the nations and must provide a standard for the awarding of arbitral decisions. Most especially, he continued, "it is necessary explicitly to proscribe attempts at violent annexation or conquest which raise permanent obstacles to future stability."[27] Argentina's reply to Colombia's invitation pushed the proposed Panama congress into the mainstream of South American power politics, for within a few months Colombia accepted Irigoyen's suggestions.

OCCUPATION OF LIMA-CALLAO; THE GARCÍA CALDERÓN GOVERNMENT

In the meantime Chile successfully renewed its military campaign in Peru. Lima was taken on January 17, 1881, and Callao the following day. By the end of January the Foreign Minister of Chile was able to inform his foreign service corps that "the military power of the alliance has been completely destroyed; its most formidable ships fly the Chilean flag and the balance of its navy is buried in the sea."[28]

But instead of producing the desired peace, the capture of Lima raised new obstacles to Chile's achievement of peace on its own terms. Peruvians, prostrate though they appeared, were less willing than ever to sign away any territory. The government that fled Lima under Chilean gunfire reorganized in the interior of the country and pledged resistance unto death. Guerrilla warfare engulfed the country, and it seemed that Chile could force Peru into submission only by a campaign fought from plaza to plaza and hacienda to hacienda. Santiago chose instead to create a puppet government in the hope that it might manage to gain enough general support to enable it to sign a peace treaty on Chilean terms. A committee of Peruvian "notables" was rounded up for the purpose of establishing a provisional government, and Francisco García Calderón was named provisional president. García then succeeded in bringing together a congress which on July 10, 1881, confirmed his position. Guerrilla warfare nevertheless continued to plague the Peruvian countryside.

THE BOUNDARY TREATY OF 1881 WITH ARGENTINA

Chile's resounding military victory over the alliance and its subsequent difficulties in imposing a peace seem to have encouraged, in both Argentina and Chile, an inclination to retreat from subbornly held positions in the boundary dispute. Although neither party was eager to take the first step, both accepted United States mediation, and a boundary treaty was signed on July 23, 1881.[29] Chile gave up the claim to Patagonia, and Argentina accepted Chilean sovereignty over the entire Strait of Magellan. Chile accepted neutralization of the strait, and Argentina agreed never to block the Atlantic access to and egress from the strait. Provision was made for the division of Tierra del Fuego between Argentina and Chile, and for the arbitration of disputes arising over interpretation of the treaty's terms. Despite substantial resistance in the legislatures of both signatories, the boundary agreement was approved and ratifications were exchanged on October 22, 1881.[30] In the not too distant future the Argentine-Chilean boundary treaty of 1881 would become a source of dangerous controversy between its signatories, but at the time of its completion it freed the Chilean government to deal with the mounting obstacles to the achievement of its peace terms in the War of the Pacific.

ANTI-CHILEAN SENTIMENT AMONG NONBELLIGERENTS

During 1881 Chilean demands, to which had now been added the outright cession of Tacna and Arica, encountered growing Peruvian opposition. Peru's resistance was further encouraged by a rising tide of anti-Chilean sentiment among the continent's nonbelligerent nations. The extent to which Chilean victory over its two larger and more populous neighbors inspired fear and hostility was exemplified in the cry of protest from distant Venezuela, whose Congress in 1881 officially resolved that "in the name of the great Bolívar, liberator also of [Peru and Bolivia], we solemnly protest against these iniquitous and scandalous usurpations of which they are the victims."[31] Venezuelan dictator Guzmán Blanco even feared, according to the Argentine envoy in Caracas, that there might exist a secret Brazilian-Chilean alliance whose countering might require "an alliance of Colombia, Venezuela, Ecuador, Argentina, Uruguay, and Paraguay against the acquisitive aims of Chile."[32]

In Venezuela's neighbor, Colombia, there were also indications of growing fear of Chile. In 1881 Adriano Páez warned that "Chile ... has destroyed the land and sea power of Peru ... and has won the predominance of the Pacific. ... Chile will be master from the strait to Ecuador for the present and, ... as neither Ecuador nor Colombia has a navy, Chile will rule from the strait to the Isthmus of Panama."[33] Páez demanded that "diplomacy put itself into the field and raise a unanimous and formidable protest against Chile's pretensions; if that country does not heed the explicit will of America then let there be formed a league of all the other republics so that insane ambition may be returned to its natural bounds."

Such sentiments as these, coming from many quarters of the continent, encouraged Peruvian resistance to Chile's peace terms and required Santiago's constant activity both in counteracting anti-Chilean attitudes and in building goodwill for Chile in countries where it was represented. At the same time, Chile's most strenuous efforts had to be directed toward frustrating the persistent attempts of nonbelligerents to intervene in the final settlement of the War of the Pacific.

UNITED STATES INTERVENTION

From the war's earliest days Washington had attempted to restore peace between Chile and the alliance, always carefully avoiding any attempt to impose its own views on the issues at stake. But in March, 1881, a change in administration led to the replacement of the previously impartial position of the United States by one openly favorable to Peru and Bolivia.

On June 26, 1881, the new secretary of state, James G. Blaine, recognized the García Calderón government in Peru, thereby giving it a status that tended to make it less dependent upon Chile and more disposed to go its own way in foreign affairs. On August 2 a new United States minister, Stephen A. Hurlbut, reached Lima. Within a few weeks he informed the commander of the Chilean army of occupation that the "United States ... do not approve of war for the purpose of territorial aggrandizement, nor of the violent dismemberment of a nation except as a last resort and in extreme emergencies."[34] Hurlbut further stated his conviction that Peru should be permitted to pay its indemnity to Chile entirely in currency. And, speaking for his own government, the minister added that "the act of seizure of Peruvian territory and annexing the same to Chile ... would justly be regarded by other nations as evidence that Chile had entered upon the path of aggression and conquest for the purpose of territorial aggrandizement."[35]

Concluding from these and similar statements that Washington was ready to aid Peruvian resistance to Chile, the García Calderón government cut the strings of Chilean control and flatly refused to consider any territorial concessions whatsoever. Chilean authorities attempted to change García's position, but to no avail; then they imprisoned him and removed him to Chile. Public indignation over Chile's abusive treatment of its former puppet, together with optimism inspired by new Hurlbut pronouncements, rekindled the fires of Peruvian resistance to Chile.

Rear Admiral Lizardo Montero, vice-president in the García regime, led his followers out of Lima and set up a government in an area that the Chilean army of occupation did not control. Together with several caudillos from various regions of Peru, Montero intensified hostilities against the Chileans. Throughout the remainder of 1881 and the early part of 1882, as events in Peru became more threatening to Chile, Chile blamed its difficulties on the United States, especially on its minister in Lima, charging that "García Calderón would have accepted the conditions of a peace with Chile if the minister of the United States had not revealed desires and even made statements which . . . modified the situation. . . . It is necessary to be in the theater of events, seeing or evaluating intimately the details and the whole of the manifestations of Mr. Hurlbut's policy, to measure in all their magnitude the complications and damages produced."[36]

AN ARGENTINE MISSION TO COLOMBIA AND VENEZUELA

At the same time that Chile attempted to deal with a deteriorating Peruvian situation, it was required to anticipate the possibility of Argentina's success in arranging a joint mediation offer on a "no-conquest" basis. Brazil was unwilling to participate in so transparent an anti-Chilean move, but persistent Buenos Aires began to look farther north for support, and in May, 1881, sent Miguel Cané to Colombia and Venezuela with instructions first to secure their approval of the principle of the preservation of the territorial integrity of the South American nations,[37] and then to seek their participation in a joint mediation of the War of the Pacific on the basis of that principle. Two months after Cané's appointment Argentina again approached Brazil, still insisting on the preservation of territorial integrity.[38]

As Argentina's success in arranging for a joint mediation would seriously embarrass Chile and would encourage the continued resistance of Peru, Santiago sought by every possible means to thwart Buenos Aires' efforts in that direction. But as it did so, the question of the proposed Panama congress became dominant and threatened to place in the way of Chile's peace plans even more formidable obstacles.

THE STILLBORN CONGRESS OF PANAMA

After its transmission to Santiago by chargé d'affaires Valdés, the Chilean-Colombian arbitration convention had languished, unsubmitted for legislative approval. Nor had Chile bothered to reply to Colombia's invitation to the Panama congress. Santiago was, however, disturbed by reports of growing anti-Chileanism in Colombia. A new minister, José Antonio Soffia, was accredited to Bogotá for the primary purpose of expounding Chile's position in the War of the Pacific. Arriving in May, 1881, he immediately encountered strong pressure for approval of the arbitration convention and for participation in the Congress of Panama. Soffia advised Santiago that Colombia's wishes would have to be granted if Chile hoped to continue friendly relations with Bogotá and to uphold its international prestige.[39]

While its minister in Bogotá was bearing the direct brunt of Colombia's pressures, the Chilean government was reaching decisions on both the convention and the congress. For Chile the proposed meeting was doubly ominous because it began to seem that it would be well attended, and because the government of Colombia had indicated its acceptance of Argentine Foreign Minister Irigoyen's suggestions concerning the agenda. Such a meeting might succeed in passing otherwise laudable "no-conquest" resolutions which, under the circumstances, would constitute a condemnation of Chilean policy, and that might have the gravest consequences for the interests of Chile. Chile would not, therefore, participate in the congress. More, Chile would attempt either to abort the congress altogether or to weaken it to the point where its deliberations would carry no weight.

On September 26, 1881, the Chilean minister in Bogotá was ordered to inform the Colombian government that Chile would neither approve the arbitration convention nor participate in the Panama congress. He was further instructed to urge the Bogotá agents of other invited nations to discourage their governments' participation in the Panama meeting. During the following month Chilean diplomats in Rio de Janeiro, Paris, and Washington were called upon to make every possible effort to frustrate the proposed meeting. A chargé d'affaires was sent to Quito to keep Ecuador away from Panama, and another Chilean agent departed for Mexico and Central America on a similar mission. After the exchange of ratifications of the Chilean-Argentina boundary agreement, the Chilean consul in Buenos Aires was instructed to discuss his government's view of the congress with both Argentina and Uruguay. As a result of Chile's efforts, Ecuador and Nicaragua agreed not to attend, and Honduras and Guatemala consented to give their delegates instructions that would prevent any possible embarrassment of Chile. Several other nations decided not to participate, for reasons of their own. On January 5, 1882, after a long and miserable wait in the heat of Panama for the arrival of other possible participants, the four plenipotentiaries who had been accredited decided that the meeting could not possibly be held with the attendance of so few nations. The Panama congress, which had boded so ill for Chile, was stillborn.

THE UNITED STATES RETREATS

In January, 1882, the threat that the United States might seek to impose a peace unsatisfactory to Chilean interests lessened. A few weeks earlier Frederick T. Frelinghuysen had replaced James G. Blaine as secretary of state of the United States, and Washington's policy was undergoing modification. United States diplomats in the warring countries were instructed to confine their activities to impartial mediation attempts, without seeking to dictate peace terms.[40] In January, when Chile learned of the new instructions, its government was able to relax so far as the United States was concerned, though the latter maintained a strong interest in seeing an end to Pacific hostilities. This interest, combined with the evolving Latin-American policy of the United States, presented an important challenge to Chilean policy and diplomacy.

Blaine had envisioned an international conference at which representatives of the American nations would devise and discuss means for preserving peace.[41] In November, 1881, United States envoys in Latin America had been instructed to issue invitations to such a conference, to be held in Washington just a year later. Although Frelinghuysen disliked Blaine's proposal for a conference, the Chilean government, on February 22, 1882, received a formal invitation to the Washington meeting. The prospect raised fears similar to those that had so recently been laid to rest with the stillborn Congress of Panama, but when Chile's minister in Washington assured his government that Frelinghuysen would not carry through the plans for the conference, the chancellery took no action on the invitation.[42]

But in April, 1882, Frelinghuysen, unwilling to bear alone the responsibility for abandoning a plan so important to his predecessor, asked Congress to approve a change in the plans for an inter-American meeting. Chile, envisioning a possible reactivation of the Washington conference idea, promptly advised its legations throughout North and South America and Europe that such a conference would be most undesirable at a time when Chile was still attempting to reach a peace settlement in the War of the Pacific. The Chilean chancellery instructed its agents to "undertake, with the government and with the most important social and political circles of the country [to which you are accredited], the most effective, persistent, and discreet crusade ... against the idea of a conference at Washington."[43] A vigorous Chilean campaign against the conference proved unnecessary, for in August, 1882, the United States withdrew its invitations.

Within a few months, however, it again seemed likely that the United States might frustrate Chile's settlement of the War of the Pacific.

James Partridge, now United States minister in Lima, had for some time sought a mediation in accord with Frelinghuysen's modified policy. But on January 22, 1883, to the complete surprise of Santiago, Partridge abandoned impartiality and went openly to the support of Peru, joining with the Lima agents of France, Italy, and Great Britain in issuing a strong memorandum demanding an end to the war, the preservation of Peru from "annihilation," and, if necessary to secure these demands, the joint intervention of the Great Powers whose representatives had signed the memorandum.[44]

For a short time it appeared that Washington had reverted to Blaine's policy, but in fact the government of the United States was just as surprised as that of Chile when it learned of the four-power Lima memorandum. As Partridge had in fact acted without instructions, Washington immediately repudiated the note. The prompt response of the United States seems to have convinced Chile that there no longer existed any danger that Washington would go to the help of Peru and Bolivia. Santiago, moreover, was persuaded that Buenos Aires would probably abandon its efforts to arrange a joint mediation. By mid-March, 1883, Chile's foreign minister believed that "the general disillusion produced among our neighbors by the explicit and circumspect declarations of the Washington chancellery has removed any probability that the governments of those republics will persist in efforts or suggestions that cannot gain effective approval and would end by putting them in a situation of a sterile and ridiculous loss of prestige."[45]

THE TREATY OF ANCÓN

As the danger of foreign intervention receded, Chile concentrated its diplomatic energies on the task of achieving a peace that would legalize and make permanent the changes in the territorial status quo its statesmen desired. In early 1883 the possibility that Peru would accept such a peace seemed remote. Chilean forces did hold Lima and much of the coast, but a large resistance force under Cáceres held out in the interior; and the area around Arequipa was controlled by Admiral Montero who claimed to be the legal president of the country. In Cajamarca, however, a feeble "government" headed by General Iglesias had evidenced willingness to come to terms. As an alternative to the costly attempt to occupy all Peru, Chile reluctantly threw its support to Iglesias, and in May negotiated with him a preliminary treaty of peace.

In July Chilean forces decisively defeated Cáceres, although the General himself escaped, remaining the chief symbol of Peruvian resistance. Preparations were speeded up for subduing Admiral Montero, and although it appeared that Iglesias would soon be the sole major political force in Peru, the Chilean government was sufficiently unsure of both his strength and his intentions to withhold its official recognition until October 18, 1883. Two days later, on October 20, 1883, a formal treaty of peace between Chile and Peru was signed at the seaside resort of Ancón, a few miles from Lima.[46]

The Treaty of Ancón effectively diminished Peru's potential as a threat to the American equilibrium and augmented the power of Chile. Its second article ceded to Chile "in perpetuity and unconditionally" the rich mineral-producing province of Tarapacá, subtracting from Peru and adding to Chile a tremendously important source of national wealth and foreign exchange.

Article III dealt with the Peruvian provinces of Tacna and Arica, which lay to the north of Tarapacá. Although the natural resources of these barren and undeveloped provinces were considered virtually worthless, Chile was intent upon their annexation for two reasons. First, Peru would thereby be deprived of a base for any attempt to retake Tarapacá. Second, Chile wanted to speed peace with Bolivia by offering it the port of Arica in compensation for its captured littoral. But Peru, stubbornly resisting the demand for outright cession, had rather surprisingly managed to obtain a compromise; Tacna and Arica were to remain in Chile's possession "subject to Chilean laws and authority during a period of ten years," at the end of which time their definitive sovereignty would be determined by a plebiscite whose loser would be consoled by the payment of 10 million Chilean silver pesos. However unpalatable this compromise was to victorious Chile, it did give her ten years in which to maneuver for permanent domination, and Peru had at least saved some face and could still hope to regain jurisdiction in the future. The drafters of the Treaty of Ancón committed a major error of omission by leaving the establishment of the procedural details of the Tacna and Arica plebiscite to a later separate protocol, but for the time being both parties seemed to be well satisfied.

Closely related to the treaty's territorial provisions were those concerning the disposition of Peru's debt. Chile would have to assume a part of the debt as a result of its territorial acquisitions. It will be remembered that in the 1860's Peru began to borrow heavily from European sources, and in the 1870's further increased its already enormous debt by nationalizing a substantial part of the Tarapacá nitrate industry, whose ousted owners were issued, in compensation, interest-bearing certificates. But the guano and nitrate revenues upon which Lima had counted to fulfill its obligations proved insufficient, and in 1876 Peru defaulted. Payments had not been resumed prior to the time when Chilean seizure of Tarapacá made their resumption a virtual impossibility.

At that point Peru's creditors turned upon Chile and demanded that it assume some responsibility. To quiet their outcries, the Chilean government ordered that a million tons of guano be sold and that the proceeds be divided equally between the Chilean treasury and those Peruvian creditors whose claims had been guaranteed by guano monopoly revenues. Article IV of the Treaty of Ancón retroactively approved that arrangement, and Chile agreed to continue the marketing of guano under the same procedure, either until existing guano deposits had been exhausted or until the guano market had collapsed. It was stipulated that Peru's creditors would have no claims upon hitherto undiscovered guano deposits.

During the course of the war Chile had further attempted to mitigate the Peruvian debt problem by returning nationalized Tarapacá nitrate properties to the holders of certificates issued in compensation for their seizure. Article VIII of the treaty approved such action, further specifying that "Chile will recognize no debts, whatever their nature or source, which may affect the new territories acquired by virtue of this treaty."

In spite of Chile's assumption of some of its obligations, Peru remained burdened with a foreign debt of staggering proportions. The loss of Tarapacá not only severely damaged Peru's national pride, but also seriously handicapped its ability to repay its debts and to get back on its feet. With the signing of the Treaty of Ancón, Peruvian power was so diminished that its potential as a major influence in South American affairs fell to a low point.

Promptly upon the signing of the Treaty of Ancón, Chilean troops left Lima and Iglesias entered the city to establish his government. Within a week Chilean forces had felled the last major center of Peruvian resistance by defeating Admiral Montero and occupying the city of Arequipa. Chile then set about the task of bringing Bolivia to terms.

NEGOTIATIONS WITH BOLIVIA

Bolivia's situation was completely untenable. Peru had crumbled. Bolivia's commerce with Peru had been choked off by Chile, whose forces stood ready to march upon the Altiplano. Bolivia made some defensive motions, but had already decided to sue for peace. In November, 1883, two Bolivian commissioners went down from La Paz toward Santiago to discuss a settlement. In formal peace negotiations, which began in December, Bolivian commissioner Salinas vehemently declared that "inasmuch as Bolivia has been deprived of its seacoast, *it is indispensable that Chile open for it an outlet to the Pacific* under penalty of [Bolivia's] being condemned to the fate of a landlocked nation, destined to suffocate, languish, and die."[47]

Salinas asked that Chile supply Bolivia with an outlet to the Pacific either through Chilean territory or by modification of the Treaty of Ancón so as to give Tacna and Arica to the Altiplano. Chile's foreign minister rejected the idea of Chilean sacrifice of territorial continuity; nor could Chile, he believed, give to Bolivia in a treaty something that it did not yet legally possess. Peru would not, the Foreign Minister felt, agree to modification of the Ancón treaty so as to award Tacna and Arica to Bolivia, because Peru had "prolonged the war by two long years [with] enormous future sacrifices, with no aim or intention but that of resisting the cession of Tacna and Arica. . . . The representatives of Bolivia should understand that it is absolutely improbable that Peru would accept such an idea . . . and that Chile can neither suggest nor support the idea."[48]

When the Bolivian commissioners insisted that any peace treaty include seaport provisions, Chile proposed an indefinite truce, pending future resolution of the Pacific outlet matter. At this point negotiations were suspended to permit the commissioners to consult La Paz, and were resumed on February 13, 1884, with Bolivian presentation of a draft proposal whose terms were unacceptable to Chile. Talks were again suspended to allow the Bolivian envoys to consult their government.[49]

RATIFICATION OF THE TREATY OF ANCÓN

In Peru, meanwhile, President Iglesias had taken concrete steps toward reëstablishment of constitutional government. Elections had been held for representatives to a constitutional assembly which was to convene in March, 1884. The assembly, it was hoped, would ratify the Treaty of Ancón, thus giving it the semblance of legality and the appearance of popular approval. But on the eve of the assembly Peru and Chile received protests against the Peruvian debt provisions of the treaty from the governments of France, Great Britain, Italy, Belgium, and Holland, which charged that the articles in question "contain serious derogations of rules generally accepted in similar matters and of agreements which have been freely made between Peru and its various creditors." The protesting creditor nations further insisted that "said clauses either be postponed in view of a friendly agreement which would be verified between the two governments and the interested parties, or that a more satisfactory solution, based upon respect for the contracts made by the creditors of Peru, be immediately proposed for examination and acceptance by the congress that is to meet in Lima."[50]

Preparing to meet the possibly disastrous consequences of these protests on the treaty, Chile immediately readied its forces for the reoccupation of Lima, informing the Peruvian government of its plans.[51] On March 4, 1884, the Constitutional Assembly convened and overwhelmingly ratified the Treaty of Ancón.[52] The ratification did not, however, solve the serious problems raised for Chile by the European protests. The Lima envoys of the five protesting nations had flouted diplomatic custom by absenting themselves from the assembly's opening session on the ground that their governments did not recognize the government of Peru. Chile, viewing that behavior as simply an additional protest against the Treaty of Ancón,[53] appeared to be more disturbed by the fact that in presenting the treaty to the assembly the Peruvian foreign minister had maintained that "with the cession of Tarapacá to Chile, Peru has ended its responsibility as a debtor to the bondholders."[54]

THE BOLIVIAN TRUCE OF 1884

The circumstances surrounding the ratification of the Treaty of Ancón boded ill not only for Chile's relations with the nations of Europe but also for its management of the Bolivian question. Chile moved swiftly to stifle any Bolivian resistance that might result from its hope of European intervention by closing Bolivia's frontier with Peru pending the Altiplano's capitulation.[55] During resumed peace negotiations, however, Bolivia failed to bow before Chilean pressures, and the foreign minister of Chile was convinced that "the true cause of the refusal of Bolivia's emissaries to sign the truce pact is the instruction from their government, which came to them in the latest mail, to gain time and to sign no agreement until the coercive nature of the European protest may be known.... [President] Campero and all the press of Bolivia are declaring with great rejoicing that the situation has completely changed, and that Bolivia neither can nor should accept a conditional truce but merely a legal suspension of hostilities."[56]

In his irritation the Chilean foreign minister characterized Bolivians in a manner that accurately reflected the views of his fellow countrymen: "The suspicious nature of that people and the characteristic perfidy of its diplomacy impel it as always to confide in the unknown, to live on false mirages, and to convince itself that the advantages of its geographical position make it possible to resist our legitimate demands."[57] Convinced that Bolivia was desperately playing for time, Chile planned to renew military operations even as its negotiators demanded that the representatives of Bolivia either sign an acceptable truce or instead affix their signatures to a protocol summarizing past discussions. Chile believed the protocol would make clear Bolivia's responsibility for delaying the conclusion of hostilities.[58] Unable any longer to resist such relentless pressures, the Bolivian commissioners, on April 4, 1884, signed a formal truce pact with Chile.

Chile gained almost everything it had hoped to achieve in a formal treaty of peace.[59] The state of war was terminated. Chile remained, pending the future signing of a peace treaty, in occupation of the entire Bolivian littoral which it was empowered to govern in accordance with its own laws. Commercial relations were reëstablished on Chile's terms, with each country's natural products and their by-products reciprocally freed of any tariff. Bolivia had strongly objected to this provision on the ground that it sold almost nothing to Chile, while its own producers for the domestic market would suffer disastrous competition from such Chilean products as wheat and wines.[60]

Chile attempted at least partly to solve the problem of Bolivia's loss of outlets to the sea by agreeing to establish ports through which foreign merchandise could pass duty-free en route to Bolivia. The former Bolivian port of Antofagasta was specified as one such port; the vastly more active Arica was not so designated. The truce pact stipulated that at Arica all Bolivian-bound goods would be subject to imposition of regular Chilean duties, and that three-fourths of the total collected would be credited to the account of Bolivia, and one-fourth, to the account of Chile. Of Bolivia's share, 40 per cent would be applied to settlement of Chilean damage claims and indemnification and to the service of a loan floated by Bolivia in Chile in 1867. The remaining 60 per cent would be used for ordinary costs of government operation. Only when all Bolivia's obligations to Chile had been liquidated would Arica become, like Antofagasta, a free port providing Bolivia with a source of revenue in the taxes it could impose upon goods when they had reached Bolivian soil.

Résumé

In the Bolivian truce Chile gained the territorial and economic goals for which it had fought Bolivia. But neither the Bolivian armistice nor the peace treaty with Peru was able to assure the future tranquillity of the Pacific Coast. Bolivia would remain restless and resentful in the absence of a seaport. The uncertain status of Tacna and Arica would constitute a constant source of tension in relations between Chile and Peru. Chile's physical possession of the former Bolivian littoral had not been written into law, and Chile would not be satisfied until that had been accomplished.

Chile had to a limited degree succeeded in recasting the South American power structure; it had, *de facto*, greatly enlarged its territory and resources, and it had reduced Peru to the status of a third-rate power. But to the extent that Chile had desired, in attempting to recast the continent's power structure, to create a stable international situation it was doomed to disappointment. For the War of the Pacific, and the international agreements that followed immediately upon it, produced serious problems for Chilean diplomacy in the years to come.

Chapter X

TOWARD AN ARMED PEACE

The end of the War of the Pacific found Chile's leadership firmly resolved to retain for Chile the undisputed hegemony of the Pacific Coast of South America which it had affirmed in more than four years of struggle. In the immediate postwar years that resolve was not difficult to carry out. The Chilean army, notwithstanding its postwar demobilization, remained formidable.[1] The navy was the continent's most powerful, save for that of a friendly Brazil.[2] The morale of the Chilean people, their sense of pride and their sentiments of patriotism were all stronger after the war than before it. Chileans were happy to lay down their guns at the end of the conflict, and enjoyed the peace that followed it, but at the same time they were clearly ready to go back to the lists if their nation's preëminence was challenged. Chile's control of Tarapacá and the Bolivian littoral gave it a source of incalculable wealth which could, if necessary, be used to strengthen its military power. Chilean government revenues doubled in the postwar decade, as compared with the prewar decade,[3] and Chile, whose prewar rate of economic growth had fallen behind that of other countries, had gained control of the economic means of preserving its status as a South American great power.

The international power structure of the early postwar period also augured well for Chile's maintenance of both its Pacific hegemony and its preëminence in Spanish-speaking South America. From the lesser South American states there was no challenge whatsoever. The challenge of Peru as a great power had been virtually eliminated. In sharp contrast with the prostrate condition of Peru, however, was the situation of a second great power—Argentina.

Although Argentina's military and naval strength was inferior to Chile's, its population had already outstripped that of its western neighbor by several hundred thousand.[4] Federalization of Buenos Aires had dissolved a major internal dispute, and the Argentine nation was experiencing phenomenal economic expansion. In fact, it would one day possess the resources with which to challenge Chile. The boundary with Chile had not been demarcated, as provided for in the treaty of 1881, but it was believed that the line would be established with little controversy. In any event, Argentina was not in the immediate postwar years disposed to make trouble for Chile. Its dominant opinion viewed Argentina's path to glory as an economic rather than a military one.[5] Buenos

Aires therefore reluctantly accepted the Pacific Coast *fait accompli,* and toward the end of the war the distinguished diplomat, José Uriburu, was sent to Santiago to establish more cordial relations.[6] Late in 1883 Chile responded by naming its first minister to Argentina since the outbreak of war and instructing him "to coöperate toward the realization of the laudable aim which the Argentine chancellery appears to pursue."[7]

Nor did South America's third great power, Brazil, challenge Chilean hegemony in the immediate postwar period. In fact, the policies and interests of the Empire seemed to support that hegemony, and its friendly and benevolent neutrality toward Chile during the War of the Pacific had strengthened their harmonious relationship. But more permanently and importantly, Brazil and Chile shared an interest in containing their common antagonist, Argentina. The Chilean government had displayed its confidence in Brazil by asking it to name the neutral member of several arbitral tribunals established to adjudge European war damage claims against Chile; and the Emperor had agreed.[8] Moreover, in 1884 Brazilian-Argentine relations were experiencing one of their recurrent periods of disturbance, this time over the disputed Misiones boundary, a question which the Chilean foreign minister regarded as "one of the many variants of the eternal rivalry that divides . . . [Argentina and Brazil]."[9] As long as that "eternal rivalry" persisted, Chile could reasonably expect Brazilian sympathy in its own difficulties with Argentina.

Chile's Pacific Coast hegemony, however, was dependent not only upon its domestic situation and the South American international power structure, but also upon the posture of the non–South American Great Powers. Their substantial interference in the continent's political affairs could hamper Chile's defense of vital interests and thwart fulfillment of her role as a great power in South American politics. In the immediate postwar period Chile could obviously cope with the Great Powers of Europe and the United States less effectively than it would have liked, and yet even during the War of the Pacific their efforts to intervene had come to naught, for several reasons. First, Chile's attempts to protect the interests of Great Power nationals had paid dividends.[10] Second, rivalries among the European Great Powers, and between them and the United States, had prevented their presentation of a united front; for example, Germany had failed to participate in protesting the Treaty of Ancón.[11] Third, Chile's firm resistance to United States intervention when its vital interests appeared to be at stake had been convincing. With the end of the war Chile was better able both to protect Great Power interests and to resist Great Power intervention. Moreover, as the rivalries among the European Great Powers became more intense, and as their interests focused upon Africa and the Far East,[12] the danger of a Great Power threat to Chilean hegemony appeared to be minimal.

Chile's favorable postwar power position did not, however, free it of serious international problems. Of these, the most basic derived from the fact that Chile had only partly succeeded in recasting the South American power structure so as to create a new equilibrium favorable to its interests. Total success would have found Chile in possession of definitive sovereignty over the nitrate littorals of Peru and Bolivia, and Bolivia in possession of a Chilean-donated port access through Tacna and Arica. Definitive legal realization of Chile's maximum goals would have created a new and stronger Bolivia, friendly to Chile and hostile to Peru.[13]

But after the war Chile was only in *de facto* control of the nitrate littoral, and could legally continue to occupy the Bolivian sector of the littoral only while the armistice remained in effect. Definitive Chilean sovereignty was dependent upon a formal treaty of peace, a treaty Bolivia refused to sign until and unless it was compensated for the loss of its littoral by a satisfactory outlet to the Pacific Ocean. Moreover, Bolivia's understandable determination to have a seaport was greatly reinforced by the deep hatred with which Bolivians regarded Chile.

Although Chilean policy favored Bolivian acquisition of Tacna and Arica in principle, the terms of the Treaty of Ancón seriously limited Chile's ability to fulfill the Altiplano's aspirations, for it provided that Chile's occupation of Tacna and Arica must be terminated within ten years by the holding of a plebiscite to determine definitive sovereignty. Chile, pending hoped-for legal incorporation of that region, could satisfy Bolivia's port demands only with the consent of Lima, which it was not likely to obtain. For in Peru, too, hatred of Chile was strong, and the people of that vanquished land, where viceroys and nitrate kings had once held sway, were resolved both to avenge themselves against Chile and to regain the provinces of Tacna and Arica.

Chile's efforts to regularize relations with its former enemies were hampered not only by the hostile attitude of Peru and Bolivia but by the existence throughout the continent of anti-Chileanism which had arisen during the course of the War of the Pacific as a result of fears inspired by Chilean conquests. From the far corners of South America demands had been voiced for joint action to contain Chilean expansion and restore the South American power structure to its prewar status.

Attempts to contain Chile had failed, but they indicated the existence of a continental system of power politics whose members were aware of the significance to their own interests of shifts in the continent's power structure. Chileans were well aware of the sentiments that they inspired. The Chilean minister to Colombia reported in August, 1884, on the "repeated proofs of bad will toward Chile which the government of Caracas . . . has given."[14] In 1885 Chile's envoy in Buenos Aires reported that "in the countries of the Atlantic . . . many think that our government, made proud by its great success . . . , wishes to extend its influence and test its strength in the region of the Plata."[15] The persistence of such fears suggested that the nations of South America, either separately or in concert, might seek to correct the balance of power which they believed Chile guilty of upsetting. Especially might they be inclined to act if Santiago encountered a crisis in relations with its former enemies, or with one or more of the non–South American Great Powers, which the war had brought into close contact with Chile.

RELATIONS WITH NON–SOUTH AMERICAN GREAT POWERS

Chile's efforts to regularize relations with its former enemies were further hampered by early postwar complications in its relations with the Great Powers. The difficulties lay in the financial interests of the latters' citizens, which fell into two broad categories: (1) war-damages claims, and (2) Peruvian government obligations. In 1882 and 1883 a solution had presumably been found for the first of these questions. In separate agreements with France, Italy, and Great Britain, Chile secured their assent to the establishment of three-member war-damages arbitral tribunals.[16] But the tribunals, which began to function in 1884, were destined to encounter serious obstacles.

The financial obligations of the Peruvian government, a disputed share of which devolved upon Chile after its conquest of Peruvian territory, were of two kinds. One was backed by *certificates* issued in the 1870's in compensation for Tarapacá's expropriated and nationalized nitrate industry; the other was represented by *bonds* issued, beginning in 1869, to finance internal improvements, and totaling an overwhelming £51 million.[17] Chile had attempted a partial solution of the Peruvian debt problem while the war was still in progress. Owners of certificates had been given the opportunity either physically to recover expropriated property or to accept in lieu thereof the proceeds from the sale of such properties at auction. Holders of bonds had been offered half the proceeds from sales of guano taken from deposits under Chilean control. The Ancón treaty had retroactively approved those arrangements and had also absolved Chile of responsibility for other Peruvian financial obligations, save those itemized in the peace agreement.

But Peru's creditors were not satisfied, for while some took advantage of Chile's offer in order to gain control of the best nitrate properties, there remained outstanding many certificates covering marginal and abandoned deposits whose worth was far less than the face value of the certificates. Furthermore, guano sales proved insufficient to reimburse the holders of bonds. When, over their protests, the Treaty of Ancón went into force, several European governments continued strongly to support the claims of their nationals. Chile was in a predicament. Submission to Great Power demands would damage both its treasury and its pride, and would deal a sharp blow to Chilean prestige throughout the continent. But resistance might produce a conflict with one or more of the Great Powers, a conflict of which Chile's South American antagonists would certainly take every possible advantage. Chile therefore sought to remove complications in its Great Power relations, primarily to clear the way for action in the South American arena.

BOLIVIA REJECTS ROLE AS CHILEAN SATELLITE

Chile continued to believe that the best solution to the Peru-Bolivian problem lay in Bolivia's transformation into a satellite. Toward that end Santiago sought to promote commercial relations with the Altiplano and to encourage the construction of road, rail, and telegraph communication between the Chilean-occupied littoral and the highlands of Bolivia.[18] Moreover, Santiago attempted to buy Tacna and Arica from Peru, at a price it hoped would be irresistible to hard-pressed Lima, in order to turn the two provinces over to Bolivia and complete the recasting of the South American power structure which had been initiated during the War of the Pacific.[19] But in 1885 Bolivia's Senate denied a concession for construction of a railroad to the port of Antofagasta on the ground that it would be an instrument of Chilean penetration and conquest of the Altiplano,[20] and the government of Peru refused to consider the sale of Tacna and Arica.[21] Chile was unable to attract Bolivia into its orbit.

RELATIONS WITH ARGENTINA

As Chile attempted to arrange its Pacific affairs, it behaved with caution toward the other South American nations, for it wanted to calm their suspicions and lessen the chance of their supporting Peru and Bolivia. As the most potentially troublesome, Argentina was the special object

of Santiago's concern. In the immediate postwar years the Chilean
government avoided even the mention of possibly controversial matters.
Thus, when Buenos Aires expressed its doubt that Bolivia held legal
right to its claimed Puna de Atacama territory, which was occupied
by Chile under the terms of the 1884 truce pact, the Chilean chancellery
chose to avoid any discussions of the matter until and unless the territory in question came under Chilean sovereignty.[22] And again, when,
without consulting Santiago, the Chilean minister in Buenos Aires suggested a modification of the 1881 boundary treaty, he was reprimanded
on the grounds that "even today, after three years of diplomatic tranquillity, animosity, far from being completely dead, produces feelings in
the press and in the clubs on the most futile pretexts. It behooves the
diplomatic action of both nations to help their respective governments in
the task, not easy in the present instance, of reëstablishing harmony and
friendship between their peoples. In order to accomplish this end there
is undoubted convenience in avoiding the very statement of ideas that
tend to arouse mutual national distrust."[23]

THE QUESTION OF REPRESENTATION IN PARAGUAY

Chile also avoided any action that might provide Argentina or any
other South American country with justification for intervening in
Pacific affairs. In this connection the Chilean chancellery backed away
from an otherwise sound diplomatic move, the establishment of a legation in Asunción. The Chilean minister in Buenos Aires advocated such
a step, through which he believed that Chile could exert its "moral force
in South America" to help lift Paraguay "from its prostration and
return to it a certain manner of independence of action which it has lost
as a result of the disasters of the war of 1865 to 1870." The minister
argued that Paraguay, since its defeat by the triple alliance, had played
"the role of a Poland with only the appearance of sovereignty. Her con-
querors have dominated her completely, sometimes in agreement with
one another, sometimes disputing for influence in Asunción, having
submitted its government to a guardianship which deprives it of all
prestige abroad and impairs its authority within the country. It is then
just, as well as good, politics to help that unfortunate people ... to
recover its full international personality."[24]

But it was altogether obvious that Paraguay was not the only defeated and prostrate nation on the continent, and the Foreign Minister
of Chile opposed his Argentine minister's argument by pointing out
that "the results of the recent War of the Pacific, and the hostile sentiments which our triumphs aroused in the different American sections,

counsel us to abstain from agreeing, for the present, though it may be with simple manifestations of adherence or sympathy, to the sanction of proceedings which can later have, because of the marked analogy of the situations, a moral reverberation against us."[25]

THE VISIT OF THE SPECIAL UNITED STATES COMMISSIONER

Chile's wish to avoid any South American intervention in the settlement of the Pacific question was echoed in its negative reaction to renewed United States interest in an international American conference. Notwithstanding its withdrawal in 1882 of invitations to such a conference, the idea of closer ties with Latin America was still alive in Washington, and in 1885 congressional agitation for stronger commercial relations led to the Latin-American tour of a special commissioner. In May, 1885, the President of Chile and several cabinet officers met with the commissioner for a discussion primarily concerned with economic matters. But during that meeting the specter of a Washington conference returned to haunt the Chilean chancellery, for the commissioner asked whether or not the government of Chile would favor the "convocation of an international congress of delegates from the American republics to arrange measures destined to guard the peace and promote the prosperity of this hemisphere."[26] In reply the President of Chile pessimistically declared that "long experience has made it evident that such congresses provide occasion for arousing suspicions and provoking agreements contrary to the views and aims with which their meeting was ostensibly promoted. Chile could not participate in the meeting of [such a] congress without prior assurances . . . that the principles of international policy which it has upheld and which are compatible with its interests would be maintained."[27] As in the instance of the ominous but stillborn Panama Congress, the government of Chile was firmly opposed to the convocation of any international gathering which, under the guise of developing machinery to keep the peace, might provide its adversaries with an open and influential forum wherein to discuss the problem of the Pacific.

DEMANDS OF THE NITRATE CERTIFICATE HOLDERS

Although Chile was vitally concerned in the immediate postwar period with South American relations, the problems posed by relations with the non–South American Great Powers proved to be a more constantly pressing challenge. Several of them, almost immediately after exchange of ratifications of the Ancón peace treaty between Chile and Peru, stepped forward to support the allegedly slighted claims of their nationals. First Italy, in June, 1884, upholding the position of the "Italian Nitrate Certificate Holders of Lima," demanded that Chile assume obligations identical to those formerly agreed to by Peru, obligations that included both interest and amortization on the certificates as well as back interest to 1879.[28] In the wake of Rome's demand came similar requests from France, Germany, Austria-Hungary, Belgium, and Holland,[29] but not, however, from Great Britain, whose government contented itself with advising Chile that it "accepts with satisfaction the security given by Chile that the government will take into equitable consideration the situation created for the creditors of Peru by the cession of a part of its territory."[30] Perhaps emboldened by Europe's apparent disunity, the Chilean chancellery procrastinated in answering these demands for payment on the Peruvian nitrate certificates.

ARBITRAL TRIBUNALS

Meanwhile the arbitral tribunals established to adjudicate the war-damages claims of Great Power nationals were encountering serious obstacles to their work. Their first awards had, by the end of 1884, stirred such heated protests from both the Chilean press and Great Power nationals that the Emperor of Brazil removed his neutral appointee, the major target of the criticism. In August, 1885, with a new Brazilian neutral member, the tribunals again commenced to function. Their subsequent awards met with Chilean approval, but Europeans charged that unfair standards were being applied. By early October the appointees of France, Italy, and Great Britain had notified the Chilean government that they would take no further part until more satisfactory award procedures had been adopted. This move placed the Chilean government in a difficult position. Dissolution of the tribunals would lead to direct diplomatic pressures under which settlement of damage suits would not only prove more costly but would be delayed to an extent incompatible with the interests of Chile, still under pressure from the nitrate certificate holders. Moreover, Chile's failure to support the decisions of the neutral arbiter would strain its relations with Brazil. Chilean agents in Europe therefore sought resumption of the tribunals' activities, but Italy, France, and Great Britain remained adamant.

Germany, which had not hitherto agreed to settlement of its nationals' claims by the tribunals, was now, however, favorably inclined toward an accommodation with Chile. Although the damage claims of German citizens were relatively small, their nitrate holdings were large enough to interest Berlin greatly. In exchange for Germany's participation in the activities of the tribunals, Santiago was prepared to treat its war-damages claims with generosity and to negotiate a settlement of the nitrate certificate claims. In September, 1886, Chile and Germany signed two agreements: one committed Chile to pay 50 per cent of the nominal value of the nitrate certificates owned by German citizens; the other established a Chilean-German abritral tribunal.

When the other European powers learned of the Chilean-German negotiations, they agreed to resumption of the tribunals' deliberations, though resolutely refusing to accept the 50 per cent payment agreed to by German nitrate certificate holders. In November, 1886, Italy sent a special mission to Santiago to seek a more favorable settlement for its nationals, and early the next year Chile bowed to Italian pressures, assenting to a figure to 66 per cent.

THE BALMACEDA REGIME

By this time a new administration, headed by José Manuel Balmaceda, had been inaugurated in Chile. The new president was experienced in affairs of state, possessed intelligence of a very high order, and was endowed with a vigorous and commanding personality. In the domestic sphere Balmaceda was committed to a nationalistic program designed to ensure the economic strength and independence of his country. Using the extraordinary revenues from the recently acquired nitrate industry, Balmaceda planned to finance an extensive program of internal improvements upon which it was hoped an increasing Chilean productive capacity might be based.

FOREIGN POLICY

As a corollary to its nationalistic domestic program, the Balmaceda administration supported an energetic foreign policy based upon recognition of certain obvious facts of Chilean domestic and international life. One of those facts was that both the internal development program of the country and its international power position were greatly dependent upon Tarapacá nitrate revenues. At the same time Tarapacá was isolated from the governmental and population center of Chile by the Atacama Desert, was inhabited by only a few Chileans, and was defensible only by sea; in short, the control of Chile over that immensely valuable territory was far from invulnerable. A great naval power could easily bring Chile to its knees by cutting off the Tarapacá sources of Chilean government revenues. Great Britain in particular loomed as a potential menace, for by the time Balmaceda assumed office a group of British investors, under the leadership of the notorious Colonel John North, had acquired ownership of Tarapacá's most productive nitrate works and were erecting a monopoly which seemed destined to come into conflict with the Chilean state.[31]

A further factor whose recognition was to be of influence in the development of Balmaceda's foreign policy was the danger inherent in the unsettled Peruvian and Bolivian problems. Until those questions were resolved, Chile would remain poised on a powder keg which might at any moment explode, leaving its relations with all South America in a shambles and providing other nations, especially Argentina, with a splendid opportunity to advance their own interests at the expense of Chile.

MILITARY AND NAVAL POWER

Responding to these realities, Balmaceda adopted a policy of investing, to the extent permitted by the demands of the internal development program, in the expansion of military and naval power. Chile's goal was armed might sufficient to cope with any conceivable threat to its Pacific Coast hegemony and to secure a definitive settlement of its South American problems on favorable terms. As Balmaceda explained, "In conformity with the plan for our future national security, I desire that Chileans be able to resist [the attack of] any possible coalition upon their territory, and that, if ... they are not able to equal the maritime strength of the Great Powers, they may prove, upon a strong military base and with a navy in keeping with their wealth, that there is no possible profit in undertaking war against the Republic of Chile."[32]

Balmaceda's policy represented an additional, and giant, step away from the policy that in the early days of the republic guided Chile's South American and Great Power international behavior. Once Chile had sought to perpetuate among the powers of its system an equilibrium favorable to its interests. Later, when an enriched Peru and forward-surging Argentina so acted as to change the nature of the system, Chile moved to establish a new equilibrium through the dismemberment of Peru and the creation of a Bolivian satellite. Having fallen short of achieving that goal while at the same time arousing the hostility of its neighbors and continent-wide distrust, Chile was now discarding the idea of maintaining any equilibrium whatsoever within its system. Instead, it was proposing to use its recently acquired resources in the creation of armed power able to "resist any possible coalition." With regard to the Great Powers, the position of Chile had undergone an even more dramatic change. In 1841 the Foreign Minister of Chile resignedly bemoaned the fact that "the Great Powers ...

hold in their hands the fate of the universe ..., a state of things which we can neither prevent nor ignore." Now Balmaceda called for sufficient naval power to "prove ... [to the Great Powers] that no profit is possible in undertaking war against the Republic of Chile."

THE ARMY AND EMIL KÖRNER

As one phase of the implementation of its defense policy, the Balmaceda administration moved strongly ahead with its predecessor's plans to improve the army's efficiency. Emil Körner,[33] a young professor of tactics and military history, arrived from Germany to instruct cadets at the Chilean military academy. Plans were pushed forward for a war college which would provide advanced specialized training for army officers. A few months after Balmaceda's inauguration, the curriculum of the military academy was reorganized to ensure greater professionalization. Shortly thereafter, in July, 1887, Körner delivered his first lectures, and at about the same date the war college offered its first courses.[34]

THE NAVY

Balmaceda's overriding interest, however, was the navy. He believed it urgently necessary to acquire faster, mightier ships of war and to fortify several strategically situated harbors. At the same time Balmaceda sought to reduce the nation's dependence upon Europe and to increase the efficiency of its naval operations by constructing a modern dry dock for the repair and renovation of Chilean ships. In 1887 the new administration's naval program was placed before Congress in the form of an initial request for £400,000 for the construction of one powerful ironclad.[35] The Chamber of Deputies displayed remarkable unanimity in its support of Balmaceda's naval policy. One of its members exemplified the chamber's grasp of the President's intent by pointing out that "since Chile has found itself under the indispensable obligation of requiring, as an indemnity of war, the appropriation of territories, it is necessary firmly to reconcile ourselves to an armed peace and to being in a position to defend ourselves."[36]

Another member of the lower house would have preferred a more ambitious program. Unsuccessfully proposing an appropriation of £1 million to be spent within six years, he insisted that Chile's location would impel it to assume an offensive posture in any South American war, and that the administration's essentially defensive program was therefore inadequate. He further argued that in any war with a European nation escort strength, which the administration had not demanded, would be required to prevent virtually immediate capture of Chilean warships, and that there would be a "distinctly different outcome if we were able to display, at the head of a squadron of cruisers, any two ships of the first order as formidable machines of war. The European antagonist would then have to send at least a double number of ships of great power and a double number of cruisers, which would make it think seriously before undertaking an enterprise that would cost it several millions and would at the same time weaken its naval forces in Europe."[37]

Balmaceda's naval program was overwhelmingly approved by Congress and won the support of the influential Círculo Naval, an organization of naval officers which had been advocating the maintenance of Chilean naval supremacy in the pages of its *Revista de Marina*.[38] The journal's editor regarded the proposed new ironclad as "a formidable answer to those who distrust our growth and our influence upon the destinies of . . . South America,"[39] and further claimed that, in combination with the exigencies of European power politics, the proposed warship would prevent any European nation from embarking upon an anti-Chilean venture.

Having secured the £400,000 naval appropriation, the Balmaceda administration ordered designs prepared for a 6,900-ton ironclad which would be the Western Hemisphere's most powerful ship; for two 2,100-ton cruisers; and for several smaller vessels.[40] The construction of those ships was begun in 1889. The fortification of the harbors of Valparaíso and Talcahuano was undertaken, and in 1888 a contract was awarded for the construction of a dry dock in the latter port.[41] In the same year the Chilean government awarded a subsidy to the Compañía Sudamericana de Vapores in return for the company's agreement to augment its fleet with vessels that could be converted to the service of the Chilean navy in wartime.[42]

TACNA-ARICA POLICY

Radically departing from the position of the preceding administration, Balmaceda sought to gain permanent sovereignty over Tacna and Arica, not for the ultimate benefit of Bolivia,[43] but in order to make those provinces a permanent and integral part of Chile and thus to make feasible the defense of Tarapacá in the event that Peru might later seek to reassert itself there. Moreover, in Balmaceda's view, Bolivia had to be persuaded permanently to cede its littoral to Chile without the compensation of Tacna and Arica. Balmaceda hoped to achieve that goal through economic and political agreements designed to fix Bolivia firmly within the Chilean orbit in the role of a satellite.

THE ARANÍBAR-TYLER CONTRACT

Chile first attempted to implement its new Peru-Bolivian policy in connection with the serious Peruvian debt question. Peru's British creditors, represented by a "Bondholders' Committee," and its French creditors, for whom the house of Dreyfus was spokesman, had in March, 1886, agreed to join in requesting the protection of their respective governments. But when Great Britain refused to coöperate with France,[44] the Bondholders' Committee presented to Peru an independent proposal ultimately embodied in a document called the Araníbar-Tyler contract, signed in London on May 26, 1887. The contract provided that the Bondholders' Committee would organize a corporation to which the Peruvian government would grant enormous concessions, including the ownership of the nation's railroads for sixty-six years and rights to exploit state-owned lands. In return the corporation would build specified rail lines, pay Peru a small sum in cash, and relieve it of its obligation in regard to the bonds. The contract provided for cancellation of only half the outstanding bonds; the remainder were to be retained by the corporation with the explicit understanding that it might attempt to collect their value from "other interested parties,"[45] meaning Chile.

Santiago moved swiftly to thwart Peruvian legislative approval of a contract that might lead to demands that it assume half of the huge bonded indebtedness of bankrupt Peru. Chile based its official objections on the contract's concession of "a large part of the [Peruvian] national sovereignty"[46] and its alleged violation of the Treaty of Ancón, which specifically relieved Chile of financial obligations not therein itemized.[47] Chile not only handed a direct protest to the Peruvian government,[48] but also tried to marshal the opinion of other American governments[49] against an arrangement that gave a foreign corporation such immense power. The strong stand of Chile, together with opposition inside Peru, succeeded in consigning the Araníbar-Tyler contract to oblivion; the government did not even submit it to the legislature.[50]

Great Britain, at the behest of the disappointed Bondholders' Committee, asked Chile what it proposed to do about its "responsibility for the claims in the province of Tarapacá, and about putting an end in this way to the permanent complaints of British creditors."[51] Chile responded by giving a detailed history of the Peruvian debt question, a history designed to support its contention that Chilean obligations were limited to those items specified in the Treaty of Ancón. But Santiago knew very well that, history or no history, it would continue to be subject to strong pressures from London so long as Peru's British creditors remained unpaid.

CHILE SEEKS TO PURCHASE TACNA AND ARICA

At this juncture Chile seized upon an idea for solving several problems with one large payment to the government of Peru: for 10 million pesos Chile would secure Lima's permanent cession of Tacna and Arica. With that sum Peru could make considerable inroads on its obligations to the British bondholders. Such an arrangement would rid Chile of the Tacna-Arica problem while terminating London's pressure on behalf of the bondholders. Moreover, as the Foreign Minister of Chile explained to his Lima envoy, through definitive acquisition of the two provinces "the power and influence of our country will gain greater vigor and extension."[52] Chile's agent in Peru was ordered to deal directly with the President and to inform him that "given the situation established by the peace treaty, the territories of Tacna and Arica are under the provisional dominion of Chile only *pro forma*, for it is certain that in reality they already form an integral part of Chilean national territory. It is therefore preferable that we terminate the question immediately in a manner satisfactory to both republics."[53]

Hoping to attract British support for its plan to purchase Tacna and Arica, as the deal would affect the financial interests of British citizens, the Foreign Minister of Chile held talks with London's minister in Santiago. In April, 1888, the Matte-Frazer Protocol,[54] which specified Chilean objections to the Araníbar-Tyler contract and contained the British envoy's agreement to the validity of those objections, was signed. During his conversations with the British minister, the Chilean foreign minister suggested that Great Britain inform the bondholders of Santiago's 10-million-peso offer to Peru and of the obvious fact that Peru might transfer that sum to its creditors.[55] This bold scheme for swinging London to the support of permanent Chilean acquisition of Tacna and Arica came to naught, however, for the Foreign Office would not transmit any proposal involving Peruvian territorial cession. On June 27 Great Britain so informed Peru, and gave assurances that London would take no action affecting Peruvian interests without prior consultation.[56]

The Peruvian government, supported by British firmness and national public sentiment, refused even to discuss Chile's purchase offer, and proceeded to negotiate with the British Bondholders' Committee for a revised contract which, like the first, failed to absolve Chile of obligations other than those listed in the Treaty of Ancón.

So vehement were Chile's objections to the revised contract that in November, 1888, Great Britain protested that continued Chilean opposition "will be considered by the government of Her Britannic Majesty as an unjustifiable intervention in the affairs between an independent state and British subjects."[57] When the revised contract nevertheless failed to win Peruvian congressional sanction,[58] Chile made a more favorable offer for Tacna and Arica,[59] but with no more success than before.

THE ASPILLAGA-DONOUGHMORE CONTRACT

Finally, in October, 1889, the Congress of Peru did approve a debt-cancellation arrangement known as the Aspillaga-Donoughmore contract. Again, while Chile was not specifically named, the British Bondholders' Committee had made it abundantly clear that it would demand Chilean payment of £4 million in order to relieve itself of obligations incurred as a result of its acquisition of Peruvian territory.[60] It was, however, to be the responsibility of the government of Peru to collect that £4 million from Santiago.

The interplay of Chilean, and British, and Peruvian interests which preceded the signing of the Aspillaga-Donoughmore contract revealed Chile's resolve to perpetuate control over Tacna and Arica, and Peru's equally strong resolve to resist that intention. When the contract was completed Chile once again found itself the unwilling target of demands to assume financial obligations which it had specifically disclaimed in the Treaty of Ancón. Thus, during the slightly more than three years it had been in office, the Balmaceda government had not succeeded in solving the Peruvian problem. But that problem was not the only one that had occupied Santiago during that time, for even as it negotiated with Lima, Chile was pursuing the development of a new Bolivian policy.

RELATIONS WITH BOLIVIA

Still officially at war, Bolivia and Chile were coexisting under the armistice agreement of 1884 which legalized, pending a formal peace treaty, Chilean occupation of the Bolivian littoral. Upon first seizing that littoral, Chile claimed that it was "revindicating" the region; but the littoral was still Bolivian, if only in law. However confident the Chilean government might have been of its ultimate permanent sovereignty there, such sovereignty had to await completion of a formal peace. Toward that end Chilean diplomacy had labored for several years.

Balmaceda's Bolivian policy was inaugurated with a decision to in-

corporate the littoral into the regular Chilean governmental structure
as the Province of Antofagasta, with absolute equality with the other
provinces of the Chilean nation. Bitterly but vainly had the Altiplano
protested both the introduction[61] and the enactment of the relevant
enabling legislation, charging that "this proposal contains, under inocu-
ous appearances, exhorbitant ends, abusive of Bolivia's sovereignty over
its territory occupied by Chile."[62]

The Chilean government's new approach to the Bolivian question
was clearly expressed in May, 1888, in instructions to its agent in the
Altiplano. He was to remind the Altiplano that even before its loss
of the littoral it had lacked an adequate outlet to the sea and could
not reasonably expect to gain one in a war that it had both provoked
and lost. Furthermore, Bolivia must understand that Chile would
never provide it with a seaport so located as to interrupt its territorial
continuity. And, in addition, Chile wanted Bolivia to know that it
would brook no interference from the Altiplano in Chile's handling
of the Tacna and Arica matter. But this bitter pill was to be admin-
istered with Chile's assurances that if and when Bolivia finally came
to realize that it had been defeated in the War of the Pacific, and
would negotiate a peace treaty suitable to Chile, "the government of
Chile will examine and take into account the situation of its [Bolivia's]
commerce and the necessity of assuring its economic independence."[63]
Chile desired a treaty in which Bolivia would relinquish its littoral,
not in exchange for any outlet to the sea, but merely in return for economic concessions from its victorious enemy.

The fruits of Chile's tough new Bolivian policy ripened no more
rapidly than had those of its revised Peruvian position. An influential
sector of the Altiplano's leadership remained determined to insist upon
an outlet to the sea. Continued hatred of Chile was a formidable obstacle to a formal peace, and now the success of Chile's policy was
being threatened by a possible Bolivian-Argentine *rapprochement,*
toward which those two ill-wishers of Chile were moving even as the
dormant Chilean-Argentine boundary question threatened to spring
to life once again. The successful conclusion of a *rapprochement* between the Altiplano and Buenos Aires would provide Bolivia with an
alternative to a Pacific Coast outlet to the sea, and with a counterpoise
to Chilean influence in its affairs. And as the boundary differences between Chile and Argentina grew sharper, Bolivia's hopes for an Argentine understanding grew stronger. It therefore became even more
important for Chile to solve its Bolivian problem on satisfactory terms,
for with each passing year the rivalry between Chile and Argentina

was growing and with it the need for Chile to marshal its power to the point where it could, if necessary, stand alone against any and all challenges.

ARGENTINE-BOLIVIAN RELATIONS

Contributing importantly to Argentina's establishment of cordial relations with Bolivia and to the embitterment of its boundary conflict with Chile was its own remarkable economic growth in the 1880's, together with a mounting conviction among Argentines that their nation was destined, by virtue of its inherent superiority, to become the leading nation in South America, if not in all Latin America. From the standpoint of Chile's vital interests, therefore, the crucial element in the Bolivian-Argentine *rapprochement* and the boundary conflict was the tendency of expanding Argentina to push its influence toward, and perhaps right up to, the shores of the Pacific.

Above the general danger to Chile's vital interests which any entente between La Paz and Buenos Aires held, the threatened harmony had two aspects whose implications were especially menacing: the construction of railroads and the negotiation of a boundary treaty. As early as October, 1887, the Chilean chancellery was warned by its minister in Buenos Aires of "the purpose, sometimes admitted and sometimes hidden, in building some of these railroads. Any railroad line that leads to the Bolivian frontier invariably gains decided [government] support.... Railroad lines that may be called commercially strategic are considered matters of farsighted policy.... In its present session [the Argentine] Congress has approved three or four railroads proposed with those objectives."[64]

In explaining the readiness of La Paz to coöperate with the designs of Buenos Aires, Chile's envoy pointed out that "oppressed as it is within its deep Andean valleys and without assured communication with the Pacific,... [Bolivia] is inclined to be the favorable ally and the efficacious collaborator of any country that will offer it this anxiously sought communication with the Atlantic. For Bolivia such proposals are... the vital condition for its progress."[65] The Chilean agent in Buenos Aires therefore strongly argued that "Chile, without antagonizing the Argentine Republic, and like it freely seeking its own development, can completely frustrate designs that seek to separate Bolivia from the Pacific and from the natural influence of Chile. Bolivia... can be an aid and even a bulwark against hostile threats, and in no way is it advantageous that a powerful nation, such as Argentina would be if it were mistress of the trade and commerce of Bolivia and enlarged by the ever-increasing numbers of people coming to it from Europe, advance toward the Pacific."[66]

Underlying the above dispatch was Chile's assumption that it must dominate the Pacific Coast of South America, and with it the Pacific Ocean, "so that it may be called a Chilean lake."[67] The Chilean government could spare no effort to prevent Argentina from gaining influence over Bolivian policies and, through that influence, a possible Pacific foothold.

The menacing implications of the continuing Argentine-Bolivian boundary talks were less immediately apparent in Chilean government circles. It was suspected that Bolivia might agree to certain territorial concessions in exchange for help in acquiring Tacna and Arica,[68] and it was feared that Chilean-occupied areas might be affected.[69] In the latter respect Chilean suspicions were well founded, for in a treaty finally signed on May 10, 1889, Bolivia ceded to Argentina part of the Chilean-held Puna de Atacama in return for recognition of Bolivia's sovereignty over Tarija and over certain disputed areas in the central Chaco.[70] The terms of the Bolivian-Argentine agreement, while presumably secret, were apparently not beyond the intelligence of the Chilean chancellery, for on September 26, 1889, the Foreign Minister telegraphed his envoy in Buenos Aires: "SEND FIRST MAIL BOUNDARY TREATY ARGENTINA BOLIVIA."[71]

CHILEAN-ARGENTINE BOUNDARY DISPUTE

As indicated, the *rapprochement* between the Altiplano and Buenos Aires was of concern to Chile because of Santiago's sharpening boundary dispute with Argentina. Boundary disputes, now acute and now chronic, were the congenital international disease of Spain's former colonies. The acute phase of the Chilean-Argentina conflict in the late 1880's was owing to three circumstances: joint failure to proceed with the boundary's physical demarcation, as required in the treaty of 1881; ambiguous wording of the 1881 treaty; and growing Argentine interest, as a result of its rapid economic expansion, in gaining control of areas whose ownership had not been definitively established.

The treaty of 1881 provided that the demarcation of the frontier would be executed by "experts," but specified a date neither for beginning the demarcation nor for its completion. As early as 1883 Buenos Aires had prodded Santiago to name its experts; as the years passed, the government of Argentina became more and more irritated by Chile's failure to take action. In Buenos Aires the delay was attributed first to one and then to another motive: domestic Chilean politics; resentment over Argentina's position on the War of the Pacific; Chile's desire to evade fulfillment of a treaty that some Chileans believed had wrongfully deprived them of Patagonia.[72] In August, 1888, under severe

Argentine pressure, Chile signed a convention[73] establishing a "commission of experts" whose task it would be to conduct the boundary demarcation. But not until early 1890 was that convention even fully ratified. In the meantime disagreement mounted concerning the meaning and interpretation of the treaty itself.

The first article of the 1881 agreement declared that the "boundary between Chile and the Argentine Republic is, north to south, to the 52d parallel, the cordillera of the Andes. The frontier line will run in that length through the highest peaks ... that divide the waters and will pass between the slopes that come out from one side and the other."[74] The syntactical shortcomings of this description permitted Argentina to insist that the line must be drawn from highest peak to highest peak in the principal chain of the Andes, and allowed Chile to maintain that the line must be drawn between the highest peaks that divide the waters. When the treaty was drafted those alternative interpretive possibilities may have seemed of slight importance. But exploration carried out during the 1880's was to demonstrate that the line of *divortium aquarum* lay considerably to the east of the highest peaks of the principal chain of the Andes. And in between lay some 94,000 square kilometers of territory, an area one-third larger than the combined territories of Costa Rica and El Salvador.

But the size of the area was not the primary issue in the hot dispute that developed over the interpretation of the first article. Of greater importance was the fact that acceptance of the *divortium aquarum* line would give Chile territory in Patagonia,[75] whereas acceptance of the "highest peaks of the principal chain of the Andes" line would transform Argentina into a two-ocean power by placing it in possession of the mouths of several rivers that emptied into the Pacific.

During the 1880's the dispute over interpretation of the treaty was not diplomatically formalized. Rather, its implications were slowly pressed upon the awareness of the Chilean government by the feverish interest of Argentina in the exploration and development of remote peripheral regions. In late 1887 Chile's minister in Buenos Aires informed Santiago of the excited reports in the Argentine press about a Patagonian expedition which had discovered, so it was claimed, three very large rivers originating in Argentina territory which flowed into the Pacific and therefore would provide Argentina with ports on that ocean. The Chilean envoy, however, did not believe in the existence of those rivers, and was convinced that the newspapers in question were merely seeking to arouse support for the idea of Pacific ports for Argentina.[76]

Several months later the Chilean minister in Buenos Aires expressed fear that failure to settle the boundary matter promptly might allow "real or false interests" to entrench themselves in the disputed areas. An adventurous spirit of speculation prevailed in Argentina: syndicates were being formed to acquire lands or concessions to exploit lands; English companies had staked out locations near potentially disputable regions; from time to time explorers hailed the discovery of valuable forests and rich mines in those unknown southern areas. It was obvious that the boundary must remain unmarked no longer.[77] And as the months passed, the Chilean government did become increasingly concerned over Argentine concessions to private companies of lands in disputed territories near rivers that flowed into the Pacific.[78] Of especial seriousness was a grant to the British Argentine South Land Company, a concession clearly granting land on the Pacific Coast itself.[79]

Toward the end of 1889 Chile moved in two directions to deal with the Argentine boundary problem. It made plans to occupy part of the disputed area by establishing an installation on the Pacific Coast at the mouth of the Palena River, which originated east of the Andes.[80] It also sought a written Argentine commitment to the effect that (1) Argentina would invalidate land grants in territories proven to be Chilean, and (2) "in points which are considered near to the *divortium aquarum,* the establishment of colonies will not be permitted nor will any act of dominion be exercised by either Chile or Argentina until the experts establish to which ... these territories belong.'"[81] But the government of Argentina, quite aware of the real stakes, would not, by recognizing the validity of the *divortium aquarum* as a boundary determinant, risk its potential position as a Pacific power. It therefore refused to grant Chile the requested commitment.[82]

CHANGE IN THE BRAZILIAN GOVERNMENT

At the same time that Argentina's expansive tendencies and its *rapprochement* with the Altiplano were making it increasingly important for Chile to reach a peace settlement with Bolivia, two events were taking place which gave that task added urgency. One was an international conference; the other was a shift in the South American power structure occasioned by events in Brazil.

In November, 1889, with the forced abdication of its monarch, the Brazilian empire expired. The nation's new provisional government met with little serious opposition, but neither did it have any strong support. It was therefore eager to obtain quick recognition from foreign countries. On November 18 and 19 its foreign minister informed the nations that had maintained relations with the empire that a federal republic had been established, that it recognized the preceding regime's obligations, that it wanted cordial relations, and that it would welcome recognition. The world's Great Powers were somewhat slower to respond than the new government would have liked,[83] but the nations of South America—above all Argentina—welcomed the new republic to their midst with great speed.

BRAZILIAN-ARGENTINE RAPPROCHEMENT

Within a few days of the Emperor's abdication, Buenos Aires recognized the provisional government and designated December 8 as a national holiday for celebration of "the advent of the Republic of the United States of Brazil."[84] The new republic's provisional president, Deodoro da Fonseca, reciprocated by ordering similar ceremonies in honor of Argentina, but more than ceremony marked the coming *rapprochement* between the ancient rivals of the Plata. Negotiations were commenced to end the long-standing Misiones boundary dispute, and on January 5, 1890, after two hours of telegraphic negotiations between Buenos Aires and Rio de Janeiro, a tentative agreement was reached under which the area would be almost equally divided.[85] It was then announced that Brazil's foreign minister and his Argentine counterpart would meet in Montevideo to sign the definitive treaty ending the Misiones conflict.[86]

CASTELLÓN-ELÍAS CONVENTION

Although there is no formal record of the cold chills that those Platine events sent down the spine of the Chilean government, the Chilean chancellery moved hastily to pull around its shoulders the warm blanket of improved relations with Peru and, indirectly, with Great Britain. On January 8, 1890, in Santiago, Chile and Peru signed a convention in which the former assumed certain obligations to Peruvian bondholders, obligations that it had hitherto tenaciously rejected. Chile's concessions in the Castellón-Elías convention satisfied the Bondholders' Committee and made it possible to proceed with implementation of the Aspillaga-Donoughmore contract of 1888, relieving Peru of an unbearable financial burden. In defending the convention to the legislature, the Chilean foreign minister admitted that his country had relinquished resources that were its legal property, but argued that "this act has infused new life into the organism of a neighbor nation and friend which found itself utterly prostrate, and has completely removed the possibility that its creditors might press a claim against

us which, although it would lack a strict juridical basis, might have
created a dangerous situation."[87]

As Brazil and Argentina sped toward an apparent *rapprochement,*
Chile sought to hasten the solution of its Argentine boundary conflict.
On January 11, 1890, there were exchanged the long-delayed ratifications of the August, 1888, convention providing for the appointment
of experts to demark the boundary. Two days later Diego Barros Arana
was named as Chile's expert. He would work with the Argentine who
had received his appointment many months earlier.[88]

THE FIRST INTERNATIONAL AMERICAN CONFERENCE
IN WASHINGTON

The potential danger to Chile in the Argentine-Brazilian accord crys-
tallized during the First International American Conference, which
convened in Washington in October, 1889. A year earlier, upon receiving Washington's invitation, Santiago had raised objections to the
conference in general and, in particular, to its proposed discussion of
"a definitive plan of arbitration for all questions, disputes, and differences which may exist or can arise." Such a discussion would permit
Chile's enemies to air their grievances and views concerning the un-
finished business of the War of the Pacific, and was therefore contrary
to Chilean policy. But the United States had persisted and had elicited
from Chile a reluctant acceptance, with the understanding that Santiago's delegation would participate only in economic and commercial
deliberations.[89]

From October until the middle of January, 1890, during which period
the Empire of Brazil had collapsed and had been replaced by the
Federal Republic, nothing occurred at the conference to displease Chile.
Delegates occupied themselves with discussions of rules and procedures,
traveled about the United States as guests of the government, explored
noncontroversial matters of substance, and got to know one another
better. But in January, "to demonstrate their bilateral solidarity,"[90]
the delegates of Argentina and Brazil submitted to the conference an
arbitration proposal whose approval would both censure Chile[91] and
paralyze its action in respect to its immediate neighbors. The joint
Argentine-Brazilian proposal affirmed that "international arbitration
is a principle of American public law to which the nations in this conference bind themselves, for decision, not only in their questions on
territorial limits, but also on all those in which arbitration is compatible
with sovereignty."[92]

The Chilean delegates, opposed in principle to compulsory arbitration, were seriously alarmed by the assumptions that were proposed as guides to arbitral proceedings. Among them were the following: "in event of war, a victory by arms shall not convey any right to the territory of the conquered; . . . the treaties of peace which end hostilities may fix pecuniary indemnifications . . . but, if they contain cessions or abandonment of territory, they may not be made final . . . without the prior evacuation of the territory of the conquered power by the troops of the other belligerent; . . . acts of conquest, whether the object of war or its consequence, shall be considered a violation of the public law of America."[93]

But the purpose of joint Argentine-Brazilian proposal was more than censure, for it also stated that "the present declarations are applicable not only to differences that may arise in the future, but also to those that . . . are now under actual discussion."[94] Approval of the proposal could thus substantially damage Chilean interests. At the least it would provide Bolivia and Peru with a strong talking point which they might attempt to use as a basis for reopening the entire question of the war settlement. Moreover, the joint nature of the proposal hinted that Argentina and Brazil might together seek to take a hand in the affairs of the Pacific Coast. The Platine *rapprochement* did indeed seem to bode ill for Chile.

In committee the joint proposal was broken down into (1) a treaty for compulsory arbitration, and (2) a separate set of principles. Chile advanced strong objections to the proposal, while Peru vehemently supported it and lauded "the representatives of two of the most powerful nations of South America" for having initiated it.[95] After modifications that made them applicable only to future conflicts, both parts of the proposal were unanimously approved by the conference, with the abstention of Chile.

Notwithstanding the proposal's temporal limitations, the Washington conference was far from a victory for Chile. Its inability to prevent discussion of arbitration led, as the chancellery had feared, to manifestations of hostility against Chile in the form of anticonquest declarations. Although these statements were modified, they were approved by every Latin-American nation represented. Furthermore, the conference had revealed the sinister possibility of Argentine-Brazilian coöperation in Pacific affairs. Quick to grasp the significance of such a denouement, Peru sought to cling to the original proposal, and indulged in flattery of those "powerful nations of South America."

Nonparticipants in the conference were equally aware of the implications of the Argentine-Brazilian *rapprochement* for Pacific Coast affairs. Rumors circulated, and reached Chile, that an alliance had been formed among Argentina, Brazil, and Peru. So widespread was the rumor that, to allay the fears it aroused, the Chilean chancellery at the end of April, a few days after adjournment of the Washington conference, published Argentina's denial of such an alliance in the *Diario Oficial.*[96]

Renewed Efforts To Solve the Peru-Bolivian Problem

The Balmaceda administration, faced with multiplying difficulties in foreign relations, proceeded resolutely toward the implementation of its tough Peruvian and Bolivian policies. Again Peru was approached on the sale of Tacna and Arica, but this time it was the aid of France, rather than of Great Britain, which Chile sought in helping to complete the purchase. The French minister in Santiago had complained that Peru's French creditors had not received the adequate satisfaction provided to the British. The Chilean government therefore raised its previous offer for Tacna and Arica by 4 million pesos, with the understanding that the additional sum be used by Peru to meet the demands of its French creditors. Informed of the plan, the Peruvian minister to Chile told the Foreign Minister that it produced "a painful impression,"[97] for, as he pointed out, the Peruvian government had already made clear its intention to accept no modification in the plebiscite provision of the Treaty of Ancón.

In Lima the Peruvian foreign minister, approached by the Chilean envoy with the new purchase proposal,[98] reacted strongly against it. He, too, spoke of the "painful impression" that it occasioned, and announced "Peru's firm and irrevocable intention . . . neither to cut short the term of ten years fixed by the Treaty of Ancón for the definitive resolution of the fate . . . of Tacna and Arica, nor to alter the form of the plebiscite established by the treaty."[99] The Foreign Minister of Peru added force to his point by declaring that "the stated resolution of my government . . . cannot be modified in the least by any type of consideration, either pecuniary or political, inasmuch as the Constitution of the Republic prohibits absolutely the signing of pacts that may be opposed to its sovereignty and territorial integrity."[100]

Frustrated in its purchase attempts, Chile sought to secure the permanent incorporation of Tacna and Arica through victory in the plebiscite stipulated by the Treaty of Ancón. Balmaceda is said to have told the Peruvian minister in Santiago, after his purchase plan failed, that the "Chileanization" of the two provinces would be undertaken; twenty thousand Chilean citizens would be sent into the region, and millions of pesos would be spent there upon public works, for which the local population would have Chile to thank.[101]

BALMACEDA'S FOUR-POINT PROPOSAL TO BOLIVIA

At the same time, Balmaceda sought Bolivia's aid in securing permanent possession of Tacna and Arica. In September, 1890, a new minister was sent to the Altiplano bearing personal and confidential instructions prepared by the president himself.[102] The new envoy's mission was negotiation of a peace treaty encompassing four major points which well reflected the nature of Balmaceda's Peru-Bolivian policies: (1) Bolivia was to assist Chile in obtaining Tacna and Arica by renouncing its own pretensions and using its influence upon commercially important Bolivian elements in the two provinces to obtain a pro-Chilean plebiscite vote. (2) Although Chile would gain permanent sovereignty over Bolivian territory currently under occupation, it would do so in such a way as to avoid violation of Bolivian pride and patriotism, and as to provide Bolivia with an outlet to the Pacific. To this end, Chile would buy the Bolivian littoral instead of seizing it as a war indemnity, the purchase price being the construction of a railroad connecting La Paz with Tacna and Arica. (3) There would be created a virtual binational common market through which Bolivia would be brought intimately and permanently into the commercial sphere of Chile. (4) Bolivia and Chile would mutually guarantee each other's territorial integrity against any Peruvian threat.

Such a treaty, notwithstanding guarantees of territorial integrity, would transform Bolivia into a Chilean satellite, for, instead of becoming a stronger and more independent state, the Altiplano would become dependent upon a Chilean-built railroad through a Chilean-controlled Tacna and Arica. It is thus clear that the Balmaceda administration had renounced the concept of a South American equilibrium and replaced it with a concept of armed peace under which Chile, in possession of the Bolivian littoral, of Tarapacá, and of Tacna and Arica, and maintaining a highly trained army and a powerful navy, would be strong enough to prevent Great Power intervention and to maintain Chilean hegemony against any possible coalition of South American powers.

Bolivia's president, tormented by the usual complex of serious domestic problems which plagued the Altiplano, was anxious to reach a definitive settlement with Chile. Moreover, there was currently a crisis in relations between Peru and Bolivia, and Argentina had not yet ratified the Bolivian-Argentine boundary treaty which had been signed a year and half before. The government of Bolivia therefore accepted Chile's terms for a final treaty of peace. But dramatic and tragic events within Chile itself acted to prevent the fruition of Balmaceda's forceful Bolivian policy.

CHAPTER XI

REVERSION TO EQUILIBRIUM

As THE YEAR 1890 ended, Chile completed a decade in which its power position had been improved, first by victory in the War of the Pacific and then by energetic exploitation of the fruits of that victory. Chile's increased power was accomapnied by its abandonment of a long-held policy favoring South American equilibrium and its adoption of a policy of armed might as the best deterrent to any possible anti-Chilean coalition. Chile's Tacna-Arica and Bolivian policies revealed the change that its international views had undergone. During and immediately after the war Chile still sought to secure a continental equilibrium by strengthening Bolivia, but it abandoned that policy in favor of transforming the Altiplano into a landlocked satellite. The viability of its revised policy was evidenced by its almost successful attempt, in late 1890 and early 1891, to secure a peace treaty in which La Paz renounced any claim to Tacna and Arica.

But as a definitive imposed peace with Bolivia was within its grasp, Chile began to suffer a subtle decline in its power position, in the wake of which the Chilean government reverted to its earlier policy of equilibrium, seeking to establish a favorable international environment wherein Bolivia would constitute a strong and independent ally.

THE REVOLUTION OF 1891

The deterioration of Chile's power position was related to both international and domestic developments; the latter concerned a malady to which Chileans had long proudly considered themselves immune—civil war. Nevertheless, such a war ravaged Chile from January to October, 1891, and was followed by a critical period of internal reorganization, which in turn was accompanied by a conflict with the United States which threatened to take the country again to war.

A constitutional question plunged Chile into civil war:[1] Was the nation to be ruled by presidential or parliamentary government? This issue, which had long smoldered just beneath the surface of Chile's apparently well-functioning political system, burst into flame after Balmaceda failed to gain congressional approval for his energetic program of economic development through governmental intervention.

In January, 1891, congressional leaders, having secretly won the support of key naval officers, threw down the gauntlet and declared that President Balmaceda was deposed for having failed to abide by the constitution. While the army remained loyal, the defection of a significant part of the navy was to prove tactically decisive. By April, 1891, the Congressionals had seized control of the crucial nitrate regions of the north and established a government at the city of Iquique. Balmaceda was thus deprived of vital revenues which the Congressionals were in their turn able to use to bring the remainder of Chile under their control.

In the wartime conduct of Chile's international affairs, Balmaceda was immediately forced into a defensive position and remained there throughout the conflict. Chile's stature was sufficient to ward off overtly aggressive attempts by rival nations to settle their disputes with Chile during a civil war, but the Balmaceda government did suffer diplomatic rebuffs and defeats which hastened the victory of the Congressionals.

The Great Powers, with the exception of the United States, were notoriously sympathetic with the revolutionary cause, partly because they disapproved of the repressive measures that Balmaceda had instituted to combat his enemies, but even more because they believed that Balmaceda favored nationalization of the nitrate industry. None of the Great Powers went so far as to recognize the belligerency of the Congressional Junta of Iquique, but they did take action that contributed to the success of the revolution. In early April, 1891, after a futile attempt to destroy northern nitrate-processing plants, Balmaceda, in order to prevent Congressional receipt of both military supplies and nitrate revenues, declared the region's ports closed to commerce.[2] Great Britain, Germany, and France strongly protested, and France sent two warships into Chilean waters, threatening to recognize the Congressional Junta's belligerency if the ports were not reopened. Deserted by the navy and confronted with the display of European solidarity, Balmaceda reopened the ports.

THE MATTA-REYES PROTOCOL

In relations with South American governments, too, the Balmaceda regime suffered diplomatic reverses. Colombia failed to control shipments of war matériel to the Congressionals via Panama.[3] Authorities in Mollendo, Peru, were bold enough to deny permission to Chilean naval officers to send a telegram to Santiago and to order their departure within twenty-four hours.[4] Disregarding Santiago's protests, Peru interned a unit of the pro-Balmaceda army which had escaped across its border. As for Argentina, its technically correct attitude covered a hotbed of revolutionary sympathies and activities.

It was Bolivia, however, which inflicted upon Balmaceda his most notable diplomatic setback. When Congressional forces gained control of the north, the favorable peace treaty negotiations of the Balmaceda government collapsed. The junta, now in control of ports through which Bolivia's commerce flowed and from which the Altiplano derived certain important revenues, began to bring pressure for recognition upon La Paz. Notwithstanding Santiago's assurances that Bolivian interests would be fully protected,[5] Bolivia received an agent of the junta and after some vacillation recognized its belligerency and commenced to negotiate a preliminary agreement on the terms of a peace treaty. That agreement, the Matta-Reyes protocol, granted Chile not only commercial privileges but, more important, sovereignty over all the territory it was occupying under the terms of the armistice. For its part, Bolivia obtained Chile's promise to assume more than 5 million pesos of Bolivia's obligations, largely to Chilean citizens, and to convert both Arica and Antofagasta into free ports for the transit of Bolivian commerce. The Matta-Reyes protocol failed to mention the matter of a railroad; nor was Bolivia asked to renounce its pretensions to Tacna and Arica.[6] The junta's success was Santiago's failure, and Balmaceda's envoy asked for his passports, warning Bolivia that it would be sorry for its unfriendly actions after the rebellion had been suppressed.

But the Congressional army was on the offensive, and in September, 1891, invaded the Central Valley, seized Santiago, and forced José Manuel Balmaceda to flee for asylum to the Argentine embassy. There he waited until his legal term of office had come to an end and then put a bullet through his head. The Chilean civil war had come to an end, but not so the diplomatic problems that it had set in motion.

THE BALTIMORE AFFAIR

The United States minister in Santiago had made no secret of his friendship for the Balmaceda regime, and when the Congressionals entered Santiago many Balmacedistas took refuge in the United States legation. Serious tension developed when the United States envoy refused the new government's demand that the refugees be turned over to it for trial. In Santiago anti–United States sentiment ran so high that Washington's legation had to be provided with a strong armed guard. In a riot in Valparaíso in October, 1891, one sailor from the United States naval vessel *Baltimore* was killed and five others were wounded. The United States protested and demanded reparations, but its representations went unheeded. In December President Benjamin Harrison reported in detail on the entire question of political asylum and on the

Baltimore affair, promising to call a special session of Congress should Chile fail to make adequate reparations. By January 25, 1892, Chile had still failed to reply satisfactorily, and Harrison asked congressional authorization to use force if necessary.[7]

THE ARGENTINE-BOLIVIAN BOUNDARY TREATY

At the same time that Chile's relations with Washington were taking an unfortunate turn, its relations with its South American neighbors also deteriorated. In Bolivia the Matta-Reyes protocol aroused such intense opposition that Santiago, at the request of the Bolivian foreign minister, agreed to delay its submission to the Chilean Congress.[8] In Argentina a move was under way to deal with the Chilean boundary question from a position of strength. In that connection, and unknown to the government of Chile, Buenos Aires turned to Bolivia, whose representative was in the Argentine capital to expedite approval of the 1889 boundary treaty, which, in late 1891, was still pending in the Argentine Senate. The Altiplano's envoy had at first attributed the treaty's failure to win approval to the fact that it granted to Argentina certain Chilean-occupied territory in the Puna de Atacama, and that the Senate was withholding sanction in order to avoid conflict with Chile. But when he offered to assume full responsibility for securing Chilean evacuation of the area, he discovered that his interpretation was incorrect[9] and that Argentina had failed to approve the treaty because it wished to change it so as to conform with its legal argument in the case of the Chilean boundary question.

THE BOUNDARY CONFLICT WITH ARGENTINA

While the differing Argentine and Chilean interpretations of their 1881 boundary treaty had not yet been thrown into the diplomatic arena,[10] Buenos Aires was aware of the existence of a difference of opinion, and of its significance.[11] Chile proposed to insist upon the *divortium aquarum* line; Argentina demanded the "highest peaks of the principal chain of the Andes" line. It developed, however, that in its 1889 boundary treaty with Bolivia Argentina had not adhered to the principle that it upheld in respect to Chile. The Bolivian treaty specified that in "Atacama [the boundary] will follow the cordillera of the same name from the head of Devil's Gorge toward the northwest, through the eastern slope of the same cordillera, to where the Sierra of Zapalegui begins."[12] The Atacama cordillera referred to above lay well to the east of the cordillera of the Andes, thus involving a considerable territorial difference; but even more important to Argentina was the treaty's failure to maintain "the same line as the treaties with Chile from one end to the other."[13] It was for this reason that the Bolivian boundary treaty had not been approved in Buenos Aires. The government of Argentina now sought to repair its mistake, and on November 12, 1891, after discussions with the Bolivian envoy, an adjusted agreement was approved by the Argentine Senate. It stated that "the definitive boundaries between the Argentine Republic and the Republic of Bolivia are established in this manner: for the west, the line that joins the highest peaks of the cordillera of the Andes, from the northernmost point of the boundary of the Argentine Republic with that of Chile to the intersection with the 23d parallel."[14] Argentina believed that it had strongly buttressed its precedential-legal position in the Chilean boundary controversy. It had, in addition, laid claim to a far larger portion of the Chilean-occupied Puna de Atacama—a claim whose effectuation would bring the Argentine Republic uncomfortably close to Chile's littoral province of Antofagasta.

Still, during the period of severe tension in relations between the United States and Chile, Buenos Aires took two further measures designed to consolidate its Chilean position. First, in response to intimations from the Secretary of State of the United States, the Foreign Minister of Argentina promised his country's support to the United States, should it become involved in a war with Chile over the *Baltimore* affair. In the event that United States forces were to seize Antofagasta as a base, the Foreign Minister "categorically promised to supply cattle and other goods to the United States at Antofagasta within six days."[15] Second, Buenos Aires seized the opportunity provided by the dislocations of the new post-Balmaceda government and Chile's problems with Washington to bring into the open, for the first time, interpretive differences concerning the 1881 treaty.

On January 3, 1892, the Argentine expert on the boundary commission arrived in Santiago. No sooner had he and his Chilean colleague started to work on the actual boundary demarcation than they disagreed over instructions to be given to the workers in the field. The Argentine insisted that the field technicians be explicitly ordered to draw the boundary through the "highest peaks," while Chilean Barros Arana was equally firm in demanding adherence to the principle of the *divortium aquarum,* maintaining steadfastly that the line was never meant to run from "highest peak" *to* "highest peak," but only *between* the "highest peaks that divide the waters."[16] These differences were fundamental. At stake were possible Argentine ports on the Pacific and possible Chilean control of extensive Patagonian territories. The work of the boundary commission was suspended, and the Argentine expert contacted his government for further instructions.

At the end of January the Argentine foreign minister, now seeking a direct settlement, suggested that the boundary experts and the foreign ministers of Chile and Argentina meet at Mendoza, Argentina, to revise the 1881 treaty.[17] Two days later the President of Argentina froze his government's position by taking his expert's request for further instructions to a cabinet meeting, where Chile's interpretation of the treaty was rejected.[18]

Chile was equally stubborn. Its boundary expert vehemently opposed participation in the proposed Mendoza conference, insisting that "we would merely cede certain territory we believe to be ours at one point, in order to obtain in compensation an equal portion of territory at another point."[19] Accepting its expert's position, Santiago advised Buenos Aires that "Chile . . . does not wish in any way to alter a treaty signed in the friendliest spirit, whose terms, in the judgment of those who drafted it, would give no occasion for vacillation in implementation."[20]

As Chile reached a tense impasse in its dispute with Argentina, it was already enjoying the results of a relaxation in its problem with the United States. After reports of possible Argentine coöperation with Washington in the event the *Baltimore* affair should lead to war, Santiago withdrew a request for the recall of the United States minister,[21] disavowed an offensive statement by its own Washington envoy, and suggested that the Supreme Court of the United States adjudge the question of damages suffered in the *Baltimore* matter. By the end of January, 1892, Washington had accepted Santiago's offer, and the threat of open conflict had virtually vanished.[22]

Upon the heels of that settlement, Argentina and Chile reached an understanding which temporarily delayed a serious crisis. At the suggestion of the Argentine envoy in Santiago, the boundary commission experts omitted from their formal minutes any reference to differences concerning treaty interpretation. And it was further agreed that, pending ultimate resolution of differences, the technical crews would go into the field and begin marking the actual boundary.[23]

A SLACKENING OF CHILEAN POWER

With relaxation of its Argentine dispute, Chile's relations with its immediate neighbors appeared superficially to have been restored to their pre–civil war condition, but in reality the Congressional victory had inaugurated internal political changes which would slowly but relentlessly erode the power position of the Chilean nation. The strong presidential government of previous decades was replaced by a parliamentary regime in which cabinets held office at the pleasure of Congress. The Congress, lacking the political polarization that might have developed had there existed at least one significant national issue, disintegrated into many fragments which struggled fiercely among themselves over power, patronage, and principle. As no single congressional clique was large enough to dominate the legislature, government by coalition became the rule. Because all congressional coalitions proved to be fluid and highly unstable, cabinet changes were frequent, governmental efficiency declined, and continuity of policy was difficult to achieve.

To be sure, foreign policy did not inspire the acrimonious disputes which over domestic concerns toppled one government after another. The Chilean leadership, politically divided though it was, agreed upon the basic goals of the nation's foreign policy, and in times of crisis was able to rally broad popular support. But the inherent instability of Chile's post-1891 parliamentary system persistently, if subtly, weakened the nation's influence and effectiveness in intra–South American affairs.

A further source of post-1891 Chilean debility lay in the refusal of those who had opposed Balmaceda's economic program to reconsider their position after the Congressional victory. Balmaceda had advocated a planned, government-sponsored, nationalistic program of long-term internal economic development and diversification, to be supported by the extraordinary revenues that were flowing into the national treasury from the northern nitrate deposits acquired in the War of the Pacific. The Chilean aristocratic leadership had rejected Balmaceda's economic concepts, and continued to reject them, deceived by steadily growing nitrate revenues into thinking that Chile was enjoying satisfactory economic growth, and that there was no need for economic planning. The myopia evident in such willingness to rely upon the extraordinary nitrate revenues represented a decline in the dynamic vision, vitality, and enterprising spirit which had, since the colonial period, characterized the Chilean elite and had been an important factor in raising Chile to a preëminent position upon the continent. The vigor of Chile's action in intra–South American affairs was inevitably affected by such relaxation.[24]

RELATIONS WITH BRAZIL

Foreign trends also played a part in clouding Chile's preëminence, and of these the most subtle and persuasive was a shift in Brazil's fortunes, which, indeed, affected the power structure of the entire continent.

In the eighth and ninth decades of the nineteenth century, Chile's strong South American power position was based in part upon its community of interests with Brazil, and upon the latter's rivalry with Argentina. It was precisely for this reason that the Argentine-Brazilian *rapprochement* of 1890 seriously threatened Chilean interests. That *rapprochement* collapsed, however, when the Brazilian Congress rejected the Misiones boundary treaty which had been signed in Montevideo with such fanfare. Simultaneously, a new, if transient, sympathy arose between the Chilean Congressionals, struggling against Balmaceda, and their Brazilian counterparts, who were locked in a struggle with authoritarian President Deodoro da Fonseca. Upon Balmaceda's defeat the Brazilian parliament formally congratulated the Congressionals.[25] And for its part, the Chilean Chamber of Deputies, at the height of the Brazilian presidential-parliamentary conflict, unanimously resolved to extend "to the Congress of the Brazilian Republic expressions of sincere adhesion and sympathy for its defense of its institutions."[26]

The downfall of Deodoro late in 1891 brought to power in Brazil a government friendly to Chile. The new Brazilian foreign minister was reported to believe that "the most impolitic act of the founders of the Republic was the direction which they impressed upon its international relations, a direction called upon to alienate from Brazil the friendship and former sympathies of the Chilean people."[27] By mid-1892 the Chilean chargé d'affaires in Rio was able to write that "the Foreign Minister of Brazil . . . spoke at length of the sympathy of Brazil for Chile, of the common cause of both countries against the Argentine Republic. He went so far as to tell me that he 'was hoping that the day would not be distant when the squadrons of our countries might work together in the Plata estuary.' "[28]

But imperial and republican sympathies were two different matters. The collapse of Brazil's monarchical government brought with it a decline of political stability and of consistency in foreign policy. Brazil had exchanged the evil of monarchical rule for the evils of financial difficulty, deep domestic discontent, open rebellion, and frequent ministerial changes, which in the new republic's early days tended to neutralize its diplomatic action.[29] However great its sympathy toward Chile, Brazil could no longer be regarded as the reliable entente partner of earlier decades.

THE SITUATION OF PERU

The painful, and at times barely perceptible, convalescence of Peru wrought further subtle changes in the South American power structure and in Chile's power position. Peru's slow economic recovery from the

effects of its prewar spending orgy and of its defeat in the War of the
Pacific began with settlement of the British bondholders' demands.
From 1890 on, although progress was hampered by lack of a needed
radical economic reorientation and by threats to internal political stability, improvement could be discerned. Peru was still unable to buttress
its diplomacy with the threat of force, but it did shift somewhat from a
purely defensive position vis-à-vis Chile.

In attempting to affirm its international position as a precondition
to the recovery of Tacna and Arica, Peru moved in three directions, at
each point encountering Chilean opposition. To remove the difficulties
inherent in its disputed Ecuadoran boundary,[30] the Peruvian government, on May 2, 1890, signed an agreement with Ecuador known as
the García-Herrera Treaty. Behind that pact lay an old and acrimonious
dispute, which in 1887 Peru and Ecuador had agreed to settle by one
of two alternative methods: direct negotiations or arbitration by the
Queen of Spain. Peru, choosing the latter alternative, prepared its case
and in December, 1889, presented it to the arbiter, confident that the
award would deprive Ecuador of any territory in the disputed provinces of Jaén and Maynas and therefore of any rights in the vital
Amazon region. Ecuador, preferring a direct settlement, suggested that
an attempt in that direction be made, but with the participation of
Colombia, because of Bogotá's interest in the disputed region. Although
Peru refused to include Colombia in the negotiations, it did proceed
with bilateral discussions from which issued the García-Herrera agreement.

The boundary treaty of 1890 unexpectedly granted Ecuador extensive concessions, including lands whose position gave Quito rights
on Amazonian tributaries, making of Ecuador what Peruvian policy
had long opposed—an Amazon power. Peru made those surprising concessions to allow it single-mindedly to deal with Tacna and Arica, free
of the threat of possible Chilean-Ecuadoran coöperation. In Quito the
treaty was almost immediately approved, but in Peru congressional
opposition was strong. Finally, in October, 1891, conditional legislative
approval was secured,[31] but when Ecuador resisted certain suggested
changes in the treaty, relations between the two nations began to deteriorate.

Aware of its stake in negotiations between Quito and Lima, Chile
observed them with great interest. Having agreed to sell Ecuador some
surplus war matériel,[32] Chile ordered its envoy in Peru to "express to
the Ecuadoran minister in Lima the desirability of delaying the signing
of the boundary treaty between his country and Peru."[33] A critical point
in Ecuadoran-Peruvian relations was reached in October, 1893, when,

after Quito's rejection of treaty changes and subsequent Peruvian congressional insistence upon them, the Peruvian consulate in Quito was stormed by an enraged mob. A Peruvian mob retaliated in Lima,[34] and an open break was averted only through the prompt mediation of Colombia and the Holy See. In the temporary calm after the storm, Bogotá successfully pressed for a tripartite solution of disputed Amazonian boundaries. In December, 1894, Colombia, Ecuador, and Peru agreed to submit their differences to arbitration by the Queen of Spain.[35] The relaxation in its Ecuadoran relations enabled Peru to cope with Chile more effectively.

Another maneuver in Peru's offensive to regain Tacna and Arica was a proposal made to Santiago in September, 1892, under which Peru would regain the provinces without either a plebiscite or a consolation payment but in exchange for commercial privileges which would in effect create a common market highly beneficial to Chilean shipping and commerce. Peru further offered to assist in the solution of the Bolivian problem by allotting two thirds of Arica's customs receipts to the Altiplano and to the building of railroads to improve Bolivia's communications with the outside world.[36] Although this proposal was approved by the Chilean agent in Lima—who may even have helped to formulate it[37]—it was rejected in Santiago, whose envoy in Lima was ordered to inform Peru that Chile was pleased with its recognition of the mutual benefits of a free-trade policy, but deplored the linking of commerce with the controversial question of Tacna and Arica. Above all, Peru was to be made to understand that "it is not the aim of Chilean policy to renounce the expectations that the Treaty of Ancón assures Chile with regard to the acquisition of the designated territory."[38]

Peru's proposal of September, 1892, was, however, a minor part of its offensive to regain control of its two lost provinces. Between 1890 and 1895 its major efforts were directed toward securing the plebiscite guaranteed in the Treaty of Ancón, for Lima was convinced that any fairly conducted vote would be favorable to it because the predominantly Peruvian population of the two provinces had remained unmoved by Santiago's "Chileanization" program.[39] If, as required by the Ancón pact, a plebiscite were held before March, 1894, there could be little question as to its outcome. As early as 1890 Lima asked its envoy in Rome to collect and forward historical records of plebiscites that had taken place on the Italian peninsula, together with copies of regulations governing their conduct. That same year, anticipating an important dispute, the Peruvian Foreign Office prepared a policy paper on "Who Ought To Vote in International Plebiscites."[40]

After the Chilean civil war the Peruvian government began actively and openly to work for a plebiscite, and for victory in that plebiscite. In August, 1892, the Peruvian foreign minister formally requested that Chile set a date for the opening of negotiations on the matter,[41] thus launching a series of futile Peruvian attempts to implement the plebiscite clause in the Treaty of Ancón. In April, 1893, having waited in vain for Santiago's reply to his August request, the Foreign Minister indicated to the Chilean envoy that more than sufficient time had elapsed for the receipt of instruction from Santiago, and asked him to set the date for the start of negotiations.[42] Cornered, the Chilean replied that his government had several times previously attempted to solve the Tacna-Arica question, and that he would be pleased to resume negotiations on the day and at the hour indicated by Peru.[43]

Having committed himself, the Chilean minister in Peru then wired his chancellery: "MINISTER FOREIGN RELATIONS DEMANDING REPEATED NOTES DISCUSSION TACNA ARICA PROTOCOL. INSTRUCTIONS URGENT. ANSWER."[44] In its reply the chancellery indicated its intentions with unmistakable clarity. The minister in Lima was told to insist upon four points: voter lists must be drawn up by special qualifying boards; permission to vote must not be denied on the basis of nationality; Chilean authorities alone would conduct the vote; and, should Chile lose, it would not evacuate the provinces until Peru had completed payment of the stipulated cash consolation. Chile was obviously not prepared to liquidate the Tacna-Arica question by means of a plebiscite, and its four points were clearly designed to force Peru into an alternative solution which might leave Chile in control of the two provinces. The Chilean foreign minister candidly stated:

Chile seeks to place Peru in the position of being unable to accept [the four points] and of obliging it, indirectly, to enter into negotiations of another order. . . . This chancellery judges it advisable to take the matter to another sphere of action, convinced that . . . it must minimize the possibility that Chile may be dispossessed of these provinces, which would not be improbable were the plebiscite held under conditions acceptable to Peru. I recommend especially that you endeavor to exchange as many notes as possible [with Peru] in order to gain time, and that you insist upon consistency in minor details.[45]

The negotiations to which the above instructions referred, dragging on throughout 1893, served primarily to throw into relief the issues that divided Peru and Chile. There was disagreement concerning control of the provinces in the likely event that the ten-year period stipulated in the treaty expired before the plebiscite was held. Peru insisted that its citizens alone should vote, whereas Chile, counting on support from both Chilean and Bolivian residents, demanded that nationality constitute no barrier to participation. Chile, rejecting Peru's demand for joint plebiscite supervision, insisted that it alone must conduct the vote. And, finally, Chile even refused to consider Peru's suggestion that their differences of opinion be submitted to arbitration.[46] In spite of the differences, however, an agreement was signed in Lima on January 26, 1894, consisting of two major points: (1) the plebiscite would be conducted under "conditions of reciprocity which both governments shall deem necessary to obtain an honest election";[47] and (2) the loser would receive, in addition to the stipulated monetary consolation, strategically valuable territorial compensation.

The Chilean foreign minister rejected the January agreement, accusing his Lima envoy of disregarding instructions. "Reciprocity," he insisted, implied equality, and Chile would allow Peru only one representative to Chile's two on a plebiscite supervisory board. The Foreign Minister asserted that Chile would not alter its position, and that any further talks must take place in Santiago.[48] But no agreement had been reached when the relocated discussions were halted by a Chilean cabinet crisis which was still unresolved when the ten-year plebiscite deadline stipulated in the Treaty of Ancón was reached and passed.

On March 27, 1894, Lima's envoy informed Chile that Peru no longer recognized Chile's right to occupy Tacna and Arica, and urged the Chilean government to proceed with implementation of the January agreement. At this point the Peruvian envoy first learned, from the newly named foreign minister, that the agreement had been officially disavowed and that Chile requested entirely new negotiations. The Foreign Minister suggested that the plebiscite date be delayed to allow for procedural planning.[49] While a new Chilean agent went to Lima to seek either a four-year postponement or an outright cession of Tacna and Arica,[50] talks continued in Santiago between the Chilean foreign minister and Peru's envoy. The latter finally accepted, as a basis for discussion, a Chilean proposal that the two disputed provinces be divided into three parts; the southernmost would be annexed to Chile, the northernmost to Peru, and the middle to the winner of an 1898 plebiscite. Such a compromise was not acceptable to Lima. But the fact that it had been advanced at all by Chile indicated that Santiago was responding to the realities of a changing South American power structure. Brazilian unreliability and Peruvian resistance played their parts in that change; but more important by far was the burgeoning power of the Argentine Republic.

ARGENTINE PROGRESS

As the decade of the 1890's opened, it was becoming obvious that in the elements that constitute potential international power Chile was being outdistanced by Argentina. Augmented by a high birthrate and a vast influx of immigration, the population of Argentina rose by almost 1 million between 1885 and 1895, when it was approaching a total of 4 million. In the same period Chile's smaller initial population had grown by scarcely 200,000, so that in 1895 there were three Argentines for every two Chileans. The economy of Argentina, responding to a growing population and accelerating integration into the world economy, was also expanding more rapidly than that of Chile, a circumstance reflected in the respective governmental revenues of the two nations.

In 1894 a former minister of the Chilean treasury, viewing the mounting disparity between the economic situations of Chile and Argentina, pointed out that

In 1878 the financial situation of the Republic [of Argentina] was virtually identical to that of Chile. The government receipts of Chile were $15.5 million, and those of the Argentine Republic were $18 million.... Neither nation then possessed extraordinary income independent of its inhabitants' labor and capital; it may thus be calculated that the wealth and the productive capacity of the two peoples were in balance, given the fact that with almost equal populations their production and budgets were also similar. As of 1894 the situation is very different. Chile has acquired extraordinary income from nitrate and iodine, which in 1892 produced a net income of $26,535,759 in common currency. The Argentine Republic has acquired no exceptional resources. Its entire income is from taxation borne completely by its inhabitants, their capital and their labor. Nevertheless Chile, even with nitrate, had a total income in 1892 of $64 million, and the Argentine Republic, without nitrate, had a total income in 1893 of $124 million.[51]

THE BOUNDARY QUESTION

Argentina's improved position was reflected in its relations with Chile. Notwithstanding the 1892 agreement temporarily to submerge differences of interpretation of the 1881 boundary treaty, the issue remained unresolved. During 1893, as Chile uneasily observed the enlargement of Argentina's army and navy,[52] emerging disagreements led to a new crisis. A binational technical team attempting to place boundary markers in Tierra del Fuego under the terms of the 1892 agreement was unable to make any progress, for its members could not even agree upon maps to serve as the basis for their work. Another binational field crew did manage to place a single marker at San Francisco Pass, but Argentina objected to the marker's location because it had been placed at the "highest peaks of the Andes which divide the waters" in the eastern rather than the western range of the cordillera. That meant that the Chilean-occupied portion of the Puna de Atacama would now have to be recognized by Argentina as belonging to Chile—and this Argentina was not prepared to do. Buenos Aires therefore claimed that the marker's position was incorrect under the terms of the treaty of 1881, and that the phrase "cordillera de los Andes" referred to the "principal chain of the Andes," and that "principal" meant the western rather than the eastern branch of the cordillera. To the applause of the Buenos Aires press, the government of Argentina demanded immediate removal of the marker.[53]

Even as an aroused Chilean public was demanding its government's rejection of Argentina's demand, a new Argentine boundary expert arrived in Santiago. His mid-January, 1893, meetings with the Chilean expert produced a recapitulation of existing differences, together with the Chilean's insistence that "Argentine ports on the Pacific [are] completely unacceptable."[54] Regarding agreement impossible, the Argentine expert informed his government that minutes would be drafted making clear the respective irreconcilable positions.[55] In view of the greatly disturbed public emotions on either side of the Andes, official confession of these differences as irreconcilable would have produced a dangerous crisis, but in February a new Argentine envoy reached Santiago who seemed eager to settle matters at the diplomatic rather than the military level. Tension eased, and at a March 10 meeting of the new envoy with the Chilean foreign minister and with the boundary experts of both countries, a tentative agreement was reached and promptly approved in Santiago. But Buenos Aires, while first giving its telegraphic approval in principle, raised questions that were resolved only after six weeks of suspenseful diplomatic activity during which the Chilean government dismissed its boundary commission expert for his persistent refusal to move from a strict *divortium aquarum* position.

While frantic boundary negotiations were in progress the protagonists were acutely aware of the intense public interest in both countries. When a Chilean newspaper erroneously claimed a victory for the principle of *divortium aquarum,* the Argentine boundary expert warned Chile that such reports "could serve to misguide public opinion, and that although what was published might soothe and satisfy the public spirit of Chile, it might equally disturb that of Argentina, alarming it and raising obstacles to the success of negotiations."[56] Santiago seemed to share this view, for during the weeks of negotiations it devoted much effort to calming a Chilean public opinion very much disturbed about the possibility of Argentine ports on the Pacific.[57]

PROTOCOL OF MAY, 1893

Finally, on May 1, 1893, Chile and Argentina signed a protocol to the treaty of 1881. From Chile's point of view the second article was the most important:

The undersigned declare that in the judgment of their respective governments, and in accordance with the spirit of the boundary treaty, the Argentine Republic exercises dominion and sovereignty over all the territory that lies to the east of the principal chain of the Andes, as far as the coast of the Atlantic, and the Republic of Chile over the territory west of the principal chain, as far as the coast of the Pacific; it being understood that, by the dispositions of said treaty, *the sovereignty of each state over the respective coastline is absolute,* and such that Chile may not aspire to any point near the Atlantic, nor the Argentine Republic to any point near the Pacific.[58]

The above clause seemed to promise Chile that Argentina would not endanger its Pacific hegemony. From Argentina's viewpoint, however, the designation of spheres of influence was less important than the terminology of the clause, for, while the first article repeated the original treaty's "highest peaks . . . which divide the waters," the second made clear reference to the "principal chain of the Andes." Argentines might therefore, if they wished, consider themselves to have triumphed over Chile's *divortium aquarum* principle.[59] Article VIII, which provided for Chile's review of the San Francisco marker location, was also regarded as an Argentine triumph. Finally, the protocol's negotiators, in view of the inflamed public opinion in both nations, agreed to keep its terms secret until approval had been completed. Almost eight months later, toward the end of December, 1893, ratifications were exchanged.

But the May protocol did not end Chile's problems with Argentina. Early in 1894 technical teams returned to the field and immediately began to dispute the location of boundary markers. Argentina's hope that Article II's reference to "principal chain" excluded the *divortium aquarum* doctrine was simply not shared by Chile, whose foreign minister insisted that "we . . . have taken care to note, each time that the opportunity presents itself, that the words 'principal chain of the Andes' . . . mean merely the uninterrupted line of peaks that divide the waters and form the separation of the valleys or hydrograhpic regions tributary to the Atlantic on the east and to the Pacific on the west.'"[60]

Moreover, the results of Chile's reconsideration of the San Francisco marker location proved totally unsatisfactory to Argentina, who was notified, at the end of September, 1894, that there appeared to be no reason to change the marker's position.[61] The San Francisco marker question led to a public debate which raised tempers to the boiling point on both sides of the cordillera.

As the boundary question grew more and more dangerous, Chile was forced to counteract the efforts of Buenos Aires to strengthen its bonds with Chile's Pacific Coast antagonists. Because of the general hostility aroused by the conquests of the War of the Pacific, Chile lived in fear of the formation of a South American coalition against it. Chilean leaders tended to be alarmed by the slightest indications and merest rumors of closer relations between and among nations they regarded as unfriendly. Chile's extreme sensitivity was responsible for its reaction to a May, 1893, address made by the Argentine minister to Peru upon accepting membership in a Peruvian veterans' organization known as a center of anti-Chilean sentiment. Because the Argentine envoy "condemned our actions ... and praised the Peruvian spirit"[62] on the very anniversary of Chile's famous naval victory at Iquique and during the Tacna-Arica negotiations, the Chilean foreign minister instructed his Argentine envoy to protest that the action of the minister to Peru "cannot possibly be understood at a time when Chileans are removing from their international relations all sources of their weakening or obstruction."[63] Sensitivity to the finest nuances of Argentine-Peruvian relations inspired the Chilean minister in Buenos Aires to report by telegraph to his chancellery that *"La Nación* ... is publishing a long study on the Tacna-Arica situation with the purpose of influencing Argentine public opinion against the interests and the foreign policy of Chile."[64] *La voz del Perú,* a pro-Peruvian magazine published in Buenos Aires, was a further source of concern to the Chilean foreign minister[65] who, by early 1894, was sufficiently suspicious of Argentine intentions to telegraph the Chilean minister in Lima asking him to verify a rumor that Argentina was providing Peru with 15,000 rifles.[66]

While hints of an Argentine-Peruvian rapport merely stirred malaise along the Mapocho, indications of a growing Argentine-Bolivian understanding spurred the Chilean chancellery into action. Although anti-Chilean sentiment among the Bolivian populace was of long standing, and was accepted in Santiago as a fact of international life, persistent reports late in 1893 and early in 1894 of anti-Chileanism in high government circles seriously perturbed Chile.[67] Those reports, together with news of difficulties being encountered by Chilean business interests in Bolivia,[68] were regarded as all the more ominous because La Paz and Buenos Aires were apparently drawing closer together just as Santiago and Buenos Aires were moving farther apart.

MODIFICATION OF THE BOLIVIAN-ARGENTINE BOUNDARY TREATY

Two signs of Argentine-Bolivian *rapprochement* especially alarmed the Chilean government: a boundary treaty and a commercially stra-

tegic railroad project.⁶⁹ Late in 1893 Santiago learned the terms of the
May, 1889, secret Bolivian-Argentine boundary treaty, as modified in
November, 1891. The Chilean minister in La Paz was at first more
concerned than his chancellery, insisting that Chilean rights in the
Puna de Atacama, which had been guaranteed in the 1884 truce with
Bolivia, had been violated. Chile's minister to the Altiplano wanted
his government to participate in the Bolivian-Argentine boundary
demarcation procedure in order to protect its rights and interests;
but, above all, he was disturbed by his belief that the Bolivian-Argentine treaty was "designed to weaken our rights and influence in this
part of the Pacific."⁷⁰ Aroused to action, Chile asked Bolivia for an
explanation in writing of the implications of the boundary treaty with
Argentina.⁷¹

The disturbing Bolivian-Argentine railroad project, formalized in
a treaty of June, 1894, would connect an existing Buenos Aires–Jujuy
line with the Bolivian town of Oruro, which was also the terminus of
the Chilean Antofagasta railway.⁷² Such a link had been previously
proposed by private interests; it was the Argentine government's promised financial assistance that now made the matter significant to Chile,
for it began to appear that the line might actually be constructed; such
a line represented a genuine threat to Chilean commercial and political
interests. In the first place, the Altiplano's possession of an alternative and competitive Platine-Atlantic outlet would adversely affect
the economic health of the port of Antofagasta and reduce the income
of the Antofagasta railway. Second, given the depth of the anti-Chilean
sentiment that pervaded the Altiplano, it was not unreasonable to suppose that Bolivian commercial ties with Argentina would be followed
by political bonds between Buenos Aires and La Paz. Third, should
these highly unfavorable possibilities materalize before Chile had solved
the Tacna-Arica question with Peru, and while Brazilian friendship
was uncertain, then the Pacific Coast hegemony of Chile would indeed
be subject to pressures that it might be unable to resist. This triple
threat determined the Chilean government to replace at all costs its
ten-year-old Bolivian truce pact with a permanent treaty of peace.

THE MAY, 1895, TREATIES WITH BOLIVIA

On May 18, 1895, after several months of negotiations in Santiago,
three separate Chilean-Bolivian agreements were signed.⁷³ The first,
a treaty of peace, officially ended the state of war between the signatories. In it Chile assumed certain financial obligations of the Bolivian
government in exchange for recognition of Chilean sovereignty over

the former Bolivian littoral and over the area in the Puna de Atacama which, although under Chilean occupation, had been ceded by La Paz to Argentina. The second, a treaty of commerce, combined a reciprocal trade agreement with guarantees for mutual protection of the nationals of one signatory doing business in the territory of the other, and included provisions for railroad construction. The third, and by far the most important, was a secret commitment under which Chile promised to give Tacna and Arica to Bolivia when and if it secured definitive possession of those provinces; or if it ultimately proved impossible to acquire Tacna and Arica, to provide Bolivia with a seaport at Vitor Bay which lay in the southern part of the province of Arica, and was itself not yet legally owned by Chile.

With the Bolivian treaties of May, 1895, Chile, pressed by its deteriorating international power position, reverted to a policy of establishing a new South American equilibrium. Once again Chile proposed to create a relatively strong Bolivia, at once independent of Argentina and unfriendly toward Peru, a Bolivia whose self-interest would require it to assist Chile in the maintenance of the latter's Pacific Coast hegemony.

CHAPTER XII

TOWARD RAPPROCHEMENT
WITH ARGENTINA

DURING THE WAR OF THE PACIFIC Chile formulated the policy of creating a favorable South American equilibrium by means of a strong Bolivian ally. That policy, although it was not implemented, was in accord with the international realities of the time. Supported by Chile, Bolivia might have constituted a counterpoise to weakened Peru, leaving Chile to enjoy its Pacific hegemony and enabling it to uphold its interests with respect to Argentina, which was then a nation comparable to Chile in population and economy. Moreover, Argentina's diplomatic action with respect to Chile was restricted not only by its Bolivian boundary question, but more importantly by its traditional rivalry with the stable Brazilian monarchy. But sixteen years later, when the Chilean government reverted to the equilibrium policy and attempted to implement it in the three treaties of May, 1895, it was far less in accord with the realities of South American power politics.

By 1895 reincorporation of Tacna and Arica had become the rallying point for resurgent Peruvian patriotism, and it was most unlikely that, short of force, Chile could implement the secret treaty providing for transfer of the provinces to Bolivian sovereignty. Nor was it realistic to suppose that the Altiplano would settle for less, in spite of the fact that provisions for such a contingency were contained in the secret treaty. Bolivia's improved bargaining position, a result of its Argentine *rapprochement,* made acceptance of any port other than Arica virtually unthinkable. But the reality of South American international life, which in 1895 boded most ill for the success of Chile's reactivated equilibrium policy, was the change that had taken place in the power position of Argentina.

By 1895 the diplomatic position of Buenos Aires had significantly improved. Its Bolivian boundary dispute was eliminated, and its rivalry with Brazil was mitigated not only by the relative internal instability of the new republic's early years, but also by the approaching settlement of the Misiones boundary dispute through United States arbitration.[1] In 1895 Argentina had a direct interest in the settlement that Chile was seeking to reach with Bolivia, for the peace treaty had recognized as Chilean the Puna de Atacama, and the Puna de Atacama had been recognized by Bolivia as Argentine in the Argentine-Bolivian treaty of 1893.

Most responsible for Argentina's diplomatic strength, however, was the fact that it had overtaken Chile in terms of resources and population. Argentinians were becoming convinced that their nation would and should play the leading role in South American affairs. As an Argentine citizen who had recently visited Chile stated in 1894, "Argentina should march at the head of the South American nations. . . . It should closely follow, with dignity and generosity, their international affairs, because its interests are bound to all of them. Today Buenos Aires is the intellectual and commercial center of South America. . . . We are in a historical moment, and we must make the voice of the Argentine chancellery clearly heard."[2]

The realities of power politics in 1895 clearly indicated that a stable South American equilibrium could best be achieved, not through implementation of Chile's old Bolivian policy, but rather by means of an entente with Argentina. Understandably, the very idea of such an arrangement, much less its execution, was difficult for Chileans to grasp. Argentina was a strong, confident, and expanding nation with which Chile was involved in a dangerous boundary dispute. And Chileans were convinced that their own record of order and progress marked them as the leading South American nation. Nevertheless, as its Bolivian policy encountered one obstacle after another, and as its relations with Argentina assumed an increasingly ominous character, Chile came to realize that its Pacific Coast hegemony depended upon an understanding with Buenos Aires.

ARGENTINE REACTION TO THE MAY TREATIES

Even before the Chilean-Bolivian treaties of May, 1895, had been signed there arose Argentine objections to their rumored provisions. Fiery nationalist Ernesto Quesada predicted dire consequences, declaring in *El Tiempo* of Buenos Aires that

Chile . . . has consolidated its conquests, has satisfied Peru, and has made a vassal of Bolivia. The concession of a port to the latter, and the construction of a railroad to La Paz, complemented by a Chilean-Bolivian customs union, has converted Bolivia . . . into a commercial possession of Chile. ∴ . . Chile has thus become the England of this continent and has transformed Bolivia into a nearby India. . . . Peru, deprived of the natural riches that once made its fortune, has been converted into a poor country, surrounded by nations under the direct influence of Chile, so that it . . . has become the Ireland of the new American England. From the economic and political hegemony that Chile is coming to exercise, it is but a step to the establishment of a great confederation of the United States of the Pacific in which Chile would play a role like that of Prussia in the present German empire. The extraordinary significance of Chile's actions for the South American equilibrium cannot be concealed from anyone. Chile would become . . . the foremost nation not

only of the Pacific but of all South America. . . . On the Atlantic there would remain
two large but not great nations—Brazil and Argentina—counterbalancing each
other.[3]

La Prensa of Buenos Aires, after the terms of the peace and commerce treaties had been published, reacted with greater moderation.
But it was fully aware of the implications of the treaties for future
Argentine-Chilean relations, and saw the connection between their
timing and Chile's deteriorating relations with Buenos Aires:

Chile is discussing an important boundary matter with the Argentine Republic and
has met with difficulties. . . . In these moments the diplomats in La Moneda [the
Chilean chancellery] . . . initiate something called the international policy of the
Pacific which identifies the destinies of Peru and Bolivia with that of Chile. . . .
And is it not a grand policy, a truly international policy, aimed at disarming those
clear enemies and transforming them into friends bound to the commerce of Chile . . .
at a time when the Argentine-Chilean boundary demarcation is subject to such disagreements that they [Argentina and Chile] are hastening their military organization?[4]

Concerned particularly about the threat to its Puna de Atacama
interests, the Argentine government reacted sharply against the Bolivian-Chilean negotiations. To frustrate Chilean designs, Buenos Aires
sent to the Altiplano a prominent senator who was familiar with the
boundary question.[5] Upon learning of this, Santiago abruptly canceled
its own minister's plans to return home and ordered him, in a coded
telegram, to "REMAIN UNTIL TREATIES DISPATCHED. ARGENTINA MAKING
ACTIVE EFFORTS OBSTRUCT. . . . YOU MAY RETURN CHILE SEPTEMBER."[6]
A letter followed explaining that "Argentina is taking steps to . . . obstruct the approval of these pacts, having already designated Señor
Dardo Rocha . . . to aid such objectives. . . . Your presence in [Bolivia]
is required to thwart plans whose execution has doubtless been confided
to the new Argentine minister."[7]

BOLIVIAN REACTION TO THE MAY TREATIES

The presence of an Argentine agent was not needed, however, to arouse
Bolivia's opposition to the pacts with Chile. From the first La Paz was
reluctant to submit the treaties to legislative debate. A substantial element of Bolivian opinion was committed to a policy of coöperation with
Argentina, as opposed to Chile, and the Altiplano was on the eve of
a national election in which foreign policy was a major issue.[8] Of greater
impact upon Bolivia's attitude, however, was the fact that the treaty
of peace was not directly tied to the seaport provisions of the secret
treaty of territorial transfer.[9] Responsible Bolivian opinion doubted
that Chile would secure Tacna and Arica, in which event Bolivia would

have relinquished its littoral in vain; and even if Bolivia did get Tacna and Arica, claimed some critics of the treaties, it would come into subsequent conflict with Peru without having secured sufficient assurances of Chilean assistance.[10]

It was against this unpromising background that Chile moved to secure the approval of the May pacts, an approval badly wanted as Chile's complications with Argentina mounted. Convinced that the agreements would certainly be approved if the Altiplano was confident of getting Tacna and Arica, Chile instructed its Peruvian minister to "consider as the principal and, for the moment, the only objective of your mission . . . to obtain from the government of Peru a settlement that gives us the ability to comply with contractual obligations," and further informed him that "the success of the entire negotiation with Bolivia depends upon our acquisition" of Tacna and Arica. The Chilean envoy in Lima was told that, "by deflecting the current from the riverbed that the Argentine Republic is trying to open, we may definitively minimize the danger of a possible understanding between the two countries that might be united by their common hostility toward Chile. . . . The treaties recently concluded . . . close to Argentine policy the vein of hatred easily exploitable in countries forced to suffer the consequences of an unfortunate war. . . . All our diplomatic action must be concentrated on the acquisition of . . . Tacna and Arica."[11]

Chile's Peruvian envoy was provided with detailed negotiating instructions. He was first to seek direct cession to Bolivia of Tacna and Arica, using the argument that Peru could thus demonstrate its true friendship for its former ally. If Peru rejected direct cession to Bolivia, as Chile was certain it would do, the envoy was to ask for direct cession to Chile, if not of the two provinces totally, then at least of the essential parts of them, in exchange for "an immediate, direct, indemnification sufficient to compensate national pride and adequate to the needs of the government . . . in Lima."[12] If, as was not unlikely, a direct cession such as that could not be agreed upon, the Chilean envoy was to proceed to a discussion of plebiscite conditions, remembering that "the stipulations . . . must produce the desired result."[13] To its familiar conditions of total Chilean control and eligibility for Chilean and Bolivian nationals, Chile added two requirements: (1) in the event of Peruvian victory, Chile would receive sovereignty over southern Arica, including the Bay of Vitor, site of the alternative Bolivian port; and (2) also, in the event of its victory, Peru must pay the stipulated indemnity within thirty days, together with a large sum still due Chile for occupation costs. In view of Peru's financial plight, the Chilean envoy was to obtain proof of ability to pay before agreeing to hold a plebiscite. The Chilean negotiator was warned to prevent Argentine assistance to Peru in connection with the indemnity payment, as that would lead to stronger insistence upon a plebiscite. In short, Chile's conditions were designed to push Peru into a direct settlement.

On August 9, 1895, not long after the opening of negotiations, the Peruvian foreign minister declared that "just as Chile seemed determined to cherish the expectations that had been created in her favor by the Treaty of Ancón so also was Peru resolved to maintain hers,"[14] and flatly rejected any direct transfer whatsoever. On August 20 the negotiators proceeded to a discussion of the plebiscite and, when Chile insisted upon indemnity payment guarantees, Peru indicated that it could not meet that demand. The talks lost their impetus, although officially they dragged on into the following year.[15]

For Chile the period was filled with anxious suspense. Negotiations with Peru were going badly just when Bolivia was demanding assurances concerning Tacna and Arica, and when Buenos Aires was not only showing marked interest in Chile's Peru-Bolivian relations and opposing Chile's boundary position, but was also arming itself for possible war with Chile. In August, 1895, the Chilean government asked congressional approval for a £6 million armaments purchase loan.[16] At the same time General Emilio Körner initiated a study of army reorganization.[17] Chile asked its ministers to France and to Great Britain to impede Argentina's rumored European debt consolidation, planned for the purpose of obtaining new funds for armaments purchases.[18] And Chile's minister to Italy was ordered to deal with a report that Rome's minister in Buenos Aires had "said that, in the event of war between ... [Argentina] and Chile, his government would ... aid the Argentine Republic, ... and was offering the cruiser *Parese* and military contingents."[19]

To strengthen its South American diplomatic position, Chile reorganized its diplomatic services in the Plata region. Before 1895 Santiago was entirely unrepresented in Asunción, and one minister served in both Uruguay and Argentina. Relieving its Buenos Aires envoy of his duties in Montevideo, Chile named a new agent to represent it in both Montevideo and Asunción.[20] Santiago's more intensive Platine representation was wise at a time when Buenos Aires' envoy in Montevideo was attempting to assure Uruguay's neutrality in the event that Argentina and Chile went to war. If Argentina could seek to influence the Pacific, then Chile could do likewise in the Plata. The two rivals were wading ever more deeply into the continent's swelling diplomatic waters.

Faced with mounting Bolivian resistance to the May treaties, Chile requested Brazil's help in securing their approval[21] and sought also to exploit a threatened break in Peruvian-Bolivian relations[22] "for the purpose of making more viable the approval of the recent treaties."[23] But by this time the Altiplano's opposition to the Chilean pacts had become so widespread that not a single member of the joint legislative committee considering them was willing to recommend them to Congress as drafted. A substantial minority of the committee advocated a renegotiation tantamount to rejection, but a majority was willing to recommend them with certain changes, though even then it appeared that they would pass the legislature with the slimmest of margins.[24]

THE CHILEAN-BOLIVIAN PROTOCOL OF DECEMBER 9, 1895

Concluding that its only, if faint, hope for the treaties lay in their modification, Chile rapidly made concessions and changes embodied in a protocol signed in Sucre on December 9, 1895. Chile agreed that "the definitive cession of the Bolivian littoral ... will be voided if, within a period of two years, Chile does not turn over to Bolivia the port on the Pacific Coast mentioned by the treaty of transference."[25] Chile obligated itself to use all possible legal means to secure Tacna and Arica, and the protocol specified that "Chile's obligation shall not be considered fulfilled until [Bolivia has received] a port and zone adequate to its present and future commercial and industrial needs. ..." The addition of the December protocol to the May treaties secured the latter's unanimous approval in the Bolivian Congress.

THE ROCHA-CANO PROTOCOL BETWEEN ARGENTINA AND BOLIVIA;
CHILEAN-BOLIVIAN PROTOCOL OF DECEMBER 28, 1895

But within three days of the vote of approval, a formidable new complication arose in Chilean-Bolivian relations. The Argentine minister to the Altiplano had secured the signing of a document, known as the Rocha-Cano protocol, in which Bolivia reaffirmed Argentina's right to the Puna de Atacama.[26] The Chilean chancellery promptly protested to the Bolivian minister in Santiago, charging that Bolivia had conceded to Argentina territory of which Chile was the legal owner.[27] In a protocol signed in Santiago on December 28 the Bolivian minister admitted that Bolivia might have ceded part of the Puna de Atacama to Argentina, but stated explicitly that "there is ... nothing in the [Rocha-Cano] protocol which can directly or indirectly affect Chile."[28] That declaration, whatever its meaning, did not alter the fact that the Bolivian government, between the Rocha-Cano protocol and the May treaties, had recognized both Argentina's and Chile's rights to the same plot of ground. But the exigencies of Chile's international situation forced it for the moment to accept the "assurances" of the December 28 protocol, and the Chilean Congress proceeded promptly to approve the three treaties with Bolivia.

But the legislature had approved the May treaties with Bolivia in ignorance of the protocol of December 9, and when news of that document reached Santiago a wave of anger rocked the Chilean Congress, many of whose members properly felt that the original treaties had been fundamentally changed. The Foreign Minister of Chile was forced to advise Bolivia that treaty ratifications would be delayed until the matter was clarified, and to this the Altiplano responded by demanding the Chilean legislature's specific approval of the December 9 protocol. As an already complicated situation became even more so, the governments of Chile and Bolivia began discussions[29] in an effort to clarify matters. And as those talks continued, Argentina and Chile moved closer to war.

THE PROTOCOL OF SEPTEMBER 6, 1895

Demarcation of the boundary between Chile and Argentina was proceeding at a snail's pace amid sharp conflicts within the technical field team over the location of boundary markers, and these conflicts threatened to bring the entire operation to a complete standstill, thereby stirring an inflamed public to the point where maintenance of relations would be endangered. The field disputes were not susceptible to resolution by the boundary commission, for they arose from still-unsettled differences in interpretation of Article I of the boundary treaty of 1881. In an effort to stave off final rupture, on September 6, 1895, there was signed a complementary protocol to the 1881 treaty which sought to keep open channels to peaceful solution by providing that field disagreements be turned over to the respective governments while the technicians proceeded with their work.[30] No provision was made with regard to disagreement between the governments, but an article in the 1881 agreement stated that disputes "will be submitted to the decision of a friendly power."[31] Santiago therefore asked Buenos Aires to agree to arbitration of differences between the boundary commission experts.[32] At a private luncheon in late October the Chilean foreign minister suggested to the Argentine envoy in Santiago that the position of the San Francisco marker be settled by a compromise, and the other disagreements, by arbitration. Encouraged by Argentina's reaction, the foreign minister optimistically made plans for further talks.[33]

But the Argentine boundary matter was not to be amicably settled over luncheon. In December the Puna de Atacama issue flared up to exacerbate the complex and emotion-laden dispute. Argentina refused to modify its position, convinced that its title to the Puna—in compensation for its Tarija concessions to Bolivia—was above question. In the words of the President of Argentina, "the question is one of national pride; ... it cannot be submitted to arbitration."[34] Nor was Chile genuinely eager to expose the matter to arbitration, as its original claim derived from the weak "principle of revindication" invoked at the outset of the War of the Pacific. Few arbiters were likely to approve that principle, and its refutation would endanger Chile's case for the remainder of its frontier. Chile was therefore prepared to make concessions,[35] in spite of the hysterical agitation of the Chilean public after publication of the news of Argentina's preparations for war.[36] At the risk of mob violence in the capital city, the Chilean government would concede the Puna to Argentina in exchange for the latter's agreement to submit all other issues to arbitration.[37]

THE GUERRERO–QUIRNO COSTA PROTOCOL OF APRIL 17, 1896

Buenos Aires was suspicious of Chile's offer, fearing that Santiago might manage to secure arbitral acceptance of the principle of *divortium aquarum* and thus force an advantageous settlement for Chile.[38] Negotiations concerning the Chilean proposal were nevertheless commenced and bore fruit in the Guerrero–Quirno Costa protocol of April 17, 1896.[39] With respect to the Puna de Atacama, the document enabled Argentina to effectuate its claim in a manner that saved face for the Chilean government. This feat was cleverly accomplished by embracing the previously excluded region of the Puna with the area covered by earlier agreements and by stipulating that, if they wished, Bolivian experts might participate in its boundary determination. As the Altiplano had already recognized Argentine sovereignty in the Puna, it was assumed that its experts would vote against Chile and would thus bring about the desired end without having forced on open retreat on the part of the Chilean government.[40] With regard to the San Francisco marker, another Chilean concession provided that it "shall not be considered a point of departure nor an obligatory precedent in determining the boundary." On the other hand, Chile gained Argentina's consent to submit all other boundary disagreements to British arbitration. And as, in accepting that arrangement, Buenos Aires had failed to insist upon "the principal chain of the cordillera," the Chilean chancellery had some reason to be satisfied with the Guerrero–Quirno Costa protocol.

April 30 Protocol with Bolivia

With the momentary relaxation of tensions with Argentina, Chile
turned its concentrated attention to the Bolivian problem, which now
centered on the impasse created by Chile's rejection of the protocol of
December 9. That impasse was cleared in a protocol of April 30, the
very day the three May treaties were due to expire for lack of exchange
of ratifications. Chile accepted the December 9 protocol in exchange
for the protection presumably granted by a more specific description
of the port to be given Bolivia if Chile could not secure Tacna and
Arica from Peru. The alternative port was now stated to be "Vitor
Bay or a similar harbor suitable for a port, adequate for the needs
of commerce ... where a town may be founded which, [linked] by
railroad to Bolivia, may be of economic and financial service to it."[41]
The April protocol provided also that the Bolivian government would
seek its legislature's approval of still another protocol concerning
liquidation of Chilean claims against Bolivia. Chile agreed in turn
to request legislative approval of the December 9 protocol, but only
after Bolivia had formally approved the April 30 protocol just signed.
This extensive protocolary patchwork having been completed, ratifications of the May treaties were duly exchanged; the government of
Chile promulgated the treaties of peace and commerce, keeping hidden
the treaty of territorial transference.[42]

Sensational Disclosure of the Secret Treaty

Chile's disputes with Argentina and Bolivia seemed on their way to
solution, but there still remained the single most formidable obstacle
to the plans of the Chilean government—permanent acquisition of
Tacna and Arica. In an effort to surmount Peruvian resistance, the
Chilean minister in Lima went directly to the President, and, after
conversing with him at length, came away feeling that a way might
have been found to acquire the provinces without inflicting undue
damage upon Peruvian pride. But the matter was delicate and required
consultations in Santiago. The Chilean minister left Lima, traveled
south, and was engaged in conferences with his government when any
chances for an agreement with Peru were destroyed by the publication in Buenos Aires of the terms of the secret Chilean-Bolivian treaty
of territorial transference.

In furious protests, handed to both Chile and Bolivia, Peru vowed
that it would never relinquish hope of reincorporating Tacna and
Arica, and that it would never cede any part of that territory to an-

other power. If Peru was to be taken at its word, not only the big prize—all of Tacna and Arica—but the little one as well—Vitor Bay—would be withheld from Chile and thus from Bolivia. This was a position from which Lima obviously would not soon retreat, for the public of Peru was so enraged that the government could reconsider[43] only if it wanted, forcibly and prematurely, to be relieved of power. The furies unleashed by disclosure of their secret territorial treaty raised doubts in both Chile and Bolivia concerning the wisdom and viability of the May treaties in general.

CHILE'S NEW PRESIDENT

In Santiago, where President-elect Federico Errázuriz assumed office in September, 1896, the unyielding stance of Peru was to have an important effect upon the new government's approach to the urgent Bolivian problem. The Errázuriz administration, reviewing the state of Chile's relations with the countries it had defeated in the War of the Pacific, could discern several disquieting facts: Bolivia would probably reject all previously advanced alternatives to a port in Tacna-Arica; Peru would not relinquish Tacna-Arica without the holding of a plebiscite which it was almost certain to win; Chilean policy must oppose satisfaction of Bolivia's port needs by means of a corridor through Chilean territory; Chile's persistent antiplebiscite policy might throw Lima into the arms of Buenos Aires; Chile was committed, like it or not, to the provision of a port for Bolivia, for upon such an arrangement depended legal sanction for its possession of the former Bolivian littoral, already incorporated into Chile as the province of Antofagasta. In sum, Chile's Peru-Bolivian policy was not only failing to accomplish its original purposes, but was creating new problems with each passing year.[44]

As Chile reviewed its Peru-Bolivian policy, new impetus was given to revision by a resolution passed in December, 1896, by the Altiplano legislature. It reserved to Bolivia the right to determine unilaterally the acceptability of any port offered by Chile. Although the meaning was obvious, Chile asked for "clarification" of the resolution, and ensuing discussions convinced its statesmen that the Bolivian port problem was under all existing circumstances absolutely insoluble. At this juncture—January and February, 1897—the Chilean government might have acknowledged the realities of the situation and, wiping the slate clean, proceeded to a frank revision of its Bolivian policy. But it did not so act, for the May peace treaty did, after all, sanction Chilean sovereignty over the littoral, even if only conditionally. But even more important, if Chile did not now proceed with its various Bolivian agreements, however unsatisfactory and impossible to implement, the Altiplano might turn to Argentina for assistance.

ARGENTINE-CHILEAN NOTES OF MARCH, 1897

Relations with Argentina had not been noticeably improved by the Guerrero–Quirno Costa protocol. Its negotiation had momentarily calmed fears of war, but mutual hatreds remained. During succeeding months reports of proposed Argentine land grants in disputed territory[45] and of Argentine discrimination against Chilean nationals[46] revived and fortified the mistrust with which Chile's press and public regarded its eastern neighbor. Chile, moreover, began to have second thoughts about the face-saving device invented for the protocol, fearing that Bolivia's inclusion in the Puna de Atacama demarcation might cost more than it was worth. Seizing upon a question raised by the Bolivian chancellery, Chile attempted to secure Argentine agreement to Bolivia's exclusion from all but the last phase of the demarcation. Relevant notes were drafted in Santiago in March, 1897, and were transmitted by the Argentine envoy to Buenos Aires for approval. But the months began to pass with no word of Argentine action;[47] Buenos Aires, too, was seeking to distort the implementation of the Guerrero–Quirno Costa protocol in a manner favorable to its interests. In an apparent play for time in which to strengthen its military position,[48] and thus force Chile to accept, at gun's point as it were, an imposed interpretation of the boundary treaty of 1881, Argentina assiduously procrastinated in the fulfillment of the arbitration provisions of the protocol.

GENERAL SOUTH AMERICAN DIPLOMACY

In 1896, as the government of Chile groped its way through the dangerous maze of its Peru-Bolivian-Argentine questions, it took care to preserve and improve its diplomatic position in other South American countries. Provision was made for Paraguayan youths to study at Chile's naval[49] and military[50] academies. For the first time in almost a decade Chile accredited an envoy to Central America, Colombia, and Ecuador,[51] and with the last negotiated a convention on the reciprocity of professional degrees.[52] But the most determined of Chile's efforts was reserved for Brazil. The Chilean minister in Rio was ordered to resume negotiation of a commercial treaty and was informed that "Chile ... will make any financial sacrifice ... to assure the development of projected commercial bases and the strengthening of every kind of political relation ... with Brazil.'"⁵³ The international problems of Brazil also elicited sympathetic Chilean interest. Santiago offered Brazil its coöperation in obtaining an amicable solution of a conflict with Uruguay over the free navigation of Lake Merín and the Yaguarón River.⁵⁴ And when, late in 1896, Brazil became embroiled in a conflict with Italy, Chile stood firmly at its side, convinced that "in these moments of difficulty for Brazil our chancellery must assume, with discretion and prudence, an attitude that may enable us increasingly to consolidate our relations with ... [Brazil]; and we must follow most attentively the course of events so that, if complications between Italy and Brazil continue, we may at the opportune moment exercise a mediation action calculated to attract decidedly to us the friendship [of Brazil] and to add prestige in America to our international policies.'"⁵⁵ The Chilean government's interest in cementing relations with Brazil was emphasized by its April, 1897, appointment of Isidoro Errázuriz, a leading elder statesman, as minister to Brazil.⁵⁶ Before his departure the new envoy discussed the important matter of a Brazilian-Chilean anti-Argentine alliance with his cousin, the President, and it was decided that such an alliance should be sought as soon as possible.⁵⁷

TACNA AND ARICA

And now Chile turned again to the northwest, and in one further effort to implement the unrealistic policy of creating a strong Bolivian ally, it once more approached the government of Peru on the question of Tacna and Arica. At the very start of the new discussions the Peruvian foreign minister turned the tables on Chile by proposing a direct settlement in which the two provinces would be returned intact to Peru. When Peru refused even to discuss exclusion of Vitor Bay from such a settlement, Santiago's envoy was stung into the declaration that the stubbornness of Peru would compel Chile "to make superhuman efforts—as we Chileans know how to do—to win the plebiscite. And ... win it we will, cost what it may, for we must win it to straighten things out with Bolovia."⁵⁸ Unmoved, the Foreign Minister of Peru did not retreat from his position.

Nor was the Altiplano in a mood for compromise. The Chilean envoy, after advising Bolivia that Chile was seeking plebiscite terms that would assure its victory, asked that Bolivia assist in that effort by agreeing to compensate Peru for the loss of Tacna and Arica with disputed territory of comparable extent in the Amazon region, and by encouraging Bolivian citizens to move into Tacna and Arica in time to vote for Chile in the plebiscite. Not only did Bolivia withhold a

commitment of assistance, but it also informed Chile that Vitor Bay
would not be an acceptable alternative port. In addition, the Bolivian
government stood firmly upon the congressional resolution of December, 1896, and now indicated, as predicted by certain Chilean statesmen, that an acceptable alternative to Tacna and Arica would be the
port of Pisagua in Tarapacá, which could be reached only by a corridor through Chilean territory.[59]

At the same time that Chile's envoys in Peru and Bolivia were meeting with so conspicuous a lack of success, Santiago was edging toward
policy modification. Chile was most irritated by the intransigence of
Bolivia, which it found far less understandable than that of Peru.[60]
Between August, 1897, and April, 1898, this irritation, together with
the ominous Argentine situation and the part that Peru might play
in the event of war, served to bring about a moderation of Chile's
Tacna-Arica policy and to cause the Chilean government to seek an
understanding with Peru. Chilean statesmen realized that Lima, de-
spairing of a satisfactory solution of the Tacna-Arica problem, might
seek and secure an entente with Buenos Aires, an entente that would
encircle Chile and place Peruvian ports at Argentina's disposal.

THE THREAT OF WAR WITH ARGENTINA

The implications of a Peruvian-Argentine entente were particularly
grim in late 1897 and early 1898, for war with Argentina never seemed
distant during that period. In August the Argentine government, whose
continued apparent reluctance to expedite the boundary demarcation
was causing grave apprehension in Chile, caused outright alarm by
rejecting at long last the March, 1897, notes regarding curtailed Bolivian participation in the Puna de Atacama boundary demarcation.
When, shortly thereafter, Bolivia began to press for a definition of
its Puna role, the Chilean chancellery became certain that Buenos Aires
and the Altiplano were coöperating against Chile in a sinister sense.
In November and December, 1897, rumors of a Peruvian-Argentine
alliance, under which Argentina would send a fleet into the Pacific
and Peru would attack Chile with 8,000 men, sent a spasm of fear
through Santiago. Chile's minister in Lima was convinced the alliance
existed; his chancellery tentatively satisfied itself that no formal arrangement had yet been made, but the dreaded possibility lurked just
behind the scenes and pressed the Chilean government into preparations for war.

Without abandoning its strong determination to resolve its problems
peacefully, the government placed its military and naval forces on

a combat footing. General Körner himself participated in a series of cabinet meetings at which strategy and procurement were discussed in great detail. Congress was asked to authorize a loan of £3 million ostensibly to complete the trans-Andine railroad, and a "secret commission" was sent to Europe to arrange the loan and to buy war matériel with the proceeds.

As successive war scares shook the Chilean nation, it became increasingly difficult to preserve the public calm which the government deemed necessary for the success of its diplomacy. In January the Argentine boundary expert visited Santiago and was subjected to a hostile attack in the press and to noisy street demonstrations which were clearly directed against Argentina as a whole.[61] Upon the expert's departure for Buenos Aires it was rumored that either boundary demarcation procedures had collapsed altogether, or Argentina, with evil motives, was seeking to delay a solution to the boundary question. In February the President of Argentina publicly stated that Argentina must arm itself to meet any contingency. With the passing of each week Chile feared increasingly that its eastern neighbor was not disposed to settle the boundary peacefully. Santiago's distrust of Buenos Aires rose even higher in March, when it was learned that Argentine troops had founded a town on Lake Lacar in Chilean territory. Following an equivocal reply to the chancellery's protest, the Chilean cabinet met in emergency sessions which were taking place when the government of Peru began strongly to press for a definitive solution to the problem of Tacna and Arica.

THE BILLINGHURST-LATORRE PROTOCOL OF APRIL 9, 1898

Certain Peruvians in very high places were anxious to reach an agreement with Chile concerning Tacna and Arica. Those people, among them the country's president and vice-president, entertained designs upon Bolivian territory and wished both to thwart possible Bolivian-Chilean *rapprochement* and to be rid of a diplomatically paralyzing problem. Vice President Guillermo Billinghurst, an intimate of many prominent Chileans, first approached the matter informally and then traveled to Santiago to negotiate officially. As the Chilean-Argentine crisis increased, Billinghurst resisted both a Chilean purchase offer and other previously advanced "compromise" proposals, insisting firmly upon a fairly conducted plebiscite as promised in the Treaty of Ancón. On April 9, as an unwanted war with Argentina loomed near, Chile retreated from its tough position and signed a compromise agreement, the Billinghurst-Latorre protocol, which stipulated that plebis-

cite voter eligibility would be decided by Spain and that the election
would be conducted by a three-man board composed of one Chilean, one
Peruvian, and one neutral member designated by Madrid.[62]

The Billinghurst-Latorre agreement signaled a major shift in Chilean policy, for with its signing Chile virtually abandoned the possibility of an early *rapprochement* with Bolivia in exchange for a more
stable and amicable association with Peru. The protocol did not constitute a technical violation of the May, 1895, treaties with Bolivia;
a plebiscite would be held, and if Chile won the provinces they would
be turned over to Bolivia. But Chile could not win a fairly conducted
vote. Chile knew it; Bolivia knew it. And as Peruvians hailed their
diplomatic victory, Chile began to sound out Bolivia on a peace settlement that would relieve Santiago of its seaport obligations. For the
time being the protocol staved off a possible anti-Chilean Peruvian-
Argentine alliance, and, fortunately for Chile, did so without catapult-
ing Bolivia into the Argentine camp. Bolivians were not, in this instance at least, as out of touch with reality as Chileans supposed them
to be; they had known all along that Peruvian intransigence constituted a powerful obstacle to their Tacna-Arica hopes. And now, confronted with a *fait accompli,* the Altiplano settled into a policy of
wistfully waiting in the hope that some miracle might produce a Chilean
plebiscite victory.[63]

AN ARMS RACE

Meanwhile Buenos Aires and Santiago moved swiftly, and apparently
inevitably, toward an open break. Chile, constitutionally unable to
impute to Argentina any but the basest of motives, was certain that
nefarious schemes lay behind its delay in referring the boundary question to British arbitration and its reluctance to agree upon a target date
for completing the work of the boundary commission. Such a supposi-
tion seemed reasonable to Chileans, for their rival's military posture
was becoming ever more formidable, threatening to outstrip that of
Chile. An arms race was, in fact, under way. In May, 1898, when
Chilean intelligence learned that Argentina was planning to purchase
the Italian cruiser *Garibaldi,* Chile protested that such a move was
inappropriate during a time of friendly boundary negotiations; the
protest was answered by the President of Argentina himself, who insisted that the warship's sole purpose was to reassure the public of
Argentina, which was greatly disturbed by Chile's recent naval acquisitions. Shortly after that ominous reply, Chile learned that Argentina
was seeking to buy still another cruiser and that its army chief of staff
was in Europe procuring equipment for a corps of Bolivians. Any re-

maining Chilean doubt now vanished, and the government prepared for war as rapidly as possible, simultaneously attempting to force the boundary dispute into arbitration before the arrival of Argentina's new warships.

THE "YES" OR "NO" WAR SCARE

Fighting against time, the Chilean foreign minister met with the Argentine envoy to Santiago and, using every persuasive arrow in his quiver, attempted to secure an agreement to arbitrate the boundary, including the Puna de Atacama. But the Argentine minister remained adamant. Then, on September 19 Chile demanded a plain "yes" or "no" answer to the demand for arbitration, implying that an unfavorable response would result in a break in relations. As the Chilean chancellery tensely waited for Argentina's reply, the news of the challenge spread throughout the Chilean capital and across the Andes. By the next day the southern part of South America was in the grip of a hysterical war scare.

The Argentine cabinet, hurriedly meeting to deal with the crisis, proposed a compromise for which the Chilean foreign minister had cleverly laid the groundwork by his unrelenting insistence upon inclusion of the Puna de Atacama: the Puna would be set aside for the future, but the southern boundary would be submitted to British arbitration. Chile promptly accepted that proposal and on September 22, 1898, as the frightened peoples of both countries breathed sighs of relief, four acts were signed setting forth the details of the compromise.[64]

PIGEONHOLING OF THE BILLINGHURST-LATORRE PROTOCOL

As the threat of war with Argentina faded, the Chilean Chamber of Deputies dealt harshly with the April 9 agreement with Peru.[65] That protocol was opposed on many different grounds, the most telling of which was its lack of guarantees against "unfair" competition from any future Peruvian-controlled Tacna-Arica nitrate industry. Although Peru agreed to an export tax no smaller than Chile's,[66] and even promised to operate its deposits under the same conditions as those in Chile were operated,[67] Congress remained unconvinced. Upon learning of the acts signed with Argentina, it pigeonholed the Billinghurst-Latorre document pending specific assurances that Chile's nitrate monopoly would be protected and perpetuated. The Chilean government subsequently asked for a Peruvian commitment "with regard to future nitrate discoveries . . . to take no steps toward working the deposits or selling or transferring rights thereto which might in any way impair the Chilean monopoly."[68] Peru rejected that demand as restrictive of its sovereignty, [69] and there the matter stood as of late 1898.

THE NOVEMBER PACTS WITH ARGENTINA; A MEETING AT THE SUMMIT

At this point, however, the Chilean government was less concerned with the fate of the Peruvian protocol than with the conclusion of a peaceful settlement with Argentina, toward which the four acts had pointed the way. While the definitive delineation of the southern frontier was now in sight, however, there still remained the difficult Puna de Atacama question, and it was to the solution of that problem that the Argentine and Chilean chancelleries now directed their efforts. When negotiations at the foreign minister level appeared to flag, President Errázuriz decided to cut red tape and deal directly with President Roca of Argentina.

The two presidents managed to reach a devious compromise which had the dual virtue of saving face and delaying the moment of truth while at the same time providing for the eventual definitive settlement of the Puna de Atacama dispute. In two pacts, signed in Santiago on November 2, 1898, it was stipulated that each nation would send a five-member delegation to a conference in Buenos Aires at which agreement would be sought on the Puna boundary. If, however, as was virtually certain, the conference failed to agree, each nation would appoint one delegate who, with the assistance of the United States minister to Argentina, would draw the boundary line. This compromise, in effect, designated the United States envoy as arbitrator.[70]

On November 23 the Chilean Congress approved the pacts, and on the same day the Chilean and Argentine ministers in London requested that Her Majesty's government commence the southern boundary arbitration. Two days later the date was fixed for the Buenos Aires conference on the Puna de Atacama.

Then, dramatically to symbolize their countries' reconciliation, Presidents Roca and Errázuriz, each borne upon a warship of his own nation, made a voyage to the Strait of Magellan where, on February 12, 1899, in moving ceremonies aboard ship, they solemnly pledged their peoples to eternal peace. Amid the general good feeling created by the summit meeting, the Puna de Atacama conference convened, failed, and turned the matter over to the three-member committee whose March 24 decision awarded most of the Puna de Atacama to Argentina. Despite murmers of dissatisfaction on both sides of the Andes, the new *rapprochement* remained intact.[71]

Having failed, through reliance solely upon its own strength, to maintain unchallenged Pacific Coast hegemony, Chile had reverted in the May, 1895, Bolivian treaties to a policy of establishing a South American equilibrium favorable to Chilean interests through the creation of a relatively strong ally on the Altiplano. But for two primary reasons Chile had been unable to implement that plan. In the first place, Peru adamantly refused to diminish or to relinquish its Tacna-Arica claim, thereby preventing a Chilean gift to the Altiplano of the port that would make it both stronger and more friendly. Second, and more important, Chile's ability to deal with its Pacific antagonists was progressively impaired by an increasingly powerful Argentina, which not only threatened a direct boundary conflict with Chile but also menaced Chile with coöperation with Peru and Bolivia. Under such pressures Chile sought a *rapprochement* with Buenos Aires which would give it a freer hand in dealing with its Pacific Coast problems. The resulting *rapprochement* in 1899 was to become the first timid step along a path at whose end lay a South American equilibrium entirely different from that earlier conceived by Chilean statesmen. But before the new equilibrium was reached, the Chilean-Argentine *rapprochement* was to be ruptured, and Chile was to be faced with hostile encirclement.

Chapter XIII

TOWARD ENCIRCLEMENT

AFTER THE BUENOS AIRES CONFERENCE on the Puna de Atacama, during the more than a year in which British arbitrators were occupied with the delineation of the southern frontier, relations between Chile and Argentina showed marked improvement. Suspicion and hostility were far from dead on either slope of the cordillera, but no serious incident broke the relative calm. Chile took advantage of the situation to press for a favorable settlement of its problems with Bolivia and Peru.

A strong and friendly Bolivia, with a Chilean-provided port, was no longer the goal of Chilean policy. In December, 1899, Abraham König Velásquez was sent to the Altiplano to secure a definitive peace treaty which would recognize Chile's sovereignty over the littoral in exchange for Santiago's assumption of certain debts and its help in constructing a railroad that would link the Altiplano with a Chilean port through which Bolivian commerce might pass free of duty.[1] Bolivia, just emerged from a serious civil war and involved in a grave dispute with Brazil over the rubber-producing Acre territory, seemed hardly in a position to resist,[2] but resist it did. In spite of Chile's offer of assistance in the Brazilian problem,[3] months of negotiations failed to produce a definitive treaty ending the war between Bolivia and Chile.

With respect to Peru, Chile renewed its determination to retain Tacna and Arica and took measures in those provinces to "put Chile in a favorable position for the realization of the plebiscite."[4] Peruvian-operated schools were closed, and Peruvians resentfully concluded that Santiago was renewing its Chileanization policy.[5] Chile, its Congress having pigeonholed the Billinghurst-Latorre protocol, sent a new envoy to Lima with instructions to arrange either for outright purchase or for a plebiscite that would assure Chile's victory.[6]

But Peru, with four years of internal order and honest government behind it, was able to resist Chile's demands more effectively.[7] And the Peruvian public, in the flush of the short-lived Billinghurst-Latorre triumph, had become, and remained, more determined than ever to recover its conquered provinces. Their determination was reflected in Peru's appointment, in January, 1900, of a special envoy to Chile with instructions to make every possible effort to secure approval of the Billinghurst-Latorre document.[8] When Chile's new minister reached Lima, he therefore found it virtually pointless to discuss the objectives of his mission, encountering only continued insistence upon approval of the protocol.[9]

Although Peru was willing to stand by the plebiscite compromise embodied in the Billinghurst-Latorre protocol, certain influential private citizens pressed for direct and forceful action. During 1900 and 1901 their influence upon Peruvian policy was strengthened by the Chilean legislature's rejection of the protocol, and by the Chilean government's implementation of the Chileanization policy in Tacna and Arica. During the same period it began to appear that Peru might succeed in an effort to regain the provinces, for the United States was again interested in the Pan-American movement. Tension between Chile and Argentina had also come to the fore, and Chile's aggressive Bolivian policy had extremely damaging repercussions.

THE GARLAND TRACT

Outstanding among the Peruvians demanding forceful action to regain Tacna and Arica was Alejandro Garland, who was influential in Peru's ruling political party and a close friend of the Foreign Minister. In *South American Conflicts in Relation to the United States*,[10] a tract that received continent-wide circulation and attracted widespread comment, Garland persuasively argued that Chile planned to retain Tacna and Arica by illegal means, if necessary. Starting with a long description of Chilean "perfidy" during and after the War of the Pacific, Garland maintained that

Chile ... accepted the [Billinghurst-Latorre] agreement only to neutralize Peru ... in the face of an approaching break with Argentina and, therefore, with the deliberate intention of not fulfilling it. Now it peremptorily demands that ... arbitration be dispensed with and threatens to retain Tacna and Arica by force; and the Chilean press, betraying the intimate sentiments of the government, will once again call for the taking up of arms, and the cost will be covered ... by the conquest of Moquegua, whose wealth in the wine industry, together with its richess in borates, sulfates, copper, and coal mines recently discovered, arouses that country's envy.[11]

Peru, Garland insisted, should ask Washington's help. The United States was in fact obliged to assist Peru, he felt, because it wanted peace in the Western Hemisphere and because Peru's present problems were largely the fault of the United States, which during the War of the Pacific had urged Peru's resistance to Chilean demands and had then failed to back up Peru. As the very existence of the problem of Tacna and Arica could be traced to a United States lapse, Washington was morally compelled to rescue Peru. That moral obligation notwithstanding, Garland would encourage United States aid with extensive commercial concessions. Garland did not expect Washington to use force, but envisioned an American Congress in which Peru's position would be supported by "the great Republic of the North," whose agreement was required "for the success of any international plan ... in this hemisphere." Garland demanded that, after Peru's expected failure to achieve any satisfaction from Santiago, Peru proceed to "formulate a protest before the chancelleries of America, denouncing Chile for refusing to fulfill international pacts and for persisting in its intentions of conquest. If the United States seconded our demand, it would clearly have a strong reason for inviting the republics of this hemisphere to a congress that would ... put an end to the latent war."[12]

Garland proposed that Brazil, Argentina, Colombia, and Mexico be asked to second Peru's demand for Washington's good offices, so that "when the President of the United States hears the Peruvian minister's demand he will hear the voice of all America." He reminded those who feared Chilean refusal to attend an American congress that "powerful Russia was compelled to be present at the last European congress in Berlin which stripped her of the fruits of her victories over the Turks." Garland, to counter possible doubts concerning the support of South American nations, enumerated the reasons that they would side with Peru, noting, among other things, that "Argentina ... knows that if Chile had not seized Tarapacá's millions it could not have accumulated the armaments that it possesses today, and that they were ... acquired in order to impose a boundary in the Andes. ... There is today no Argentine who fails to understand that without Tarapacá Chile would be impotent."[13]

Garland's influential tract actually contained two different proposals: one for a congress; another for United States good offices and/or assistance. The latter suggestion met with wide approval in Peru. In May, 1900, *El Comercio*, one of Lima's leading newspapers, even proposed a formal alliance with the United States. Santiago, becoming fearful of possible United States intervention, asked Washington for policy clarification and was assured that the United States would not interfere in the Tacna-Arica question unless its mediation was requested by both Chile and Peru.[14]

A Proposed Inter-American Meeting

The suggestion that the Tacna-Arica dispute be placed before an American congress was potentially more dangerous to Chilean interests than United States intervention, for Washington was becoming actively interested in such a meeting. During the decade since the Washington conference of 1889–1890 Pan-American activity had been largely limited to support of the Commercial Bureau of the American Republics, established in 1891 for a period of ten years to facilitate the exchange of commercial information. As the bureau's life span drew to a close, President William McKinley of the United States suggested that another conference be held, and in February, 1900, his secretary of state officially proposed the idea to the Latin-American diplomatic corps in Washington. The next month Washington's envoy in Santiago asked for the reaction of the Chilean chancellery.

Because McKinley, in suggesting a meeting, had referred to "many matters of general interest and common benefit to all the American Republics,"[15] it was obvious to Chile that the proposed conference might have a dangerously broad agenda. Nor had Chile forgotten the problems of the first conference, ten years earlier, when Argentina and Brazil sponsored a joint resolution of censure for Chile's conduct in the War of the Pacific. A new meeting would be fraught with peril, for recent intelligence indicated that Argentina might second Peruvian demands for an open discussion of Tacna and Arica. The press, the public, and even the Foreign Minister of Argentina seemed to favor Lima's position,[16] and the nationalistic Estanislao Zeballos, a former foreign minister, believed that Chile's continued military readiness was due to its planned rejection of any unfavorable award in its boundary dispute with Argentina. Zeballos, advocating the diplomatic isolation of Chile, insisted that "Peru and Bolivia are natural and spontaneous allies" of Argentina. "Shall we in addition," asked Zeballos, "fully participate in the diplomatic negotiations of the Pacific?" He answered himself affirmatively, explaining that "we are part of them because of a common Atacama boundary with the affected territories and ... because of the pacifying principle of continental equilibrium."[17]

But however perilous a public airing of the Tacna-Arica question might be, Chile could not risk the adverse public opinion of a flat refusal to participate. It therefore assured the United States that "Chile, by nature and self-interest a lover of peace, ... can do no less than accept in general the idea ... of a congress." Chilean statesmen, however, did want to know the precise nature of the agenda so they could "judge whether the matters to be treated are ... capable of practical solutions and genuinely advantageous to the American states, or the kind that might create disturbing situations."[18]

Even as Chile's reluctant conditional reply was en route to Washington, the Executive Committee of the Commercial Bureau, one of whose three members was the Argentine minister, was preparing an agenda. By May 22, 1900, the committee had agreed upon a list of five major topics which, together with copies of the proceedings of the first Washington conference, it distributed to representatives of invited nations. The committee, at the suggestion of its Argentine member, then asked the United States to telegraph the invited countries, asking both for their replies and for their authorization to Washington representatives to fix the time and place for the meeting. On May 29 the Chilean chancellery found itself in receipt of the United States telegram, but, as it had not seen the proposed agenda, it withheld acceptance of the invitation, although authorizing its Washington envoy to discuss time and place for the conference. In June, as those discussions commenced, it became apparent that there was a growing trend toward coöperation between Peru and Argentina.[19]

Arrangements for the proposed international conference lasted for many months. During that period a series of events increased the probability of Peruvian-Argentine coöperation in the conference, brought Bolivia actively into their camp, strengthened their case against Chile, and caused growing Chilean apprehension that the conference would seek to take a hand in the solution of Pacific questions.

THE LACAR MATTER REOPENED

In May, 1900, the Chilean government learned that Argentine soldiers had reëntered the Lacar Valley, claimed by Chile, and with this knowledge the strain of waiting for the British arbiter's award became evident. The diplomatic exchanges which followed Chile's resulting protest were not acrimonious, but in the legislatures and the press of both nations virulent charges were hurled, charges that might endanger the cordial relations officially established not long before. In the Chilean Chamber of Deputies Joaquín Walker Martínez, who had opposed the November, 1898, settlement with Argentina, began a supposedly secret interpellation of the government concerning what he termed "the Argentine invasion." Charging that the government was soft on Argentina, he demanded that Argentine troops be driven out by force. To that demand the opposition press gave its vigorous applause, and, although the government did secure a vote of confidence, the damage had already been done. Argentine distrust of Chile, never far below the surface, was sharply reawakened by news of the interpellation; even the President of Argentina, who might have been expected to understand the nature of the interpellation as a domestic Chilean political matter, was believed to have completely changed his attitude toward Chile on account of it.[20]

Chile's other adversaries, encouraged by the reactivated Chilean-Argentine hostility, exploited the situation. In Peru there was a flowering of public demonstrations in honor of Argentina, a prominent feature of which was anti-Chilean sentiment.[21] In Bolivia, as the Chilean envoy noted during the event, "there are fireworks in the plaza. A popular demonstration is being organized [carrying] the flags of the Argentine and Peruvian legations. . . . Shouts of 'Long live!' for both those countries and of "Down with Chile!' "[22] And, after handing a protest to the Bolivian government, the Chilean minister wrote a letter to a friend in Chile telling him of the serious damage being caused to Chilean interests in the Altiplano by the "criminal and agitating" Walker interpellation.[23]

THE KÖNIG NOTE

It was now, however, the Chilean minister to Bolivia, Abraham König Velásquez, who was to become a focal point for Bolivian anti-Chileanism and to supply a *cause célèbre* for those throughout South America who wanted to brand Chile as an aggressor. König, exasperated by months of fruitless bargaining in the culturally, politically, and climatically hostile Altiplano, handed the Bolivian government a long note[24] which he hoped would serve to force the issue of a final peace treaty. Believing the seaport matter to be the major single obstacle, König sought to convince Bolivia that it did not need a port; that even if it did need one, Chile could not give it one; and that even if it had a port,

. . . in wartime Chile could seize Bolivia's single port as easily as it had occupied all Bolivia's seaports in 1879. . . . This is not empty boasting, for all who know my country's resources are aware that its offensive power has increased a hundred-fold during the past twenty years. . . . It is a widespread error . . . to say that Bolivia has the right to demand a seaport in compensation for its coast. That simply is not true. Chile has occupied the coast and seized it with the same right that Germany had to seize Alsace and Lorraine, . . . and the United States, . . . Puerto Rico. Our rights are born of victory—the supreme law of nations.

The disastrous repercussions of the note were not immediately evident. The Bolivian government delayed its protest, although its Santiago minister informed the Chilean chancellery that his government considered the note an ultimatum, and the Chilean foreign minister considered it necessary to write König to ask him what was happening in La Paz. Bolivia's envoy in Washington, seconded by his Argentine and Peruvian colleagues, unsuccessfully attempted to use the note to secure United States support against Chile.[25] The storm broke when the full text of the König note became known in diplomatic and journalistic circles. Estanislao Zeballos described the memorandum as "without precedent in diplomatic literature, on account of its lack of good style and [failure to] respect men and forms."[26] He predicted that "Chile's

... prestige in Christian nations will suffer," and advised Peru and Bolivia to settle their Amazon boundary dispute and unite against Chile, pressing them onward with assurances that "Chile's shortsighted and insensate masses, with their unjustifiable outbursts against the Argentine Republic, have provoked a profound reaction in our country, and Peru and Bolivia no longer stand alone."

Awakening to König's blunder, the Chilean chancellery, on September 26, 1900, telegraphed its legations abroad advising them of the note's "true meaning," and followed the telegrams with a long and detailed memorandum "which, if necessary, may serve to justify Chile's actions."[27] Chile claimed that it had long sought a peace treaty with Bolivia and that, in order to implement its peace policy, its minister to the Altiplano had prepared the controversial note. It was not an ultimatum but merely the most recent of many peace proposals. And as for "observations concerning the style of its writing," the Chilean chancellery reminded its critics that "it is not discreet to judge a nation's foreign policy by the form of an isolated document."

CHILE OBJECTS TO THE AGENDA OF THE PROPOSED CONFERENCE

Chile next moved to thwart discussion of its foreign policy at the meeting of American nations. Having received the proposed agenda, the Foreign Minister, charging that it was too vague "to avoid discussion of points that might be unpleasant or offensive," asked not only for a more specific and satisfactory agenda but for virtual veto power over conference proceedings. He declared that "the only thing that, by making [Chile] completely tranquil will induce it to accept the invitation ... , would be the inclusion ... of a clause whereby it is established ... that no matters whatsoever may be discussed, nor agreements made, if a delegate of any one of the republics objects."[28]

While Chile waited for such assurances, its international position continued to deteriorate, for the circular justifying the König note had not convinced any of Chile's enemies that its cause was just. Former Argentine Foreign Minister Zeballos, speaking in Buenos Aires[29] to a group that included the ministers from Peru, Bolivia, Paraguay, and Portugal and the consuls general of Russia and the United States, traced the history of Chilean-Bolivian relations and told his listeners that in König circular "Chile shows itself ... possessed of unction, humanity, and tolerance comparable only to the eternally comforting and infinite goodness of Jesus Christ." Zeballos then accused Chile of maliciously instigating rivalries among the South American nations in order to achieve the aggressive objectives of its foreign policy.

VIRTUAL RUPTURE OF RELATIONS WITH PERU

The Chilean circular was countered by one from Peru which sought to place upon Chile the guilt for the War of the Pacific and denied that Lima had frustrated the final solution of the international problems of the Pacific. Chile bore the full responsibility for the delay, Peru charged, because it had refused Bolivia a port and had denied Peru a fair plebiscite on Tacna and Arica.[30] The Peruvian circular was followed shortly by a widely influential analysis by the historian Carlos Paz Soldán. Paz Soldán noted that the Chilean circular had been designed primarily to counteract unfavorable reaction to the König note, but he was mainly concerned with refuting its alleged historical distortions. It was necessary, he claimed, to establish the "truth" because the issue involved had been thwarting the peaceful progress of three nations and "today threatens that of the others of the continent, leading them to establish a condition of *armed peace*."[31]

Peru, stirred by the hostility it sensed in the König note and distrustful of Chile's evasion of a plebiscite and its tactics concerning the Billinghurst-Latorre protocol, tried once more to bring the matter of Tacna and Arica to a head.[32] On November 15, 1900, the Peruvian minister in Santiago handed the Chilean government a note protesting the Chileanization of Tacna and Arica. The protest went unanswered for several weeks, and then its receipt was merely acknowledged. On December 24 Peru repeated its protest. Again there was no reply.

Finally, on January 14, 1901, the Chilean Chamber of Deputies buried the Billinghurst-Latorre protocol,[33] upon which Peruvians had placed great hope for their eventual recovery of Tacna and Arica. Chile now expected that Peru would be willing to accept a large indemnity in exchange for direct cession of the two provinces.[34] Chile was wrong. The Peruvian minister promptly protested rejection of the protocol as "a delaying procedure designed to prevent the plebiscite,"[35] and strongly denounced continued Chilean occupation of Tacna and Arica.

As Peru's protest was being dispatched, the Chilean chancellery replied to the previous protest of November 15 against the Chileanization policy, insisting that the criticized measures were required in the interests of the area's inhabitants and that Chile had the right to exercise sovereign powers there. To this note the Peruvian envoy again protested, charging that the justification of the Chileanization policy, together with rejection of the Billinghurst-Latorre protocol, "seems to confirm the unswerving purpose of Chile to postpone the plebiscite until she might hold it under conditions that would inevitably cause the triumph of her hopes."[36]

By March 9, 1901, a further exchange of notes had produced no change in the position of either government, and the Peruvian minister requested his passports. In Lima a newly arrived Chilean envoy failed to present his credentials, and left his legation in charge of a secretary. Relations between Peru and Chile were for all practical purposes broken.

PREPARATIONS FOR THE INTERNATIONAL AMERICAN CONGRESS

Lima and Santiago immediately began to contend for support among the participants in the forthcoming international American congress scheduled to convene in October in Mexico City. The goal of Peru, clearly revealed in an article by Carlos Paz Soldán,[37] was to bring its dispute with Chile to the floor of the conference and force it from there into arbitration. Chile, the historian charged, had distorted the institution of the plebiscite, twisting it into a tool with which to annex and dismember the territory of another nation. The honor and liberty of America, he claimed, were at stake in the Tacna and Arica question and could be saved only by the hemisphere's adherence to the plebiscite principle and to the principle of arbitration, the occasion for which would be offered at Mexico City. Peru especially sought the support of Colombia, sending Alberto Ulloa to Bogotá to cultivate its friendship and carry on a diplomatic offensive against Chile.[38] Ulloa was received on March 23, 1901,[39] and shortly thereafter presented to the National Library a collection containing many books of great scholarly and literary value, as well as numerous works stating the Peruvian case against Chile.[40]

The Chilean chancellery, which believed that the closing of Peru's Santiago legation was part of a premeditated plan to embarrass Chile at Mexico City,[41] attempted to counter Peruvian propoganda in South America and to neutralize the damage that Peru might inflict upon Chile at Mexico City. Having received no reply to its request for veto power over the conference program, Chile pressed the Executive Committee of the Commercial Bureau of American Republics to act favorably upon its agenda recommendations.[42] A few days later, on May 2, 1901, Chile named a recent former foreign minister as envoy to Mexico with instructions to persuade its government, which appeared to favor the five-point agenda approved the preceding year, to Chile's point of view.[43]

The Executive Committee that met in Washington on May 6, 1901, to consider Chile's agenda suggestions was not the same committee that had prepared the draft agenda the year before, a fact that had a direct bearing upon the matter's outcome. Its members were now the United States' secretary of state and the ministers of Colombia, Costa Rica, Ecuador, and Bolivia. Not only was the Argentine minister no longer a member of the committee, but on the day of the meeting the Bolivian envoy failed to appear. A new report was prepared which stated that "on the agenda ... no troublesome question should be included."[44] And the committee specifically declared that any arbitration agreement reached at the conference would "apply to the future and would in no way be retroactive," and that the committee "explicitly abstains from any idea of proposing ... any existing questions."

On May 13 Santiago cabled Washington its acceptance of the conference program,[45] which remained unaltered despite a further May 16 meeting called to hear the protests of Peru and of the previously absent Bolivian minister. The Chilean foreign minister, who devoted more than half of his June 1, 1901, report to Congress to the forthcoming international meeting, considered the arbitration victory to be of great importance. It must therefore have been with tongue in cheek that he commented, toward the end of the long and copiously documented exposition, that "under I know not what unusual concept of the rights and duties implied in relations among peoples, the Executive Committee's definition of the conference program ... has been considered by some as a triumph of our diplomacy; and I can understand even less the heated and open campaign of Peru and Bolivia against what they term Chile's pretensions."[46]

THE CIRCULAR OF PERU

The Executive Committee had not solved Chile's problems. Peru took up its campaign with new vigor, issuing on May 26 a long and forceful anti-Chilean circular[47] which effectively argued that Chile was determined illegally to retain Tacna and Arica. Peru also made the grave new charge that Chile had offered to compensate Peru for Tacna and Arica by assisting Lima to conquer and divide Bolivia.[48] The circular, which demanded Chilean evacuation of the provinces, an impartial plebiscite, and the fixing of dates for indemnity payments, was virtually the brief upon which Peru would base its case at Mexico City. Chile was deeply disturbed by the document, expressing the belief that its "altogether baseless charges ... and the aggressive form of its language [are] unmistakable indications that the government of Peru was breaking diplomatic relations."[49]

Peru, like Chile, sought to influence opinion at the site of the approaching conference, hinting to the Mexican government that acceptance of a restricted agenda, as desired by Santiago, would prevent its participation. And tirelessly speaking and writing in their nation's behalf were such Peruvian propagandists[50] as Carlos Paz Soldán, who declared that "I would consider myself fortunate and amply rewarded if what I have written were in some measure to contribute to reaching the desired goal of the Pan-American Congress of Mexico, ... that our nations may be joined with the only ties that endure: the mutual respect of their reciprocal rights and a common effort for the progress and growth of all the nations."[51]

RENEWED TENSION WITH ARGENTINA

As Peru waged its valiant diplomatic and literary offensive throughout the hemisphere, Chile was confronted by progressively deteriorating relations with Argentina. To prevent further border incidents of the kind that had led to the damaging Walker interpellation of mid-1899, Buenos Aires and Santiago had agreed to respect the 1889 status quo, a move that Chilean nationalists denounced as "capitulation." Chilean public opinion was further agitated in the summer of 1901 by reports of Argentine troop movements in Chilean-claimed Ultima Esperanza. Again Joaquín Walker Martínez summoned the Foreign Minister to the Chamber of Deputies and demanded, as before, that force be used against Argentina.[52] In April, 1901, Buenos Aires protested Chilean road-building operations in a disputed region.[53] The entire complex of Chilean-Argentine relations was, moreover, disquieted by a Chilean presidential campaign and reports that Argentina was rapidly augmenting its armaments. In July the Chilean Congress established a special committee to study the question of arms procurement, and appropriated additional funds for naval expansion and modernization.[54]

Chile, encouraged by United States support for its agenda position, moved to cultivate the closer friendship of Washington. In July, 1901, Henry Lane Wilson, the United States minister to Chile, was introduced at a private dinner party to President-elect Germán Riesco, who informed him that war would result from Argentina's policy and argued that peace could best be maintained through Chilean naval predominance. Riesco urged Wilson to press for a favorable decision on Santiago's request to purchase two warships from the United States.[55]

As Argentina moved away from Chile, it drew closer to Peru and Bolivia. In May, 1901, *La Prensa* of Buenos Aires thrice demanded that Argentina refuse to participate in the Mexico City congress if Chile's preferences for the agenda were accepted. Some Argentine legislators expressed fears that their government might not insist upon full discussion,[56] but Argentina did join with Peru and Bolivia in a strenuous, and partly successful, effort to keep the agenda open for a debate on unrestricted arbitration. In August, when a new Chilean envoy reached Mexico, he discovered that the Mexican government, reacting to pressures from Argentina, Bolivia, and Peru, had decided not to notify the nations invited to the conference of the May 6 report of the Executive Committee, in which controversial questions had been eliminated from the agenda. The Foreign Minister of Mexico explained to the Chilean agent that a telegram had been received "from the Foreign Minister of Argentina protesting in passionate terms the said May 6 agreement and invoking Mexico's neutrality in this grave matter as a necessary guarantee in order to attend the congress."[57]

As Peru and Bolivia also threatened to boycott the meeting if the May 6 report was circulated, Mexico had decided to avoid any appearance of partiality. The Chilean minister's argument that distribution of the Executive Committee's report was a procedural matter which could not compromise Mexican neutrality did not sway the Foreign Minister. "If that were so," he replied, "the Executive Committee itself could have sent it out." This reply gave the Chilean envoy an idea which he promptly discussed with the United States minister in Mexico: Mexico would inform the United States that, although wishing to remain neutral, it would not oppose distribution of the Executive Committee report, and that it did not want the conference to discuss controversial matters; that having been done, the Executive Committee itself would distribute its report of May 6. The United States agreed, and the plan was carried out.[58] On September 26, 1901, the Chilean government telegraphed its official acceptance of the invitation to the conference, but surrounded it with conditions indicating Chile's firm intention to deal only with noncontroversial topics.[59]

As the time for the conference drew near, the entire hemisphere understood that Chile would not participate in any meeting that discussed the liquidation of the problems that had resulted from the War of the Pacific. Its position was supported in the May Executive Committee report; and the United States and Mexico had expressed their opposition to the raising of controversial questions. It was also possible that Chile might secure Colombian assistance. Francisco Herboso, a new Chilean envoy to Colombia, was received on September 11, 1901, [60] and by September 29 had concluded an agreement.

THE HERBOSO–ABADIA MÉNDEZ PROTOCOLS OF SEPTEMBER, 1901

Herboso's task was eased by the fact that since 1899 Colombia had been immersed in a tragic, bloody, and destructive civil war. Its relations with Venezuela and Ecuador, both of which it had accused of intervention,[61] were hostile in the extreme; and Bogotá may have seen in ties with Chile a means to strengthen its position vis-à-vis those unfriendly neighbors. In the Herboso–Abadia Méndez protocols[62] of September, 1901, Chile and Colombia dealt with a broad range of matters: bases were established for negotiation of exchange of publications and of commercial treaties; Chile agreed to encourage its good friend Ecuador to reëstablish harmony with Colombia as a first step in a planned close working relationship among the three nations; Chile would deliver a second-class ironclad cruiser to Colombia; and, above all, Colombia would support Chile's position at the international conference in Mexico.

But what support Chile had managed to secure was not certain to carry the day for her. The opposition of Peru, Bolivia, and especially Argentina was intense, the latter's role becoming crucial because of the belief of many Argentines that the conference could affect the outcome of their continental rivalry with Chile,[63] and because the Argentine-Chilean boundary crisis was again approaching an acute phase. In September, 1901, Argentina renewed its protest against road construction in disputed areas. On October 22, while these protests were being discussed, the International American Conference convened. During the more than three months in which the conference was in session Argentine-Chilean relations steadily deteriorated. By the end of the year talk of war was on every tongue. A January 7, 1902, agreement designed to prevent war was damned in both countries as capitulation to the "enemy." And after the agreement had been signed, the Chilean Congress appropriated £3 million for increased naval armaments and authorized a loan for further defense preparations.[64]

THE INTERNATIONAL AMERICAN CONFERENCE OF 1901–02

Conflict between Chile and Argentina lay heavy in the atmosphere at Mexico City. The delegation from Argentina was large and illustrious;[65] that of Chile was as brilliant, and even larger.[66] Their first clash occurred on the second day when Argentina, speaking for a bloc composed of Peru, Bolivia, Brazil, Uruguay, and Paraguay, introduced a resolution asking that Colombia and Venezuela submit their dangerous dispute to arbitration. The Chilean delegation viewed the resolution as menacing, for if the conference considered one pending dispute it could consider another. But not wishing to appear opposed to conciliation, Chile's delegation moved that consideration of the proposal be postponed until procedural regulations had been approved. Chile's motion was defeated; the Argentine resolution was put to an immediate vote and carried, with the abstention of Haiti, Venezuela, Colombia, and Chile.

As the resolution was being transmitted to the Venezuelan and Colombian governments by cable, the Chilean delegation sent the news to Santiago, whereupon the Chilean chancellery apparently cabled its minister in Bogotá to offer Chilean mediation in the dispute with Caracas. When the replies of the disputants reached Mexico City they were read in secret session. Venezuela, pointing out that its question with Colombia was not on the agenda, asserted that it could not renew relations until it had received satisfaction for claimed injuries. Colombia assured the conference that in spite of its serious grievances against Venezuela it desired a peaceful solution, and had accepted a Chilean mediation offer.[67] The Venezuelan reply so displeased the delegates, according to Bello of Chile, that the president of the conference suspended the session. When it reconvened Chile suggested, and the meeting approved, that the replies be filed without discussion. Venezuela's subsequent acceptance of Chilean mediation was regarded by Bello as placing "Chile ... in a prestigious position, exercising an efficacious and practical influence in the service of the reëstablishment of peace and cordiality [between Colombia and Venezuela], in sharp contrast to the failure of those who attempted to induce the conference improperly to intervene in the difficulties now dividing those two republics."[68]

But their failure in the Colombian-Venezuelan matter did not stop Chile's adversaries from attempting to secure conference action on the question of the Pacific. To their proposal that arbitration be made compulsory for all disputes, past, present and future, Chile countered with a demand for voluntary arbitration, asking specifically that the conference adhere to the three relevant conventions signed in 1899 at The Hague Peace Conference.[69] At this juncture the question of arbitration, voluntary versus compulsory, became the central issue of the Mexico City conference.

As it prepared to do battle for voluntary arbitration, the Chilean delegation assessed its situation. Of nineteen delegations only five were inalterably committed to compulsion—Peru, Bolivia, Argentina, Uruguay, and Paraguay; several other delegations favored future, but not retroactive, compulsory arbitration. It was therefore the task of the Chileans to prevent the latter group from falling under the influence of the five-power bloc favoring all-inclusive compulsory arbitration.[70] Toward that end the Chilean delegation fought during the entire meeting, in formal sessions and in private conversations. It used parliamentary tactics, legalistic argumentation, and direct pressures upon the home governments of some uncommitted delegates. And both the Chilean delegation and the delegations of its opponents held over the heads of neutral nations the threat of a walkout.

Of the neutral participants in the conference, Mexico and the United States were of particular importance, the latter because of its wealth, size, and military might, so recently displayed in the Spanish-American War, the former because it was the host nation and was enjoying a period of material splendor and political stability. Moreover, Mexico had been the first Latin-American nation to sit with the United States and the Great Powers of Europe at an important international meeting, The Hague Peace Conference. Hoping to preserve the international luster gained at The Hague, Mexico sought to prevent the wreck of the conference on the rocks of the Pacific dispute. Toward that end, it proposed the acceptance of general compulsory arbitration, but with two exceptions: disputes involving national honor and/or independence; and pending disputes specifically excluded by any signatory to the proposed agreement.

Precisely because Mexico's proposal was a compromise, it satisfied neither the Chilean nor the anti-Chilean faction. As Peru prepared to pack up and leave the meeting, and Chile to work for modification of the proposal, the United States delegation made known its opposition to the principle of compulsory arbitration,[71] suggesting that the Mexican plan be modified to make it conform to The Hague Convention on voluntary arbitration. The opponents of Chile remained adamant, Argentina informing the United States government in Washington that "the Conference will prove a failure should the United States fail to employ legitimate influence on behalf of obligatory arbitration."[72]

When Argentina, Peru, and Bolivia prepared to rush to the floor of the conference with an unrestricted compulsory arbitration agreement, Mexico, to meet that threat to the life of the conference, offered another compromise. The conference would adhere to The Hague conventions, but, in addition, its Committee on Arbitration would prepare a report in which each delegation might state its position. Moreover, in connection with that report, nations desiring to arrange extraconference treaties might do so, making it possible for Chile's adversaries to return home with a compulsory arbitration treaty which had not, however, been officially sanctioned.

Informed that its adversaries had agreed to the compromise plan, Chile too gave its approval, for from its viewpoint the plan was highly advantageous. But then Chile was dismayed to learn that the Argentine-Peruvian-Bolivian bloc had managed to secure approval of its unlimited compulsory arbitration pact by seven other nations, including Mexico, together with their consent that "this agreement will be raised to the rank of treaty and signed in order to include it in the final act of the conference."[73]

The Chilean delegation protested first to the Mexican foreign minister and then to President Porfirio Díaz himself, charging that Mexico had abandoned its neutrality and had thereby enabled the enemies of Chile to win the support of a conference majority. Inclusion of the compulsory agreement in the final act, Chile claimed, was designed only to give offense to Chile, as any nations wanting to secure compulsory arbitration could do so outside the conference, as contemplated in the Mexican compromise proposal. Under Chile's threat to withdraw from the conference, Mexico announced that it would erase its signature unless the final clause was removed. To this Argentina, Peru, Bolivia, Paraguay, Venezuela, and Santo Domingo reacted by threatening to withdraw, and underlined their warning by an ostentatious collective absence from the plenary session of January 10, 1902.

The United States and Mexico next jointly advanced a new compromise. Two proposals would be drawn up outside the conference, one for adherence to The Hague conventions, the other for compulsory arbitration. The first would be signed by all delegates; the second, by those who wished to do so. Both proposals would be communicated to the conference president, read, and sent without discussion to the Mexican secretary of foreign affairs for incorporation into the final act. Chile protested that the Mexican–United States compromise would actually give the proposal of its enemies official conference sanction, but sponsors of the compromise remained determined to seek its approval.

Chile, seconded by Ecuador, then took the battle to the floor of the plenary session by moving for approval of The Hague conventions. As one of the compromise proposals called for the very same thing and had already been signed by fifteen delegations, there was little that the conference could do except unanimously approve the Chilean resolution. Then, at the same session, what remained of the United States–Mexican resolution was carried out and sent to the secretary for inclusion in the final act.

Because Chile's proposal became an official "resolution" of the international conference at Mexico City, Chile could claim triumph. But a paper victory, gained through a clever parliamentary maneuver, could not conceal the fact that Chile's position in South America was a perilous one. As the conference ended Chile stood in danger not only of Argentine-Bolivian-Peruvian encirclement, but of moral isolation upon the continent.

The *rapprochement* with Argentina of 1899 did not produce the desired results. Relaxed relations with Buenos Aires were not enough to ensure the success of a stiffer Chilean policy toward both Bolivia and Peru. On the contrary, those nations opposed increased resistance to

Chile's demands, and Peru mounted a highly promising campaign to force the Tacna-Arica dispute into arbitration. Moreover, when Argentine-Chilean relations once again deteriorated under the strain of border incidents during the long arbitral proceedings, a basis for anti-Chilean coöperation on the part of Peru, Bolivia, and Argentina was established; the Pan-American Conference at Mexico City provided the opportunity for such coöperation. Although Chile's opponents there failed to gain their full objectives, Chile was nevertheless left in danger of moral and military encirclement.

Chapter XIV

A NEW SOUTH AMERICAN EQUILIBRIUM

THE PERIL OF ISOLATION and encirclement which confronted Chile at the start of 1902 lasted through the early months of the year. The question of the Pacific was no nearer solution than ever. Bolivia, although discouraged by the failure of the Mexico City conference to censure Chile and force it to accept compulsory arbitration, and harried by the mounting bitterness of its dispute with Brazil, continued stubbornly to reject Chile's terms for peace. Relations with Peru had been broken for nearly two years, and their early reëstablishment seemed improbable. But for Chile the major single obstacle to ultimate solution of the Pacific question, and at the same time its most immediate source of physical danger, lay in the crisis of its relations with Argentina, for that crisis now seemed certain to lead to war.

RELATIONS WITH ARGENTINA IN 1902

The Argentine-Chilean agreement of January, 1902, regarding occupation of disputed territory completely failed to assuage the mistrust obsessing both countries. Having received the pertinent congressional authorization, Chile ordered two new cruisers to compensate for the naval superiority now being attributed to Argentina. But European bankers, anticipating war between Chile and Argentina, would lend funds for military procurement only on excessively harsh terms, so that the Chilean government, without awaiting legislative permission, diverted to the navy funds earmarked for the conversion of paper currency. Later approved by Congress, Chile's effort to gain on Argentina came to naught, for Buenos Aires in its turn ordered two more cruisers. No end to the naval race seemed in sight, and each new move increased the almost intolerable tension.[1] Concurrently, the Chilean chancellery feared Argentine intervention in the Pacific question.[2] A tendency in that direction had clearly been indicated at Mexico City; such Argentine nationalists as Estanislao Zeballos were demanding drastic action; and even President Roca, coauthor of the 1898–99 *rapprochement,* seemed committed to forcing Chilean fulfillment of the treaties with Peru and Bolivia.[3]

RELATIONS WITH ECUADOR AND COLOMBIA IN 1902

As the Argentine threat mounted Chile reached out to the northern republics. The 1901 Herboso–Abadia Méndez protocols with Colombia

had been a preliminary step which their negotiators now followed with
further accords, certain of whose aspects would assist Chile in the event
of war with Argentina. The cruiser that Chile was to sell to Colombia
would be returned in the event of open hostilities, and Colombia secretly
promised "to allow the free transit at all times through the Isthmus
of Panama of armament for the government of Chile."[4] Chile had
changed its position on that matter; during the War of the Pacific it
had fought valiantly for the "principle" of isthmian neutrality, but
then it was Peru that benefited from Colombia's failure to prevent
transshipment of arms. Now, because Chile's use of the route would
involve Colombia in difficulties with Peru or Argentina or Bolivia, or
with all three, the secret protocol in question contained Chile's promise
"to forestall whatever difficulty might ensue to the Government of
Colombia as a result of this concession; and especially to aid it with
loans, subsidies and assistance."[5]

Two further agreements dealt with a desired *rapprochement* between
Colombia and Ecuador; the disputing nations would attempt to solve
their differences in Chilean-assisted bilateral negotiations, and, if these
failed, would accept Chilean arbitration. There existed, however, a
major obstacle to direct Colombian-Ecuadoran agreement in the form
of the tripartite convention of 1894 which bound Colombia, Ecuador,
and Peru to submit their common boundary disputes to Spanish arbitration.[6] Alone among the signatories, Ecuador had not ratified the
convention, although failure to do so would throw the dispute back
upon a less favorable treaty, signed in 1887. To circumvent the pre-
existing treaties—for their implementation would deny Chile a role—
the 1902 Chilean-Colombian protocols provided that (1) Colombia
would not exploit Ecuador's failure to ratify the 1894 convention in
order to gain the more favorable 1887 terms, and would assist Ecuador
to evade the 1887 commitment in respect to its dispute with Peru; and
(2) the foregoing having been accomplished, Bogotá and Quito would
either reach a direct settlement or submit to Santiago's mediation.
Until and unless Chile's formal mediation proved necessary, the protocol provided that "in view of the cordial relations which Chile main-
tains with Ecuador, it will inform that country of . . . the close friendship which from this date binds it to Colombia and . . . shall invite
it to sign a Treaty which shall stipulate the most perfect and close
harmony between the three Republics."[7]

In accordance with its new Colombian agreement, Chile invited
Ecuador to sign with Bogotá a treaty "stipulating the most perfect
harmony between the contracting parties, the governments of Colombia

and Ecuador being bound to arrange their difficulties . . . [or] submit them . . . to the resolution of the government of Chile."⁸ And in negotiating with Ecuador, as it had with Colombia, Chile offered Quito a warship—pending legislative approval.

Peru was to regard Chile's Colombian-Ecuadoran diplomacy as part of a plan to disrupt Lima's peaceful settlement of its boundary disputes with those two countries, in order to prevent Peru's concentration on the question of Tacna and Arica.⁹ But the Foreign Minister of Chile saw the far-northern policy of his country in a different light. Although noting that the cruiser agreement with Colombia "would . . . tend to give it greater military influence in the Pacific,"¹⁰ he stressed that upon completion of the treaties "Chile will . . . have taken another step forward toward the recovery of the influence in America which rightly belongs to it because of its organization and progress."¹¹ But in the early months of 1902 Chile's far-northern policy was an ancillary one at best. It could harass Peru but not paralyze her. And in any event Chile's greatest danger lay to its east.

THE ARGENTINE CRISIS REACHES FEVER PITCH

Until the British arbiters had drawn and secured acceptance of the long-disputed Chilean-Argentine boundary, there would continue the incursive incidents, any one of which might serve as the spark that would ignite war. Although such incidents aroused public outcries and let to the exchange of angry official protests, there was a far more fundamental source of conflict between Argentina and Chile. As an able Argentine jurist observed, "the boundary question has never been a serious motive for conflict. . . . The only question that has agitated the two countries is that of the influence of each in the South American equilibrium."¹²

Argentine nationalism, using as a foundation the nation's recent forward strides, had constructed castles in the air. Argentina, in nationalist opinion, was destined to be a future leader in South America; perhaps it would reign supreme. Chilean nationalism was equally intransigent, if differently based; Chile, because of its long and brilliant history of political stability and steady material progress, crowned by the well-deserved victory it had gained in the War of the Pacific, was superior to all other Latin-American nations. Having long since "arrived," as its reputation in the world proved, Chile would brook no challenge from the trans-Andine parvenu. The nationalists of each country were quick to see dire threats in the actions of the other country, and to demand that those threats be stamped out by

military force. Their paranoid voices were strident; they had strong
popular followings; and their very strength made a general settlement
both more necessary and more difficult.

Responsible moderate elements did, however, exist in both countries.
They felt that a peaceful solution was imperative. The arms race was
becoming so costly as sharply to restrict productive spending; war,
beyond the disaster of death, injury, and material damage, would place
both countries in financial bondage for decades to come. But in the
face of powerful nationalism in both Chile and Argentina, moderates
found it impossible to speak out publicly. A *deus ex machina* was
clearly needed; and one was found.

GREAT BRITAIN'S ROLE

Great Britain had been observing the Chilean-Argentine crisis with
concern.[13] Its commerce with both nations was important; many British
citizens held substantial public and private investments in them;
British nationals resided in both Chile and Argentina and engaged
in commercial, business, and professional activities. The continuance
of the arms race, and even more so war, would damage those interests.
Great Britain was, moreover, already involved in the Chilean-
Argentine conflict as boundary arbitrator. Perhaps, too, having recently recognized United States hegemony in the Caribbean in the
Hay-Pauncefote Treaty, the British may have sensed an opportunity
to consolidate their South American position.

London's first move was an attempt to accelerate the boundary
arbitration. Early in January, 1902, Thomas Holdich, a member of
the arbitral tribunal, departed for South America accompanied by
a technical staff to observe the disputed territory at first hand. Stopping first in Buenos Aires, Holdich sent his staff to explore the southern
area while he remained in the Argentine capital to explore the possibility of a direct settlement. Holdich moved on to Santiago at the end
of February and, while his staff reconnoitered the San Francisco Pass,
Ultima Esperanza, and Lake Lacar, he met with the Chilean foreign
minister and advised him that Argentina might not oppose a direct
settlement. The Foreign Minister firmly replied that "in 1881, when
Chile was at war against two nations, she relinquished the sovereignty
of the extensive region of Patagonia to which she considered herself
to hold indisputable title, thus giving up the possession of a territory
larger than that of some European nations. . . . [Chile's] only compensation for that was the fixing of the *divortium aquarum* as its boundary
[with Argentina], . . . and it therefore cannot now accept any change."[14]

Although Holdich was made to understand that Chile was not immediately prepared to accept a direct settlement, he was also urged to
secure an arbitral decision as soon as possible in the interest of peace.

In the absence of a prompt, direct settlement, Great Britain tried
to bring an end to the armaments race. The destructive competition was
not only having unfortunate economic consequences for the countries
involved, but also threatened to precipitate a war before the British
agents could complete their work and hand down a boundary decision.
At the beginning of April a new British minister, Lord Lowther,
arrived in Santiago to seek acceptance of His Majesty's good offices
"toward the objective of arriving at a limitation of armaments." He
informed the Chilean foreign minister that the British envoy in Buenos
Aires was similarly approaching the Argentine government. The Foreign Minister, who believed that the British envoy's approach had
been solicited by Buenos Aires, declared that the Chilean navy was no
larger than required by national tradition and the need to protect a
very long coastline from Argentine attack. The situation of the Argentine navy was, according to the Chilean, altogether different; it had
little coast to defend, and the country was living far beyond its means
"in order to erect a military power superior to that of any other South
American nation." Moreover, the Foreign Minister explicitly charged
that "Chile's . . . difficulties in arranging pending questions with Peru
and Bolivia are due in large part to the influence of Argentina. . . .
Any overt Argentine attempt to intervene in the liquidation of Pacific
affairs would be . . . an immediate *casus belli*."[15]

Undaunted, the British minister took at their face value the Chilean's
polite parting remarks to the effect that he would welcome British
efforts to end existing Chilean-Argentine difficulties. After consultation with his colleague in Buenos Aires, Lord Lowther formally
offered His Majesty's good offices to Chile. The terms of the offer
indicated a primary interest in halting the arms race. Characterizing
that competition as potentially disastrous, Great Britain asked Argentina and Chile to abstain from further preparations for war until
London had completed work on the boundary arbitration.[16]

Chile accepted the British offer and in doing so expressed its conviction that a general settlement would be a necessary precondition to
suspension of arms procurement. Santiago advanced two suggestions
for eliminating Argentine-Chilean discord: first, a treaty of compulsory
arbitration; second—without this, Chile declared, a treaty would be
meaningless—a change in Argentina's Pacific Coast policy. Chile proposed "a declaration of reciprocal neutrality which confirms each

nation's absolute independence to develop its proper sphere of action."[17]

The Foreign Minister of Chile, while insisting that Chile's financial position would permit payment for ships under construction and more, without need of foreign loans, assured Lowther that Chile would gladly reduce its armaments if its ideas for a settlement were accepted. On the other hand, the Foreign Minister insisted, Chile would continue to arm itself "unless it becomes convinced that Argentina rejects the idea of general [retroactive] arbitration and of seeking to intervene in the arrangement of Pacific affairs which we wish quickly to conclude under existing treaties."[18] The claim of a strong financial position was of course designed to warn England that it could not disarm Chile through its influence in the financial world, but would have to secure from Argentina the commitments that Chile deemed prerequisite to arms reduction. But Chile, in speaking of "Pacific affairs which we wish quickly to conclude under existing treaties," was offering Argentina a *quid pro quo*.

The importance of that *quid pro quo* became increasingly evident as the British, having gained acceptance by both nations of their good offices, hastened completion of the boundary arbitration. Argentine nationalism, losing the boundary dispute as a basis for its demand for war, turned to Chilean Pacific policy, alleging that Chile was certain to attempt new conquests which Argentina must prevent in order to preserve the balance of power essential to its security and continued leadership.[19] Such nationalist newspapers as *La Prensa* and *La Tribuna* demanded that Argentina insist upon Chilean fulfillment of the terms of the Treaty of Ancón.[20]

But as the British government groped for a solution to the Chilean-Argentine conflict, moderate elements in Argentina, including the newspapers *La Nación* and *El País,* owned by former Presidents Mitre and Pellegrini respectively, spoke up in opposition to the war cries of the nationalists. On April 9, 1902, a *La Nación* editorial denied charges that war was necessary because the boundary award would fail to solve the Pacific question, insisting that

The Republic would present a sorry sight if the day after the solution of its own case it charged forth bearing on high a foreign case upon which to base its right to live in perpetual malaise and alarm, to bankrupt itself with armaments, and to cut off its sources of progress, sacrificing all in the name of an ... intervention justified neither by history, nor by geography, nor by economic interests, nor by the example of the greatest nations on earth. ... The Argentine Republic is not party to the questions of the Pacific, nor does it have any business with them unless its own security, now or later, is threatened.[21]

Attempting to calm fears concerning Chilean power, *La Nación* pointed out, on at least three separate occasions, that Chile's control of the nitrates of Peru and the ports of Bolivia since the War of the Pacific had posed no threat to Argentina, and that therefore formalization of such control would not change the situation. Nor would Chile, *La Nación* claimed, dare to seek dismemberment of Peru and Bolivia, for those nations would resist with tenacity, and the United States and Brazil would not be indifferent. Moreover, if and when the occasion arose, Argentina would adopt the policy best suited to its interests; meanwhile, upon completion of the boundary arbitration, Argentina should accept peace with Chile on the basis of Argentine naval superiority, or at least parity, and take advantage of peace to develop its own resources, leaving Chile to deal with the question of the Pacific. Through the achievement of peace with Chile, declared *La Nación*, "the Republic will take its proper path toward power and grandeur."[22]

El País, supporting the general thesis of *La Nación*, set forth additional arguments against Argentine intervention on the Pacific Coast, reminding its readers that since Argentina had opposed United States intervention in the War of the Pacific, it could hardly justify its own. Claiming that Argentine intervention would be tantamount to imperialism, *El País* asked whether or not "Brazil would regard with indifference an imperialist policy that would tend to make Argentina the arbiter of all American questions."[23] And the journal further counseled that it is an "obligation of political honesty . . . that Peru and Bolivia not be misled . . . into believing that Argentine policy may be based upon and directed by unreflecting advice and passions."[24]

SEARCH FOR A SOLUTION

The moderate policy advocated by Argentine ex-presidents Mitre and Pellegrini gained adherents outside and within the Argentine government,[25] including the new minister to Chile, José Antonio Terry. Terry's official instructions, however, betrayed no softening. He was ordered merely to watch and wait, and warned to say or do nothing that might be interpreted as weakness. Moreover, he was instructed to make it clear that Buenos Aires could "not . . . be indifferent to the conquests of Chile and the augmentation of its power."[26] Two days after Terry's arrival, Chile was deprived of a foreign minister by a cabinet crisis, and his official reception had to be delayed. In the meantime Terry conversed privately with President Riesco, and their talks were the beginning of negotiations that ultimately led to a major settlement. On May 9 the new foreign minister, José Francisco Vergara Donoso, joined in the discussions. And working behind the scenes assiduously, but saying little, was the British envoy, Lord Lowther.

Negotiations for a direct general settlement between Chile and Argentina proved to be extremely difficult. Buenos Aires, kept constantly informed by telegraph, was primarily concerned over arms limitation, believing that Chilean insistence upon other agreements was merely a delaying action designed to permit completion of warships under construction. Many days and much argumentation were required to convince Buenos Aires of Chile's genuine desire for a broad settlement covering the entire range of pending problems, including Argentina's relationship to the question of the Pacific. Finally the last obstacle— Argentina's belief that mere discussion of the Pacific matter would constitute its *de facto* recognition of Chile's conquest—was overcome. On May 28, 1902, the Chilean foreign minister, Vergara Donoso, and the Argentine envoy, Terry, signed three agreements and exchanged several supplementary notes designed to place their nations' relations on a basis of permanent friendship.

THE PACTOS DE MAYO

The first of these important agreements, which became known as the Pactos de Mayo,[27] was a preliminary act which was in effect a preamble to the second pact, a general treaty of arbitration. The preliminary agreement expressed the usual desire to settle differences amicably, and willingness to do so in an arbitration treaty. The preliminary act, however, contained extremely significant clauses prohibiting both Argentine intervention in Pacific affairs and future Chilean conquests, and it was these mutual guarantees that paved the way for further negotiation.

The guarantees were contained in general statements of good intentions. Argentina affirmed that its policy had always been to resolve conflicts with other nations in a friendly manner, and that "the government of the Republic of Argentina has achieved this result by . . . respecting the sovereignty of other nations, interfering in neither their internal nor their foreign affairs; that consequently there was no place in its spirit for aims of territorial expansion; that it would adhere to this policy and that . . . it was making these declarations now that the moment had come for Chile and the Argentine Republic to remove all causes of alarm in their international relations." Chile stated that its purposes had always been the same high purposes expressed by Argentina, and that "Chile . . . does not harbor aims of territorial expansion, excepting such as may result from the fulfillment of existing treaties or as might later be celebrated."

The general treaty of arbitration bound Chile and Argentina to "submit to arbitration all controversies of whatever nature which for any reason might arise between them, so long as they do not affect the precepts of either nation's constitution." Questions already settled between the two countries were excepted from arbitration. The British government was named as first choice to act as arbiter, with the Swiss Confederation as alternate. The third agreement, a convention on naval armaments, committed the signatories not to take possession of warships under construction or to make further purchases and, in addition, to reduce their existing fleets to a "reasonable parity" under an agreement to be reached within one year. It was also agreed not to dispose of excess warships by allowing nations potentially unfriendly to either signatory to acquire them; this provision assured Chile that Argentine warships would not one day appear flying the Peruvian flag. A supplementary exchange of notes recognized the difficulty of defining "reasonable parity" by providing that any dispute on the point would be handled under the provisions of the arbitraton treaty. And, to ensure the permanence of the naval reduction pacts, it was agreed that for a period of five years neither nation would make any increase in naval armaments without giving the other advance notice. In addition to the foregoing major agreements, Argentine and Chilean negotiators approved several documents designed to speed final demarcation of the boundary by the British arbiter.

The first news of the Pactos de Mayo brought a sharp drop in tensions between Chile and Argentina, but nationalists in both countries soon raised their voices to protest the settlement. Argentine nationalists criticized it for its naval reduction aspects, and Chilean nationalists, for its allegedly insufficient guarantees against Argentine intervention. Moreover, some Chilean nationalists were disturbed by Chile's renunciation of "territorial expansion, excepting such as may result from the fulfillment of existing treaties," for they feared that Argentina, claiming that the interpretation and fulfillment of the treaties with Peru and Bolivia were its concern, might force Chile to submit the Tacna and Arica question to arbitration under the general arbitration treaty.

Negotiators Terry and Vergara, recognizing both the political strength and the merit of certain objections, prepared an "additional act" which sought to clarify the Pactos de Mayo and to "remove the slight doubts raised in both nations."[28] To meet Chilean objections it

was agreed "that the execution of existing treaties or of those that are
a consequence of them, to which the preliminary act refers, cannot be
subject to arbitration, . . . and that consequently neither of the contracting governments has the right to interfere in the form chosen to
fulfill those treaties." To meet Argentine objections it was agreed that
"reasonable parity . . . does not require the alienation of ships, as
reasonable parity can be sought in disarmament or by other means,
. . . in order that both governments may conserve the squadrons necessary for *Chile's natural defense and permanent destiny in the Pacific,
and for the Argentine Republic's natural defense and permanent destiny in the Atlantic and the Río de la Plata"* (italics added).

The additional act to the Pactos de Mayo clearly did much more than
"remove slight doubts." It superimposed upon the mutual no-territorial-
conquest commitments of the original agreements, which were its necessary precondition, an almost formal delineation of spheres of interest.
At last the negotiators had reached the heart of the Chilean-Argentine
conflict. Each nation now granted the other, short of territorial conquest, carte blanche in the international political manipulation of its
own back yard. From Chile's viewpoint the demarcation of spheres of
interest was of tremendous importance; Chile could now proceed, without Argentine interference, to consolidate the hegemony it had wrested
in the War of the Pacific. But even more, Chile had gained the definition
of spheres of influence despite Argentina's strong power position.

The Pactos de Mayo and the additional act represented a Chilean
diplomatic triumph. A few months earlier Chile had appeared in
danger of Argentine-Bolivian-Peruvian encirclement and of moral
isolation, as well as of a war with Argentina which it could not be sure
of winning. It was scraping the bottom of the financial barrel to wage
an arms competition which it would inevitably lose to Argentina's
mounting economic strength. Against that unfavorable background,
Chile succeeded in creating a new South American equilibrium favorable to its interests.

The new South American equilibrium was to be perpetuated by
several devices. In addition to naval parity between Chile and Argentina and to the territorial status quo provisions of the Pactos, the
general treaty of arbitration would act powerfully in that direction.
Either power could call the other promptly to account before an
arbiter in the event of a threat to the equilibrium; this arrangement
was obviously advantageous to Chile, which was losing ground in the
power struggle with Argentina. Even the fact that no cognizance was
taken of Brazil in the Pactos operated to create a new equilibrium

favorable to Chile. Although it was true that at the time the agreements were signed Brazilian-Argentine relations were cordial, Brazil was far more likely to act as a counterpoise to Argentina than to Chile in the future. Finally, Chile's Pacific power position was affirmed and enhanced by the spheres-of-influence agreement. The budding entente with Ecuador and Colombia, and the dashing of Peru-Bolivian hopes for Argentine assistance, combined with Chile's inherent power and a new favorable continental equilibrium, would seem to provide assurance of its Pacific hegemony.

The additional clarifying act, however, did not quiet the opposition that was to stand for a time between the Pactos and their legislative approval and public acceptance. In Buenos Aires, interventionist *La Prensa* charged that "Argentine diplomacy has been drugged by Chilean diplomacy," claiming that Chile had outwitted Argentina by first convincing it to accept naval parity and then making a concession that it would have been willing to make all along—Argentina's right to maintain its existing navy. In exchange for that concession, *La Prensa* added, "Chile ... has received ... carte blanche in the Pacific."[29] Estanislao Zeballos declared that because Argentina was afraid of war it had relinquished its South American supremacy to Chile. But on July 30, 1902, the Argentine Chamber of Deputies approved the Pactos de Mayo by a vote of 62 to 5.

Chilean legislative opposition was slower to collapse, culminating on August 8 with a "Manifesto to the Country," in which five deputies charged that experience had shown that Argentina was not to be trusted, that Chile was abandoning its traditional stand against compulsory arbitration so recently defended in Mexico City, that the pacts made Chile a virtual protectorate of Great Britain, and that Chile would now be relegated to a position of naval inferiority.[30] But on August 11, 1902, the Chilean Chamber of Deputies approved the treaties by a large majority.

To dramatize the rebirth of Argentine-Chilean friendship and to help erase the rancor of the past, it was decided to exchange ratifications of the Pactos de Mayo in Santiago on September 18, Chile's Independence Day. Argentina sent to Chile, aboard the cruiser *San Martín,* a large and distinguished delegation which was greeted with friendly street demonstrations, parades, balls, banquets, and ceremonies which lasted for several days. Ratifications were exchanged. Speeches were made in praise of the eternal friendship that would exist between Argentina and Chile.

In succeeding months the new "eternal" friendship was put to the test, first by the handing down, on November 20, 1902, of King Edward VII's boundary award. Rejecting both Chile's *divortium aquarum* and Argentina's "highest peaks of the principal chain of the Andes" interpretations of Article I of the treaty of 1881, the British arbitral tribunal drew the line at an intermediary point. Of the approximately 94,000 square kilometers in dispute, Chile was awarded about 54,000 and Argentina, about 40,000. From both sides of the Andes complaints arose and charges were leveled against the supposedly responsible governments. But the storm of protest did subside, and on January 9, 1903, Argentina and Chile signed an agreement officially requesting the British government to proceed with physical demarcation of the boundary.[31]

Another test of the new Chilean-Argentine *rapprochement* was met when the two countries succeeded in negotiating the naval disarmament protocol envisioned in the Pactos de Mayo. In that agreement, signed in Buenos Aires on January 9, 1903, the two governments agreed to sell the ships that each had under construction in England and Italy, and not to incorporate the ships into their fleets even if sale should prove impossible. And the first steps toward naval armaments reduction were taken with Chile's agreement to disarm the cruiser *Capitán Prat* and Argentina's willingness to disarm the *Garibaldi* and the *Pueyrredón.*[32]

In May, 1903, Chile returned Argentina's courtesies of the preceding September by sending a distinguished delegation to Buenos Aires for the celebration of Argentina's Independence Day. During the ceremonies there was some talk of "international alliances, of the necessity of agreement among the South American republics to defend themselves against possible aggressions, and of a concert of powers to maintain peace in this continent,"[33] indicating a desire to turn the *rapprochement* into an instrument of positive coöperation.

The Chilean and Argentine governments also took concrete steps to bring their peoples closer to each other. On January 9, 1903, a convention was signed expanding an existing agreement on the reciprocity of scholarly and professional degrees. On February 6 an agreement was reached to facilitate telegraphic communications.[34] Plans were made to join the railway systems of Chile and Argentina through completion of the Chilean section of the long-envisioned trans-Andine railroad.[35] The *transandino*, threading its way perilously up and into and through the cordillera's high passes, was eventually completed and stands now as a monument to the Argentine-Chilean *rapprochement.*

THE BOLIVIAN QUESTION

The effects of the *rapprochement* upon Chile's Pacific Coast interests soon became apparent. Even before the pacts had been signed, Bolivia's bargaining position had been weakened by its serious dispute with Brazil.[36] Early in 1902, while the Pactos were being negotiated, an "unofficial" Bolivian agent appeared in Santiago to discuss peace terms with Chile's foreign minister. After the signing of the Chilean-Argentine agreements a new Bolivian minister, Alberto Gutiérrez, was sent to Santiago to negotiate replacement of the truce pact of 1884 with an official treaty of peace. Arriving in the wake of celebrations held to exchange ratifications of the Pactos de Mayo, Gutiérrez reported to his government that "there could still be heard the echo of the applause and joy with which the high society of Chile and the common people had welcomed the delegates of the Argentine government."[37]

For many months the Bolivian envoy negotiated with the Chilean government. And in La Paz, on August 30, 1903, the same Bolivian foreign minister who had flatly rejected the König proposals reported to his Congress that during the past year negotiations with Chile had been proceeding in both Santiago and La Paz. He emphasized the fact that Chile's power position required Bolivians to be prepared to relinquish their aspiration for a seaport on the Pacific, but he attempted to console them with the assurance that the negotiations in progress would provide other forms of compensation for the loss of the coastal region. The Foreign Minister poignantly confessed that "in view of our numerous questions with the Republic of Chile, and that nation's financial and military preponderance in relation to us, I have never shared the attitude toward these affairs of some Bolivian political groups ... who feed upon illusory hopes. A statesman does not have the right to live out of contact with reality; he must tell the people the truth, however painful and sad it may be, and suggest solutions that will allow them to go forward on the road of progress."[38] Bolivia had finally accepted its defeat in the War of the Pacific.

THE BOLIVIAN PEACE TREATY OF 1904

By December, 1903, Bolivian and Chilean negotiators succeeded in preparing two draft treaties which dealt separately with major pending questions. The drafts were then consolidated into a comprehensive treaty signed on October 20, 1904. On March 10, 1905, after the exchange of several clarifying notes, ratifications were exchanged.[39] The

Bolivian-Chilean 1904 peace treaty reëstablished the peace that was shattered in 1879. In it Chile gained one minor and one major concession. The former guaranteed Chile reduced freight rates on railroads to be built in Bolivia under the terms of the treaty; the latter gave Chile permanent sovereignty over the former Bolivian littoral.

Bolivia obtained a broad range of concessions. Chile agreed to construct and pay for a railroad connecting the port of Arica with La Paz and to turn over to the Bolivian government, at the end of fifteen years, that part of the railroad lying within Bolivian territory. Chile also guaranteed, in perpetuity, free transit for Bolivian commerce across Chilean territory, as well as Bolivia's right to establish customs houses in designated Chilean ports. Bolivia was thus not only assured of a commercial outlet to the sea but also of improved international communications via the future Arica–La Paz railroad. Chile further agreed to guarantee the interest on the investment required for construction of five domestic Bolivian railroads, without which commitment Bolivia could not have secured the necessary foreign capital. Chile also granted Bolivia commercial independence by relinquishing the special privileges it held under the truce pact and by permitting Bolivia to charge the same customs duties on Chilean products as upon those of other nations. To relieve Bolivia's drastic financial problem, Chile agreed to pay its government £300,000 in currency during the succeeding eighteen months and to assume Bolivia's obligations to both private and commercial Chilean interests, which totaled approximately 6.5 million pesos. Finally, Bolivia and Chile agreed to submit to the arbitration of the Emperor of Germany all disputes that might arise concerning the fulfillment of the terms of the peace treaty.

The Chilean-Bolivian treaty of peace was an instrument of great importance to Chile's maintenance of its Pacific Coast hegemony. Not only did it end the threatening impasse with Bolivia, but it also tied Bolivia's fortunes to those of Chile in the still-unsettled Tacna and Arica matter. Only if Chile could permanently secure sovereignty over those provinces would Bolivia be assured a free port of entry at Arica. Moreover, in the contemplated future demarcation of the frontier between Bolivia and Tacna-Arica, only Chilean sovereignty would guarantee to Bolivia—as promised in a secret additional agreement to the 1904 treaty—a favorable delineation. The peace treaty paid Chile a further, if unspecified, dividend, but one not unforeseen by Chilean negotiators. Because Chile had, in a diplomatic agreement with another nation, committed itself to the building of a railway through Arica, and had made provision for the demarcation of the boundaries of both

Tacna and Arica, it would now be able to point to those acts as evidence of effective exercise of sovereignty in the two provinces and thereby, so it hoped, strengthen its legal claim to them.[40]

RELATIONS WITH PERU

The settlements with Argentina and Bolivia greatly improved Chile's position with respect to its Peruvian problem. That position was even further strengthened by current cordial relations with the northern Pacific Coast republics of Colombia and Ecuador, and by the fact that these two nations seemed to be drawing closer together while they were at the same time at odds with Peru over unsettled boundaries and various incidents arising from rubber-collecting activities in disputed areas. In early 1905 there was no open conflict between Peru and Colombia or between Peru and Ecuador, but the peace was distinctly uncertain, and Peru's simultaneous involvement in a dispute with Brazil put it in a position of virtual isolation as it faced Chile.

Peru well knew what the settlements between Chile and Argentina and between Chile and Bolivia implied for its own position. It had bitterly but fruitlessly objected to both agreements. In February, 1905, it formally protested against Chile's exercise of sovereignty over Tacna and Arica. Chile replied that the Treaty of Ancón had in reality ceded the two provinces to it; the plebiscite had merely been added to mollify public opinion and was not intended to be taken seriously. At the same time Chile invited Peru to send a diplomatic representative to Santiago for the purpose of discussing the unsettled business between them. Peru had no alternative. In May, 1905, its new envoy arrived in the capital of Chile, reopened the doors of his country's legation, and prepared to negotiate from a position of weakness.[41] Bolivia had already accepted the reality of its defeat; it was Peru's turn to do the same.

Three-quarters of a century had passed since the victory at Lircay cleared the way for the reforms of the Portalian era. The dream of a Chilean nation-state preëminent upon the continent's Pacific Coast had been realized. Chile's position had been challenged without success. Now, finally, her preëminence seemed to be definitely established. Affirmed by the new favorable South American equilibrium created in the Pactos de Mayo, reinforced by the overdue capitulation of Peru and Bolivia, the Pacific Coast hegemony of the Republic of Chile seemed to be assured.

Chapter XV

CONCLUSION

Between 1830 and 1905 Chile consistently behaved as though it were a nation-state operating within a system of power politics. Throughout that period Chilean leadership, assuming that significant shifts in the international power structure embodied a potential threat to vital national interests, sought to maintain a favorable power structure. Striving to augment its power and to advance its interests, Chile competed with other nations within its system for commercial preëminence; for control of such resources as guano, nitrates, and silver; for possession of territory with strategic or agricultural potential; and for military and naval superiority. Both in the effort to maintain a favorable power structure and in the process of competing with other countries for elements of power, Chile showed herself willing to employ the full range of the policies and techniques of power politics, such as reprisals, economic coercion, ultimatums, alliances, the *divide et impera* principle, and armed force.

The particular policy or technique chosen by Chilean leaders from the arsenal of European methods to deal with individual situations was a significant indicator of contemporary Chilean assumptions concernin the spatial limits of Chile's system of power politics. The fact that threats of force were largely confined to the sphere of intra–South American affairs revealed Chile's belief that she was part of a system composed of South American nations. Within that system Chile could hope to be an influential determinant of the power structure.

Chile knew that she could not play a forceful role in respect either to the individual Great Powers of the non–South American world or to their system(s). On the other hand, those powers might, if they chose, decisively influence Chile's system, so that it was necessary to keep them at bay. As coercion was not a viable tool in this connection, Chile based her Great Power policy on the assumption that the rivalries among the Great Powers would tend to keep them in rein, and employed generally accommodative policies designed to hold the Great Powers at arm's length. There evolved, with time, a *modus operandi* under which Chile provided economic opportunities and protection of nationals in exchange for freedom from intervention.

Only when a Great Power appeared to threaten the South American power structure, in a way potentially damaging to Chilean interests, did Chile assume a posture of open resistance. She did so when

Spain backed a Flores expedition; when a United States protectorate over Ecuador was proposed; when Spanish seizure of the Chincha Islands seemed to threaten the continental territorial status quo; when United States intervention in the War of the Pacific threatened to frustrate Chile's efforts to recast the South American power structure; or when British control of the nitrate industry, together with its naval power, posed a potential threat to the source of wealth upon which Chile was dependent for her South American power superiority.

Chile's Great Power policy was generally, therefore, subordinate to her South American policy. Chile sought, in relations with the non–South American Great Powers, to acquire the resources and to ensure the freedom requisite to her assumption of a leading role within the South American system. The importation of capital, technology, and skilled individuals from the United States and Europe, and the expansion of Chilean commerce with the Great Powers, were important in promoting Chile's aggrandizement and thus in improving her ability to compete with the nations in her system. But Chile sought Great Power trade and technology free of Great Power intervention, for such intervention would have nullified her ability to play the role of a great power within the area of her vital interests.

Within the area of Chile's vital interests—that is, within South America—Chilean policy decisions reflected progressively expanding systemic spatial limits and a continually shifting and evolving relative power position. In the early 1830's, as a weak nation struggling to establish itself, Chile was enabled by a favorable South American power structure, resulting from the anarchy of its neighbors, to adopt a policy of nonintervention and no entangling alliances, a policy based upon the assumption that there was in operation an automatically self-regulating balance of power mechanism.

When the unification of Peru and Bolivia demonstrated the deficiencies of that mechanism, and at the same time threatened to disrupt a power structure favorable to Chilean interests, Chile resorted to force. In the course of its military destruction of the Peru-Bolivian Confederation, Chile abandoned the policy of relying upon a self-regulating balance of power mechanism and adopted a policy of attempting positively to maintain a power structure favorable to Chilean hegemony. For a brief moment after the war this objective was sought through the negotiation of bilateral security pacts and the promotion of an American congress. When those efforts failed, Chile assumed the role of regulator of the balance of power in the area of her immediate vital interests.

In acting as regulator of the balance of power, Chile was at first ready to employ force only to maintain the territorial status quo in Peru and Bolivia. But as her power increased and her commerce expanded northward along the Pacific Coast, and as Peruvian strength mounted, Chile moved to become the regulator of the balance of power along the entire Pacific Coast. The power structure of which Chile was the regulator permitted her to extend her influence over the Atacama Desert and the Strait of Magellan. Chile now had hegemony on the Pacific Coast.

But, beginning in the 1860's, the South American power structure under which Chile enjoyed her hegemony began to change under the impact of South America's increasing integration into the world economy. Argentina emerged as a fourth great South American power, and Peru's efforts to attract it into a tripartite anti-Chilean alliance with Bolivia forced Santiago to recognize the possible effect of the new South American power structure upon Chile's vital interests.

Responding to the changed structure, Chile sought first to make of Brazil a counterpoise to Argentina; and then, when war broke out between Chile and the Peru-Bolivian alliance, the government of Chile sought to establish a new equilibrium that would compensate for the change effected in the power structure by the rise of Argentina. Chile would recast the structure by dismembering Peru and Bolivia, keeping for herself their nitrate resources and giving Bolivia the Peruvian provinces of Tacna and Arica, so that a stronger Bolivia might be Chile's ally against Peru and/or Argentina. But Chile's attempt in that respect was only partly successful; and at the same time her conquests had aroused widespread mistrust throughout the continent. Thus, Chile's leaders sought briefly to use the nation's newly acquired nitrate wealth to maintain an armed peace under which Chile might be sufficiently strong to ward off all possible coalitions. When that policy failed as a result of Chile's deteriorating power position—a result in turn of Chile's internal problems, the uncertainty of its Brazilian entente, and the continued growth of Argentina—Chile reverted to the policy of establishing a new South American equilibrium. The new equilibrium was sought first, and unsuccessfully, through creation of a strong and allied Bolivia; then, and successfully, in an understanding with Argentina which permitted Chile to maintain her hegemony on the Pacific Coast of the continent.

The evolution of Chile's South American policy between 1830 and 1905 demonstrates two salient characteristics of Chilean international life during that period. First, Chilean policy was consistently and intimately dependent upon the broad trends in Chile's internal development and upon the totality of her international situation. As Chile and the other South American nations matured and developed internally, their contacts with other South American nations expanded. At first interested only in herself, and then only in herself and Peru and Bolivia, Chile had by the beginning of the twentieth century become a nation that maintained diplomatic contacts with all the continent's countries, and one that was actively involved in attempting to shape the mutual or conflicting interests of those nations into a form that would create a favorable power structure for Chile. The process of the expansion of Chilean interests was a reflection of the evolution of South American power politics from the regional to the continental. Second, Chile's South American policy between 1830 and 1905 revolved consistently about the leitmotiv of maintaining a balance of power in South America which would be favorable to Chilean interests. And during that long period Chilean leadership was remarkably successful in securing and maintaining Chile's hegemony on the Pacific Coast, whether by reason or by force.

NOTES

ABBREVIATIONS

ChDC, 1889	Diplomáticos chilenos, 1889
ChDC, 1890–1891	Diplomáticos chilenos, 1890–1891
ChDC, 1891–1893	Diplomáticos chilenos, 1891–1893
ChDC, 1893–1894	Diplomáticos chilenos, 1893–1894
ChDC, 1894	Diplomáticos chilenos, 1894
ChDC, 1895, I	Diplomáticos chilenos, 1895, I
ChDC, 1895, II	Diplomáticos chilenos, 1895, II
ChDC, 1896	Diplomáticos chilenos, 1896
ChDC, 1897	Diplomáticos chilenos, 1897
ChDC, 1898, I	Diplomáticos chilenos, 1898, I
ChDC, 1899	Diplomáticos chilenos, 1899
ChGACol, 1851–1876	Gobierno y agentes diplomáticos de E. U. de Colombia en Chile, 1851–1876
ChLBraz, 1891–1892	Legación de Chile en el Brasil, 1891–1892
ChLCol, 1879–1880	Legación de Chile en Colombia, 1879–1880
ChLCol, 1881–1882	Legación de Chile en Colombia, 1881–1882
ChLEc, 1836–1840	Legación de Chile en el Ecuador, 1836–1840
ChLEc, 1852–1865	Legación de Chile en el Ecuador, 1852–1865
ChLP, 1823–1853	Legación de Chile en el Perú, 1823–1853
ChLP, 1887, II	Legación de Chile en el Perú, 1887, II
ChLPlat, 1836–1838	Legación de Chile en las Repúblicas del Plata, 1836–1838
ChPlat, 1887–1888	Legación de Chile en el Plata, 1887–1888
ChLUrug, 1885–1886	Legación de Chile en el Uruguay, 1885–1886
ChT, 1885	Telegramas, 1885
ChT, 1888–1889	Telegramas despachados, 1888–1889

COLOMBIA, MINISTERIO DE RELACIONES EXTERIORES

ColADC 174	No. 174. Archivo Diplomático y Consular. [Correspondence of the Colombian minister in Chile, Pablo Arosemena]

UNITED STATES, GENERAL RECORDS OF THE DEPARTMENT OF STATE

USDespChile 48	Diplomatic Despatches, Vol. XLVIII, Chile
USDespCol 33	Diplomatic Despatches, Vol. XXXIII, Colombia

NOTES

Chapter I: Introduction

[1] Robert N. Burr, "The Balance of Power in Nineteenth-Century South America: An Exploratory Essay," *Hispanic American Historical Review*, XXXV (Feb., 1955), 37–60; and Robert N. Burr, *The Stillborn Panama Congress: Power Politics and Chilean-Colombian Relations during the War of the Pacific* (Berkeley and Los Angeles: University of California Press, 1962).

Chapter II: The Foundations of National Power

[1] Because the boundaries of the South American nations had not been demarcated as of 1830, it is impossible to know their exact extent at that date. Today Chile is larger than it was in 1830, and yet its territory is smaller than that of six of the ten South American countries: Peru, Argentina, Bolivia, Brazil, Colombia, and Venezuela. As Venezuela was in early 1830 still part of Great Colombia, it may be assumed that Chile was then smaller than at least five of the then-existing South American countries. For the present territorial extent of the South American nations, see *Statistical Abstract of Latin America, 1960*, Center of Latin American Studies, University of California (Los Angeles, 1961), p. 2. Reliable figures for the 1830 populations of South American nations are unobtainable. Angel Rosenblat, *La población indígena y el mestizaje en América* (2 vols.; Buenos Aires: Editorial Nova, 1954), I, 36–37, gives population estimates for all of them except Paraguay in approximately 1825. I have assumed little change in the relative sizes of those populations between 1825 and 1830. Rosenblat (*op. cit.*, II, 171–212) discusses a variety of population estimates for the period between 1810 and 1825. For a discussion of Latin American censuses see *Bibliography of Selected Statistical Sources of the American Nations*, Inter-American Statistical Institute (Washington, 1947).

[2] Ricardo Montaner Bello, *Historia diplomática de la independencia de Chile* (Santiago de Chile: Prensas de la Universidad de Chile, 1941), pp. 455–472.

[3] C. K. Webster, *Britain and the Independence of Latin America, 1812–1830* (2 vols.; London: Oxford University Press, 1938), pp. 23–25; Alan K. Manchester, *British Preëminence in Brazil: Its Rise and Decline* (Chapel Hill: University of North Carolina Press, 1933), pp. 186–219.

[4] Montaner Bello, *op. cit.*, pp. 391–394. For Britain's recognition policy toward Chile see also Theodore E. Nichols, "The Establishment of Political Relations between Chile and Great Britain," *Hispanic American Historical Review*, XXVIII (Feb., 1948), 137–143, and Charles W. Centner, "El fracaso chileno de obtener el reconocimiento británico (1823–1828)," *Boletín de la Academia Chilena de la Historia*, IX, no. 27 (1943), 33–44.

[5] John White to the Earl of Aberdeen, Valparaíso, Jan. 4, 1830, Webster, *op cit.*, p. 368.

[6] For an analysis of the development of the Chilean hacienda see George M. McBride, *Chile: Land and Society* (New York: American Geographical Society, 1936), pp. 61–122; for the Chilean aristocracy see Alberto Edwards Vives, *La fronda aristocrática: historia política de Chile* (Santiago de Chile: Editorial del Pacífico, 1945), pp. 11–67.

[7] For evidence of this tendency in the late colonial period see Sergio Villalobos R., *Tradición y reforma en 1810* (Santiago de Chile: Ediciones de la Universidad de Chile, 1961), pp. 61–63.

[8] For discussions of Portales' political ideas and policies see Edwards Vives, *op. cit.*, pp. 50–62; Francisco A. Encina, *Historia de Chile desde la prehistoria hasta 1891* (20 vols.; Santiago de Chile: Editorial Nascimento, 1949–1952), X, 460–509; and Jorge Basadre, *Chile, Perú y Bolivia independientes* (Barcelona and Buenos Aires: Salvat Editores, S.A., 1948), pp. 121–123.

[9] *El Araucano*, Oct. 2, 1830, p. 3.

[10] *Sesiones de los cuerpos legislativos de la República de Chile, 1811 a 1845*, ed. Valentín Letelier (37 vols.; Santiago de Chile, 1887–1908), XX, 353.

[11] *Ibid.*, XXIII, 389–390.

[12] Daniel Martner, *Historia de Chile: historia económica* (Santiago de Chile: Establecimientos Gráficos de Balcells, 1929), pp. 149–150.

[13] Francisco Frias Valenzuela, *Historia de Chile* (4 vols.; Santiago de Chile: Editorial Nascimento, 1949), IV, 7–11.

[14] *El Araucano*, Sept. 17, 1830, p. 1.

[15] Alberto Cruchaga Ossa, *Los primeros años del ministerio de relaciones exteriores* (Santiago de Chile: Imprenta Universitaria, 1919), p. 91.

[16] Guillermo Feliú Cruz, *Andrés Bello y la redacción de los documentos oficiales administrativos, internacionales y legislativos de Chile: Bello, Irisarri y Egaña en Londres* (Caracas: Fundación Rojas Astudillo, 1957), p. 153.

[17] A[ndrés] B[ello], *Principios de derecho de gentes* (Santiago de Chile, 1832). A valuable study of various aspects of Bello's text and its significance, including an analysis of the author's modifications and revisions in two succeeding editions, has been made by Eduardo Plaza A. in his preface to *Derecho internacional* (Caracas: Ministerio de Educación, 1954), Vol. X of Andrés Bello, *Obras completas*.

[18] Bello, *Derecho internacional*, pp. cxci, clxvi.

[19] Feliú Cruz, *op. cit.*, pp. 116, 251–273, 315.

[20] *El Araucano*, Aug. 25, 1837, p. 4.

[21] Octavo Gil Munilla, *El Río de la Plata en la política internacional. Génesis del virreinato* (Sevilla: Escuela de Estudios Hispanoamericanos de Sevilla, 1949).

[22] Montaner Bello, *op. cit.*, pp. 441–442, 468, 487, 492, 509–522, 600; Alberto Cruchaga Ossa, *La jurisprudencia de la cancillería chilena hasta 1865, año de la muerte de Don Andrés Bello* (Santiago de Chile: Imprenta de Chile, 1935), pp. 40–43.

[23] Quoted in Encina, *op. cit.*, XI, 128.

[24] For the colonial conflict between Chile and Peru see Néstor Meza Villalobos, *La conciencia política chilena durante la monarquía* (Santiago de Chile: Universidad de Chile, 1958), pp. 226–245.

[25] A. Bascuñán Montes, ed., *Recopilación de tratados y convenciones celebrados entre la República de Chile y las potencias extranjeras* (2 vols.; Santiago de Chile: Imprenta Cervantes, 1894), I, 6–13, 168–177.

[26] No reliable figures are available on Chile's foreign trade in this period. These generalizations are based on approximations from Encina, *op. cit.*, X, 153–154, 173–174, and from Charles Centner, "Relaciones comerciales de Gran Bretaña con Chile, 1810–1830," *Revista Chilena de Historia y Geografía*, no. 103 (July–Dec., 1943), pp. 96–107.

[27] See Alberto Cruchaga Ossa, "Don Pedro Trujillo y su misión diplomática en Lima," *Boletín de la Academia Chilena de la Historia*, IX, no. 20 (1942), 79–100.

[28] Diego Portales to Minister Zañartu in Peru, no. 4, Santiago de Chile, July 31, 1830, ChC, 1826–1839; see also Encina, *op. cit.*, X, 92.

[29] Diego Portales to Minister Zañartu in Peru, no. 4, Santiago de Chile, July 31, 1830, ChC, 1826–1839.

[30] *Ibid.;* Diego Portales to Minister Zañartu in Peru, no. 8, Santiago de Chile, Aug. 19, 1830, ChC, 1826–1839.

[31] Carlos Pedemonte [Minister of State, Department of Foreign Relations, Peru] to Juan Bautista de Lavalle, Minister Plenipotentiary of Peru, Lima, Jan. 5, 1831, *Colección de los tratados, convenciones ... y otros actos diplomáticos y políticos celebrados desde la independencia hasta el día, precedida de una introducción ... por Ricardo Aranda*, Peru, Ministerio de Relaciones Exteriores (14 vols.; Lima, 1890–1919), IV, 778–781.

[32] *Ibid.*, XIII, 323.

[33] Encina, *op. cit.*, X, 596.

[34] Diego Portales to Minister Zañartu in Peru, no. 22, Santiago de Chile, April 2, 1831, ChC, 1826–1839.

[35] *Colección de los tratados* ..., II, 176–186.

[36] R. Errázuriz to the Minister of Chile in Peru, Zañartu, no. 39, Santiago de Chile, March 8, 1832, ChC, 1826–1839.

[37] R. Errázuriz to the Minister of Chile in Peru, no. 40, Santiago de Chile, March 10, 1932, ChC, 1826–1839.

[38] *Ibid.*

[39] *Ibid.*

[40] For the growing commercial conflict between Chile and Peru see Ramón Molina Guzmán, "Las relaciónes chileno-peruanas (1819–1837)," *Boletín de la Academia Chilena de la Historia*, I, no. 4 (1934), 125–194; Jorge Basadre, *La iniciación de la República* (2 vols.; Lima, 1929–1930), II, 10–11; Encina, *op. cit.*, XI, 130–136.

[41] Joaquín Tocornal to the Minister of Chile in Peru, no. 53, Santiago de Chile, Aug. 11, 1832, ChC, 1826–1839.

[42] Benjamín Vicuña Mackenna, *Obras completas* ... (16 vols.; Santiago de Chile: Universidad de Chile, 1939–1940), VI, 684–687; Encina, *op. cit.*, XI, 133–134.

[43] Joaquín Tocornal to Ventura Lavalle [González], Consul General of Chile in Peru, no. 1, Santiago de Chile, June 24, 1833, ChC, 1826–1839.

[44] Ramón Sotomayor Valdés, *Historia de Chile durante los cuarenta años transcurridos desde 1831 hasta 1871* (4 vols.; Santiago de Chile: Imprenta de "La Estrella de Chile," 1875–1903), I, 413 n. 8.

[45] For text of the treaty see *Colección de los tratados* ..., IV, 18–32.

[46] *El Araucano*, July 30, 1835, p. 4.

CHAPTER III: CHAMPION OF THE AMERICAN EQUILIBRIUM

[1] Jorge Basadre, *Chile, Perú y Bolivia independientes* (Barcelona and Buenos Aires: Salvat Editores, S.A., 1948), pp. 153–156; Lane Carter Kendall, "Andrés Santa Cruz and the Peru-Bolivian Confederation," *Hispanic American Historical Review*, XVI (Feb., 1936), 29–48.

[2] Oscar de Santa Cruz, comp., *El General Andrés de Santa Cruz, Gran Mariscal de Zepita y el Gran Perú: documentos históricos* (La Paz: Escuela Tipográfica Salesiana, 1924), pp. 69–71.

[3] For text of treaty see *ibid.*, pp. 395–397.

[4] For text see *El Araucano*, Aug. 29, 1835, p. 2.

[5] *Ibid.*

[6] Ramón Sotomayor Valdés, *Historia de Chile durante los cuarenta años transcurridos desde 1831 hasta 1871* (4 vols.; Santiago de Chile: Imprenta de "La Estrella de Chile," 1875–1903), II, 76.

[7] *El Araucano*, Nov. 27, 1835, p. 1.

[8] *Ibid.*, Nov. 20, 1835, p. 4, gives the justification for Chile's policy of "neutrality." See also Ramón Molina Guzmán, "Las relaciónes chileno-peruanas (1819–1837)," *Boletín de la Academia Chilena de la Historia*, I, no. 4 (1934), 166.

[9] D. Portales to the chargé d'affaires of Chile in Peru, Lavalle, no. 38, Santiago de Chile, Jan. 8, 1836, ChC, 1826–1839.

[10] Sotomayor Valdés, *op. cit.*, II, 83–84; Diego Portales to the chargé d'affaires of Chile in Peru, no. 42, Santiago de Chile, Feb. 29, 1836, ChC, 1826–1839.

[11] *Colección de los tratados, convenciones ... y otros actos diplomáticos y políticos celebrados desde la independencia hasta el día, precedida de una introducción ... por Ricardo Aranda*, Peru, Ministerio de Relaciones Exteriores (14 vols.; Lima, 1890–1919), IV, 32–33.

[12] *El Araucano*, Feb. 26, 1836, p. 4.

[13] D. Portales to the chargé d'affaires of Chile in Peru, no. 43, Santiago de Chile, March 16, 1836, ChC, 1826–1839.

[14] Ventura Lavalle to the Minister of State and Foreign Relations of Chile, Lima, April 8, 1836, ChCAP, 1833–1836.

[15] *El Araucano*, May 27, 1836, p. 3.

[16] Ventura Lavalle to the Minister of State and Foreign Relations of Chile, no. 54, Lima, July 4, 1836, ChCAP, 1833–1836.

[17] *Sesiones de los cuerpos legislativos de la República de Chile, 1811 a 1845*, ed. Valentín Letelier (37 vols.; Santiago de Chile, 1887–1908), XXV, 229–233.

[18] *Ibid.*, p. 233.

[19] *El Araucano*, June 24, 1836, p. 7.

[20] *Ibid.*, July 29, 1836, p. 1.

[21] Luís Uribe Orrego, *Nuestra marina militar, desde la liberación de Chiloé (1826) hasta la guerra con España (1865)* (Valparaíso: Imprenta de la Armada, 1914), pp. 56–59.

[22] Basadre, *op. cit.*, p. 168.

[23] *Collección de los tratados ...*, IV, 35–37.

[24] Ernesto de la Cruz and Guillermo Feliú Cruz, eds., *Espistolario de Don Diego Portales, 1821–1837* (3 vols.; Santiago de Chile: Imprenta de la Dirección General de Prisiones, 1936–1937), III, 452.

[25] For text see Sotomayor Valdés, *op. cit.*, II, 188–189.

[26] Joaquín Prieto to Andrés Santa Cruz, Santiago de Chile, Oct. 3, 1836, *ibid.*, II, 190–195.

[27] *Sesiones de los cuerpos legislativos ...*, XXV, 228–229.

[28] As quoted in Sotomayor Valdés, *op. cit.*, II, 240–241 n. 35.

[29] Uribe Orrego, *op. cit.*, pp. 69–70.

[30] Casimiro Olañeta to Diego Portales, Santiago de Chile, Dec. 8, 1836, *El Araucano*, Dec. 23, 1836, p. 3.

[31] Diego Portales to the minister of Peru, Santiago de Chile, Dec. 10, 1836, *ibid.*, p. 4.

[32] Casimiro Olañeta to Diego Portales, Santiago de Chile, Dec. 14, 1836, *ibid.*, Dec. 30, p. 1.

[33] Diego Portales to Casimiro Olañeta, Santiago de Chile, Dec. 15, 1836, *ibid.*, pp. 1–2.

[34] For the text of the President's message see Alberto Cruchaga Ossa, *La jurisprudencia de la cancillería chilena hasta 1865, año de la muerte de Don Andrés Bello* (Santiago de Chile: Imprenta de Chile, 1935), pp. 123–126.

[35] *El Araucano*, Dec. 30, 1836, p. 2.

[36] Santa Cruz, *op. cit.*, p. 125.

[37] Sotomayor Valdés, *op. cit.*, II, 246 n. 37.

[38] Andrés Bello, *Principios de derecho internacional* (2d ed., corr. and aug.; Lima, 1944), pp. 127–128.

[39] Cruchaga Ossa, *op. cit.*, pp. 129–130; Jorge Basadre, *La iniciación de la República* (2 vols.; Lima, 1929–1930), II, 96–97.

[40] Ventura Lavalle to the Minister of State and Foreign Relations of Chile, Guayaquil, Nov. 22, 1836, ChLEc, 1836–1840.

[41] For the text of this treaty see Santa Cruz, *op. cit.*, pp. 401–404.

[42] Ventura Lavalle to the Minister of State and Foreign Relations of Chile, Quito, Dec. 14, 1836, ChLEc, 1836–1840.

[43] Ventura Lavalle to the Minister of State and Foreign Relations of Chile, Quito, Feb. 2, 1837, *ibid.*

[44] Ventura Lavalle to Francisco de Paula Santander, Quito, Dec. 19, 1836, copy, attached to Ventura Lavalle to the Minister of State and Foreign Relations of Chile, Quito, Dec. 22, 1836, *ibid.*

[45] Francisco de Paula Santander to Ventura Lavalle, Bogotá, Nueva Granada, Jan. 31, 1837, *ibid.*

⁴⁶ Enrique M. Barba, "Las relaciones exteriores con los paises americanos," in *Historia de la Nación Argentina*, Academia Nacional de la Historia, VII, *Rosas y su época* (2d ed.; Buenos Aires: Librería y Editorial "El Ateneo," 1951), 213–270.

⁴⁷ José Joaquín Pérez to the Minister of Foreign Relations of Buenos Aires, charged with those of the Argentine Confederation, Buenos Aires, Feb. 3, 1836, copy, enclosed in José Joaquín Pérez to the Minister of Foreign Relations of Chile, Buenos Aires, Feb. 20, 1836, ChLPlat, 1836–1838.

⁴⁸ Ernesto Restelli, comp., *La gestión diplomática del General de Alvear en el Alto Perú (Misión Alvear–Díaz Vélez, 1825–1827)*: *documentos* ... (Buenos Aires, 1927), XV–XVII, 35–55.

⁴⁹ José Joaquín Pérez to the Minister of Foreign Relations of the Republic of Chile, Buenos Aires, April 21, 1837, ChLPlat, 1836–1838; Barba, *op. cit.*, pp. 235–236.

⁵⁰ Barba, *op. cit.*, p. 218.

⁵¹ *El Araucano*, June 23, 1837, p. 3.

⁵² *Ibid.*, June 19 (pp. 3–4), 30 (pp. 5–6), 1837.

⁵³ J. Tocornal, foreign minister of Chile, to the chargé d'affaires of Chile in Buenos Aires, Santiago de Chile, July 21, 1837, ChC, 1826–1839.

⁵⁴ Joaquín Tocornal to the Foreign Minister of Ecuador, Santiago de Chile, Aug. 4, 1837, ChCGMexColEU, 1826–1855.

⁵⁵ J. Tocornal to the chargé d'affaires of Chile in Ecuador, Santiago de Chile, Aug. 4, 1837, ChC, 1826–1839.

⁵⁶ *El Araucano*, Aug. 25, 1837, p. 4.

⁵⁷ J. Tocornal to General Manuel Blanco Encalada and Colonel Antonio José de Irisarri, Santiago de Chile, Sept. 6, 1837, ChC, 1826–1839.

⁵⁸ For text of treaty see *Colección de los tratados* ..., IV, 40–43.

⁵⁹ *Ibid.*

⁶⁰ *El Araucano*, Dec. 30, 1837, p. 3.

⁶¹ Francisco A. Encina, *Historia de Chile desde la prehistoria hasta 1891* (20 vols.; Santiago de Chile: Editorial Nascimento, 1949–1952), XI, 357–359.

⁶² J. Tocornal to the chargé d'affaires of Chile in Buenos Aires, Santiago de Chile, March 26, 1838, ChC, 1826–1839.

⁶³ J. Tocornal to the chargé d'affaires of Chile in Buenos Aires, Santiago de Chile, Dec. 19, 1837, ChC, 1826–1839.

⁶⁴ José Joaquín Pérez to the Minister of Foreign Relations of Buenos Aires, Buenos Aires, Jan. 3, 1838, copy, ChLPlat, 1836–1838; Felipe Arana, foreign minister of Buenos Aires, to the chargé d'affaires of the Republic of Chile, Buenos Aires, Jan. 18, 1838, copy, *ibid.*

⁶⁵ Ventura Lavalle to the Minister of State and Foreign Relations of Chile, Ecuador, Feb. 24, 1838, ChLEc, 1836–1840.

⁶⁶ Joaquín Tocornal to the Minister of Foreign Relations of the Republic of Nueva Granada, Santiago de Chile, April 28, 1838, ChCGMexColEU, 1826–1855.

⁶⁷ Joaquín Tocornal to the Minister of Foreign Relations of the Republic of Nueva Granada, Santiago de Chile, May 19, 1838, *ibid.*

⁶⁸ Encina, *op. cit.*, XI, 362–363.

⁶⁹ El Araucano, Jan. 19 (pp. 3–4), Feb. 9 (pp. 3–4), 1838.

⁷⁰ *Ibid.*, Jan. 19, 1838, p. 4.

⁷¹ For text of Irisarri's charges, dated January 20, 1838, see *Antonio José de Irisarri, Escritos polémicos*, ed. Ricardo Donoso (Santiago de Chile: Imprenta Universitaria, 1934), pp. 171–205.

⁷² These articles are reprinted in *Sesiones de los cuerpos legislativos* ..., XXV, 434–455.

⁷³ "Exposición de los motivos que ha tenido el presidente de Chile para desaprobar el tratado de paz celebrado en Paucarpata ... i renovar las hostilidades interrumpidas por él" (March 4, 1838), in *Sesiones de los cuerpos legislativos* ..., XXV,

428–434. The exposition does not seem to have been published in *El Araucano* until May, 1838. The Chilean objections to the treaty, as discussed above, are found in this message and in a series of editorials in *El Araucano*, Dec. 22, 30, 1837; Jan. 5, 12, 19, Feb. 9, 1838.

⁷⁴ Encina, *op. cit.*, XI, 428–430.

⁷⁵ J. Tocornal to Mariano de Egaña, Santiago de Chile, Oct. 5, 1838, ChC, 1826–1839; Encina, *op. cit.*, XI, 425–427.

⁷⁶ Encina, *loc. cit.*

CHAPTER IV. ASPIRATION VERSUS REALITY

¹ Jorge Basadre, *Chile, Perú y Bolivia independientes* (Barcelona and Buenos Aires: Salvat Editores, S.A., 1948), p. 175.

² *Sesiones de los cuerpos legislativos de la República de Chile, 1811 a 1845,* ed. Valentín Letelier (37 vols.; Santiago de Chile, 1887–1908), XXVIII, 417.

³ Basadre, *op. cit.*, p. 201.

⁴ Theodore E. Nichols, "The Establishment of Political Relations between Chile and Great Britain," *Hispanic American Historical Review,* XXVIII (Feb., 1948), 141.

⁵ Luís Uribe Orrego, *Nuestra marina militar, desde la liberación de Chiloé (1826) hasta la guerra con España (1865)* (Valparaíso: Imprenta de la Armada, 1914), pp. 181–211; Luís Langlois, *Influencia del poder naval en la historia de Chile desde 1810 a 1910* (Valparaíso: Imprenta de la Armada, 1911), pp. 135–138.

⁶ Antonio José Uribe, ed., *Anales diplomáticos y consulares de Colombia* (6 vols.; Bogotá, 1900–1920), III, 146.

⁷ Ramón Cavareda to Sr. Lavalle, chargé d'affaires of Chile in Ecuador, Santiago de Chile, March 17, 1840, and Ramón Cavareda to Sr. Vial, chargé d'affaires of Chile in Bolivia, Santiago de Chile, April 23, 1840, ChC, 1840–1843.

⁸ Joaquín Tocornal to Ventura Lavalle, Santiago de Chile, Aug. 22, 1839, ChC, 1826–1839.

⁹ Ricardo Montaner Bello, *Negociaciones diplomáticas entre Chile y el Perú: primer período (1839–1846)* (Santiago de Chile: Imprenta Cervantes, 1904), p. 30 n. 16.

¹⁰ Joaquín Tocornal to Ventura Lavalle, Santiago de Chile, Aug. 22, 1839, ChC, 1826–1839.

¹¹ Ventura Lavalle to the Minister of State and Foreign Relations of Chile, Quito, Nov. 15, 1839, ChLEc, 1836–1840.

¹² Robert N. Burr and Roland D. Hussey, eds., *Documents on Inter-American Cooperation 1810–1948* (2 vols.; Philadelphia: University of Pennsylvania Press, 1955), I, 56.

¹³ See Art. 14 in A. Bascuñán Montes, ed., *Recopilación de tratados y convenciones celebrados entre la República de Chile y las potencias extranjeras* (2 vols.; Santiago de Chile: Imprenta Cervantes, 1894), I, 14–27.

¹⁴ Joaquín Tocornal to the Minister Plenipotentiary of the United Mexican States, Santiago de Chile, July 17, 1834, *Documentos parlamentarios. Discursos de la apertura en las sesiones del congreso, y memorias ministeriales* (9 vols.; Santiago de Chile: Imprenta del Ferrocarril, 1858–1861), I, 144–147.

¹⁵ R. Cavareda to the Minister of Foreign Relations of Mexico, Santiago de Chile, April 9, 1840, ChCGMexColEU, 1826–1855.

¹⁶ "Memoria del ministro de relaciones exteriores al congreso nacional de 1840," *Documentos parlamentarios,* I, 188.

¹⁷ *Sesiones de los cuerpos legislativos ...,* XXVI, 71, 336.

¹⁸ M. Montt to the Minister of Foreign Relations of Ecuador, Santiago de Chile, Nov. 5, 1840, ChCGMexColEU, 1826–1855. Similar notes were sent to Colombia, Venezuela, and Mexico.

¹⁹ Montt to Sr. Vial, Santiago de Chile, Nov. 14, 1840, ChC, 1840–1843.

²⁰ For examples see the reports of the Ministry of Foreign Relations to Congress for 1842 and 1843, in *Documentos parlamentarios*, II, 13–19, 131–136.

²¹ Ramón Luís Yrarrázaval to the Chilean chargé d'affaires in France, Santiago de Chile, Dec. 31, 1842, ChC, 1840–1843.

²² For the history of international politics in the Plata area see Pelham H. Box, *The Origins of the Paraguayan War* (Urbana: University of Illinois Press, 1927); Ramón J. Cárcano, *Guerra del Paraguay: orígenes y causas* (Buenos Aires, 1939); Efraím Cardozo, *Vísperas de la guerra del Paraguay* (Buenos Aires: Librería "El Ateneo" Editorial, 1954); Julio César Chaves, *El Presidente López: vida y gobierno de Don Carlos* (Buenos Aires, 1955), chaps. v–x.

²³ For discussions of the Eucadoran-Peruvian boundary dispute see Gordon Ireland, *Boundaries, Possessions and Conflicts in South America* (Cambridge: Harvard University Press, 1938), pp. 219–221; Oscar Efrén Reyes, *Breve historia general del Ecuador* (5th ed.; 3 vols.; Quito: Editorial "Fray Jodoco Ricke," 1955–1956), III, 867–885; Alberto Ulloa, *Posición internacional del Perú* (Lima, 1941), pp. 1–61.

²⁴ Ventura Lavalle to the Minister of State in the Department of Foreign Relations of Chile, Quito, Dec. 9, 1839, ChLEc, 1836–1840.

²⁵ Quoted in *ibid.*

²⁶ *Ibid.*

²⁷ A copy of the instructions to the Ecuadoran chargé d'affaires is enclosed in Ventura Lavalle to the Minister of State in the Department of Foreign Affairs of Chile, Quito, March 10, 1840, *ibid.*

²⁸ Ventura Lavalle to the Minister of State and Foreign Relations of Chile, Quito, March 20, 1840, no. 21, *ibid.;* Richard Pattee, *Gabriel García Moreno y el Ecuador de su tiempo* (Quito: Editorial Ecuatoriano, 1941), pp. 65–66.

²⁹ Basadre, *op. cit.,* p. 239.

³⁰ Ramón Cavareda to Sr. Lavalle, Santiago de Chile, March 17, 1840, ChC, 1840–1843.

³¹ R. Renjifo to the Minister of Foreign Relations of New Granada, Santiago de Chile, July 4, 1842, ChCGMexColEU, 1826–1855.

³² R. L. Yrarrázaval to the consul of Chile in Ecuador, Santiago de Chile, July 21, 1842, ChC, 1840–1843.

³³ R. L. Yrarrázaval to S. Lavalle, Minister of Chile in Lima, Santiago de Chile, Aug. 23, 1842, no. 52, *ibid.*

³⁴ The complete text of the note is quoted in Montaner Bello, *op. cit.,* pp. 54–57.

³⁵ Ramón Cavareda to Sr. Vial, chargé d'affaires of Chile in Bolivia, Santiago de Chile, April 23, 1840, ChC, 1840–1843.

³⁶ R. L. Yrarrázaval to Sr. Lavalle, minister plenipotentiary of Chile in Peru, Santiago de Chile, Dec. 3, 1841, *ibid.*

³⁷ Montaner Bello, *op. cit.,* p. 112.

³⁸ Ramón Renjifo to Sr. Amunátegui, consul of Chile in Lima, Santiago de Chile, Jan. 22, 1842, ChC, 1840–1843.

³⁹ For text of treaty see *Colección de los tratados, convenciones ... y otros actos diplomáticos y políticos celebrados desde la independencia hasta el día, precedida de una introducción ... por Ricardo Aranda*, Peru, Ministerio de Relaciones Exteriores (14 vols.; Lima, 1890–1919), II, 283–286.

⁴⁰ Montaner Bello, *op. cit.,* pp. 98–99.

⁴¹ R. L. Yrarrázaval to the consul of Chile in Arica, Santiago de Chile, Nov. 28, 1843, ChC, 1840–1843.

⁴² For text see *Colección de los tratados ...,* IV, 53–57.

⁴³ "Memoria del ministro de hacienda al congreso nacional de 1861," *Documentos parlamentarios,* VIII, 389–440.

⁴⁴ Basadre, *op. cit.,* p. 201.

⁴⁵ For a detailed discussion of the establishment of the Pacific Steamship Naviga-

tion Company see J. B. Alberdi, *Life and Industrial Labors of William Wheelwright in South America* (Boston: A. Williams and Co., 1877), chaps. vi–x.

⁴⁶ Armando Braun Menéndez, *Fuerte Bulnes* (Buenos Aires: Emecé Editores, S.A., 1943); Benjamín Valdés A., "¿Pretendió el gobierno francés tomar posesión del Estrecho de Magallanes?" *Revista Chilena de Historia y Geografía* (July–Dec., 1943), pp. 5–16.

⁴⁷ "Memoria del ministro del interior al congreso nacional de 1844," *Documentos parlamentarios*, II, 223.

⁴⁸ "Memoria del ministro de guerra y marina al congreso nacional de 1844," *ibid.*, pp. 309–321.

⁴⁹ *Sesiones del los cuerpos legislativos ...*, XXXVII, 328.

CHAPTER V: PACIFIC COAST BALANCE OF POWER

¹ Francisco A. Encina, *Historia de Chile desde la prehistoria hasta 1891* (20 vols.; Santiago de Chile: Editorial Nascimento, 1949–1952), XIII, 555.

² *Ibid.*, chaps. lvi, lvii.

³ Based upon Chilean government revenues reported in Daniel Martner, *Historia de Chile: historia económica* (Santiago de Chile: Establecimientos Gráficos de Balcells, 1929), pp. 224, 298.

⁴ "Exposición que el General Don Manuel Bulnes dirije a la nación chilena," Sept. 18, 1851, *Documentos parlamentarios. Discursos de la apertura en les sesiones del congreso, y memorias ministeriales* (9 vols.; Santiago de Chile: Imprenta del Ferrocarril, 1858–1861), III, 784.

⁵ Encina, *op. cit.*, XIII, 554–555.

⁶ Based upon Vicente Pérez Rosales, *Ensayo sobre Chile*, trans. from French into Spanish by Manuel Miguel (Santiago de Chile: Imprenta del Ferrocarril, 1859), p. 481.

⁷ "Memoria del ministro de guerra y marina al congreso de 1851," *Documentos parlamentarios*, III, 760.

⁸ *Statistical Abstract of Peru, 1919*, Perú, Dirección de Estadística (Lima: Imprenta Americana, 1920), p. 89.

⁹ For the Flores expedition see Mark J. Van Aken, *Pan-Hispanism: Its Origin and Development to 1866* (Berkeley and Los Angeles: University of California Press, 1959), chap. vi.

¹⁰ Manuel Camilo Vial to the minister of Chile in the United States, Santiago de Chile, Nov. 26, 1846, ChC, 1844–1846; Manuel Camilo Vial to the chargé d'affaires of Chile in France, Santiago de Chile, Nov. 26, 1846, *ibid.*

¹¹ Manuel Camilo Vial to the minister of Chile in Peru, Santiago de Chile, May 27, 1847, *ibid.*

¹² Manuel Camilo Vial to the chargé d'affaires of Chile in Madrid, Santiago de Chile, Dec. 26, 1846, *ibid.*

¹³ "Memoria del ministro de guerra y marina al congreso nacional de 1847," *Documentos parlamentarios*, III, 93–94.

¹⁴ *Congresos y conferencias internacionales en que ha tomado parte el Perú: coleccionados sus trabajos por Ricardo Aranda*, Perú, Ministerio de Relaciones Exteriores (5 vols.; Lima, 1909–1920), I, 83–84.

¹⁵ For instructions to the Chilean delegate see Manuel Camilo Vial to the Minister Plenipotentiary of Chile in Peru, Santiago de Chile, July 24, Aug. 17, 27, 1847, ChC, Ind, 1847–1851. For Chilean policy see also "Memoria del ministro de relaciones exteriores al congreso nacional de 1847," *Documentos parlamentarios*, III, 23–25.

¹⁶ For text see *Congresos americanos de Lima: recopilación de documentos precedida de un prólogo por Alberto Ulloa*, Vols. II–III of *Archivo diplomático del Perú*, Perú, Ministerio de Relaciones Exteriores (2 vols.; Lima, 1938), I, 301–311. Translations of excerpts from this treaty are found in Robert N. Burr and Roland

D. Hussey, eds., *Documents on Inter-American Cooperation, 1810–1948* (2 vols.; Philadelphia: University of Pennsylvania Press, 1955), I, 102–108.

[17] Salvador Sanfuentes to the Minister Plenipotentiary of Chile in Peru, Santiago de Chile, Aug. 12, 1848, ChC, Ind, 1847–1851.

[18] *Ibid.*

[19] *Ibid.*

[20] *Ibid.*

[21] Jorge Basadre, *Historia de la República del Perú* (2 vols.; Lima: Editorial Cultura Antártida, S.A., 1946), I, 218–220.

[22] Luís Uribe Orrego, *Nuestra marina militar, desde la liberación de Chiloé (1826) hasta la guerra con España (1865)* (Valparaíso: Imprenta de la Armada, 1914, p. 202.

[23] José Joaquín Pérez to the chargé d'affaires of Chile in Peru, Santiago de Chile, Oct. 29, 1849, ChC, Ind, 1847–1851.

[24] José Joaquín Pérez to the chargé d'affaires of Chile in Peru, Santiago de Chile, Jan. 29, 1850, *ibid.*

[25] Antonio José Uribe, ed. *Anales diplomáticos y consulares de Colombia* (6 vols.; Bogotá, 1900–1920), III, 230.

[26] Victoriano de D. Paredes, foreign minister of New Granada, to the Minister of Foreign Relations of Ecuador, Bogotá, May 29, 1850, ChGACol, 1851–1876.

[27] *Ibid.*

[28] José Joaquín Pérez to the chargé d'affaires of Chile in Peru, Santiago de Chile, March 27, 1850, ChC, Ind, 1847–1851.

[29] Antonio Varas to the chargé d'affaires of Chile in Peru, Santiago de Chile, June 26, 1850, *ibid.*

[30] Antonio Varas to the chargé d'Affaires of Chile in Peru, Santiago de Chile, July 29, 1850, *ibid.*

[31] Antonio Varas to the consul of Chile in Guayaquil, Santiago de Chile, Aug. 23, 1851, ChC, 1851–1855; B. J. de Toro to the Minister of Foreign Relations of Chile, Lima, March 9, 1851. ChCAP, 1849–1856.

[32] Jesús María Henao and Gerardo Arrubla, *Historia de Colombia* (6th ed.; Bogotá: Librería Colombiana, Camacho Roldán y Cía., 1936), pp. 644–645; Oscar Efrén Reyes, *Breve historia general del Ecuador* (5th ed.; 3 vols.; Quito: Editorial "Fray Jodoco Ricke," 1955–1956), III, 548–550.

[33] Victoriano de D. Paredes to General José M. Obando, Bogotá, June 3, 1851, ChGACol, 1851–1876.

[34] Victoriano de D. Paredes to the Minister of Foreign Relations of Chile, Bogotá, Sept. 10, 1851, *ibid.*

[35] B. J. de Toro to the Foreign Minister of Chile, Lima, July 9, 1851, ChCAP, 1849–1856.

[36] Basadre, *op. cit.*, I, 265–266.

[37] B. J. de Toro to the Foreign Minister of Chile, Lima, June 2, 1852, ChCAP, 1849–1856.

[38] Antonio Varas to Carlos Bello, chargé d'affaires of Chile in Peru, Santiago de Chile, July 14, 1852, ChLP, 1823–1853.

[39] *Ibid.*

[40] Antonio Varas to the chargé d'affaires of Chile in Peru, Santiago de Chile, Aug. 30, 1852, *ibid.*

[41] Antonio Varas to the chargé d'affaires of Chile in Lima, Santiago de Chile, Aug. 14, 1852, *ibid.*

[42] Antonio Varas to the chargé d'affaires of Chile in Ecuador, confidential, Santiago de Chile, Sept. 14, 1852, ChC, 1851–1855.

[43] "Memoria del ministro de guerra y marina al congreso nacional de 1853," *Documentos parlamentarios*, IV, 416.

[44] Antonio Varas to the chargé d'affaires of Chile in Ecuador, Santiago de Chile, Nov. 30, 1852, ChC, 1851–1855.

[45] "Memoria del ministro de relaciones exteriores al congreso nacional de 1853," *Documentos parlamentarios*, IV, 273–274.

[46] Antonio Varas to the chargé d'affaires of Chile in Peru, Santiago de Chile, June 14, 1853, ChC, 1851–1855.

[47] Antonio Varas, foreign minister of Chile, circular to the South American governments and several governments of Europe, Santiago de Chile, Jan. 30, 1855, in Antonio Varas, *Correspondencia de Don Antonio Varas: cuestiones americanas ...*, ed. Alberto Cruchaga Ossa (Santiago de Chile: Talleres Imprenta, 1929), pp. 131–135.

[48] José F. Gana to Antonio Varas, Quito, May 12, 1855, *ibid.*, pp. 154–155.

[49] José F. Gana to the Minister of State in the Department of Foreign Relations of Chile, Quito, May 10, 1855, ChLEc, 1852–1865.

[50] Minister Yrarrázaval to the Minister of Foreign Relations of Chile, Lima, July 12, 1856, ChCAP, 1855–1857.

[51] Gustave A. Nuermberger, "The Continental Treaties of 1856: An American Union 'Exclusive of the United States,'" *Hispanic American Historical Review*, XX (Feb., 1940), 32–55.

[52] Antonio Varas to the chargé d'affaires of Chile in Peru, Santiago de Chile, Aug. 16, 1860, ChCRes, 1858–1866.

[53] Antonio Varas to the chargé d'affaires of Chile in Peru, Santiago de Chile, Sept. 29, 1860, ChC, 1856–1861.

[54] Antonio Varas to the chargé d'affaires of Chile in Peru, Santiago de Chile, Nov. 2, 1860, *ibid.*

[55] Frederick George Howe, "García Moreno's Efforts To Unite Ecuador and France," *Hispanic American Historical Review*, XVII (May, 1936), 257–262.

[56] Luís Robalino Dávila, *García Moreno* (Quito, 1948), pp. 505–506.

[57] Encina, *op. cit.*, XIV, 110–111.

[58] Pérez Rosales, *op. cit.*, p. 22.

[59] For text of treaty see A. Bascuñán Montes, ed., *Recopilación de tratados y convenciones celebrados entre la República de Chile y las potencias extranjeras* (2 vols.; Santiago de Chile: Imprenta Cervantes, 1894), I, 227–251.

[60] *Memoria ... al congreso nacional de 1863*, Chile, Ministerio del Interior y Relaciones Exteriores (Santiago de Chile, 1863), pp. 24–29.

[61] Basadre, *op. cit.*, I, 348.

[62] "Memoria del ministro de relaciones exteriores al congreso nacional de 1861," *Documentos parlamentarios*, VIII, 77–79; Manuel Alcalde to the Foreign Minister of Peru, Santiago de Chile, Nov. 30, 1861, in *Memoria ... al congreso nacional de 1862*, Chile, Ministerio del Interior y Relaciones Exteriores (Santiago de Chile, 1862), pp. 127–129.

[63] M. A. Tocornal to the chargé d'affaires of Chile in Mexico, Santiago de Chile, July 30, 1862, ChC, 1861–1863.

[64] The following account of the war against Spain is based upon Jorge Basadre, *Chile, Perú y Bolivia independentes* (1st ed.; Barcelona and Buenos Aires: Salvat Editores, S.A., 1948), pp. 338–363. See also Van Aken, *op. cit.*, pp. 107–114.

[65] Uribe Orrego, *op. cit.*, p. 310.

[66] Manuel A. Tocornal, "Circular a los gobiernos de América," Santiago de Chile, May 4, 1864, in *Memoria ... al congreso nacional de 1864*, Chile, Ministerio del Interior y Relaciones Exteriores (Santiago de Chile, 1864), pp. 69–72.

[67] Uribe Orrego, *op. cit.*, p. 312.

[68] For the second Lima congress see Robert W. Frazer, "The Role of the Lima Congress, 1864–1865, in the Development of Pan-Americanism," *Hispanic American Historical Review*, XXIX (Aug., 1949), 319–348, and *Congresos americanos de Lima*.

[69] For the state of the Peruvian navy, as reported by Chileans, see Varas, *op. cit.*, pp. 35–42.

[70] Victorino Garrido to Antonio Varas, Lima, April 18, 1853, *ibid.*, pp. 310–312.

[71] William Marion Gibson, *The Constitutions of Colombia* (Durham: Duke University Press, 1948), pp. 273–296.

[72] Manuel Montt to the Foreign Minister of Chile, Lima, Feb. 3, 1865, in *Memoria ... al congreso nacional de 1865*, Chile, Ministerio del Interior y Relaciones Exteriores (Santiago de Chile, 1865), pp. 65–68.

[73] *Ibid.*

[74] *Ibid.*

CHAPTER VI: THE BRIDGE THAT TWO WARS BUILT

[1] *Memoria ... al congreso nacional de 1865*, Chile, Ministerio del Interior y Relaciones Exteriores (Santiago de Chile, 1865), p. 14.

[2] Alvaro Covarrubias to J. N. H., chargé d'affaires of Chile in Ecuador, Santiago de Chile, Oct. 17, 1865, ChC, 1865–1866.

[3] Alvaro Covarrubias to R. Sotomayor, confidential agent of Chile to Bolivia, Santiago de Chile, Oct. 4, 1865, *ibid.*

[4] For text see *Colección de los tratados, convenciones ... y otros actos diplmáticos y políticos celebrados desde la independencia hasta el día, precedida de una introducción ... por Ricardo Aranda*, Peru, Ministerio de Relaciones Exteriores (14 vols.; Lima, 1890–1919), IV, 69–72.

[5] Alvaro Covarrubias to José Nicolás Hurtado, chargé d'affaires of Chile in Ecuador, Santiago de Chile, Feb. 15, 1866, ChC, 1865–1866.

[6] Alvaro Covarrubias to Aniceto Vergara Albano, minister of Chile in Bolivia, Santiago de Chile, March 2, 1866, ChC, 1866–1867.

[7] For text of treaty see A. Bascuñán Montes, *Recopilación de tratados y convenciones celebrados entre la República de Chile y las potencias extranjeras* (2 vols.; Santiago de Chile: Imprenta Cervantes, 1894), II, 22–28.

[8] Francisco A. Encina, *Historia de Chile desde la prehistoria hasta 1891* (20 vols.; Santiago de Chile: Editorial Nascimento, 1949–1952), XIV, 330–333.

[9] For the history of international politics in the Plata area see Pelham H. Box, *The Origins of the Paraguayan War* (Urbana: University of Illinois Press, 1927); Ramón J. Cárcano, *Guerra del Paraguay: orígenes y causas* (Buenos Aires, 1939); Efaím Cardozo, *Vísperas de la guerra del Paraguay* (Buenos Aires: Librería "El Ateneo" Editorial, 1954).

[10] Julio César Chaves, *El presidente López: vida y gobierno de Don Carlos* (Buenos Aires, 1955), chaps. v–x.

[11] For the Anglo-French intervention see John F. Cady, *Foreign Intervention in the Río de la Plata, 1838–1850* (Philadelphia: University of Pennsylvania Press, 1929).

[12] As quoted in H. Sánchez Quell, *La diplomacia paraguaya de Mayo a Cerro-Cora* (3d ed.; Buenos Aires: Editorial Guillermo Kraft, 1957), pp. 219–220.

[13] Alvaro Covarrubias to J. V. Lastarria, Santiago de Chile, April 15, 1865, ChC, 1865–1866.

[14] *Memoria ... de 1865*, Chile, p. 22.

[15] Encina, *op. cit.*, XV, 38–39.

[16] Alvaro Covarrubias to J. V. Lastarria, Santiago de Chile, June 14, 1865, ChC, 1865–1866.

[17] Alvaro Covarrubias to the Minister of Chile in Argentina, Santiago de Chile, Nov. 12, 1865, *ibid.*

[18] For text of the memorandum adopted at this meeting see *Colección de los tratados ...*, Peru, X, 455–460.

[19] Alvaro Covarrubias to José Victorino Lastarria, Santiago de Chile, April 29, 1866, ChC, 1866–1867.

[20] J. V. Lastarria to the Foreign Minister of Chile, Buenos Aires, May 26, 1866, in *Colección de los tratados* ..., Peru, X, 480–482.

[21] Alvaro Covarrubias to D[on] J. V. Lastarria, Santiago de Chile, July 31, 1866, ChC, 1866–1867; "Memorandum," Oct. 9, 1866, signed by Rufino Elizalde, foreign minister of Argentina, and J. V. Lastarria, in *Colección de los tratados* ..., Peru, X, 62–64.

[22] For texts of treaty and additional protocols see *Colección de tratados, convenciones y otros pactos internacionales de la República Oriental del Uruguay*, Uruguay, Ministerio de Relaciones Exteriores (5 vols.; Montevideo: Imprenta "El Siglo Ilustrado," 1923), II, 65–85.

[23] Ramón J. Cárcano, *Guerra del Paraguay: acción y reacción de la triple alianza* (2 vols.; Buenos Aires: Editores Domingo Viau y Cía., 1941), I, 270.

[24] *The Paraguayan Question. The Alliance between Brazil, the Argentine Confederation and Uruguay, versus the Dictator of Paraguay. Claims of the Republics of Peru and Bolivia in Regard to the Alliance* (New York, 1866), pp. 53–56.

[25] *Colección de los tratados* ..., Peru, X, 467–475.

[26] *Ibid.*, X, 535.

[27] Alvaro Covarrubias to D[on] Marcial Martínez, minister of Chile in Peru, Santiago de Chile, July 24, 1866, ChC, 1866–1867.

[28] Alvaro Covarrubias to Aniceto Vergara Albano, minister of Chile to Bolivia, Santiago de Chile, July 9, 1866, *ibid.*

[29] Alvaro Covarrubias to D[on] Marcial Martínez, Santiago de Chile, Aug. 16, 1866, *ibid.*

[30] "Memorandum," Oct. 9, 1866, signed by Rufino Elizalde, foreign minister of Argentina, and J. V. Lastarria, in *Colleción de los tratados* ..., Peru, X, 62–64.

[31] Alvaro Covarrubias to Guillermo Blest Gana, chargé d'affaires of Chile in Brazil, Santiago de Chile, Sept. 3, 1866, ChC, 1866–1867.

[32] *Memoria ... al congreso nacional de 1866*, Chile, Ministro del Interior y Relaciones Exteriores (Santiago de Chile, 1866), pp. 29–30.

[33] A. Covarrubias to Guillermo Blest Gana, chargé d'affaires of Chile in Argentina, Santiago de Chile, June 1, 1867, ChC, 1867–1869.

[34] Encina, *op. cit.*, XV, 48–49.

[35] *Memoria ... al congreso nacional de 1867*, Chile, Ministerio del Interior y Relaciones Exteriores (Santiago de Chile, 1867), p. 14.

[36] *Ibid.*, p. 15.

CHAPTER VII: CONTINENTAL POWER POLITICS

[1] Sanford A. Mosk, "Latin America and the World Economy, 1850–1914," *Inter-American Economic Affairs*, II (Winter, 1948), 53–82.

[2] H. S. Ferns, *Britain and Argentina in the Nineteenth Century* (Oxford: Clarendon Press, 1960), pp. 289–290.

[3] For foreign investments in South America see J. Fred Rippy, *British Investments in Latin America, 1822–1849* (Minneapolis: University of Minnesota Press, 1959), and Leland H. Jenks, *The Migration of British Capital to 1875* (New York: Knopf, 1927).

[4] See J. Fred Rippy, *Latin America and the Industrial Age* (New York: Putnam, 1944).

[5] John Melby, "Rubber River: An Account of the Rise and Collapse of the Amazon Boom," *Hispanic American Historical Review*, XXII (Aug., 1942), 452–469.

[6] Brazil's rubber production rose from 978,360 kilos, valued at £45,525, in 1849 to 10,136,417 kilos, valued at £1,659,418, in 1879. See J. P. Wileman, comp. and ed., *The Brazilian Year Book, Second Issue—1909* (London: McCorquodale and Co., 1909), p. 639.

[7] Uruguay, though rapidly integrated into the world economy, did not become a great power because of its small population and territory.

[8] As quoted in Antonio José Uribe, *Anales diplomáticos y consulares de Colombia* (6 vols.; Bogotá, 1900–1920), III, 565.

[9] *The Economic Development of the Argentine Republic in the Last Fifty Years* (Buenos Aires: E. Tornquist and Co., 1919), pp. 276–277.

[10] Jenks, *op. cit.*, pp. 421–424.

[11] Rippy, *Latin America and the Industrial Age*, p. 160.

[12] *The Economic Development of the Argentine Republic*, pp. 276–277.

[13] Antonio Varas, *Correspondencia de Don Antonio Varas: cuestiones americanas* ..., ed. Alberto Cruchaga Ossa (Santiago de Chile: Talleres Imprenta, 1929), p. 305.

[14] Vicente Pérez Rosales, *Ensayo sobre Chile*, trans. from French into Spanish by Manuel Miguel (Santiago de Chile: Imprenta del Ferrocarril, 1859), pp. 501–502.

[15] Domingo Santa María to Miguel Luís Amunátegui, Panama, Dec. 21, 1859, in Domingo Amunátegui Solar, ed., *Archivo epistolar de Don Miguel Luís Amunátegui* (3 vols.; Santiago de Chile, 1942), I, 69–70.

[16] Alan K. Manchester, *British Preëminence in Brazil: Its Rise and Decline* (Chapel Hill: University of North Carolina Press, 1933), chaps. x, xii.

CHAPTER VIII: FROM COÖPERATION TO CONFLICT

[1] Alvaro Covarrubias to D[on] Marcial Martínez, chargé d'affaires of Chile in Peru, Santiago de Chile, May 16, 1866, ChC, 1866–1867.

[2] Alvaro Covarrubias to D[on] Marcial Martínez, minister of Chile in Peru, Santiago de Chile, March 2, 1867, *ibid.*

[3] The Chilean government sought information from its minister in Peru on the implications of this revolutionary movement (F. Vargas Fontecilla to Marcial Martínez, Minister of Chile in Peru, Santiago de Chile, Oct. 9, 1867, ChC, 1867–1869). The minister later claimed that he had assured the government that the revolutionary group would pose no threat to Chile should it succeed in overthrowing the government of Peru (*Sesiones de 1868*, Chile, Congreso, Cámara de Diputados [Santiago de Chile, 1868], p. 255). For the attitude of the chief clerk of the Chilean Department of Foreign Relations, as he later remembered it, see Abdón Cifuentes, *Memorias* (2 vols.; Santiago de Chile: Editorial Nascimento, 1936), I, 179–185.

[4] F. Vargas Fontecilla to Joaquín Godoy, chargé d'affaires of Chile in Peru, Santiago de Chile, March 17, 1868, ChC, 1867–1869; F. Vargas Fontecilla to Alberto Blest Gana, minister of Chile in Great Britain, Santiago de Chile, May 1, 1868, *ibid.*; Francisco Encina, *Historia de Chile desde la prehistoria hasta 1891* (20 vols.; Santiago de Chile: Editorial Nascimento, 1949–1952), XV, 17–24.

[5] F. Vargas Fontecilla to Joaqúin Godoy, chargé d'affaires of Chile in Peru, Santiago de Chile, May 14, 1868, ChC, 1867–1869.

[6] J. A. García to the Minister of Foreign Relations of Peru, Washington, D.C., April 8, 1869, as quoted in Mariano Felipe Paz Soldán, *Narración histórica de la guerra de Chile contra el Perú y Bolivia* (Buenos Aires, 1884), pp. 10–14.

[7] June 30, 1868, *Sesiones de 1868*, p. 242.

[8] Jorge Basadre, *Historia de la República del Perú* (2 vols.; Lima: Editorial Cultura Antártida, S.A., 1946), II, 113–114; Encina, *op. cit.*, XV, 35.

[9] Belisario Prats to Floridor Rojas, chargé d'affaires of Chile in Bolivia, Santiago de Chile, March 2, 1871, ChC, 1869–1872.

[10] Belisario Prats to Floridor Rojas, chargé d'affaires of Chile in Bolivia, Santiago de Chile, June 9, 1871, *ibid.*

[11] Pedro Yrigoyen, *La alianza perú-boliviana-argentina y la declaratoria de guerra de Chile* (Lima, 1921), p. 42.

[12] For the text of the law see Ignacio Santa María, *Guerra del Pacífico* (Santiago de Chile: Imprenta Universitaria, 1919), pp. 307–309.

[13] Encina, *op. cit.*, XV, 137–142; Cifuentes, *op. cit.*, I, 408–411.

[14] For the text of the naval officers' report see Dec. 28, 1871, *Sesiones extraordi-*

narias de 1871, Chile, Congreso, Cámara de Diputados (Santiago de Chile, 1871), pp. 511–512.

[15] Arturo García Salazar, *Resúmen de historia diplomática del Perú, 1820–1884* (Lima: Talleres Gráficos Sanmartí y Cía., 1928), p. 142.

[16] *Memoria ... al congreso nacional de 1873*, Chile, Ministerio de Relaciones Exteriores y Colonización (Santiago de Chile, 1873), pp. vi–ix.

[17] As quoted in Encina, *op. cit.*, XV, 142.

[18] *Ibid.*

[19] Adolfo Ibáñez to Guillermo Blest Gana, minister of Chile to the republics of the Plata, Santiago de Chile, March 20, 1872, ChC, 1872–1873.

[20] *Ibid.*

[21] Adolfo Ibáñez to Santiago Lindsay, minister of Chile in Bolivia, Santiago de Chile, April 10, 1872, *ibid.;* Basadre, *op. cit.*, II, 114.

[22] Adolfo Ibáñez to Santiago Lindsay, Santiago de Chile, June 18, 1872, ChC, 1872–1873.

[23] *Memoria ... de 1873*, Chile, pp. 75–103.

[24] Adolfo Ibáñez to Joaquín Godoy, minister of Chile in Peru, Aug. 20, 1872, ChC, 1872–1873.

[25] J. de la Riva-Agüero to the minister of Peru in Chile, Lima, Aug. 29, 1872, as quoted in García Salazar, *op. cit.*, pp. 159–160.

[26] *Ibid.*

[27] For text see Yrigoyen, *op. cit.*, p. 42.

[28] "Actas del consejo de ministros del Gobierno del Perú, sesión de 19 de noviembre de 1872," as reprinted in Santa María, *op. cit.*, pp. 282–284.

[29] As quoted in Gonzalo Bulnes, *Guerra del Pacífico* (3 vols.; Valparaíso and La Paz, 1911–1918), I, 64.

[30] *Ibid.*

[31] Santiago Lindsay, the Chilean negotiator of the agreement, attributed Bolivian opposition to internal political considerations and to the urgings of Bolivians writing for the Peruvian press (Aug. 14, 1873, *Sesiones ordinarias de 1873*, Chile, Congreso, Cámara de Diputados [Santiago de Chile, 1873], pp. 343–346).

[32] Basadre, *op. cit.*, pp. 115–116. For text of the secret treaty see Yrigoyen, *op. cit.*, pp. 381–385.

[33] Adolfo Ibáñez to Guillermo Blest Gana, minister of Chile in Argentina, Santiago de Chile, Feb. 28, 1872, ChC, 1872–1873.

[34] For a discussion of Chilean attitudes toward Patagonia see Alejandro Magnet, *Nuestros vecinos argentinos* (Santiago de Chile: Editorial del Pacífico, S.A., 1956), pp. 295–314; Encina, *op. cit.*, XV, chap. 12.

[35] Belisario Prats to Guillermo Blest Gana, Santiago de Chile, Oct. 25, 1870, ChC, 1869–1872.

[36] As quoted in Encina, *op. cit.*, XV, 161.

[37] For Manuel Yrigoyen's instructions see Yrigoyen, *op. cit.*, pp. 64–66.

[38] *Ibid.*, p. 67.

[39] For a detailed discussion of the post–Paraguayan War rivalry between Argentina and Brazil, see Ramón J. Cárcano, *Guerra del Paraguay: acción y reacción de la triple alianza* (2 vols.; Buenos Aires: Editores Domingo Viau y Cía., 1941).

[40] Adolfo Ibáñez to Guillermo Blest Gana, Santiago de Chile, Oct. 24, 1873, ChC, 1872–1873.

[41] Juan José Fernández Valdés, "El tratado secreto peruano-boliviano de 1873 y la diplomacia brasileña," *Boletín de la Academia Chilena de la Historia*, XXIII, no. 55 (1956), 5–18.

[42] Bulnes, *op. cit.*, I, 29.

[43] *Ibid.*, p. 37.

[44] Adolfo Ibáñez to Carlos Walker Martínez, Santiago de Chile, Sept. 7, 1873, ChC, 1872–1873.

⁴⁵ Adolfo Ibáñez to Guillermo Blest Gana, minister of Chile in Argentina, Santiago de Chile, Oct. 24, 1873, *ibid.;* Adolfo Ibáñez to Joaquín Godoy, minister of Chile in Peru, Santiago de Chile, Oct. 24, 1873, *ibid.*

⁴⁶ Adolfo Ibáñez to the minister of Chile in France, Santiago de Chile, Dec. 19, 1873, ChC, 1873–1877.

⁴⁷ Fernández Valdés, *op. cit.*

⁴⁸ *Ibid.;* Adolfo Ibáñez to the minister of Chile in the republics of the Plata, confidential, Santiago de Chile, March 12, 1874, ChC, 1873–1877.

⁴⁹ *Colección de los tratados, convenciones … y otros actos diplomáticos y políticos celebrados desde la independencia hasta el día, precedida de una introducción … por Ricardo Aranda*, Perú, Ministerio de Relaciones Exteriores (14 vols.; Lima, 1890–1919), II, 578–579, 611–613.

⁵⁰ Yrigoyen, *op. cit.*, pp. 141–142.

⁵¹ For text of the Bolivian-Chilean treaty of 1874 see A. Bascuñán Montes, ed., *Recopilación de tratados y convenciones celebrados entre la República de Chile y las potencias extranjeras* (2 vols.; Santiago de Chile: Imprenta Cervantes, 1894), II, 101–111.

⁵² J. Alfonso to the minister of Chile in Peru, Santiago de Chile, June 18, 1875, ChC, 1873–1877.

⁵³ *Memoria … al congreso nacional de 1876, Chile, Ministerio de Relaciones Exteriores y Colonización* (Santiago de Chile, 1876), p. xxiii.

⁵⁴ José Alfonso to Pedro Nolasco Videla, chargé d'affaires of Chile in Bolivia, Santiago de Chile, April 23, 1877, ChC, 1877–1879.

⁵⁵ Encina, *op. cit.*, XV, 207–211.

⁵⁶ *Memoria … al congreso nacional de 1875, Chile, Ministerio de Relaciones Exteriores y Colonización* (Santiago de Chile, 1875), p. xiv.

⁵⁷ J. Alfonso to Guillermo Blest Gana, minister of Chile in the republics of the Plata and the Empire of Brazil, confidential, June 5, 1875, ChC, 1873–1877.

⁵⁸ *Memoria … 1875*, Chile.

⁵⁹ *Memoria … 1876*, Chile, pp. xxvi–xxvii.

⁶⁰ J. Alfonso to Máximo P. Lira, chargé d'affaires in the republics of the Plata, confidential, Santiago de Chile, Aug. 2, 1875, ChC, 1873–1877.

⁶¹ Yrigoyen, *op. cit.*, pp. 191–206.

⁶² *Memoria … 1876*, Chile, p. xxvii.

⁶³ For the negotiations leading up to these agreements see José Bianco, *Negociaciones internacionales: los tratados de 1876, gestiones administrativas* (Buenos Aires, 1904).

⁶⁴ Encina, *op. cit.*, XV, 519–561.

⁶⁵ J. Alfonso to Diego Barros Arana, minister of Chile to the republics of the Plata and the Empire of Brazil, Santiago de Chile, May 4, 1876, ChC, 1873–1877.

⁶⁶ Ricardo Donoso, *Barros Arana: educador, historiador y hombre público* (Santiago de Chile: Universidad de Chile, 1931), p. 128.

⁶⁷ Encina, *op. cit.*, XVI, 232–235.

⁶⁸ As quoted in *ibid.*, p. 238.

⁶⁹ *Ibid.*, p. 240.

CHAPTER IX: RECASTING THE POWER STRUCTURE

¹ Of a voluminous literature on the War of the Pacific, the following works are noteworthy. A brief, well-balanced survey of the origins and the history of the war is to be found in Jorge Basadre, *Chile, Perú y Bolivia independientes* (Barcelona and Buenos Aires: Salvat Editores, S.A., 1948), pp. 453–498. See also William Jefferson Dennis, *Tacna and Arica: An Account of the Chile-Peru Boundary Dispute and of the Arbitration of the United States* (New Haven: Yale University Press, 1931), pp. 1–193. More detailed accounts, written by Chileans, are Gonzalo Bulnes, *Guerra del Pacífico* (3 vols.; Valparaíso and La Paz, 1911–1918); Ignacio

284   *Notes to Pages 138–149*

Santa María, *Guerra del Pacífico* (Santiago de Chile: Imprenta Universitaria, 1919) ;
Francisco Encina, *Historia de Chile desde la prehistoria hasta 1891* (20 vols.; Santiago de Chile: Editorial Nascimento, 1949–1952) ; XVI, 241–572; XVII; XVIII, 1–
115. The Peruvian point of view is represented by Mariano Felipe Paz Soldán, *Narración histórica de la guerra de Chile contra el Perú y Bolivia* (Buenos Aires, 1884), and
by an English writer, Sir Clements Robert Markham, *The War between Chile and
Peru* (London, 1883), as well as by an Italian, Thomas Caivano, *Historia de la
guerra de América entre Chile, Perú y Bolivia, versión castellana de Arturo de
Ballesteros y Cotín* (Iquique, 1904). More extensive bibliographies of contemporary
and secondary materials on the War of the Pacific may be found in Jorge Basadre,
Historia de la República del Perú (2 vols.; Lima: Editorial Cultura Antártida,
1946), II, 327–332, and Encina, *op. cit.*, XVI, 241–243. A valuable collection of
printed documents on the war, ranging from war ballads and newspaper editorials
to documents from the archives of the belligerents, is in Pascual Ahumada Moreno,
ed., *Guerra del Pacífico: recopilación completa de todos los documentos oficiales,
correspondencias y demás publicaciones referentes a la guerra ...* (9 vols.; Valparaíso, 1884–1890). Among other collections on aspects of the war are Pedro
Yrigoyen, *La alianza perú-boliviana-argentina y la declaratoria de guerra de Chile*
(Lima, 1921), and Antonio Varas, *Correspondencia de Don Antonio Varas sobre la
guerra del Pacífico ...* (Santiago de Chile: Imprenta Universitaria, 1918).

[2] Manuel Irigoyen, "Manifiesto que el gobierno del Perú dirije a los estados
amigos con motivo de la guerra que le ha declarado él de Chile," May 1, 1879, in
Paz Soldán, *op. cit.*, pp. 820–834.

[3] *Memoria ... al congreso nacional de 1879*, Chile, Ministerio de Relaciones Exteriores y Colonización (Santiago de Chile, 1879), p. vii.

[4] Varas, *op. cit.*, p. 251.

[5] *Ibid.*, pp. 251–252.

[6] Mariano Muñóz, Bolivian foreign minister in 1866, charged in a letter written
in April, 1879, after the outbreak of the War of the Pacific, that Chile had made
a similar proposal to him as early as 1866 (see Paz Soldán, *op. cit.*, pp. 782–784,
for the text of this letter). Encina, *op. cit.*, XVI, 469–472, discusses early Chilean
attempts to secure an alliance with Bolivia.

[7] Unless otherwise noted, the remainder of this chapter is based upon Robert N.
Burr, *The Stillborn Panama Congress: Power Politics and Chilean-Colombian Relations during the War of the Pacific* (Berkeley and Los Angeles: University of
California Press, 1962).

[8] Domingo Santa María to Victorino Lastarria, minister of Chile to the Empire
of Brazil and the Oriental Republic of Uruguay, Santiago de Chile, May 2, 1879,
ChC, 1877–1879.

[9] J. V. Lastarria to Miguel Luís Amunátegui, Montevideo, Sept. 1, 1879, in
Domingo Amunátegui Solar, ed., *Archivo epistolar de Don Miguel Luís Amunátegui*
(3 vols.; Santiago de Chile, 1942), I, 187–191.

[10] Nicolás A. Calvo, *La cuestión argentino-chilena* (Buenos Aires, 1879).

[11] Encina, *op. cit.*, XVII, 273.

[12] Bulnes, *op. cit.*, II, 449.

[13] *Ibid.*, pp. 435–436.

[14] For the text of the decree see *Diario Oficial*, Colombia, June 15, 1879, p. 6804.

[15] Ernest Dichman to the Secretary of State [of the United States], Bogotá, June
20, 1879, USDespCol 33.

[16] D. Santa María to Francisco Valdés Vergara, Santiago de Chile, June 26, 1879,
ChC, 1879–1881.

[17] Pablo Arosemena to the Secretary of Foreign Relations of Colombia, Santiago
de Chile, Oct. 14, 1879, ColADC 174.

[18] For a good and concise description of the military action of the War of the
Pacific see Basadre, *Chile, Perú y Bolivia independientes*, pp. 478–495.

[19] For these reports see ColADC 174.

[20] Miguel Amunátegui, foreign minister of Chile, to Francisco Valdés Vergara, Santiago de Chile, May 7, 1880, ChC, 1879–1881.

[21] Herbert Millington, *American Diplomacy and the War of the Pacific* (New York: Columbia University Press, 1938), pp. 66–67.

[22] M. Amunátegui to Francisco Valdés Vergara, chargé d'affaires of Chile in Colombia, Santiago de Chile, June 12, 1880, ChLCol, 1879–1880.

[23] The text of the Chilean-Colombian arbitration convention, together with the Colombian invitation and other documents related to the proposed Panama congress, may be found in *Documentos referentes a la reunión en Panamá del congreso Americano, iniciada y promovida por el gobierno de Colombia en favor de la institución del arbitraje*, Colombia (Bogotá, 1881).

[24] For a discussion of the Conference of Arica see Millington, *op. cit.*, pp. 53–81, and previously cited general works on the War of the Pacific.

[25] For texts of the circulars sent by Peru and Bolivia to friendly governments after the Conference of Arica see Ahumada Moreno, *op. cit.*, IV, 187–197.

[26] Luís L. Domínguez, minister of Argentina to Brazil, to the Foreign Minister of Brazil, Petropolis, Dec. 25, 1880, in Ahumada Moreno, *op. cit.*, VI, 155.

[27] B. de Irigoyen, foreign minister of Argentina, to the Foreign Secretary of Colombia, Dec. 30, 1880, *Diario Oficial*, Colombia, April 2, 1881, pp. 9052–9053.

[28] Mielquíades Valderrama to the diplomatic corps of Chile abroad, Santiago de Chile, Jan. 29, 1881, ChC, 1879–1881.

[29] For the text of the Argentine-Chilean boundary treaty of 1881 see A. Bascuñán Montes, ed., *Recopilación de tratados y convenciones celebrados entre la República de Chile y las potencias extranjeras* (2 vols.; Santiago de Chile: Imprenta Cervantes, 1894), II, 120–125.

[30] For a general discussion of the Argentine-Chilean boundary treaty of 1881 see Encina, *op. cit.*, XVII, 431–441.

[31] As quoted in Adriano Páez, *La guerra del Pacífico y deberes de la América* (Bogotá, 1881), pp. 14–15.

[32] As quoted in Ricardo Sáenz Hayes, *Miguel Cané y su tiempo (1851–1905)* (Buenos Aires, 1955), p. 230.

[33] Páez, *op. cit.*, pp. 2, 8–9.

[34] United States, 47th Cong., 1st sess., S. Exec. Doc. 79, pp. 516–517.

[35] *Ibid.*

[36] J. M. Balmaceda to Marcial Martínez, Chilean minister in the United States, Santiago de Chile, Nov. 18, 1881, ChC, 1881–1882.

[37] Sáenz Hayes, *op. cit.*, pp. 226–227.

[38] Ahumada Moreno, *op. cit.*, VI, 159–161.

[39] J. A. Soffia, Chilean minister to Colombia, to M. Valderrama, foreign minister of Chile, Bogotá, Aug. 18, 1881, ChLCol, 1881–1882.

[40] For a discussion of this change in the policy of the United States see Millington, *op. cit.*, pp. 121–143.

[41] The most able analysis of Blaine's motivations for calling a conference in Washington is to be found in Russell H. Bastert, "A New Approach to the Origins of Blaine's Pan-American Policy," *Hispanic American Historical Review*, XXXIX (Aug., 1959), 375–412.

[42] *Memoria ... al congreso de 1882*, Chile, Ministerio de Relaciones Exteriores y Colonización (Santiago de Chile, 1882), pp. xxvi–xxxi.

[43] Luís Aldunate, foreign minister of Chile, circular to the legations of Chile in America and Europe, Santiago de Chile, May 12, 1882, ChC, 1881–1882.

[44] Millington, *op. cit.*, p. 134.

[45] Luís Aldunate to the minister of Chile in Colombia, Santiago de Chile, March 14, 1883, ChDC, 1882–1884.

[46] *Colección de los tratados, convenciones ... y otros actos diplomáticos celebrados*

desde la independencia hasta el día, precedida de una introducción ... por Ricardo Aranda, Peru, Ministerio de Relaciones Exteriores (14 vols.; Lima, 1890–1919), IV, 594–595.

⁴⁷ "Pro-Memoria de la Conferencia de 7 de diciembre celebrado entre el ministro de relaciones exteriores señor Luís Aldunate y los señores Belisario Salinas y Belisario Boeto, ministros plenipotenciarios de Bolivia," in Luís Aldunate, *Los tratados de 1883–1884 a propósito de las declaraciones del mensaje presidencial de 1 de junio en curso* (Santiago de Chile, 1912), p. 241.

⁴⁸ *Ibid.*, pp. 241–242.

⁴⁹ Bulnes, *op. cit.*, III, 589.

⁵⁰ I have not seen the note sent to the Peruvian government. *Colección de los tratados ...*, Peru, IV, 674–675 contains a copy of the note to Chile but does not mention that one was received by Peru. Yet the Chilean foreign minister, in reporting to the Chilean diplomatic corps on the European notes, copies of which he enclosed, said: "The same representation has been made to the government of Peru ..." (A. Vergara Albano to Chilean diplomatic agents abroad, Santiago de Chile March 1, 1884, ChDC, 1882–1884). Because the European governments concerned did not recognize the Iglesias government, it is possible that this government was given a copy of the note addressed to Chile, which is found in *Memoria ... al congreso nacional de 1884*, Chile, Ministerio de Relaciones Exteriores y Colonización (Santiago de Chile, 1884), pp. xlii–xliii.

⁵¹ Bulnes, *op. cit.*, III, 590.

⁵² Basadre, *Historia ... del Perú*, II, 211–212.

⁵³ A. Vergara Albano to Jovino Novoa, Santiago de Chile, March 24, 1884, ChDC, 1884, I.

⁵⁴ *Ibid.*

⁵⁵ Bulnes, *op. cit.*, III, 590.

⁵⁶ A. Vergara Albano to the Chilean diplomatic corps, Santiago de Chile, March 29, 1884, ChDC, 1884, I.

⁵⁷ *Ibid.*

⁵⁸ Bulnes, *op. cit.*, III, 593.

⁵⁹ For the full text of the truce see Chile, *Memoria ... de 1884*, pp. xxiv–xxviii.

⁶⁰ *Ibid.*, pp. xxxii–xxxiii.

CHAPTER X: TOWARD AN ARMED PEACE

¹ A law of 1884 limited the Chilean army to 12,410 men. In 1885 the Chilean army consisted of 1,039 officers and 7,066 men. In addition there was a national guard estimated at 53,741 (*Statesmen's Yearbook*, 1886, pp. 578–579).

² According to *ibid.*, pp. 550–551, 578–579, in 1885 the Chilean navy consisted of 3 ironclads, 1 other cruiser, 4 corvettes, 2 gunboats, 2 transports, 11 torpedo boats, and a number of small paddle-wheel and screw steamers. It was manned by 1,589 officers and men. The Brazilian navy had 9 ironclads, 6 cruisers, 18 gunboats, 9 torpedo boats, and 20 auxiliary ships, and was manned by 5,788 officers and men.

³ For Chilean governmental revenues for the decades 1885–1894 and 1869–1878, adjusted to take into account differences in value of currency, see *Sinópsis estadística de la República de Chile*, Chile, Oficina Central de Estadística (Santiago de Chile: Sociedad Imprenta y Litografía Universo, 1921), p. 66.

⁴ Chile's population in 1885 was estimated at 2,527,320; that of Argentina, at 2,880,111 (see *ibid.*; and *The Economic Development of the Argentine Republic in the Last Fifty Years* [Buenos Aires: E. Tornquist Co., 1919], p. 276).

⁵ For a good analysis of the objectives of the Argentine ruling class in the 1880's see Thomas F. McGann, *Argentina, the United States and the Inter-American System, 1880–1914* (Cambridge: Harvard University Press, 1957), pp. 35–65.

⁶ Luís Aldunate to the minister of Chile in the Argentine Republic, Santiago de Chile, Dec. 7, 1883, ChDC, 1882–1884.

[7] *Ibid.*

[8] For the appointment of Brazil to the arbitral tribunals see Alejandro Soto Cárdenas, *Guerra del Pacífico: los tribunales arbitrales (1882–1888)* (Santiago de Chile: Imprenta Cultura, 1950), pp. 40–41.

[9] A. Vergara Albano to A. Montt, Santiago de Chile, March 31, 1884, ChDC, 1884, I.

[10] For example, the efforts to satisfy Peru's creditors through the sale of guano and the return of nitrate works to the holders of certificates, as well as the agreement to submit European claims for damages against Chile to arbitration.

[11] Germany had refused to participate in a proposed joint European intervention or in a European protest against the Treaty of Ancón. The United States had sought to end the war as a means of preventing European intervention.

[12] France had conquered Indo-China by 1883, and in 1884 the Great Powers met in Berlin to discuss African affairs (Geoffrey Brunn, *Nineteenth-Century European Civilization, 1815–1914* [New York: Oxford University Press, 1960], pp. 172–180).

[13] A clear statement of this position by Carlos Walker Martínez, a member of the Chilean Chamber of Deputies, is in *Sesiones extraordinarias de 1880*, Chile, Congreso, Cámara de Diputados (Santiago de Chile, 1881), Jan. 14, 1881, p. 146.

[14] *Memoria ... al congreso nacional de 1884*, Chile Ministerio de Relaciones Exteriores y Colonización (Santiago de Chile, 1884), p. 43.

[15] A. Montt to the Minister of Foreign Relations, Montevideo, May 19, 1885, ChLUrug, 1885–1886.

[16] Soto Cárdenas, *op. cit.*, is a full study of the history of the arbitral tribunals. See also Francisco A. Encina, *Historia de Chile desde la prehistoria hasta 1891* (20 vols.; Santiago de Chile: Editorial Nascimento, 1949–1952), XVIII, 409–446.

[17] Jorge Basadre, *Historia de la República del Perú* (2 vols.; Lima: Editorial Cultura Antártida, S.A., 1946), II, 227.

[18] A. Vergara Albano to B. Alamos González, Santiago de Chile, April 25, 1885, ChDC, 1885–1886.

[19] Javier Vial Solar, *Páginas diplomáticas* (Santiago de Chile: Imprenta, Litografía y Encuadernación Barcelona, 1900), pp. 113–115.

[20] Alberto Ostria Gutiérrez, *Una obra y un destino: la política internacional de Bolivia después de la guerra del Chaco* (2d ed.; Buenos Aires: Imprenta López, 1953), pp. 40–42.

[21] Vial Solar, *op. cit.*, p. 115.

[22] A. Vergara Albano to Ambrosio Montt, Santiago de Chile, June 23, 1884, ChDC, 1884, I.

[23] *Ibid.*

[24] A. Montt to the Minister of Foreign Relations of Chile, Montevideo, May 19, 1885, ChLUrug, 1885–1886.

[25] A. Vergara Albano to A. Montt, Santiago de Chile, June 25, 1885, ChDC, 1885–1886.

[26] *Memoria ... al congreso nacional de 1885*, Chile, Ministerio de Relaciones Exteriores y Colonización (Santiago de Chile, 1885), pp. c–ci.

[27] *Ibid.*

[28] *Ibid.*, pp. xxviii–xxxvi; Encina, *op. cit.*, XVIII, 318–319.

[29] *Memoria ... de 1885*, p. xxxvii.

[30] *Ibid.*, pp. xxxvii–xxviii.

[31] For British interest and activities in Tarapacá see Encina, *op. cit.*, XIX, 386–398; J. Fred Rippy, *British Investments in Latin America, 1822–1949* (Minneapolis: University of Minnesota Press, 1959), pp. 58–63.

[32] As quoted in Encina, *op. cit.*, XIX, 336.

[33] *Memoria ... de 1885*, p. 83; Virgilio Figueroa, *Diccionario histórico y biográfico de Chile, 1800–1931* (5 vols.; Santiago de Chile, 1925–1931), III, 603.

[34] Encina, *op. cit.*, XIX, 334–338.

[35] *Sesiones ordinarias de 1887,* Chile, Congreso, Cámara de Diputados (Santiago de Chile, 1887), Aug. 13, 1887, p. 472.

[36] *Ibid.,* p. 477.

[37] *Ibid.,* pp. 475–476.

[38] For example, see the article comparing Chilean and Argentine ironclads in *Revista de Marina,* I (Sept. 1, 1885), 500.

[39] *Ibid.,* VI (1888), 203.

[40] Encina, *op. cit.,* XIX, 319–320.

[41] Luís Langlois, *Influencia del poder naval en la historia de Chile desde 1810 a 1910* (Valparaíso: Imprenta de la Armada, 1911), p. 230.

[42] Encina, *op. cit.,* XIX, 337.

[43] Vial Solar, *op. cit.,* pp. 116–120, quotes a letter from the Peruvian diplomatic agent in Santiago which makes this point.

[44] Carlos Wiesse, *El asunto de Tacna y Arica: primera conferencia histórico-geográfica sobre las negociaciones diplomáticas entre el Perú y Chile de 1887 a 1894, dada en la Sociedad Geográfica la noche del 21 de enero de 1905* (2d ed.; Lima: Empresa Tipográfica, 1917), pp. 7–8.

[45] A summary of the terms of the Araníbar-Tyler contract may be found in Encina, *op. cit.,* XIX, 444–446.

[46] M. L. Amunátegui to Benecio Alamos González, Santiago de Chile, Aug. 5, 1887, ChDC, 1887.

[47] M. L. Amunátegui to plenipotentiaries Matta, Varas, Blest Gana, and Santa Cruz, Santiago de Chile, Aug. 8, 1887, *ibid.*

[48] B. Alamos González to the Minister of Foreign Relations, Lima, Sept. 24, 1887, ChLP, 1887, II.

[49] M. L. Amunátegui to Benecio Alamos González, Santiago de Chile, Aug. 4, 1887, ChDC, 1887; M. L. Amunátegui to plenipotentiaries Matta, Varas, Blest Gana, and Santa Cruz, Aug. 8, 1887, *ibid.*

[50] Basadre, *op. cit.,* II, 228–229.

[51] *Memoria ... al congreso nacional de 1888,* Chile, Ministerio de Relaciones Exteriores y Culto (Santiago de Chile, 1888), p. li.

[52] Agusto Matte to Benecio Alamos González, Santiago de Chile, Feb. 11, 1888, ChDC, 1888, I.

[53] *Ibid.*

[54] [Chilean foreign minister] to Benecio Alamos González, Santiago de Chile, April 27, 1888, *ibid.*

[55] Demetrio Lastarria to Benecio Alamos González, Santiago de Chile, July 6, 1888, ChDC, 1888, II.

[56] Wiesse, *op. cit.,* p. 9.

[57] *Memoria ... al congreso nacional de 1893,* Chile, Ministerio de Relaciones Exteriores, Culto y Colonización (Santiago de Chile, 1893), I, xliii.

[58] *Memoria ... al congreso nacional de 1889,* Chile, Ministerio de Relaciones Exteriores y Culto (Santiago de Chile, 1889), pp. 196–199.

[59] Wiesse, *op. cit.,* pp. 11–12.

[60] *Colección de los tratados, convenciones ... y otros actos diplomáticos y políticos celebrados desde la independencia hasta el día, precedida de una introducción ... por Ricardo Aranda,* Peru, Ministério de Relaciones Exteriores (14 vols.; Lima, 1890–1919), IV, 709–711.

[61] *Memoria ... de 1888,* p. lxvii.

[62] M. Terrazas to Demetrio Lastarria, Santiago de Chile, Nov. 12, 1888, *ibid.,* p. xxiii.

[63] Demetrio Lastarria to Ramón Cerda Concha, Santiago de Chile, May 3, 1888, ChDC, 1888, I.

[64] Guillermo Matta to the Minister of Foreign Relations of Chile, [Buenos Aires], Oct. 12, 1887, ChLPlat, 1887–1888.

⁶⁵ *Ibid.*
⁶⁶ *Ibid.*
⁶⁷ *Ibid.*
⁶⁸ Demetrio Lastarria to Guillermo Matta, Santiago de Chile, July 24, 1888, ChDC, 1888, II.
⁶⁹ Demetrio Lastarria to Ramón Cerda Concha, Santiago de Chile, May 3, 1888, ChDC, 1888, I.
⁷⁰ Oscar Espinosa Moraga, *La Postguerra del Pacífico y la Puna de Atacama (1884–1899)* (Santiago de Chile: Editorial Andrés Bello, 1958), pp. 35–40.
⁷¹ Matte to Chilean minister in Buenos Aires, Santiago de Chile, Sept. 26, 1889, ChT, 1888–1889.
⁷² Luís Vicente Varela, *La República argentina y Chile: historia de la demarcación de sus fronteras (desde 1843 hasta 1899)* (2 vols.; Buenos Aires, 1899), I, 220–221; Gonzalo Bulnes, *Chile y la Argentina: un debate de 55 años* (Santiago de Chile, 1898), p. 154.
⁷³ Guillermo Matta to the Minister of Foreign Relations of Chile, [Buenos Aires], Feb. 12, 1888, ChLPlat, 1887–1888.
⁷⁴ A. Bascuñán Montes, ed., *Recopilación de tratados y convenciones celebrados entre la República de Chile y las potencias extranjeras* (2 vols.; Santiago de Chile: Imprenta Cervantes, 1894), II, 121. The original reads as follows: "El límite entre Chile y la República Argentina es, de norte á sur, hasta el paralelo cincuenta y dos de latitud, la Cordillera de los Andes. La línea fronteriza correrá en esa extensión por las cumbres más elevadas de dichas Cordilleras que dividan las aguas y passará por entre las vertientes que se despreden á un lado y otro."
⁷⁵ See Varela, *op. cit.*, I, 251.
⁷⁶ Guillermo Matta to the Minister of Foreign Relations of Chile, [Buenos Aires], Oct. 11, 1887, ChLPlat, 1887–1888.
⁷⁷ Guillermo Matta to the Minister of Foreign Relations of Chile, [Buenos Aires], Feb. 12, 1888, *ibid.*
⁷⁸ Eduardo Matte to Guillermo Matta, Santiago de Chile, Sept. 25, 1889, ChDC, 1889.
⁷⁹ Juan Castellón to Guillermo Matta, Santiago de Chile, Nov. 7, 1889, *ibid.*
⁸⁰ Bulnes, *op. cit.*, p. 156.
⁸¹ Juan Castellón to Guillermo Matta, Santiago de Chile, Nov. 7, 1889, ChDC, 1889.
⁸² See a memorandum quoted in Varela, *op. cit.*, I, 256–258 n. 115.
⁸³ C. Delgado de Carvalho, *História diplomática de Brasil* (São Paulo: Companhia Editora Nacional, 1959, pp. 166–171.
⁸⁴ *Tratado de Misiones; litigio solucionado; las repúblicas brasilera y argentina; homenajes; el ministro brasilero Bocayuva en la Plata; firma del tratado en Montevideo; resúmen general de las fiestas, 1889–1890* (Buenos Aires: A. Sommaruga y Cía., 1890), pp. 18–19.
⁸⁵ *Ibid.*, p. 35; see also Carvalho, *op. cit.*, pp. 192–194.
⁸⁶ *Tratado de Misiones ...*, p. 39.
⁸⁷ *Memoria ... al congreso nacional de 1890*, Chile, Ministerio de Relaciones Exteriores, Culto y Colonización (Santiago de Chile, 1890), p. vi.
⁸⁸ *Ibid.*, p. xxvi.
⁸⁹ Eduardo Matte to José Alfonso, Santiago de Chile, Aug. 28, 1889, ChDC, 1889.
⁹⁰ McCann, *op. cit.*, p. 145.
⁹¹ Alvaro Bianchi Tupper to the Minister of Foreign Relations, Petropolis, Jan. 26, 1892, ChLBraz, 1891–1892, viewed this plan as a censure of Chile.
⁹² United States, 51st Cong., 1st sess., S. Exec. Doc. 231, p. 107.
⁹³ *Ibid.*, p. 108.
⁹⁴ *Ibid.*
⁹⁵ *Ibid.*, p. 804.

[96] Mackenna to the Chilean minister in Buenos Aires, Santiago de Chile, April 28, 1890, ChT, 1888–1889.

[97] Carlos M. Elías to the Foreign Minister of Peru, Santiago de Chile, April 12, 1890, confidential, in *Circular sobre la cuestión Tacna y Arica*, Peru, Ministerio de Relaciones Exteriores (Lima: Imprenta Torres Aguirre, 1901), pp. 73–77.

[98] J. E. Mackenna to Benecio Alamos González, Santiago de Chile, April 12, 1890, in *ibid.*, pp. 78–79.

[99] Manuel Irigoyen to Carlos M. Elías, Lima, May 1, 1890, in *ibid.*, p. 80.

[100] *Ibid.*, pp. 80–81.

[101] Vial Solar, *op. cit.*, p. 120.

[102] My discussion of this mission is based upon Espinosa Moraga, *op. cit.*, pp. 55–64.

CHAPTER XI: REVERSION TO EQUILIBRIUM

[1] Unless otherwise noted, the ensuing account of the Chilean civil war is based upon the following: Jorge Basadre, *Chile, Perú y Bolivia independientes* (Barcelona and Buenos Aires: Salvat Editores, S.A., 1948), pp. 510–519; Francisco A. Encina, *Historia de Chile desde la prehistoria hasta 1891* (20 vols.; Santiago de Chile: Editorial Nascimento, 1949–1952), XIX, 187–327; XX; Francisco Frias Valenzuela, *Historia de Chile* (4 vols.; Santiago de Chile: Editorial Nascimento, 1949), III, 349–411; and Francisco A. Encina and Leopoldo Castedo, *Resúmen de la historia de Chile* (3 vols.; Santiago de Chile: Editorial Zig-Zag, 1954), III, 1705–1767, 1819–1899.

[2] Ricardo Cruzat to the foreign diplomatic corps, Santiago de Chile, April 10, 1891, ChDC, 1890–1891.

[3] M. M. Aldunate to the consul of Chile in Panama, Santiago de Chile, July 10, 1891, *ibid.*; José Antonio Uribe, ed., *Anales diplomáticos y consulares de Colombia* (6 vols.; Bogotá, 1900–1920), IV, 588–591.

[4] Ricardo Cruzat to B. Alamos González, Santiage de Chile, April 9, 1891, ChDC, 1890–1891.

[5] Ricardo Cruzat to Angel C. Vicuña, Santiago de Chile, May 19, 1891, *ibid.*

[6] For the text of the Matta-Reyes protocol see Oscar Espinosa Moraga, *La postguerra del Pacífico y la Puna de Atacama (1884–1899)* (Santiago de Chile: Editorial Andrés Bello, 1958), pp. 58–63.

[7] For the role of the United States in the Chilean civil war and its aftermath see Henry Clay Evans, Jr., *Chile and Its Relations with the United States* (Durham: Duke University Press, 1927), pp. 135–154.

[8] Espinosa Moraga, *op. cit.*, p. 76; Luís Pereira to Juan Gonzalo Matta, Santiago de Chile, Jan. 5, 1892, ChDC, 1891–1893.

[9] Manuel M. Pinto, hijo, *Bolivia y la triple política internacional (anexión-conquista-hegemonía)* (n.p., 1902), pp. 294–299.

[10] The joint Argentine-Chilean boundary commission had met briefly in 1890, but the work of the two experts was disrupted by the Chilean civil war before the issue had been joined.

[11] See excerpts from a memorandum of Foreign Minister Estanislao Zeballos presented to the Argentine cabinet on December 4, 1889, as quoted in Luís Vicente Varela, *La República argentina y Chile: historia de la demarcación de sus fronteras (desde 1843 hasta 1899)* (2 vols.; Buenos Aires, 1899), I, 256–258 n. 115.

[12] Horacio Carrillo, *Los límites con Bolivia* (Buenos Aires: Talleres Gráficos Argentinos L. J. Rosso y Cía., 1925), p. 37.

[13] Pinto, *op. cit.*, p. 298.

[14] Carrillo, *op. cit.*, p. 41.

[15] Thomas F. McGann, *Argentina, the United States and the Inter-American System, 1880–1914* (Cambridge: Harvard University Press, 1957), p. 173; see also Espinosa Moraga, *op. cit.*, p. 66.

[16] Ricardo Donoso, *Barros Arana: educador, historiador y hombre público* (Santiago de Chile: Universidad de Chile, 1931), pp. 185–186; Jaime Eyzaguirre, *Chile durante el gobierno de Errázuriz Echaurren, 1896–1901* (Santiago de Chile: Empresa Editora Zig-Zag, S.A., 1957), p. 94.

[17] Barros Arana, informed of the proposed Mendoza conference by the Chilean minister in Buenos Aires, wrote a long letter about it to the President of Chile (see Donoso, *op. cit.*, pp. 186–188 n. 1).

[18] Luís Vicente Varela, *La República argentina y Chile ante el árbitro: refutación a las últimas publicaciones chilenas* (Buenos Aires, 1901), p. 175.

[19] Diego Barros Arana to Jorge Montt, San Bernardo, Feb. 5, 1892, as quoted in Donoso, *op. cit.*, pp. 186–188 n. 1.

[20] Luís Pereira to Adolfo Guerrero, Santiago de Chile, Feb. 10, 1892, ChDC, 1891–1893.

[21] Espinosa Moraga, *op. cit.*, p. 66.

[22] Evans, *op. cit.*, pp. 151–152; Alvaro Bianchi Tupper to the Minister of Foreign Relations, Petropolis, Feb. 5, 1892, ChLBraz, 1891–1892.

[23] Donoso, *op. cit.*, p. 186.

[24] For a good contemporary analysis representing the above point of view see Francisco Valdés Vergara, *La situación económica y financiera de Chile* (Valparaíso: Imprenta Germania, 1894), particularly pp. 143–146.

[25] *Boletín de las sesiones ordinarias de 1891*, Chile, Congreso, Cámara de Diputados (Santiago de Chile, 1891–1892), Nov. 25, 1891, p. 108.

[26] *Ibid.*

[27] Alvaro Bianchi Tupper to the Minister of Foreign Realtions, Petropolis, Jan. 26, 1892, confidential, ChLBraz, 1891–1892.

[28] Carlos Luís Hübner to the Minister of Foreign Relations, Petropolis, July 13, 1892, *ibid.*

[29] The Chilean minister to Brazil, reflecting in 1898 upon the history of republican Brazil, noted these influences upon Brazilian foreign policy (see Isidoro Errázuriz to the Minister of Foreign Relations of Chile, Rio de Janeiro, Feb. 15, 1898, in José Zamudio Z., *Isidoro Errázuriz, ministro en Brazil, 1897–1898* [Santiago de Chile: Imprenta Universitaria, 1949], pp. 53–54).

[30] Alberto Ulloa, *Posición internacional del Perú* (Lima, 1941), pp. 64–70, discusses this attempt.

[31] Jorge Basadre, *Historia de la República del Perú* (2 vols.; Lima: Editorial Cultura Antártida, S.A., 1946), II, 240–241.

[32] V. Blanco, circular confidencial al cuerpo diplomático chileno, Santiago de Chile, Aug. 29, 1893, ChDC, 1893–1894.

[33] Isidoro Errázuriz to the minister in Peru, Santiago de Chile, Aug. 30, 1893, ChDC, 1891–1893.

[34] José Antonio Uribe, ed., *Anales diplomáticos y consulares de Colombia* (6 vols.; Bogotá, 1900–1920), IV, 724.

[35] *Ibid.*, pp. 722–724.

[36] E. Larrabure y Unanue to Javier Vial Solar, Lima, Sept. 5, 1892, in *Circular sobre la cuestión Tacna y Arica*, Peru, Ministerio de Relaciones Exteriores (Lima: Imprenta Torres Aguirre, 1901), pp. 165–167.

[37] Carlos Wiesse, *El asunto de Tacna y Arica: primera conferencia histórico-geográfica sobre las negociaciones diplomáticas entre el Perú y Chile de 1887 a 1894, dada en la Sociedad Geográfica la noche del 21 de enero de 1905* (2d ed.; Lima: Empresa Tipográfica, 1917), pp. 33–34, claims that the idea for Peru's September, 1892, proposal to Chile was suggested to the author, Wiesse, who was an official of the Peruvian Ministry of Foreign Relations, by the Chilean minister, Javier Vial Solar.

[38] Isidoro Errázuriz to the minister in Peru, Santiago de Chile, Feb. 13, 1893, ChDC, 1891–1893.

[39] See Javier Vial Solar, *Páginas diplomáticas* (Santiago de Chile: Imprenta, Litografía y Encuadernación Barcelona, 1900), pp. 124–142, for an informed contemporary description of the state of Tacna and Arica in 1891.

[40] Wiesse, *op. cit.*, pp. 29–31.

[41] E. Larrabure y Unanue to Javier Vial Solar, Lima, Aug. 10, 1892, in *Circular sobre la cuestión Tacna y Arica*, pp. 163–164.

[42] *Arbitration between Peru and Chile: Appendix to the Case of Peru in the Matter of the Controversy Arising out of the Question of the Pacific before the President of the United States of America, Arbitrator*, Peru (Washington, D.C.: National Capitol Press, 1922), p. 250.

[43] *Ibid.*, pp. 32–33.

[44] As quoted in Isidoro Errázuriz to the minister in Peru, confidential, Santiago de Chile, April 13, 1893, ChDC, 1891–1893.

[45] *Ibid.*

[46] The minutes of the meetings in which these discussions took place are printed in *Arbitration between Peru and Chile*, pp. 254–263.

[47] *Ibid.*, p. 275.

[48] [V. Blanco] to the minister in Peru, Santiago de Chile, Feb. 20, 1894, ChDC, 1893–1894.

[49] Arturo García Salazar, *Historia diplomática del Perù*, Vol. I, *Chile, 1884–1922* (Lima: Imprenta A. J. Rives Berrio, 1930), pp. 49–53.

[50] Sánchez Fontecilla to Máximo R. Lira, Santiago de Chile, Aug. 24, 1894, ChDC, 1894.

[51] Valdés Vergara, *op. cit.*, p. 146.

[52] Donoso, *op. cit.*, p. 189; Gonzalo Bulnes, *Chile y la Argentina: un debate de 55 años* (Santiago de Chile, 1898), p. 163.

[53] Bulnes, *op. cit.*, p. 165.

[54] Varela, *La República argentina y Chile*, I, 272.

[55] *Ibid.*, p. 274.

[56] *Ibid.*, p. 277.

[57] *Ibid.*, p. 281, points out that a major goal of the Chilean government, during the negotiations in question, was to keep Chilean public opinion calm.

[58] A. Bascuñán Montes, ed., *Recopilación de tratados y convenciones celebrados entre la República de Chile y las potencias extranjeras* (2 vols.; Santiago de Chile: Imprenta Cervantes, 1894), II, 385–392. Italics added.

[59] Varela, *La República argentina y Chile*, I, 329–336.

[60] V. Blanco to the Chilean diplomatic corps, Santiago de Chile, Feb. 9, 1894, ChDC, 1893–1894.

[61] Donoso, *op. cit.*, pp. 195–196.

[62] V. Blanco to the minister in Peru, Santiago de Chile, June 6, 1893, confidential, ChDC, 1893–1894.

[63] *Ibid.*

[64] V. Blanco to the minister in the Plata, Santiago de Chile, June 6, 1893, *ibid.*

[65] V. Blanco to the minister in the Plata, Santiago de Chile, Aug. 17, 1893, *ibid.*

[66] V. Blanco to the minister in Lima, Santiago de Chile, Feb. 3, 1894, *ibid.*

[67] As reported in V. Blanco to the minister in Bolivia, Santiago de Chile, Aug. 26, Nov. 23, Dec. 10, 1893; Jan. 4, 15, 1894, *ibid.*

[68] As reported in V. Blanco to the minister in Bolivia, Santiago de Chile, Nov. 9, 1893, *ibid.*

[69] Unless otherwise noted, the following discussion of the triangular relationship among Argentina, Bolivia, and Chile is based upon Espinosa Moraga, *op. cit.*, pp. 86–96.

[70] As quoted in *ibid.*, p. 89.

[71] M. Sánchez Fontecilla to the minister of Chile in Bolivia, Santiago de Chile, Dec. 4, 1894, ChDC, 1894.

[72] Luís Barros Borgoño to the minister in Bolivia, Santiago de Chile, March 18, 1895, ChDC, 1895, I.

[73] For the text of these treaties see Luís Barros Borgoño, *La negociación chileno-boliviana de 1895* (Santiago de Chile, 1897), pp. 129–135.

CHAPTER XII: TOWARD RAPPROCHEMENT WITH ARGENTINA

[1] Curtis Wilgus, ed., *Argentina, Brazil and Chile since Independence* (Washington, D.C.: George Washington University Press, 1935), pp. 460–462.

[2] Román Pacheco, *Argentina versus Chile: ¿Paz o guerra?* (Buenos Aires: Arnoldo Moen Editores, 1894), pp. 25–26.

[3] *El Tiempo*, May 14, 1895, as quoted in Ernesto Quesada, *La política chilena en el Plata* ... (Buenos Aires: Arnoldo Moen Editores, 1894), pp. 313–315.

[4] As quoted in Luís Barros Borgoño, *La negociación chileno-boliviana de 1895* (Santiago de Chile, 1897), pp. 22–25.

[5] Luís Vicente Varela, *La República argentina y Chile: historia de la demarcación de sus fronteras (desde 1843 hasta 1899)* (2 vols.; Buenos Aires, 1899), II, 316–317.

[6] As quoted in Luís Barros Borgoño to the minister of Chile in Bolivia, Santiago de Chile, June 7, 1895, ChDC, 1895, I. (The altitude and the climate of Bolivia made the post difficult, then as now.)

[7] *Ibid.*

[8] Jaime Eyzaguirre, *Chile durante el gobierno de Errázuriz Echaurren, 1896–1901* (Santiago de Chile: Empresa Editora Zig-Zag, S.A., 1957), pp. 113–114.

[9] Claudio Matte Pérez to the minister of Chile in Bolivia, Santiago de Chile, Aug. 9, 1895, ChDC, 1895, I.

[10] Claudio Matte Pérez to the minister of Chile in Bolivia, Santiago de Chile, Aug. 16, 1895, confidential, *ibid.*

[11] Luís Barros Borgoño to Máximo R. Lira, Santiago de Chile, July 5, 1895, confidential, *ibid.*

[12] *Ibid.*

[13] *Ibid.*

[14] *The Appendix to the Case of the Republic of Chile Submitted to the President of the United States as Arbitrator,* Chile, Tacna-Arica Arbitration (Washington, D.C., 1922), p. 77.

[15] The minutes of nine conferences held on this matter are in *ibid.*, pp. 78–97.

[16] Claudio Matte to the minister of Chile in Bolivia, confidential, Santiago de Chile, Aug. 16, 1895, ChDC, 1895, I.

[17] Virgilio Figueroa, *Diccionario histórico y biográfico de Chile, 1800–1931* (5 vols.; Santiago de Chile, 1925–1931), III, 602–603.

[18] Claudio Matte to Agusto Matte, minister of Chile in France and Great Britain, Santiago de Chile, Oct. 29, 1895, ChDC, 1895, II.

[19] Claudio Matte to the minister of Chile in Italy, Santiago de Chile, Nov. 13, 1895, *ibid.*

[20] Claudio Matte to Carlos Morla Vicuña, Santiago de Chile, Aug. 21, 1895, *ibid.*

[21] As reported in Claudio Matte to Juan G. Matta, minister of Chile in Bolivia, Santiago de Chile, Aug. 13, 1895, ChDC, 1895, I.

[22] Claudio Matte to Juan G. Matta, minister of Chile in Bolivia, Santiago de Chile, Aug. 8, 1895, *ibid.*

[23] Claudio Matte to the minister in Bolivia, Santiago de Chile, Aug. 10, 1895, *ibid.*

[24] Manuel M. Pinto, hijo, *Bolivia y la triple política internacional (anexión-conquista-hegemonía)* (n.p., 1902), pp. 304–315.

[25] For the text of the December 9 protocol see Barros Borgoño, *op. cit.*, pp. 137–139.

[26] For the text of the Rocha-Cano protocol see Varela, *op. cit.*, II, 328–329.

[27] *Ibid.*, p. 332.

[28] *Ibid.*

[29] Eyzaguirre, *op. cit.*, p. 115.

[30] For text of September 6 protocol see Ricardo Donoso, *Barros Arana: educador, historiador y hombre público* (Santiago de Chile: Universidad de Chile, 1931), pp. 197–198.

[31] For the text of the Argentine-Chilean boundary treaty of 1881 see A. Bascuñán Montes, ed., *Recopilación de tratados y convenciones celebrados entre la República de Chile y las potencias extranjeras* (2 vols.; Santiago de Chile: Imprenta Cervantes, 1894), II, 123.

[32] Eyzaguirre, *op. cit.*, p. 103.

[33] Claudio Matte to Adolfo Guerrero, minister of Chile in Argentina, Santiago de Chile, Oct. 24, 1895, ChDC, 1895, II.

[34] Eyzaguirre, *op. cit.*, p. 102.

[35] *Ibid.*, p. 103.

[36] Varela, *op. cit.*, I, 365–366.

[37] Eyzaguirre, *op. cit.*, p. 103.

[38] Varela, *op. cit.*, I, 391–407.

[39] For text of the Guerrero–Quirno Costa protocol see *ibid.*, I, 407–408, n. 161.

[40] Eyzaguirre, *op. cit.*, pp. 103–104.

[41] *Memoria ... al congreso nacional de 1896*, Chile, Ministerio de Relaciones Exteriores, Culto y Colonización (2 vols.; Santiago de Chile, 1897), II, 180–181, contains the text of the April 30 protocol with Bolivia.

[42] Eyzaguirre, *op. cit.*, p. 116.

[43] *Ibid.*, pp. 124–125.

[44] *Ibid.*, pp. 117–119.

[45] Adolfo Guerrero to Carlos Morla Vicuña, minister of Chile in the Argentine Republic, no. 949, Santiago de Chile, July 20, 1896, ChDC, 1896.

[46] Adolfo Guerrero to Carlos Morla Vicuña, no. 957, Santiago de Chile, July 20, 1896, *ibid.*

[47] Eyzaguirre, *op. cit.*, pp. 106–108.

[48] *Ibid.*, p. 111.

[49] Adolfo Guerrero to the minister of Chile in Uruguay and Paraguay, Santiago de Chile, Aug. 21, 1896, ChDC, 1896.

[50] Adolfo Guerrero to Vicente Santa Cruz, Chilean minister in Uruguay and Paraguay, Santiago de Chile, Sept. 3, 1896, *ibid.*

[51] Adolfo Guerrero to Beltrán Mathieu Andrews, Santiago de Chile, May 20, 1896, *ibid.*

[52] *Memoria ... de 1896*, II, 29, contains the text of the convention on the reciprocity of professional degrees.

[53] Adolfo Guerrero to Joaquín Walker Martínez, minister of Chile in Brazil, Santiago de Chile, July 18, 1896, ChDC, 1896.

[54] Adolfo Guerrero to Joaquín Walker Martínez, Santiago de Chile, Aug. 17, 1896, *ibid.*

[55] Enrique de Putrón to Francisco A. Pinto, minister of Chile in Italy, Santiago de Chile, Dec. 28, 1896, *ibid.*

[56] [Carlos Morla Vicuña] to Isidoro Errázuriz, Santiago de Chile, April 9, 1897, ChDC, 1897.

[57] Errázuriz referred to this discussion in a letter he wrote to the President from Brazil (see Isidoro Errázuriz to Federico Errázuriz, Rio de Janeiro, Jan. 31, 1898, in José Zamudio Z., *Isidoro Errázuriz, ministro en Brasil, 1897–1898* [Santiago de Chile: Imprenta Universitaria, 1949], pp. 50–51).

[58] As quoted in Eyzaguirre, *op. cit.*, pp. 127–128.

[59] *Ibid.*, pp. 119–120.

[60] Unless otherwise noted, the following discussion is based upon the relevant chapters in Eyzaguirre, *op. cit.*

[61] Varela, *op. cit.*, I, 439.

[62] *The Appendix to the Case of the Republic of Chile*, pp. 141–147, contains the text of the Billinghurst-Latorre protocol.

[63] Eyzaguirre, *op. cit.*, pp. 164–165.

[64] *Memoria ... al congreso nacional de 1899*, Chile, Ministerio de Relaciones Exteriores, Culto y Colonización (Santiago de Chile, 1899), pp. 30–34.

[65] Eyzaguirre, *op. cit.*, pp. 172–173.

[66] Manuel Francisco Benavides, chargé d'affaires of Peru in Chile, to the Minister of Foreign Affairs of Chile, Santiago de Chile, Sept. 9, 1898, in *Arbitration between Peru and Chile: Appendix to the Case of Peru in the Matter of the Controversy Arising out of the Question of the Pacific before the President of the United States of America, Arbitrator*, Peru (Washington, D.C.: National Capitol Press, 1922), p. 347.

[67] Porras-Amunátegui protocol, Sept. 14, 1898, in *ibid.*, p. 349.

[68] J. D. Amunátegui to Melitón F. Porras, Lima, Oct. 1, 1898, in *ibid.*, pp. 351–352.

[69] M. F. Porras to José Domingo Amunátegui Rivera, Lima, Oct. 2, 1898, in *ibid.*, pp. 354–356.

[70] *Memoria ... de 1899*, pp. 39–41.

[71] Unless otherwise noted, the preceding discussion of Argentine-Chilean relations has been based on the detailed account in Eyzaguirre, *op. cit.*, pp. 181–267.

CHAPTER XIII: TOWARD ENCIRCLEMENT

[1] Jaime Eyzaguirre, *Chile durante el gobierno de Errázuriz Echaurren, 1896–1901* (Santiago de Chile: Empresa Editora Zig-Zag, S.A., 1957), pp. 285–286.

[2] For the Acre dispute see Jorge Basadre, *Chile, Perú y Bolivia independientes* (1st ed.; Barcelona and Buenos Aires: Salvat Editores, S.A., 1948), pp. 594–597; Frederic William Ganzert, "The Boundary Controvery in the Upper Amazon between Brazil, Bolivia and Peru, 1903–1909," *Hispanic American Historical Review*, XIV (Nov., 1934), 427–449.

[3] Abraham König, *Memorias íntimas, políticas y diplomáticas de Don Abraham König, ministro de Chile en La Paz*, comp. Fanor Velasco V. (Santiago de Chile: Imprenta Cervantes, 1927), p. 63.

[4] *Memoria ... al congreso nacional de 1900*, Chile, Ministerio de Relaciones Exteriores, Culto y Colonización (2 vols.; Santiago de Chile, 1900), I, 18–19.

[5] *The Appendix to the Case of the Republic of Chile Submitted to the President of the United States as Arbitrator*, Chile, Tacna-Arica Arbitration (Washington, D.C., 1922), pp. 166–170.

[6] Eyzaguirre, *op. cit.*, p. 306.

[7] Basadre, *op. cit.*, pp. 552–556.

[8] Arturo García Salazar, *Historia diplomática del Perú*, Vol. I, *Chile, 1884–1922* (Lima: Imprenta A. J. Rives Berrio, 1930), p. 84.

[9] Eyzaguirre, *op. cit.*, p. 307.

[10] Alejandro Garland, *Los conflictos sudamericanos en relación con los Estados Unidos, versión castellana ampliada de la edición en inglés que lleva el mismo título* (Lima: Imprenta La Industria, 1900).

[11] *Ibid.*, p. 34.

[12] *Ibid.*, pp. 63, 64.

[13] *Ibid.*, pp. 65, 80, 78.

[14] Eyzaguirre, *op. cit.*, p. 313.

[15] From the President's annual message to Congress, as quoted in Henry L. Wilson to Rafael Errázuriz U., minister of foreign relations, Santiago de Chile, March 18, 1900, in *Memoria ... al congreso nacional de 1901*, Chile, Ministerio de Relaciones Exteriores, Culto y Colonización (Santiago de Chile, 1901), pp. 34–35.

[16] Germán Riesco, *Presidencia de Riesco, 1901–1906* (Santiago de Chile: Editorial Nascimento, 1950), p. 183.

[17] Estanislao Zeballos, "La Política exterior de Chile y las repúblicas argentina, del Perú y Bolivia," *Revista de Derecho, Historia y Letras*, VI (April, 1900), 312, 313.

[18] *Ibid.*, p. 340.

[19] Further details on the subject discussed in this paragraph may be found in *Memoria ... de 1901*, pp. 34–66.

[20] Eyzaguirre, *op. cit.*, pp. 327–336.

[21] *Ibid.*, p. 315.

[22] König, *op. cit.*, p. 71.

[23] Eyzaguirre, *op. cit.*, p. 292.

[24] For the full text of the note see König, *op. cit.*, pp. 75–84.

[25] Eyzaguirre, *op. cit.*, pp. 299–300, 302.

[26] Estanislao Zeballos, "Gravedad de la situación internacional," *Revista de Derecho, Historia y Letras*, VII (Oct., 1900), 616–631.

[27] R. Errázuriz Urmeneta to the Chilean legations abroad, Santiago de Chile, Sept. 30, 1900, in *Memoria ... de 1901*, pp. 21–31.

[28] Rafael Errázuriz Urmeneta to Carlos Morla Vicuña, minister of Chile in the United States, Santiago de Chile, Oct. 1, 1900, in *ibid.*, pp. 66–72.

[29] Estanislao Zeballos, "Bolivia y Chile," *Revista de Derecho, Historia y Letras*, VII (Dec., 1900), 259–302.

[30] García Salazar, *op. cit.*, pp. 93–96.

[31] "La circular del Señor Errázuriz Urmeneta ante la historia," in Carlos Paz Soldán, *El Perú y Chile: la cuestión de Tacna y Arica. Colección de aríulos* (Lima: Imprenta Liberal, 1901), pp. 22–23

[32] García Salazar, *op. cit.*, p. 96.

[33] For the full January 14 report of the Foreign Affairs Committee of the Chilean Chamber of Deputies see *The Appendix to the Case of the Republic of Chile*, pp. 208–209.

[34] Eyzaguirre, *op. cit.*, p. 324.

[35] As quoted in García Salazar, *op. cit.*, p. 106.

[36] *The Appendix to the Case of the Republic of Chile*, p. 239.

[37] "The Third Clause of the Treaty of Ancón and the Tacna and Arica Plebiscite," in Paz Soldán, *op. cit.*, pp. 89–129.

[38] This Peruvian mission to Colombia is described in Alberto Ulloa, *Memoria que presenta al ministerio de relaciones exteriores del Perú el enviado extraordinario y ministro plenipotenciario en Colombia* (Bogotá, 1901).

[39] *Diario Oficial* (Colombia), no. 11459, April 10, 1901, p. 277.

[40] *Ibid.*, no. 11501, June 13, 1901, p. 445.

[41] Emilio Bello C., *Anotaciones para la historia de las negociaciones diplomáticas con el Perú y Bolivia, 1900–1904* (Santiago de Chile: Imprenta La Ilustración, 1919), p. 10.

[42] *Memoria ... de 1901*, pp. 78–80.

[43] *Ibid.*, pp. 75–78.

[44] *Ibid.*, p. 82.

[45] *Ibid.*, p. 83.

[46] *Ibid.*, p. 84.

[47] Felipe de Osma to the Minister of Foreign Affairs [of ———], Lima, May 26, 1901, in *The Appendix to the Case of the Republic of Chile*, pp. 258–278.

[48] It seems clear that in 1900 partition of Bolivia was proposed and discussed, but I have been unable to find adequate documentation on the source of the proposal. Eyzaguirre, *op. cit.*, pp. 316–320, attributes it to Peru, whereas García Salazar, *op. cit.*, p. 90, attributes it to Chile.

[49] *Memoria ... al congreso nacional de 1902*, Chile, Ministerio de Relaciones Exteriores, Culto y Colonización (Santiago de Chile, 1902), p. 150.

[50] Bello C., *op. cit.*, pp. 42–43.

[51] Paz Soldán, *op. cit.*, pp. iii–iv.

[52] Eyzaguirre, *op. cit.*, pp. 340–342.

[53] *Memoria ... de 1902*, p. 13.

[54] Eyzaguirre, *op. cit.*, p. 342.

[55] Henry L. Wilson to the Secretary of State, Santiago, Chile, July 11, 1901, no. 201, USDespChile, 48. (The United States did not sell Chile the warships.)

[56] Thomas F. McGann, *Argentina, the United States and the Inter-American System, 1880–1914* (Cambridge: Harvard University Press, 1957), pp. 202–203.

[57] Emilio Bello C. to the Chilean minister of foreign relations, Mexico, Aug. 20, 1901, in Bello C., *op. cit.*, pp. 43–48.

[58] *Memoria ... de 1902*, pp. 170–172.

[59] Emilio Bello to the Foreign Minister of Mexico, Sept. 27, 1901, in Bello C., *op. cit.*, pp. 118–120.

[60] *Diario Oficial*, no. 11561, Sept. 23, 1901, p. 685.

[61] Antonio José Uribe, *Colombia, Venezuela, Costa Rica, Ecuador, Brasil, Nicaragua and Panamá* (Bogotá, 1931), p. 99.

[62] Reports concerning the Herboso-Abadia Méndez protocols appeared in the *New York Sun* on October 19, 1902, and were reproduced in *Arbitration between Peru and Chile: Appendix to the Case of Peru in the Matter of the Question of the Pacific before the President of the United States of America, Arbitrator*, Peru (Washington, D.C.: National Capitol Press, 1922), p. 53440. I was not permitted to search for the protocols in the Chilean Archives, which were closed to me for the years after 1899, nor have I been able to find a reference to them in any Chilean publication. Collateral evidence, however, indicates that the protocols did exist. The 1902 report of the Foreign Minister of Chile states that a mission to Bogotá signed a protocol for the negotiation of a commercial treaty and of one on the exchange of publications, and discusses the sale of a cruiser to Colombia (see *Memoria ... de 1902*, pp. 157–160).

[63] McGann, *op. cit.*, pp. 201–202.

[64] For a detailed discussion of Argentine-Chilean relations during this period see Riesco, *op. cit.*, pp. 184–201; *Memoria ... de 1902*, pp. 6–105.

[65] McGann, *op. cit.*, pp. 200–201.

[66] The following account of the Mexico City conference of 1901–02 is based largely upon Bello C., *op. cit.*, pp. 109–173. Bello, who was a member of the Chilean delegation, included in his work copies of a number of reports and messages sent to the Chilean chancellery during the course of the conference. Supplementary information has been obtained from McGann, *op. cit.*, from *Memoria ... de 1902*, and from García Salazar, *op. cit.*

[67] The Colombian and Venezuelan replies are in *Memoria ... de 1902*, pp. 176–177.

[68] Bello C., *op. cit.*, p. 112.

[69] For the Chilean proposal see *Memoria ... de 1902*, pp. 301–323.

[70] Bello C., *op. cit.*, pp. 151–152.

[71] *Ibid.*, pp. 131–133.

[72] As quoted in McGann, *op. cit.*, p. 202.

[73] Bello C., *op. cit.*, pp. 145–146.

CHAPTER XIV: A NEW SOUTH AMERICAN EQUILIBRIUM

[1] Germán Riesco, *Presidencia de Riesco, 1901–1906* (Santiago de Chile: Editorial Nascimento, 1950), pp. 200–203.

[2] *Memoria ... al congreso nacional de 1902*, Chile, Ministerio de Relaciones Exteriores, Culto y Colonización (Santiago de Chile, 1902), pp. 137–139.

[3] Riesco, *op. cit.*, pp. 204–205. Enrique Tagle, *Los tratados de paz entre la República argentina y Chile: la opinión argentina* (Buenos Aires: Tipo–Lito Galileo, 1902), pp. 31–47, prints a letter published in *El País* (Buenos Aires) on June 24,

1902, from ex-President Carlos Pellegrini to Indalecio Gómez in which the writer states that Roca notified Chile officially that Argentina would require its compliance with treaty obligations toward Peru and Bolivia.

[4] *Arbitration between Peru and Chile: Appendix to the Case of Peru in the Matter of the Controversy Arising out of the Question of the Pacific before the President of the United States of America, Arbitrator,* Peru (Washington, D.C.: National Capitol Press, 1922), pp. 536–537.

[5] *Ibid.*

[6] For the text of the Colombian-Ecuadorian-Peruvian tripartite convention of 1894 see *Arbitraje entre el Perú y el Eucador: documentos anexos a la memoria del Perú presentada a S. M. el Real Arbitro por D. Mariano H. Cornejo y D. Felipe de Osma, plenipotenciarios del Perú,* Peru (2 vols.; Madrid: Imprenta de los hijos de M. G. Hernández, 1905), II, 74–76.

[7] *Arbitration between Peru and Chile,* pp. 537–540, prints the text of the Chilean-Colombian agreement on the Ecuadoran question.

[8] *Memoria ... de 1902,* pp.161–162.

[9] *Arbitration between Peru and Chile: The Case of Peru in the Matter of the Controversy Arising out of the Question of the Pacific before the President of the United States of America, Arbitrator,* Peru (Washington, D.C., 1923), pp. 181–183; Arturo García Salazar, *Historia diplomática del Perú,* Vol I, *Chile, 1884–1922* (Lima: Imprenta A. J. Rives Berrio, 1930), pp. 126–127.

[10] *Memoria ... de 1902,* p. 159.

[11] *Ibid.,* p. 162.

[12] Luís Vicente Varela, *Defensa de los últimos pactos internacionales* (Buenos Aires, 1902), p. 9.

[13] Joaquín V. González, *Los tratados de paz de 1902 ante el congreso ...* (Buenos Aires: Imprenta "Didot" de Féliz Lajouane y Cía., 1904), pp. 115–117.

[14] *Memoria ... de 1902,* p. 130.

[15] *Ibid.,* pp. 137–139.

[16] *Ibid.,* pp. 140–141.

[17] *Ibid.,* p. 145.

[18] *Ibid.,* p. 146.

[19] Tagle, *op. cit.,* pp. 4–5, quotes the full text of an article in *La Nación* which mentions fear of Chilean power as a nationalist talking point.

[20] This summary of the views of *La Presna* and *La Tribuna* is that of *El País,* as quoted in *ibid.,* p. 61.

[21] As quoted in *ibid.,* p. 49.

[22] *Ibid.,* p. 50.

[23] *Ibid.,* p. 62.

[24] *Ibid.,* p. 65.

[25] The ensuing discussion of Chilean-Argentine negotiations, unless otherwise indicated, is based on Riesco, *op. cit.,* pp. 204–221.

[26] As quoted in *ibid.,* p. 209.

[27] For the texts of the Pactos de Mayo see *Memoria ... de 1902,* pp. 259–274.

[28] For the text of the additional act of July 10, 1902, see *Memoria ... al congreso nacional de 1903,* Chile, Ministerio de Relaciones Exteriores, Culto y Colonización (Santiago de Chile, 1903), pp. iv–v.

[29] As quoted in Riesco, *op. cit.,* p. 228.

[30] Based upon a brief summary of the manifesto in Riesco, *op. cit.,* pp. 229–232.

[31] *Memoria ... de 1903,* pp. xii–xiii.

[32] *Ibid.,* pp. xviii–xx.

[33] *Anexo a la memoria de 1903,* Bolivia, Ministerio de Relaciones Exteriores y Culto (La Paz, 1903), p. 233.

[34] *Memoria ... de 1903,* pp. xiv–xvii, xx–xxix.

[35] *Anexo a la memoria de 1903,* Bolivia, p. 234.

[36] See Jorge Basadre, *Chile, Perú y Bolivia independientes* (Barcelona and Buenos Aires: Salvat Editores, S.A., 1948), pp. 587–600.

[37] *Anexo a la memoria de 1903*, Bolivia, p. 227.

[38] *Memoria ... al congreso ordinario de 1903*, Bolivia, Ministerio de Relaciones Exteriores y Culto (La Paz, 1903), p. xliv.

[39] For the text of the Chilean-Bolivian peace treaty of 1904 and its additional clarifying notes see *Memoria ... al congreso nacional de 1903–1905*, Chile, Ministerio de Relaciones Exteriores, Culto y Colonización (Santiago de Chile, 1905), pp. 26–42.

[40] Emilio Bello C., *Anotaciones para la historia de las negociaciones diplomáticas con el Perú y Bolivia, 1900–1904* (Santiago de Chile: Imprenta La Ilustración, 1919), pp. 194–197; García Salazar, *op. cit.*, pp. 134–137.

[41] García Salazar, *op. cit.*, pp. 134–142.

BIBLIOGRAPHY

BIBLIOGRAPHY

MANUSCRIPT SOURCES

For manuscript sources in the archives of Chile, Colombia, and the United States, used in the preparation of this volume, see the list of abbreviations at the beginning of the section of notes.

GOVERNMENT PUBLICATIONS

Bolivia. Ministerio de Relaciones Exteriores y Culto. *Memoria de relaciones exteriores y culto presentada al congreso ordinario de 1903.* La Paz, 1903.

―――. ―――. *Anexo a la memoria de 1903.* La Paz, 1903.

Chile. Congreso. *Documentos parlamentarios. Discursos de la apertura en las sesiones del congreso, y memorias ministeriales.* Santiago de Chile: Imprenta del Ferrocarril, 1858–1861. 9 vols.

―――. ―――. Cámara de Diputados. *Sesiones de 1868.* Santiago de Chile, 1868.

―――. ―――. ―――. *Sesiones extraordinarias de 1871.* Santiago de Chile, 1871.

―――. ―――. ―――. *Sesiones ordinarias de 1873.* Santiago de Chile, 1873.

―――. ―――. ―――. *Sesiones extraordinarias de 1879.* Santiago de Chile, 1879.

―――. ―――. ―――. *Sesiones extraordinarias de 1880.* Santiago de Chile, 1881.

―――. ―――. ―――. *Sesiones extraordinarias de 1881.* Santiago de Chile, 1881.

―――. ―――. ―――. *Sesiones ordinarias de 1887.* Santiago de Chile, 1887.

―――. ―――. ―――. *Boletín de las sesiones ordinarias de 1891.* Santiago de Chile, 1891–1892.

―――. ―――. ―――. *Boletín de las sesiones ordinarias de 1901.* Santiago de Chile, 1901.

―――. Ministerio del Interior y Relaciones Exteriores. *Memoria ... al congreso nacional de 1864.* Santiago de Chile, 1864.

―――. ―――. *Memoria ... al congreso nacional de 1865.* Santiago de Chile, 1865.

―――. ―――. *Memoria ... al congreso nacional de 1866.* Santiago de Chile, 1866.

―――. ―――. *Memoria ... al congreso nacional de 1867.* Santiago de Chile, 1867.

―――. Ministerio de Relaciones Exteriores y Colonización. *Memoria ... al congreso nacional de 1873.* Santiago de Chile, 1873.

―――. ―――. *Memoria ... al congreso nacional de 1875.* Santiago de Chile, 1875.

―――. ―――. *Memoria ... al congreso nacional de 1876.* Santiago de Chile, 1876.

―――. ―――. *Memoria ... al congreso nacional de 1879.* Santiago de Chile, 1879.

―――. ―――. *Memoria ... al congreso nacional de 1882.* Santiago de Chile, 1882.

―――. ―――. *Memoria ... al congreso nacional de 1883.* Santiago de Chile, 1883.

―――. ―――. *Memoria ... al congreso nacional de 1884.* Santiago de Chile, 1884.

―――. ―――. *Memoria ... al congreso nacional de 1885.* Santiago de Chile, 1885.

―――. ―――. *Memoria ... al congreso nacional de 1886.* Santiago de Chile, 1886.

―――. ―――. *Memoria ... al congreso nacional de 1887.* Santiago de Chile, 1887.

―――. Ministerio de Relaciones Exteriores y Culto. *Memoria ... al congreso nacional de 1888.* Santiago de Chile, 1888.

―――. ―――. *Memoria ... al congreso nacional de 1889.* Santiago de Chile, 1889.

―――. Ministerio de Relaciones Exteriores, Culto y Colonización. *Memoria ... al congreso nacional de 1890.* Santiago de Chile, 1890.

―――. ―――. *Memoria ... al congreso nacional de 1892.* Santiago de Chile, 1893.

―――. ―――. *Memoria ... al congreso nacional de 1893.* Santiago de Chile, 1893.

―――. ―――. *Memoria ... al congreso nacional de 1896.* Santiago de Chile, 1897. 2 vols.

————. ————. *Memoria ... al congreso nacional de 1899.* Santiago de Chile, 1899.

————. ————. *Memoria ... al congreso nacional de 1900.* Santiago de Chile, 1900.
2 vols.

————. ————. *Memoria ... al congreso nacional de 1901.* Santiago de Chile, 1901.

————. ————. *Memoria ... al congreso nacional de 1902.* Santiago de Chile, 1902.

————. ————. *Memoria ... al congreso nacional de 1903.* Santiago de Chile, 1903.

————. ————. *Memoria ... al congreso nacional de 1903–1905.* Santiago de Chile, 1905.

————. Oficina Central de Estadística. *Sinópsis estadística de la República de Chile.* Santiago de Chile: Sociedad Imprenta y Lithografía Universo, 1921.

————. Tacna-Arica Arbitration. *The Appendix to the Case of the Republic of Chile Submitted to the President of the United States as Arbitrator.* Washington, D.C., 1922.

Colombia. *Diario Oficial.*

————. *Documentos referentes a la reunión en Panamá del congreso americano, iniciada y promovida por el gobierno de Colombia en favor de la institución del arbitraje.* Bogotá, 1881.

Peru. *Arbitraje entre el Perú y el Ecuador: documentos anexos a la memoria del Perú presentada a S. M. el Real Arbitro por D. Mariano H. Cornejo y D. Felipe de Osma, plenipotenciarios del Perú.* Madrid: Imprenta de los hijos de M. G. Hernández, 1905. 2 vols.

————. *Arbitration between Peru and Chile: Appendix to the Case of Peru in the Matter of the Controversy Arising out of the Question of the Pacific before the President of the United States of America, Arbitrator.* Washington, D.C.: National Capitol Press, 1922.

————. *Arbitration between Peru and Chile: The Case of Peru in the Matter of the Controversy Arising out of the Question of the Pacific before the President of the United States of America, Arbitrator.* Washington, D.C., 1923.

————. *Exposición de la República del Perú presentada el excmo. gobierno argentino en el juicio de límites con la República de Bolivia, conforme al tratado de arbitraje de 30 de diciembre de 1902.* Barcelona, 1906.

————. Departamento de Fomento. *Statistical Abstract of Peru, 1919.* Lima: Imprenta Americana, 1920.

————. Dirección de Estadística. *Statistical Abstract of Peru, 1919.* Lima: Imprenta Americana, 1920.

————. Ministerio de Relaciones Exteriores. *Circular sobre la cuestión Tacna y Arica.* Lima: Imprenta Torres Aguirre, 1901.

United States. 47th Cong. 1st sess. S. Exec. Doc. 79.

————. 51st Cong. 1st sess. S. Exec. Doc. 231.

Uruguay. Ministerio de Relaciones Exteriores. *Colección de tratados, convenciones y otros pactos internacionales de la República Oriental del Uruguay.* Montevideo: Imprenta "El Siglo Ilustrado," 1923. 5 vols.

OTHER PRIMARY SOURCES

Ahumada Moreno, Pascual, ed. *Guerra del Pacífico: recopilación completa de todos los documentos oficiales, correspondencias y demás publicaciones referentes a la guerre ...* Valparaíso, 1884–1890. 9 vols.

Aldunate, Luís. *Los tratados de 1883–1884 a propósito de las declaraciones del mensaje presidencial de 1 de junio en curso.* [Collection of articles published in *El Ferrocarril*, June 7–30, 1900.] Santiago de Chile, 1912.

Amunátegui Solar, Domingo, ed. *Archivo epistolar de Don Miguel Luís Amunátegui.* Santiago de Chile, 1942. 3 vols.

Barros Borgoño, Luís. *La negociación chileno-boliviana de 1895.* Santiago de Chile, 1897.

Bascuñán Montes, A., ed. *Recopilación de tratados y convenciones celebrados entre la República de Chile y las potencias extranjeras.* Santiago de Chile: Imprenta Cervantes, 1894. 2 vols.

Burr, Robert N., and Ronald D. Hussey, eds. *Documents on Inter-American Cooperation, 1810–1948.* Philadelphia: University of Pennsylvania Press, 1955. 2 vols.

Calvo, Nicolás A. *La cuestión argentino-chilena.* Buenos Aires, 1879.

Cruz, Ernesto de la, and Guillermo Feliú Cruz, eds. *Epistolario de Don Diego Portales, 1821–1837.* Santiago de Chile: Imprenta de la Dirección General de Prisiones, 1936–1937. 3 vols.

Garland, Alejandro. *Los Conflictos sudamericanos en relación con los Estados Unidos, versión castellana ampliada de la edición en inglés que lleva el mismo título.* Lima: Imprenta La Industria, 1900.

Gonzáles, Joaquín V. *Los tratados de paz de 1902 ante el congreso.* ... Buenos Aires: Imprenta "Didot" de Féliz Lajouane y Cía., 1904.

Humphreys, R. A. *British Consular Reports on the Trade and Politics of Latin America, 1824–1826.* London, 1940.

Irrisarri, Antonio José de. *Escritos polémicos.* Ed. Ricardo Donoso. Santiago de Chile: Imprenta Universitaria, 1934.

König, Abraham. *Memorias íntimas, políticas y diplomáticas de Don Abraham König, ministro de Chile en La Paz.* Comp. Fanor Velasco V. Santiago de Chile: Imprenta Cervantes, 1927.

Pacheco, Román. *Argentina versus Chile: ¿Paz o guerra?* Buenos Aires: Arnoldo Moen Editores, 1894.

Páez, Adriano. *La guerra del Pacífico y deberes de la América.* Bogotá, 1881.

Peru. Ministerio de Relaciones Exteriores. *Colección de los tratados, convenciones ... y otros actos diplomáticos y políticos celebrados desde la independencia hasta el día, precedida de una introducción ... por Ricardo Aranda.* Lima, 1890–1919. 14 vols.

―――. ―――. *Congresos americanos de Lima: recopilación de documentos precedida de prólogo por Alberto Ulloa.* Vols. II–III of *Archivo diplomático del Perú.* Lima, 1938. 2 vols.

―――. ―――. *Congresos y conferencias internacionales en que ha tomado parte el Perú: coleccionados sus trabajos por Ricardo Aranda.* Lima, 1909–1920. 5 vols.

Santa Cruz, Oscar de, comp. *El General Andrés de Santa Cruz, Gran Mariscal de Zepita y el Gran Perú: documentos históricos.* La Paz: Escuela Tipografía Salesiana, 1924.

Sesiones de los cuerpos legislativos de la República de Chile, 1811 a 1845. Ed. Valentín Letelier. Santiago de Chile, 1887–1908. 37 vols.

Tagle, Enrique. *Los tratados de paz entre la República argentina y Chile: la opinión argentina.* Buenos Aires: Tipo-Lito Galileo, 1902.

Tratado de Misiones; litigio solucionado; las repúblicas brasilera y argentina; homenajes; el ministro brasilero Bocayuva en el Plata; firma del tratado en

Montevideo; resúmen general de las fiestas, 1889–1890. Buenos Aires: A. Sommaruga y Cía., 1890.

Ulloa, Alberto. *Memoria que presenta al ministerio de relaciones exteriores del Perú el enviado extraordinario y ministro plenipotenciario en Colombia.* Bogotá, 1901.

Universidad de Buenos Aires. *La política exterior de la República Argentina.* Vol. XIX of *Estudios editados por la Facultad de Derecho y Ciencias Sociales.* Buenos Aires, 1931.

Uribe, Antonio José, ed. *Anales diplomáticos y consulares de Colombia.* Bogotá, 1900–1920. 6 vols.

Varas, Antonio. *Correspondencia de Don Antonio Varas: cuestiones americanas. ...* Ed. Alberto Cruchaga Ossa. Santiago de Chile: Talleres Imprenta, 1929.

————. *Correspondencia de Don Antonio Varas sobre la guerra del Pacífico ... con los señores Eulogio Altamirano, General Don José Francisco Gana, Don Francisco Puelma, coronel don Cornelio Saavedra, Don Domingo Santa María, Don Rafael Sotomayor, Coronel Don José Velásquez y Don Rafael Vial; actas del ministerio Varas–Santa María, abril-agosto, 1879.* Santiago de Chile: Imprenta Universitaria, 1918.

Varela, Luís Vicente. *Defensa de los últimos pactos internacionales.* Buenos Aires, 1902.

————. *El Brasil y la Argentina, confraternidad sud-americana. ...* Buenos Aires, 1901.

————. *La República argentina y Chile ante el árbitro: refutación a las últimas publicaciones chilenas.* Buenos Aires, 1901.

————. *La República argentina y Chile: historia de la demarcación de sus fronteras (desde 1843 hasta 1899). Obra escrita con motivo del arbitraje pendiente ante su magestad británica, apoyada en los documentos inéditos del archivo del ministerio de relaciones exteriores de la República Argentina.* Buenos Aires, 1899. 2 vols.

Vial Solar, Javier. *El problema del norte.* Santiago de Chile, 1898.

————. *Páginas diplomáticas.* Santiago de Chile: Imprenta, Litografía y Encuadernación Barcelona, 1900.

Webster, C. K. *Britain and the Independence of Latin America, 1812–1830.* London: Oxford University Press, 1938. 2 vols.

Zeballos, Estanislao S. "Bolivia y Chile," *Revista de Derecho, Historia y Letras,* VII (Dec., 1900), 259–302.

————. "Gravedad de la situación internacional," *Revista de Derecho, Historia y Letras,* VII (Oct., 1900), 616–631.

————. "La política exterior de Chile y las repúblicas argentina, del Perú y Bolivia," *Revista de Derecho, Historia y Letras,* VI (April, 1900).

Zegers, Julio. *La paz chileno-argentina.* Santiago de Chile, 1902.

SECONDARY WORKS

Alberdi, J. B. *Life and Industrial Labors of William Wheelwright in South America.* Boston: A. Williams and Co., 1877.

Amunátegui Solar, Domingo. "Orígen del comercio inglés en Chile," *Revista Chilena de Historia y Geografía,* no. 103 (July–Dec., 1943), 83–95.

Barba, Enrique M. "Las relaciones exteriores con los paises americanos," in *Historia de la Nación Argentina,* Academia Nacional de la Historia, VII, *Rosas y su época* (2d ed.; Buenos Aires: Librería y Editorial "El Ateneo," 1951), pp. 213–270.

Basadre, Jorge. *Chile, Perú y Bolivia independientes.* Barcelona and Buenos Aires: Salvat Editores, S.A., 1948.

———. *Historia de la República del Perú.* Lima: Editorial Cultura Antártida, S.A., 1946. 2 vols.

———. *La iniciación de la República.* Lima, 1929–1930. 2 vols.

Bastert, Russell H. "A New Approach to the Origins of Blaine's Pan-American Policy," *Hispanic American Historical Review,* XXXIX (Aug., 1959), 375–412.

B[ello], A[ndrés]. *Principios de derecho de gentes.* Santiago de Chile, 1832.

Bello, Andrés. *Obras completas.* Vol. X. *Derecho internacional.* Preface by Eduardo Plaza A. Caracas: Ministerio de Educación, 1954.

———. *Principios de derecho internacional.* 2d ed., corr. and aug. Lima, 1844.

Bello C., Emilio. *Anotaciones para la historia de las negociaciones diplomáticas con el Perú y Bolivia, 1900–1904.* Santiago de Chile: Imprenta La Ilustración, 1919.

Bernárdez, Manuel. *El tratado de la Asunción.* Montevideo, 1894.

Bianco, José. *Negociaciones internacionales; los tratados de 1876, gestiones administrativas.* Buenos Aires, 1904.

Blanco Acevedo, Pablo. *La mediación de Inglaterra en la convención de paz de 1828.* 2d ed. Montevideo: Casa A. Barreiro y Ramos, S.A., 1944.

Boletín del Instituto Geográfico Argentino. Buenos Aires, 1899–1911.

Box, Pelham H. *The Origins of the Paraguayan War.* Urbana: University of Illinois Press, 1927.

Braun Menéndez, Armando. *Fuerte Bulnes.* Buenos Aires: Emecé Editores, S.A., 1943.

Browne, Albert G., Jr., "The Growing Power of the Republic of Chile," *Bulletin of the American Geographical Society,* XVI, no. 1 (1884), 3–88.

Brunn, Geoffrey. *Nineteenth-Century European Civilization, 1815–1914.* New York: Oxford University Press, 1960.

Bulnes, Alfonso. *Errázuriz Zañartu: su vida.* Santiago de Chile: Editorial Jurídica de Chile, 1950.

Bulnes, Gonzalo. *Chile y la Argentina: un debate de 55 años.* Santiago de Chile, 1898.

———. *Guerra del Pacífico.* Valparaíso and La Paz, 1911–1918. 3 vols. [Reprinted at Santiago de Chile in 1955, with introduction by Francisco A. Encina.]

Burgin, Miron. *Economic Aspects of Argentine Federalism.* Cambridge, Mass., 1946.

Burr, Robert N. "The Balance of Power in Nineteenth-Century South America: An Exploratory Essay," *Hispanic American Historical Review,* XXXV (Feb., 1955), 37–60.

———. *The Stillborn Panama Congress; Power Politics and Chilean-Colombian Relations during the War of the Pacific.* Berkeley and Los Angeles: University of California Press, 1962.

Cady, John F. *Foreign Intervention in the Río de la Plata, 1838–1850.* Philadelphia: University of Pennsylvania Press, 1929.

Caivano, Thomas. *Historia de la guerra de América entre Chile, Perú y Bolivia, versión castellana de Arturo de Ballesteros y Cotín.* Iquique, 1904.

Cárcano Ramón J. *Guerra del Paraguay: acción y reacción de la triple alianza.* Buenos Aires: Editores Domingo Viau y Cía., 1941. 2 vols.

———. *Guerra del Paraguay: orígenes y causas.* Buenos Aires, 1939.

Carcovich, Luís. *Portales y la política internacional hispanoamericana.* Santiago de Chile, 1937.

Cardozo, Efraím. *Vísperas de la guerra del Paraguay.* Buenos Aires: Librería "El Ateno" Editorial, 1954.

Carrillo, Horacio. *Los límites con Bolivia.* Buenos Aires: Talleres Gráficos Argentinos L. J. Rosso y Cía., 1925.

Carvalho, C. Delgado de. *História Diplomática do Brazil.* São Paulo: Companhia Editora Nacional, 1959.

Center of Latin American Studies, University of California. *Statistical Abstract of Latin America, 1960.* Los Angeles, 1961.

Centner, Charles W. "El fracaso chileno de obtener el reconocimiento británico (1823–1828)," *Boletín de la Academia Chilean de la Historia,* IX, no. 27 (1943), 33–44.

———. "Great Britain and Chilean Mining, 1830–1914," *Economic History Review,* XII, nos. 1–2 (1942), 76–82.

———. "Relaciones comerciales de Gran Bretaña con Chile, 1810–1830," *Revista Chilena de Historia y Geografía,* no. 103 (July–Dec., 1943), pp. 96–107.

Chaves, Julio César. *El presidente López: vida y gobierno de Don Carlos.* Buenos Aires, 1955.

Cifuentes, Abdón. *Memorias.* Santiago de Chile: Editorial Nascimento, 1936. 2 vols.

Cortesão, Jaime, and Pedro Calmon. *Brasil.* Barcelona and Madrid: Salvat Editores, S.A., 1956.

Cruchaga Ossa, Alberto. "Don Pedro Trujillo y su misión diplomática en Lima," *Boletín de la Academia Chilena de la Historia,* IX, no. 20 (1942), 79–100.

———. *La jurisprudencia de la cancillería chilena hasta 1865, año de la muerte de Don Andrés Bello.* Santiago de Chile: Imprenta de Chile, 1935.

———. *Los primeros años del ministerio de relaciones exteriores.* Santiago de Chile: Imprenta Universitaria, 1919.

Dennis, William Jefferson. *Tacna and Arica: An Account of the Chile-Peru Boundary Dispute and of the Arbitration of the United States.* New Haven: Yale University Press, 1931.

Donoso, Ricardo. *Barros Arana: educador, historiador y hombre público.* Santiago de Chile: Universidad de Chile, 1931.

———, ed. *Antonio José de Irisarri: escritor y diplomático.* Santiago de Chile: Prensas de la Universidad de Chile, 1934.

Edwards Vives, Alberto. *La fronda aristocrática: historia política de Chile.* Santiago de Chile: Editorial del Pacífico, 1945.

Efrén Reyes, Oscar. *Breve historia general del Ecuador.* 5th ed. Quito: Editorial "Fray Jodoco Ricke," 1955–1956. 3 vols.

Encina, Francisco A. *Historia de Chile desde la prehistoria hasta 1891.* Santiago de Chile: Editorial Nascimento, 1949–1952. 20 vols.

Encina, Francisco A., and Leopoldo Castedo. *Resúmen de la historia de Chile.* Santiago d Chile: Editorial Zig-Zag, 1954. 3 vols.

Espinosa Moraga, Oscar. *La postguerra del Pacífico y la Puna de Atacama (1884–1899).* Santiago de Chile: Editorial Andrés Bello, 1958.

Espinosa y Saravia, Luís. *Después de la guerra, las relaciones boliviano-chilenas.* 2d ed. La Paz: Editorial Renacimiento, 1929.

Evans, Henry Clay, Jr. *Chile and Its Relations with the United States.* Durham: Duke University Press, 1927.

Eyzaguirre, Jaime. *Chile durante el gobierno de Errázuriz Echaurren, 1896–1901.* Santiago de Chile: Empresa Editora Zig-Zag, S.A., 1957.

Feliú Cruz, Guillermo. *Andrés Bello y la redacción de los documentos oficiales administrativos, internacionales y legislativos de Chile: Bello, Irisarri y Egaña en Londres.* Caracas: Fundación Rojas Astudillo, 1957.

Fernández Valdés, Juan José. "El tratado secreto peruano-boliviano de 1873 y la diplomacia brasileña," *Boletín de la Academia Chilena de la Historia,* XXIII, no. 55 (1956), 5–18.

Ferns, H. S. *Britain and Argentina in the Nineteenth Century.* Oxford: Clarendon Press, 1960.

Figueroa, Virgilio. *Diccionario histórico y biográfico de Chile, 1800–1931.* Santiago de Chile, 1925–1931. 5 vols.

Frazer, Robert W. "The Role of the Lima Congress, 1864–1865, in the Development of Pan-Americanism," *Hispanic American Historical Review,* XXIX (Aug., 1949), 319–348.

Frias Valenzuela, Francisco. *Historia de Chile.* Santiago de Chile: Editorial Nascimento, 1949. 4 vols.

Ganzert, Frederic William. "The Boundary Controversy in the Upper Amazon between Brazil, Bolivia and Peru, 1903–1909," *Hispanic American Historical Review,* XIV (Nov., 1934), 427–449.

García Salazar, Arturo. *Historia diplomática del Perú.* Vol. I. *Chile, 1884–1922.* Lima: Imprenta A. J. Rives Berrio, 1930.

———. *Resúmen de la historia diplomática del Perú, 1820–1884.* Lima: Talleres Gráficos Sanmartí y Cía., 1928.

Gilmore, Robert Louis. "New Granada's Socialist Mirage," *Hispanic American Historical Review,* XXXVI (May, 1956), 190–210.

Gil Munilla, Octavo. *El Río de la Plata en la política internacional. Génesis del virreinato.* Sevilla: Escuela de Estudios Hispanoamericanos de Sevilla, 1949.

Gondra, César. *La diplomacia de los tratados: Paraguay y Bolivia.* Buenos Aires: Félox Lajouane y Cía., 1906.

Henao, Jesús María, and Gerardo Arrubla. *Historia de Colombia.* 6th ed. Bogotá: Librería Colombiana, Camacho Roldán y Cía., 1936.

Howe, Frederick George. "García Moreno's Efforts To Unite Ecuador and France," *Hispanic American Historical Review,* XVII (May, 1936), 257–262.

Inter-American Statistical Institute. *Bibliography of Selected Statistical Sources of the American Nations.* Washington, 1947.

Ireland, Gordon. *Boundaries, Possessions and Conflicts in South America.* Cambridge: Harvard University Press, 1938.

Jenks, Leland H. *The Migration of British Capital to 1875.* New York: Knopf, 1927.

Jones, Tom B. *South America Rediscovered.* Minneapolis: University of Minnesota Press, 1949.

Kendall, Lane Carter. "Andrés Santa Cruz and the Peru-Bolivian Confederation," *Hispanic American Historical Review,* XVI (Feb., 1936), 29–48.

Langlois, Luís. *Influencia del poder naval en la historia de Chile desde 1810 a 1910.* Valparaíso: Imprenta de la Armada, 1911.

Lascano, Victor. *América y la política argentina.* Buenos Aires: Librería y Casa Editora de Emilio Perrot, 1938.

Library of Congress. Latin American Series no. 17. *A Guide to the Official Publications of the Other American Republics. IV. Chile.* Washington, D.C., 1947.

McBride, George M. *Chile: Land and Society.* New York: American Geographical Society, 1936.

McGann, Thomas F. *Argentina, the United States and the Inter-American System, 1880–1914.* Cambridge: Harvard University Press, 1957.

Magnet, Alejandro. *Nuestros vecinos argentinos.* Santiago de Chile: Editorial del Pacífico, S.A., 1956.

Manchester, Alan K. *British Preëminence in Brazil: Its Rise and Decline.* Chapel Hill: University of North Carolina Press, 1933.

Markham, Sir Clements Robert. *The War between Chile and Peru.* London, 1883.

Martner, Daniel. *Historia de Chile: historia económica.* Santiago de Chile: Establecimientos Gráficos de Balcells, 1929.

Maúrtua, V. M. *La cuestión del Pacífico.* Lima: Imprenta Americana, 1919.

Melby, John. "Rubber River: An Account of the Rise and Collapse of the Amazon Boom," *Hispanic American Historical Review*, XXII (Aug., 1942), 452–469.

Meza Villalobos, Néstor. *La conciencia política chilena durante la monarquía.* Santiago de Chile: Universidad de Chile, 1958.

Millington, Herbert. *American Diplomacy and the War of the Pacific.* New York: Columbia University Press, 1938.

Molina Guzmán, Ramón. "Las relaciónes chileno-peruanas (1819–1837)," *Boletín de la Academia Chilena de la Historia*, I, no. 4 (1934), 125–194.

Montaner Bello, Ricardo. *Historia diplomática de la independencia de Chile.* Santiago de Chile: Prensas de la Universidad de Chile, 1941.

———. *Negociaciones diplomáticas entre Chile y el Perú: primer período (1839–1846).* Santiago de Chile: Imprenta Cervantes, 1904.

Mosk, Sanford A. "Latin America and the World Economy, 1850–1914," *Inter-American Economic Affairs*, II (Winter, 1948), 53–82.

Nichols, Theodore E. "The Establishment of Political Relations between Chile and Great Britain," *Hispanic American Historical Review*, XXVIII (Feb., 1948), 137–143.

Nuermberger, Gustave A. "The Continental Treaties of 1856: An American Union 'Exclusive of the United States,'" *Hispanic American Historical Review*, XX (Feb., 1940), 32–55.

Ostria Gutiérrez, Alberto. *Una obra y un destino: la política internacional de Bolivia después de la guerra del Chaco.* 2d ed. Buenos Aires: Imprenta López, 1953.

Pattee, Richard. *Gabriel García Moreno y el Ecuador de su tiempo.* Quito: Editorial Ecuatoriano, 1941.

Paz, Carlos. [Bolivian.] *Bolivia y la Argentina: reseña histórica de los tratados diplomáticos. La cuestión de Tarija.* Tarija, Bolivia: Imprenta de J. Adolfo León, 1912.

Paz Soldán, Carlos. [Peruvian.] *El Perú y Chile: la cuestión de Tacna y Arica. Colección de artículos.* Lima: Imprenta Liberal, 1901.

Paz Soldán, Mariano Felipe. *Narración histórica de la guerra de Chile contra el Perú y Bolivia.* Buenos Aires, 1884.

Pérez Rosales, Vicente. *Ensayo sobre Chile.* Trans. from French into Spanish by Manuel Miguel. Santiago de Chile: Imprenta del Ferrocarril, 1859.

———. *Recuerdos del pasado, 1814–1860.* 3d ed. Santiago de Chile: Imprenta Gutenberg, 1886.

Phelp, Elizabeth. *Statistical Activities of the American Nations, 1940.* Washington, D.C.: Inter-American Statistical Institute, 1941.

Pinto, Manuel M., hijo. *Bolivia y la triple política internacional (anexión-conquista-hegemonía).* N.p., 1902.

Quesada, Ernesto. *La política chilena en la Plata.* ... Buenos Aires: Arnoldo Moen Editores, 1895.

Rennie, Ysabel F. *The Argentine Republic.* New York: Macmillan, 1945.

Restelli, Ernesto, comp. *La gestión diplomática del General de Alvear en el Alto Perú (Misión Alvear–Díaz Vélez, 1825–1827): documentos.* ... Buenos Aires, 1927.

Riesco, Germán. *Presidencia de Riesco, 1901–1906.* Santiago de Chile: Editorial Nascimento, 1950.

Rippy, J. Fred. *British Investments in Latin America, 1822–1949. A Case Study in the Operations of Private Enterprise in Retarded Regions.* Minneapolis: University of Minnesota Press, 1959.

———. *Latin America and the Industrial Age.* New York: Putnam, 1944.

Robalino Dávila, Luís. *García Moreno.* Quito, 1948.

———. "Política internacional de Rocafuerte," *Boletín de la Academia Nacional de la Historia* (Quito, Ecuador), XXIX (Jan.–June, 1949), 65–84.

Rosenblat, Angel. *La población indígena y el mestizaje en América.* Buenos Aires: Editorial Nova, 1954. 2 vols.

Sáenz Hayes, Ricardo. *Miguel Cané y su tiempo (1851–1905).* Buenos Aires, 1955.

Sánchez Quell, H. *La diplomacia paraguaya de Mayo a Cerro-Cora.* 3d ed. Buenos Aires: Editorial Guillermo Kraft, 1957.

Santa María, Ignacio. *Guerra del Pacífico.* Santiago de Chile: Imprenta Universitaria, 1919.

Silva Salas, Edulia. "Biografía de Don Adolfo Ibáñez," *Revista Chilena de Historia y Geografía,* XXXIV, no. 38 (1920), 342–388; XXV, no. 39 (1920), 326–392.

Sotomayor Valdés, Ramón. *Historia de Chile durante los cuarenta años transcurridos desde 1831 hasta 1871.* Santiago de Chile: Imprenta de "La Estrella de Chile," 1875–1903. 4 vols.

The Economic Development of the Argentine Republic in the Last Fifty Years. Buenos Aires: E. Tornquist and Co., 1919.

The Paraguayan Question. The Alliance between Brazil, the Argentine Confederation and Uruguay, versus the Dictator of Paraguay. Claims of the Republics of Peru and Bolivia in Regard to the Alliance. New York, 1866.

Torrico, Carlos. *Tratados chileno-bolivianos: ligero análisis de los celebrados en 1895. Artículos publicados en "El Comercio," segunda parte.* Cochabamba, Bolivia, 1896.

Traversoni, Alfredo. *Historia del Uruguay.* Montevideo: Editorial Medina, 1956.

Ugarteche, Pedro, and José P. S. Pareja. "Nómina de los ministros de relaciones exteriores del Perú y relación de las memorias que han presentado a las cámaras legislativas, 1821–1956," *Revista Peruana de Derecho Internacional,* XVI (Jan.–June, 1956), 44–69.

Ulloa, Alberto. *Posición internacional del Perú.* Lima, 1941.

Uribe, Antonio José. *Colombia, Venezuela, Costa Rica, Ecuador, Brasil, Nicaragua y Panamá.* Bogotá, 1931.

Uribe Orrego, Luís. *Nuestra marina militar, desde la liberación de Chiloé (1826) hasta la guerra con España (1865).* Valparaíso: Imprenta de la Armada, 1914.

Valdés A., Benjamín. "¿Pretendió el gobierno francés tomar posesión del Estrecho de Magallanes?" *Revista Chilena de Historia y Geografía* (July–Dec., 1943), pp. 5–16.

Valdés Vergara, Francisco. *La situación económica y financiera de Chile.* Valparaíso: Imprenta Germania, 1894.

Valencia Avaría, Luís, comp. *Anales de la República.* Santiago de Chile, 1951. 2 vols.

Van Aken, Mark J. *Pan-Hispanism: Its Origin and Development to 1866.* Berkeley and Los Angeles: University of California Press, 1959.

Vicuña Mackenna, Benjamín. *Obras completas.* ... Santiago de Chile: Universidad de Chile, 1939–1940. 16 vols.

Villalobos R., Sergio. *Tradición y reforma en 1810.* Santiago de Chile: Ediciones de la Universidad de Chile, 1961.

Webster, C. K. *Britain and the Independence of Latin America, 1812–1830.* London: Oxford University Press, 1938. 2 vols.

Wiesse, Carlos. *El asunto de Tacna y Arica: primera conferencia histórico–geográfica sobre las negociaciones diplomáticas entre el Perú y Chile de 1887 a 1894, dada en la Sociedad Geográfica la noche del 21 de enero de 1905.* 2d ed. Lima: Empresa Tipográfica, 1917.

Wileman, J. P., comp. and ed. *The Brazilian Year Book, Second Issue—1909.* London: McCorquodale and Co., 1909.

Wilgus, A. Curtis, ed. *Argentina, Brazil and Chile since Independence.* Washington, D.C.: George Washington University Press, 1935.

Yrarrázaval Larraín, José Miguel. *El presidente Balmaceda.* Santiago de Chile, 1940. 2 vols.

Yrigoyen, Pedro. *La alianza perú-boliviana-argentina y la declaratoria de guerra de Chile.* Lima, 1921.

Zamudio Z., José. *Isidoro Errázuriz, ministro en Brasil, 1897–1898.* Santiago de Chile: Imprenta Universitaria, 1949.

INDEX